Eric Meyer on CSS

Content Highlights:

Practical CSS techniques and advice

Understanding structure versus presentation

Transitioning sites from tables to style sheet layouts

Blending techniques to create complex designs

Advantages of CSS over raw HTML

Working with CSS-based layouts

Using basic multicolumn layout

Understanding CSS positioning

Creating non-rectangular layout effects

Organizing information with style

Creating great link effects

Styling for print and screen media

Adding visual interest to forms

Helping images and CSS work together

From the outset, the goal has been to deliver to you a project-based book that shows how to use CSS and HTML together in practical ways that aren't boring and won't break in today's browsers. From converting HTML-based layouts to re-creating a print design, from styled links to multicolumn layout, from padding to positioning, I set out to show you how CSS is really used and really useful. If you've wondered how to use CSS in today's browsers to achieve working, interesting, or even artistic effects, then this book is for you.

—Eric A. Meyer

"CSS is a powerful, elegant instrument with far more possibilities than most of us realize. That's why *Eric Meyer on CSS* is so valuable: it provides a well-balanced combination of hands-on instruction and explanatory theory. Using step-by-step projects, Eric guides readers through everyday applications and demonstrates what we can achieve by harnessing the power of CSS. When you finish a chapter, you can confidently say, 'Hey, I can do this!'"

MaKo, President, *Orion HiTek, Inc.*

"In his typical practical style, Eric Meyer successfully leads the reader through numerous real-world styling exercises that illustrate not only the judicious use of CSS for pleasing effect, but also how to avoid common implementation pitfalls."

Tantek Çelik, *Tasman Development Lead, Microsoft*

www.newriders.com

Eric Meyer on CSS

Mastering the Language of Web Design

Eric A. Meyer

www.newriders.com

1249 Eighth Street, Berkeley, California 94710
An Imprint of Pearson Education

Eric Meyer on CSS: Mastering the Language of Web Design

FIRST PRINTING: July, 2002

International Standard Book Number: 0-73571-245-X

Library of Congress Catalog Card Number: 20-01097665

07 10

Printed in the United States of America

Trademarks

All terms mentioned in this book that are known to be trademarks or service marks have been appropriately capitalized. New Riders Publishing cannot attest to the accuracy of this information. Use of a term in this book should not be regarded as affecting the validity of any trademark or service mark.

Warning and Disclaimer

This book is designed to provide information about cascading style sheets (CSS). Every effort has been made to make this book as complete and as accurate as possible, but no warranty or fitness is implied.

The information is provided on an as-is basis. The author and New Riders Publishing shall have neither liability nor responsibility to any person or entity with respect to any loss or damages arising from the information contained in this book or from the use of the programs that may accompany it.

PUBLISHER
David Dwyer

ASSOCIATE PUBLISHER
Stephanie Wall

PRODUCTION MANAGER
Gina Kanouse

MANAGING EDITOR
Kristy Knoop

SR. ACQUISITIONS EDITOR
Linda Anne Bump

DEVELOPMENT EDITOR
Laura Loveall

PRODUCT MARKETING MANAGER
Kathy Malmloff

PUBLICITY MANAGER
Susan Nixon

SENIOR EDITOR
Lori Lyons

COPY EDITOR
Amy Lepore

INDEXER
Chris Morris

MANUFACTURING COORDINATOR
Jim Conway

BOOK DESIGNER
Barbara Kordesh
bkordesh@insightbb.com

COVER DESIGNER
Alan Clements

COMPOSITION
Barbara Kordesh

Table of Contents

About the Author

Eric A. Meyer has been working with the Web since late 1993. He is currently employed as a Standards Evangelist with Netscape Communications and lives in Cleveland, Ohio, which is a much nicer city than you've been led to believe. A graduate of and former Webmaster for Case Western Reserve University, Eric is also an Invited Expert with the W3C CSS&FP Working Group and coordinated the authoring and creation of the W3C's CSS1 Test Suite. He often speaks at conferences on the subjects of CSS, Web design, Web standards, Web browsers, and how they all go together. He is the host of "Your Father's Oldsmobile," a weekly big band–era radio show heard on WRUW 91.1FM in Cleveland. When not otherwise busy, Eric is usually bothering his wife, Kat, in some fashion.

To my parents, who have meant more to me and done more for me than I can ever express or repay.

And to my wife, Kathryn, whose boundless joy suffuses my life as well as her own.

About the Technical Reviewers

These reviewers contributed their considerable hands-on expertise to the entire development process for *Eric Meyer on CSS: Mastering the Language of Web Design*. As the book was being written, these dedicated professionals reviewed all the material for technical content, organization, and flow. Their feedback was critical to ensuring that this book fits our reader's need for the highest-quality technical information.

Molly E. Holzschlag With over 20 Web development books to her credit, Molly is also a popular columnist and feature writer for such diverse publications as *Macworld, PC Magazine, IBM developerWorks*, and *Builder.com*. She is an engaging speaker and teacher, appearing regularly at such conferences as Comdex, Internet World, and Web Builder.

As a steering committee member for the Web Standards Project (WaSP), Molly works with a group of other dedicated Web developers and designers to promote W3C recommendations. Currently, she is serving as the Associate Editor for *Digital Web Magazine*. Molly also acts as an advisory board committee member to numerous organizations, including the World Organization of Webmasters.

Tobias Horvath has been involved with Web technologies since 1995, when he was just 12 years old. Growing up in the early stages of the Internet, he made his journey to become a Macintosh enthusiast. During the day, he is trying to be a student in Essen, Germany, where he lives. You can find his personal website at `www.tobyx.com`.

Acknowledgments

Linda Bump and Laura Loveall, both of New Riders, provided a great deal of support and encouragement for this entire project. Laura in particular deserves credit for spending hours on the phone with me while I obsessed over changes to the layout of the book, its cover, the fonts used, the size of the figures, and just about everything else.

Brett Merkey's early and very detailed feedback on the original project proposal helped shape the final result in very basic ways, affecting everything from its structure to the skill level at which it was aimed. This would have been a very different and probably less worthwhile book without his penetrating insights.

Major thanks are due to my technical reviewers, Molly Holzschlag and Tobias Horvath, for their input regarding points to highlight, passages to clarify, and mistakes to fix. I literally couldn't have done this without them

I'd especially like to thank Jeffrey Zeldman for agreeing to write the Foreword when he already had an overfull to-do list, and for his continued attempts to bring a measure of sanity to the subject of Web standards.

Extra-special thanks are due Tantek Çelik for his permission to include some of his discoveries in "Tricking Browsers and Hiding Styles" (on the Web site) for his incredibly useful tools, and for blazing a trail of CSS implementation that others are still following. Without Tantek and his work on Internet Explorer 5 for Macintosh, CSS support might be as bad today as it was four years ago. In that sense, without his work this book would not have been possible at all.

The first person to show me the Web, way back in the middle of 1993, was my friend and colleague Jim Nauer. At the time, I didn't see why I should care. Thank you, Jim, for being visionary enough to see the Web's promise and persistent enough to keep telling me until the message finally penetrated my skull.

Similarly, my friend and colleague Peter Murray, a highly regarded expert in the field of library automation, helped make it possible for me to unwittingly attend one of the first public demonstrations of a CSS implementation. From that coincidental chain of events grew my interest in CSS, and so I owe Peter a great debt for playing a major role in the launch of my career. And also for being a generally great guy.

And last, I'd like to express my deep gratitude to everyone who has contacted me over the years with praise, complaints, comments, suggestions, questions, and ideas regarding CSS, browsers, and my writing. Your feedback not only helps me improve my work, but it keeps me moving forward, period. Without the interest you've collectively shown, I might have given up years ago. Thank you, one and all.

Eric A. Meyer
Cleveland, Ohio, March 2002

Tell Us What You Think

As the reader of this book, you are the most important critic and commentator. We value your opinion and want to know what we're doing right, what we could do better, what areas you'd like to see us publish in, and any other words of wisdom you're willing to pass our way.

Email: `errata@newriders.com`

Foreword

When my girlfriend stops by my studio, I thrill her with the words every woman wants to hear. "I'm not going to write to Eric Meyer again today. I'm going to solve this CSS problem on my own."

She nods, peering over my shoulder at the site I've been working on. "I see you finally fixed that problem you were having with the site's menu bar," she says.

"Well, uh, actually I emailed Eric Meyer earlier today, and he hooked me up. But this new problem with these text rollovers? Gonna solve that baby on my own. No more Eric Meyer for this boy today."

"Uh-huh," she says. "So who are you writing to?"

I close the email message I was about to send to Eric Meyer.

"Just an old college buddy," I say.

My name is Jeffrey, and I'm an Eric Meyer addict.

I can't recall the first time I wrote to CSS expert Eric Meyer, begging his advice on a Web project that had bogged down in browser incompatibilities. Nor can I pinpoint the moment when I realized that my very livelihood depended on continuous access to Eric Meyer's knowledge of CSS.

It was so easy to get hooked. First there were his early books, explaining CSS in ways that anyone could understand. Then there was his personal site at Meyerweb.com, brimming with inspiring examples of advanced CSS design. Plus the tutorials Meyer wrote for a variety of online and offline magazines, including *Netscape DevEdge*. And the CSS mailing list Meyer co-ran with fellow expert John Allsopp.

I used them all—daily, nightly, and with piggish abandon. And still I craved more. I hit bottom when I realized that I could write to the guy directly and he'd actually make time to write back, providing CSS information I could not get elsewhere and solving problems I could not begin to solve myself.

In today's Web, there are perhaps a dozen people who know CSS as intimately as Eric Meyer. Of those few experts, you can count on the fingers of one hand the number who can explain even the trickiest CSS concept so that the average working Web designer can comprehend it. Most geeks at Eric Meyer's level speak in ways that hurt your brain. Meyer makes it simple even when it's quite complex. If other CSS experts share his peculiar combination of world-class knowledge and plain-speaking populism, they are too busy to write books and certainly too busy to answer email.

I don't know how he does it. All I know is that without his insights, I might still use CSS in only the most limited ways. Because of Eric Meyer's patience, practicality, and passion for teaching, I can execute the sophisticated yet simple and accessible site designs that keep my studio going.

And how do I thank him? By bugging him with endless questions.

> "Why is this layout breaking in this browser?"
>
> "How can I turn off link colors for one set of images while leaving them on for another set?"
>
> "Can I float this element *and* position it?"

I might be an addict, but I also have a conscience. I know that Eric Meyer is at least as busy as I am, so I do not allow myself to write to him as often as I'd like—which is every time I encounter a problem with CSS (which is pretty much every time I use CSS, which is pretty much every working day).

That's why I need this book, and if you design Web sites, it's why you need it, too. This book is the next best thing to having your own personal Eric Meyer on call 24–7. In some ways, it's better. The virtual Eric Meyer contained in this book won't grind pistachio shells into your carpet, won't drink your milk right out of the carton, and above all, won't laugh when you trip over tricky CSS2 selectors. Then again, neither would the flesh-and-blood Eric Meyer, and that's one more reason to admire the guy. His humility is genuine, and it comes through in the text of this book.

This book is filled with code, but it's really filled with ideas. Practical ideas that solve problems we all face as working Web designers. Unique ideas that inspire one's own creativity. You can prop this book open and use it as a crib sheet when you're facing tough deadlines, or you can read it on a sunny, secluded hillside and extrapolate its concepts into artistic ideas of your own. I plan to do both. But before I start enjoying this book, I'm compelled to do something else first.

I have to write to Eric Meyer again. This time the message will be very short, and it will be a statement instead of a question: "Thank you for writing this book."

Jeffrey Zeldman
Zeldman.com
New York City, April 2002

INTRODUCTION

As many readers are no doubt aware, I've spent a good deal of time and energy on the subject of CSS during the past six years. In addition to articles and support charts and test suites, I've also written *Cascading Style Sheets: The Definitive Guide* (O'Reilly, 2000) and *Cascading Style Sheets 2.0 Programmer's Reference* (Osborne/McGraw-Hill, 2001), which to me always felt like two legs of a three-legged stool. The first leg covered theory in detail with the intent of educating the reader how CSS works in all its details. The second leg was meant for CSS authors who needed a reference text to help them write clean CSS the first time and to remind them of value names and meanings. The missing third leg was a book that showed how CSS works in a hands-on, practical way, preferably in full living color.

Happily, the third leg is missing no longer: Thanks to New Riders, you're holding it in your hands right now.

SHOULD YOU BUY THIS BOOK?

That isn't a facetious question. As proud as I am of the work contained in these pages, I'm also keenly aware that this book is not for every reader. So let me take a moment to describe two kinds of readers: those for whom this book was written and those for whom it was not.

Those For Whom This Book Is Meant

You ought to find this book useful if you match one or more of the following criteria:

- You want a hands-on, practical guide to using CSS in real-world projects. That's exactly what this book is all about.
- You're a hands-on learner, someone who gets a lot more out of interactive experimenting than from just reading a book. Despite the fact that this is indeed a book, it's been intentionally designed to let the reader "play along at home," as it were.
- You've been meaning to increase your CSS skills for some time now, but you keep putting it off because CSS is a large, complex subject, and you don't have a roadmap for how to get to the next level.
- You've always wanted someone to show you how to convert a typical, old-school, pure-HTML design into a blend of HTML and CSS and to explain why it's to your advantage to do so. If that's the case, go to Project 1, "Converting an Existing Page," without another moment's delay.
- If asked, you would describe your HTML skill level as "intermediate" or "expert" and your CSS skill level as "basic" or "intermediate." In other words, you understand HTML fairly well and have used enough CSS to have a basic grasp of how it's written.

Those For Whom This Book Is Not Meant

You might not find this book to be useful if one or more of the following describes you:

- You've never used or even seen CSS before. Although some basic terms are defined in the text and I've included a short glossary, the assumption here is that the reader knows the basics of writing CSS and is fairly proficient with HTML authoring.
- You want to understand all of the subtleties of the theory underlying CSS and grasp the nuances of the specification. There are now many books on the market that occupy that niche. The focus here is on demonstrating effects that work.
- You've only done Web design in a point-and-click editing environment. This book assumes that you can edit (or have edited) HTML and CSS by hand, and its narrative is based on that assumption. Its projects may be easily reproducible in a point-and-click editor, but the book was not written with such editors in mind.
- You want a book that will tell you how to write CSS that will look the same in all browsers on all platforms, including Netscape 4.x and Explorer 3.x. See the following section, "What You Can Expect from This Book," for details.
- You've read my other works and hate the personal, familiar tone I take in my writing. I promise you that my writing style has changed very little.

What You Can Expect From This Book

From the outset, my intent has been to write an engaging, interactive book that focuses on practical and interesting uses of CSS that can be deployed in today's browsers. To do this, each project evolves from having no styles to being fully styled and ready for deployment on the Web. If I've done my job well, you should get the feeling of watching over my shoulder as I work on a project, with me commenting on what I'm doing as I do it.

Although you can simply read the text and look at the figures to get a sense of how a project is evolving, I think the best way to work along with the book is to have a Web browser and a text editor open as you read. That way, you can follow along with the changes I make in the text by physically making the same changes in your project file and seeing the changes in your own Web browser.

There is one point on which I want to be very clear: The techniques shown in this book are generally meant for browsers whose version number is greater than or equal to 5. If you have to design a site that looks the same in Explorer 4.x and Netscape 4.x as it does in IE6.x and NS6.x, this book is *not* for you. In fact, "Tricking Browsers and Hiding Styles" on the Web site spends a good deal of time describing ways to hide CSS from version-4 browsers. Such techniques allow you to write CSS for modern browsers and still let the content display (albeit in a much plainer way) in older browsers. That's about as far as this book goes to cater to the limitations of version-4 browsers, however.

Overview

In keeping with the practical, hands-on nature of this book, I've divided it into a series of 13 projects—each one effectively a chapter. It is possible to skip around from project to project as the spirit moves you because each project was written to stand on its own as much as possible. However, the book was still written with the linear reader in mind, and if you read from front to back, you should find that the projects build on one another.

With a few exceptions, the projects are titled in as self-obvious a way as possible. For example, Project 1 takes a page designed using only HTML markup and spacer GIFs and converts it to an HTML-plus-CSS design.

Projects 2 through 5 cover some fairly basic projects, from touching up a press release or an events calendar to making hyperlinks look better than they ever have before. Projects 6 and 7 increase the sophistication somewhat by focusing on printing and the styling of form elements in more than one medium. Then, in Projects 8 through 11, the topics of discussion are positioning, integration of various styling techniques, and how to make designs look more organic and less boxy.

Project 12 takes a look at a powerful and potentially beautiful technique that isn't widely supported but can be adapted to work in the real world. In some ways, this is a look ahead to a future in which CSS support is more widespread, but if you pick the right tools, you can flex your artistic muscles today. All work and no play makes for a boring book, I always say.

Project 13 is the most ambitious and complex of the book: It is an attempt to re-create, as closely as possible, the visual design of this book in HTML and CSS. Just as important as the ways in which the look can be re-created are the discussions of why certain things can't be exactly reproduced on the Web.

Companion Web Site

Each project in the book is based on the editing of a real project file. You can either download the project files for the entire book at once, or for each chapter individually. The project files are available on the book's companion Web site: `http://www.ericmeyeroncss.com/`. There you will find "Picking a Rendering Mode" and "Tricking Browsers and Hiding Styles" (which are of a more practical and theoretical nature than the projects themselves), a short Glossary of terms, the files that were used to produce the figures throughout the book, any errata to the book, and supplemental materials like bonus text, commentary from the author, and links to useful on line resources.

For each project, there will be an archive of all the files you need to work along with the text, which includes any graphic files needed as well as a version of the project file at its outset. These files follow a consistent naming; for example, the Project 1 file will be `ch01proj.html`. This is the file you should open up with a text editor and make changes to as the project moves forward. You can also load it into a Web browser and hit "Reload" at each step to see what effect the new styles have.

Conventions

This book follows a few typographical conventions that you should be familiar with before proceeding.

A new term is set in *italics* the first time it is introduced. There will often be a short definition of the term nearby. Program text, functions, variables, and other "computer language" are set in a fixed-pitch font. In regular text, it will also be a dark blue color—for example, when mentioning the property `margin` or a value like `10px`.

Code blocks are set entirely in a fixed-pitch font. Any red text within a code block indicates a change to the code from its previous state. Most code blocks show only a fragment of the overall document or style sheet, with the lines to be changed (or inserted) surrounded by unchanged text. This extra text provides a sense of context, making it easier to find the part you need to change if you're following along with the text. Here is an example:

```
<head>
<title>Travel Guide: Ragged Point Inn</title>
<style type="text/css">
/* temporary styles */
table {border: 2px solid red; margin: 3px;}
td {border: 1px dotted purple; padding: 2px;}
</style>
</head>
```

Every computer book has its own style of presenting information. As you flip through this book, you'll notice that it has an interesting layout. Here are the layout conventions:

▸▸ Asides

These usually contain detailed explanations that are related to the main text but are not a part of the project itself. They might also offer alternative approaches or ideas to those demonstrated in a project. In every case, they can be skipped without disrupting the project's flow.

Notes

These are meant to be helpful annotations to the main text, and there are a lot of them in this book. These are used to provide tips, asides, definitions of new terms, tangential points, or related bits of information.

Warnings

These indicate a point that might cause problems in some browsers or a similarly grave note of caution.

Web site notes provide guidance as to which files to download or load into a Web browser, or things to check out on the Web.

Finally, at the end of each project you will find a section titled "Branching Out." This will present three short exercises that invite you to try modifying the finished project in certain ways. These "branches" are certainly not the end of what you can do, but they may help you start experimenting with the concepts presented in the project. Think of them as jumping-off points for your own design ideas and also as interesting challenges in their own right. If you can match the illustrations with your own styles, then you'll be well on your way to writing creative CSS of your own.

1

Converting an Existing Page

Unlearn what you have learned.

—Yoda

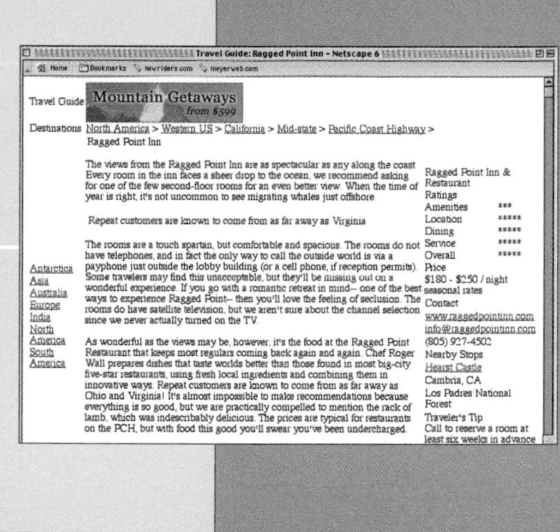

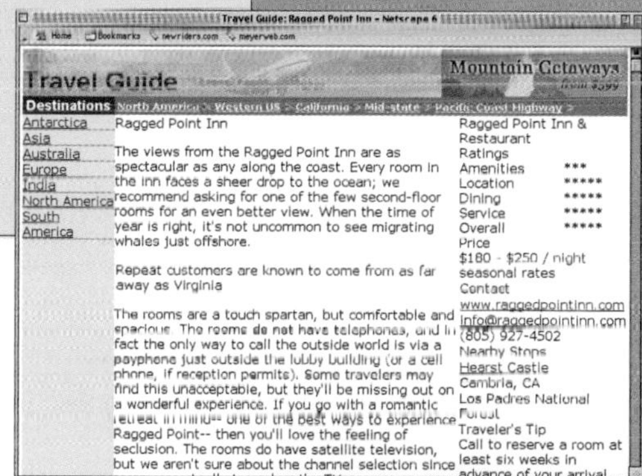

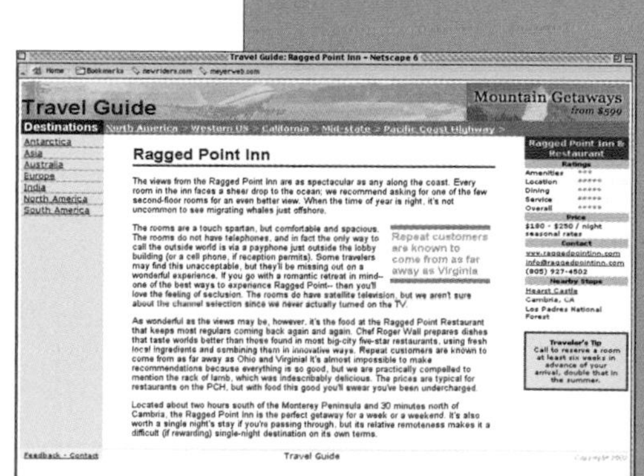

Psychology teaches us that any major trauma or unwelcome, life-changing event typically evokes four stages: denial, anger, bargaining, and acceptance. For many Web authors, such an event was the news that HTML was dropping elements like `<b>` and `<font>` and that, to make pages look good in the future, a new skill would have to be acquired: cascading style sheets (CSS).

After the refusal to believe that such useful tags could be eliminated, there is usually rage directed at the W3C ("stupid, fuzzy-headed, ivory-tower academics!") and then the silent vow to use fewer `font` tags in the future. What I hope to do in this book is hasten acceptance and show why this transition is actually cause for celebration, not sorrow. Join us and be free and happy!

A few of you are probably muttering about pod people and collectivization. Far from being some kind of "invasion of the `<body>` snatchers" scenario, CSS promises to give authors a more complex and sophisticated way of styling documents while allowing them to simplify their document structure. The end results are documents that are easier to maintain and layouts that are not only easier to create but almost infinitely easier to change at a moment's notice. Think of it as upgrading from an old mainframe terminal to a brand-new desktop system. Tasks that used to take you forever and that required a lot of complicated juggling to accomplish will now happen quickly and simply. Plus you can play "Quake" on it, whereas the mainframe only lets you play "Nethack."

And It's Invalid To Boot

Note that the HTML-based design isn't only needlessly complex, but it's also invalid: in order to get rid of the page margins, I was forced to use the proprietary attribute `marginheight` and `marginwidth`, among other invalid bits of markup. By the time we're done, we'll have a validating document that's much smaller and simpler than when we started.

A good way to ease into the new world of CSS is to compare a traditional all-HTML design to the equivalent design in HTML+CSS. The easiest way to make such a comparison is to convert an all-HTML design to use CSS for layout and a simplified structure for the actual content. This not only will let us see how traditional layout techniques are accomplished in CSS, it also will measure the savings in file sizes and server load between the old and new versions of the same design.

Project Goals

Our goal for this project is as straightforward as can be: to take an HTML-heavy design and convert it to a mixture of HTML and CSS. In so doing, we'll explore how commonly used HTML structures and tricks can be replaced with vastly simpler markup and CSS, and we'll learn how doing this makes the document markup a great deal easier to read. When we're done, we'll take some measurements to determine just how much of a savings our effort has yielded.

We'll assess each portion of the document as we reach it, so the approaches we'll take aren't known ahead of time. We can still articulate some general goals, however:

- The number of images in the page should be reduced to an absolute minimum. This will have the dual benefit of making the document structure much more clean and reducing the potential number of server hits required to display the page.
- Large-scale tables intended for overall page layout will be left in place, but smaller tables will be converted to nontable markup whenever it is practical to do so.
- The final product should look as much like the all-HTML design as possible. Although there might not be a perfect pixel-for-pixel fidelity between the two, we should do our utmost to minimize any differences.

If we can fulfill all three of these goals, we'll have done something fairly remarkable.

PREPARATION

Download the files for Project 1 from this book's Web site. If you're planning to play along at home, load the file `ch01proj.html` into the editing program of your choice. This is the file you'll be editing, saving, and reloading as the project progresses.

See the Introduction for instructions on how to download files from the Web site.

LAYING THE GROUNDWORK

First we need to take a look at the existing all-HTML page in a Web browser and then take a look at its markup. Figure 1.1 shows what the page looks like.

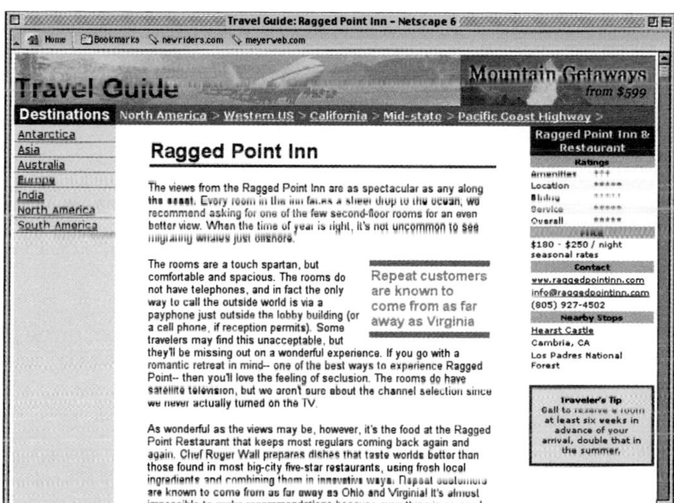

FIGURE 1.1

The page as it is displayed using only HTML for presentation.

Now it's time to look at the HTML itself. Unfortunately, we can't provide it here because a listing of the page's source code would be about seven pages long! So we'll have to consider another approach.

You can see the source code for Figure 1.1 by loading the `ch0101.html` file into your favorite text editor.

Instead of going through the HTML line by line, let's take a quick look at how the page has been put together. To do this, we're going to add a temporary style sheet to the top of the document. The first rule in this temporary style sheet will put a 2-pixel red border around the outside of any `table` elements and add 3 pixels of blank space (margin) around them. The second rule gives `td` elements a 1-pixel dotted purple border and 2 pixels of padding. The result of this addition is shown in Figure 1.2.

```
<head>
<title>Travel Guide: Ragged Point Inn</title>
<style type="text/css">
/* temporary styles */
table {border: 2px solid red; margin: 3px;}
td {border: 1px dotted purple; padding: 2px;}
</style>
</head>
```

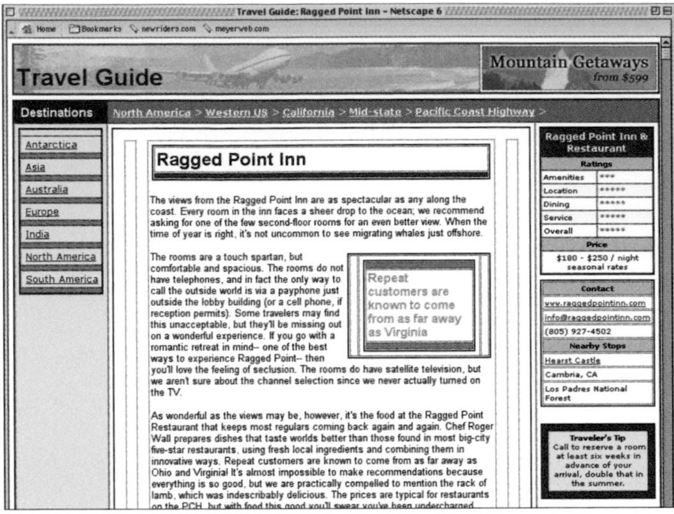

FIGURE 1.2

Adding a simple style sheet to figure out the page structure.

Spreading Out

The elements in Figure 1.2 are spread out more than those in Figure 1.1 because of the margin and padding values we added to the `table` and `td` elements, respectively. Everything will come back together when we remove the temporary style sheet.

Because every thick red border represents the outer edge of a table, we can quickly determine the page's structure. The banner (or masthead) across the top of the page is in its own table. The rest of the document is wrapped in a second table, with several tables nested within it. One point of interest is that the right-hand sidebar is actually laid out using three separate tables, the last of which has another table nested inside it.

Another layout trick revealed by these temporary styles is the use of "empty" table cells to hold open space. Look, for example, at either side of the main text column in the center of the page and also at either side of the large, grayish block of text set into the main content. (This is known as a *pullquote*). In both cases, you can see empty cells outlined by a dotted purple border.

These cells are not, in fact, empty—they contain image files called `blank.gif`. This is a 1×1 image whose sole pixel has been set to be transparent. A quick search of the HTML reveals that there are 16 `img` elements that refer to this same image file. For example:

```
<tr>
<td bgcolor="#A98763"><img src="blank.gif"
   height="1" width="1" alt=""></td>
</tr>
```

Using the Outline

It's a good idea to keep the "outlined" version of the file handy. As we come to each portion of the document, it might be helpful to refer back to the outline for visual guidance on how to proceed.

Eliminating these `img` elements will be one of our top priorities because they add wholly unnecessary clutter to the document structure and are easily replaced with CSS properties like `margin` and `padding`.

At this point, we can get rid of the temporary style sheet and start the conversion process.

Converting the Document

Going from an all-HTML design to an HTML+CSS design requires two steps:

- Shedding the HTML-based presentation
- Adding in CSS to replace it

In many cases, it's easier to do this in a gradual fashion by stripping down a small portion of the document and styling it before moving on to the next section. For this project, though, we're going to go the hard-core route and strip the file all the way down to its minimum state before we start styling. (It makes the figures look a lot better, too.)

Stripping Down to the Minimum

It's time to make a copy of the original all-HTML file and strip out nearly all of its HTML-based presentation. This is undeniably the toughest part of converting an all-HTML design to an HTML+CSS layout. A good deal of the work can be done using find-and-replace utilities, but there is still the need to go through and delete any leftover HTML-based presentation manually.

Tidying Up Your Markup

It's possible to use one of a number of utilities to clean up markup and, in the process, strip out most or all of the presentational aspects of a document. HTML Tidy is one of the most popular of these tools, and it is available for free from `http://tidy.sourceforge.net`. Syntax checking is also available in many authoring tools, and the Macintosh browser iCab even does it while rendering a page!

Things to eliminate include:

- `font` elements
- `<br>` elements
- ` ` entities
- The attributes `bgcolor` and `background`
- The attributes `align` and `valign` wherever they appear
- The `table` attributes `width`, `border`, and `cellpadding`
- Any table cell that contains only an image or that contains nothing at all
- Any attributes on the `body` element (such as `text` and `link`)

Note that we're not stripping out actual table cells that contain text or visible images. We may find as we go along that we can get rid of some tables or cells, but we'll leave them in for now. There's no sense in cutting out markup that we might have to restore later!

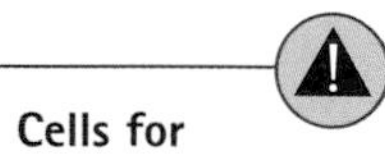

Padded Cells for Navigator 4.x

If you're concerned about layout in Navigator 4.x, you'll want to keep your `cellpadding` attribute and avoid setting `padding` for cells. NN4.x has been known to throw severe fits over `padding` on table cells, including making a table twice as wide as the browser window.

There's one thing we've left in place that you might be tempted to remove: the attribute `cellspacing`. The usual temptation is to take it out and try to replicate it with margins on table cells, but that's a bad idea because CSS2 states in section 17.5 that margins are not applied to table cells. The CSS2 way to enforce separation between table cells is the property `border-spacing`, but support for this property is pretty bad. Support for `padding` on table cells, however, is pretty good, so we can drop `cellpadding`. If this approach strikes you as a bad idea, you could leave in `cellpadding` to go with `cellspacing`.

Similarly, do *not* remove any `colspan` or `rowspan` attributes and their values. CSS does not currently provide mechanisms to make cells span rows or columns, so it is necessary to preserve these attributes.

Ultimately, you should end up with a file that consists of no more than a bare minimum of structure and the actual content. This should look rather like Figure 1.3.

FIGURE 1.3

The naked content, stripped of any presentational HTML.

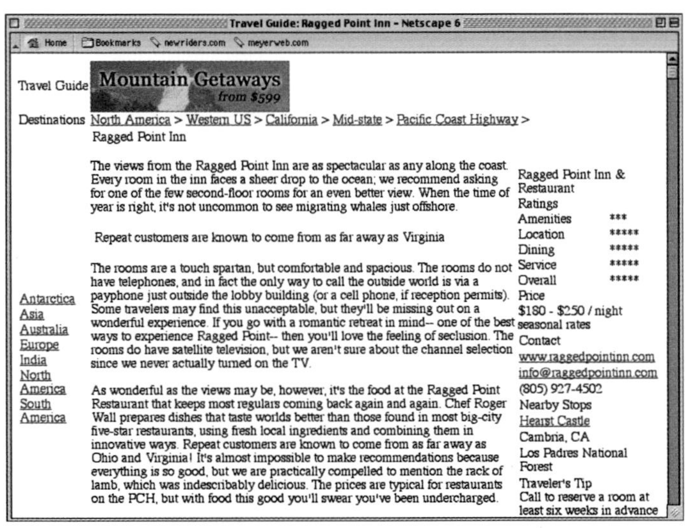

If you'd rather just skip to the end of this process, you can see the markup that gives us Figure 1.3 by loading the `ch0103.html` or `ch01proj.html` file into your favorite editor.

It might look pretty grim now, but things will get better as we begin styling. With the file pared down to a minimum, we can start re-creating the styles through CSS. We'll do this by looking at the original document's markup and the effect it was intended to create and then figuring out how to style the stripped-down design to re-create the original effect.

Healing the Body

What's a Declaration?

A *declaration* in CSS is a property-value pair. For example, `color: red;` is a declaration. One or more declarations form a *declaration block*, which is the part of a style surrounded by curly braces.

The first thing to fix is the `body` element. In the original markup, it carries a number of HTML4 and proprietary attributes. The latter include `marginheight`, `marginwidth`, and the `background` attribute on the `td` element. Then there are the valid but unnecessary attributes, like `align`, `valign`, `bgcolor`, and so forth.

```
<body marginwidth="4" marginheight="4"
  topmargin="4" leftmargin="4" rightmargin="4"
  link="#990000" vlink="#990099" text="#000000">
```

We can replace every last one of these attributes with a CSS equivalent. `marginheight` and `marginwidth` can be replaced with a single `margin` declaration, and the text and link colors are easy to re-create.

```
<html>
<head>
<title>Travel Guide: Ragged Point Inn</title>
<style type="text/css">
<!--
body {margin: 4px; color: black; background: white;}
a:link {color: #990000;}
a:visited {color: #990099;}
-->
</style>
</head>
```

At this point, you might be wondering why we would bother because the CSS we've written requires more typing than the `body` attributes did. This is true for now, but we're about to see a situation in which it takes a lot fewer characters to style the entire document.

Establishing Common Styles

We should set a global styling policy for all of the tables and table cells in the document. This will take a moment of thought.

In the first place, not every table has the same settings for the attributes `cellpadding` and `cellspacing`. Almost every table is set to have both attributes as either `0` or `1`, however. So we'll establish a global style that sets the `padding` of table cells to `0` and take care of the exceptions later on. In a similar vein, almost every table is set to `width="100%"`, so we can re-create that in our CSS.

Notice that all of the text on the page is in a sans-serif font, but not every cell uses the same sans-serif font. A few elements call for Arial, but most of the rest list Verdana first. As with the cell padding, we'll write a rule to cover the majority and worry about styling the exceptions later on.

What's a Rule?

A *rule* in CSS is a complete style statement made up of a selector and a declaration block. For example, `p {color: gray; font-weight: bold;}` is a rule.

```
body {margin: 4px; color: black; background: white;}
table {width: 100%; margin: 0;}
table td {padding: 0; border-width: 0; vertical-align: top;
  font-family: Verdana, Arial, Helvetica, sans-serif;}
a:link {color: #990000;}
```

We've also set all table cells to have a zero-width border (which effectively means no border at all) and to align their contents with the top of the cell. With these few declarations, we've replaced all of the `valign`, `border`, and `cellspacing` attributes in the old document. Similarly, the `font-family` declaration replaces at least part of the 49 `font` elements we stripped out of the markup. We can see the results in Figure 1.4.

Granted, it's still pretty ugly, but there's a lot of style still to come. Let's just work our way down through the page's contents and style things as we come to them.

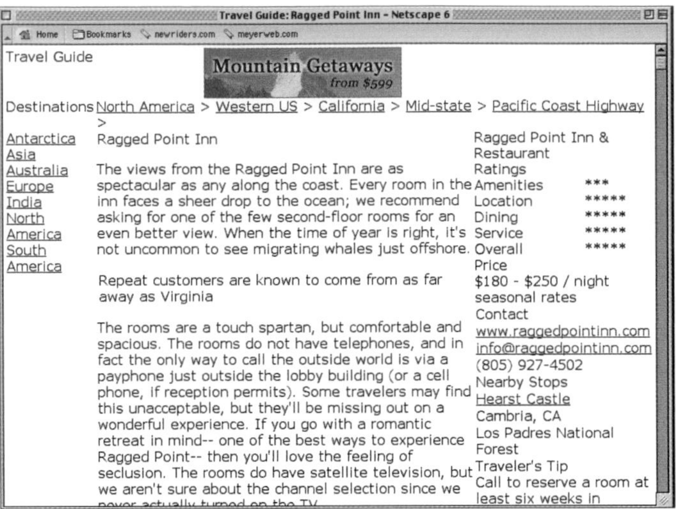

Travel Guide: Ragged Point Inn - Netscape 6
Home
Bookmarks
newriders.com
meyerweb.com
Travel Guide
Mountain Getaways
from $599
Destinations North America > Western US > California > Mid-state > Pacific Coast Highway >
Antarctica
Asia
Australia
Europe
India
North America
South America
Ragged Point Inn
The views from the Ragged Point Inn are as spectacular as any along the coast. Every room in the inn faces a sheer drop to the ocean; we recommend asking for one of the few second-floor rooms for an even better view. When the time of year is right, it's not uncommon to see migrating whales just offshore.
Repeat customers are known to come from as far away as Virginia
The rooms are a touch spartan, but comfortable and spacious. The rooms do not have telephones, and in fact the only way to call the outside world is via a payphone just outside the lobby building (or a cell phone, if reception permits). Some travelers may find this unacceptable, but they'll be missing out on a wonderful experience. If you go with a romantic retreat in mind-- one of the best ways to experience Ragged Point-- then you'll love the feeling of seclusion. The rooms do have satellite television, but we aren't sure about the channel selection since we
Ragged Point Inn & Restaurant
Ratings
Amenities ***
Location *****
Dining *****
Service *****
Overall *****
Price
$180 - $250 / night
seasonal rates
Contact
www.raggedpointinn.com
info@raggedpointinn.com
(805) 927-4502
Nearby Stops
Hearst Castle
Cambria, CA
Los Padres National Forest
Traveler's Tip
Call to reserve a room at least six weeks in

FIGURE 1.4

Some basic styles have been established.

Restoring the Masthead

First up is the masthead: the `table` at the top of the page containing the site's name and a small advertisement. In the original HTML, we had the following:

```
<table width="100%" border="0" cellpadding="0" cellspacing="0">
<tr>
<td valign="bottom" background="topbg.gif"><font size="+3"
  color="#442200" face="Arial, Helvetica, Verdana, sans-serif">
  <b>Travel Guide</b></font></td>
<td width="234" align="center" valign="middle"><img src="ad.gif"
  height="60" width="234" alt="advertisement"></td>
</tr>
</table>
```

Thanks to our stripping down of the markup, here's what we have to work with now:

```
<table cellspacing="0">
<tr>
<td>Travel Guide</td>
<td><img src="ad.gif" height="60" width="234" alt="advertisement"></td>
</tr>
</table>
```

We have two separate challenges here. The first is to replicate the styles of the Travel Guide cell so that the text looks like it did before we got rid of the `font` element, the `valign` attribute, and so on. The second challenge is to make sure the cells are the correct width.

To do all this efficiently, we should identify each cell with a unique label, thus providing us with a way to target each cell with its own unique styles. That's exactly what the `id` attribute was designed to do.

```
<table cellspacing="0">
<tr>
<td id="title">Travel Guide</td>
<td id="advert"><img src="ad.gif" height="60" width="234"
  alt="advertisement"></td>
</tr>
</table>
```

Now that each of these table cells has been uniquely tagged, we can set about styling them with `id` selectors. In the first cell, we need to re-create the text styling and place it in the bottom of the cell. You might remember that we already have a rule to set the `font-family` for all table cells, but the order of fonts in that rule was `Verdana, Arial, Helvetica, sans-serif`. The title's `font` tag called for `Arial, Helvetica, Verdana, sans-serif`. The text was also boldfaced (using the `<b>` element) and a dark brown color. Finally, its size was set to be `+3`. CSS doesn't accept that particular value, but in most cases, `+3` will be equal to about `200%`. Thus, we get the styles illustrated in Figure 1.5.

```
a:visited {color: #990099;}
td#title {vertical-align: bottom; color: #442200;
   font: bold 200% Arial, Helvetica, Verdana, sans-serif;}
</style>
```

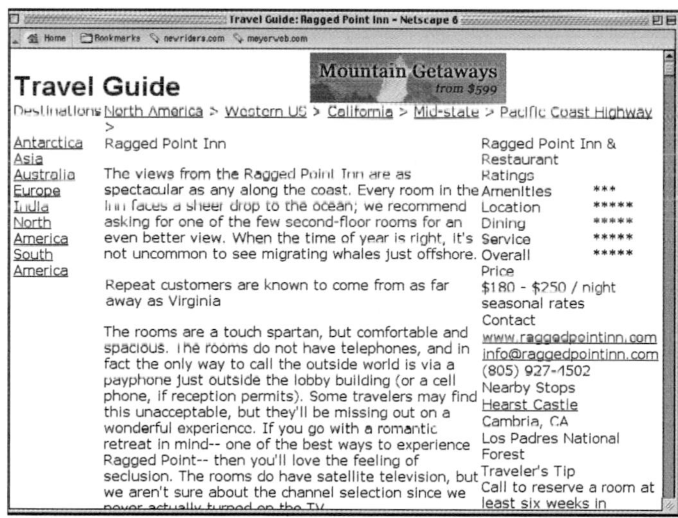

It's a good start, but we're still missing the background image. We can easily bring it back with the `background` property.

```
td#title {vertical-align: bottom; color: #442200;
   background: transparent url(topbg.gif) top left;
   font: bold 200% Arial, Helvetica, Verdana, sans-serif;}
```

What's a Selector?

A *selector* in CSS is the part of a rule that determines which element(s) is selected by that rule. For example, `div`, `table#info`, and `ol li.step` are all selectors. The declaration block that goes with a selector determines what styles will be applied to the selected element(s). Thus, `p {color: gray;}` selects all `p` elements and sets their `color` to `gray`. There are many different kinds of selectors, such as descendant selectors, class selectors, and more. See section 5 of the CSS2 specification for details.

FIGURE 1.5

The re-creation of the title text's appearance.

Position Keywords

In this declaration, we have the `background-position` keywords `top` and `left` as part of the `background` value. Because the default values for `background-position` place images in the top-left corner of the element, including `top left` was not strictly necessary. It was done here mostly for the sake of clarity and to justify the existence of a note on the default values for `background-position`.

In Figure 1.5, note that the advertisement isn't placed as we'd like. Remember that we already have a rule stating that all tables have a `width` of `100%`, so the problem isn't that the table is too narrow. The cells are just too wide: In the absence of any other information, the browser has made each cell of equal width. What we need to do is define the width of one of them, allowing the other to take up the remainder of the space.

```
td#title {vertical-align: bottom; color: #442200;
   background: transparent url(topbg.gif) top left;
   font: bold 200% Arial, Helvetica, Verdana, sans-serif;}
td#advert {width: 234px;}
</style>
```

With this rule, we've told the browser that the advertisement cell should be 234 pixels wide—the same width as the image within it. The browser will set the advertisement cell to the declared width and will make the other cell (the "title" cell) as wide as it needs to be to fill in the rest of the overall table width. Thus, we get the result shown in Figure 1.6.

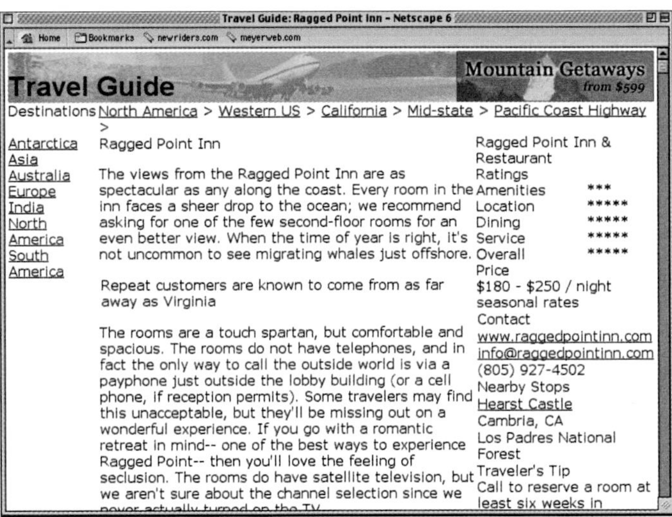

FIGURE 1.6

The masthead returns to its former appearance.

The Content and Its Top

With the masthead under control, we've taken care of the first `table` in the document. The rest of the page is contained in a second `table`, but like the first, we are not going to add an `id` to the `table` element itself. Why not? Because we'll be adding `id`s to the cells themselves, so it's not necessary to `id` the `table`.

Let's take a look at the first row of the table. It contains exactly two cells, but in the original version, a lot of markup was involved in the presentation of those cells.

Tables and `id`

There are cases in which it makes a lot of sense to `id` a `table` element, as we'll see later in the project. We just haven't yet come to a situation in which it makes sense to do so.

```
<tr>
<td bgcolor="#663300" valign="middle"><font size="+2"> </font>
  <font face="Arial, Helvetica, Verdana, sans-serif" color="#FFFFFF"
   size="+1"><b>Destinations</b></font></td>
<td colspan="2" bgcolor="#997753" valign="middle"><font size="-1"
face="Verdana, Arial, Helvetica, sans-serif" color="#FFFFFF"> <b>
<a href="/northam/">
  <font color="#FFFFFF">North America</font></a> &gt;
<a href="/northam/west/">
  <font color="#FFFFFF">Western US</font></a> &gt;
<a href="northam/west/ca/">
  <font color="#FFFFFF">California</font></a> &gt;
<a href="/northam/west/ca/mid/">
  <font color="#FFFFFF">Mid-state</font></a> &gt;
<a href="/northam/west/ca/mid/pch">
  <font color="#FFFFFF">Pacific Coast Highway</font></a> &gt;
</b></font></td>
</tr>
```

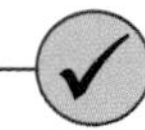

Bold Changes

The boldface code is intended to highlight HTML that gets reduced between the first and second code blocks. Since the markup is being reduced, we didn't use the red color, as that usually indicates additions to code. This boldfacing does not appear elsewhere in the book.

By contrast, here's what we have now:

```
<table cellspacing="0">
<tr>
<td>Destinations</td>
<td colspan="2">
<a href="/northam/">North America</a> &gt;
<a href="/northam/west/">Western US</a> &gt;
<a href="northam/west/ca/">California</a> &gt;
<a href="/northam/west/ca/mid/">Mid-state</a> &gt;
<a href="/northam/west/ca/mid/pch">Pacific Coast Highway</a> &gt;</td>
</tr>
```

Let's identify what these cells shared in common before working on the styles that made them different. In the first place, both were set to `valign="middle"` and featured white text (`color="#FFFFFF"`). The text in both cells was also boldfaced with the `<b>` element.

So let's `id` both cells—and also the row that contains them—in preparation for our styles.

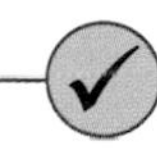

Preserving the Crumbs

The second cell contains information that identifies the page's place within the structure of the site. This is usually referred to as "breadcrumbs," named after the concept of dropping breadcrumbs to mark one's trail. Fortunately, there are no digital birds to gobble up our trail and leave us stranded in a virtual gingerbread house.

```
<tr id="content-top">
<td id="sidetop">Destinations</td>
<td id="crumbs" colspan="2">
<a href="/northam/">North America</a> &gt;
<a href="/northam/west/">Western US</a> &gt;
<a href="northam/west/ca/">California</a> &gt;
<a href="/northam/west/ca/mid/">Mid-state</a> &gt;
<a href="/northam/west/ca/mid/pch">Pacific Coast Highway</a> &gt;</td>
</tr>
```

The first thing to do is use the row's `id` to apply common styles to the content of the cells. We'll do this using a descendant selector.

```
td#advert {width: 234px;}
#content-top td {color: white; vertical-align: middle;
  font-weight: bold;}
</style>
```

Selecting Descendants

A *descendant selector* selects an element that's a descendant of another (for example, `table td` or `ul li`). In the rule we've just written, we're selecting any `td` element that's a descendant of *any* element that has an `id` with the value `content-top`. That narrows down the cells selected. In CSS1, this kind of selector was called a *contextual selector.*

Let's fill in the backgrounds and fonts of these two cells so we can get a better idea of where things stand. All we need to do is reproduce the values for `bgcolor` to get the background colors.

```
#content-top td {color: white; vertical-align: middle;
  font-weight: bold;}
tr td#sidetop {background: #663300;}
tr td#crumbs {background: #997753;}
</style>
```

Now all we have to do is add the necessary values for the font families and sizes in the two cells. The `sidetop` cell is like our title: The original markup calls for Arial before any other fonts. The `crumbs` cell, however, uses the order `Verdana, Arial, Helvetica, sans-serif`, exactly the same as the earlier rule for `table td`. Thus, we only need to define a `font-size` for the `crumbs` cell, while we can take care of the size and family of the `sidetop` font using the `font` property (see Figure 1.7).

```
tr td#sidetop {background: #663300;
  font: 115% Arial, Helvetica, Verdana, sans-serif;}
tr td#crumbs {background: #997753; font-size: 85%;}
```

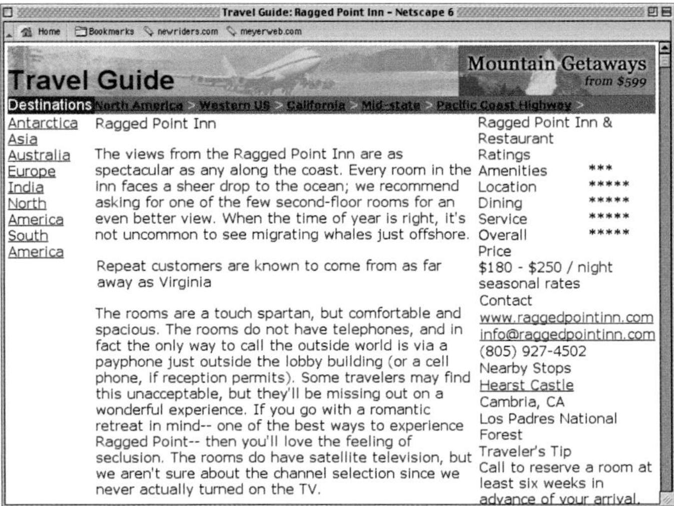

FIGURE 1.7

Backgrounds and fonts are mostly set, but the padding and links need work.

Things are a little tight in these cells, so we'll want to add some padding. There's something else to notice: The word "Destinations" is not boldfaced. This is because the declaration `font: 115% Arial, Helvetica, Verdana, sans-serif;` has the effect of making the `font-weight` of the cell `normal`. This happens because the missing keywords for the weight, style, and variant of the text are set to their defaults, and all of them are `normal`. So we need to add in the fact that we still want this text to be bold.

```
tr td#sidetop {background: #663300;
  font: bold 115% Arial, Helvetica, Verdana, sans-serif;}
```

To open a little space around the text in these cells, let's give both cells some padding. Actually, let's give them both the same padding.

```
#content-top td {vertical-align: middle; color: white;
  font-weight: bold; padding: 0.1em 0.2em 0;}
```

Now they both have `0.1em` top padding, `0.2em` left and right padding, and no bottom padding. We could have written the value as `0.1em 0.2em 0 0.2em` and gotten the same result.

The other thing we need to fix in this row is the color of the links in the `crumbs` cell. In the original design they were all white, but here they're the same red that we defined for all links in the document. That's because the rule `a:link {color: #990000;}` overrides the `color` value `white` that we assigned to the cell itself. The same would happen if any of the links had been visited, except then the visited link would be colored purple (`#990099`). Thus, the arrows turn white, but the links stay red. It's time for two more rules using descendant selectors.

```
tr td#crumbs {background: #997753; font-size: 85%;}
tr td#crumbs a:link {color: white;}
tr td#crumbs a:visited {color: gray;}
</style>
```

Between the padding and the link coloring, we get the result shown in Figure 1.8, which is very close to the original design. There might be a few pixels of difference in cell widths, but nothing anyone would ever notice.

What's an em?

In CSS, `1em` is equivalent to the value of the element's `font-size`. Thus our rule makes the top padding one-tenth the value of `font-size` for the cell, and the left and right padding each one-fifth the `font-size` value.

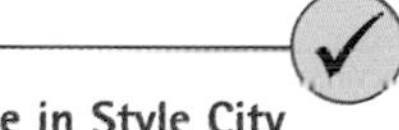

Trouble in Style City

When you want to declare all four values for any box-model shorthand property like `padding`, `margin`, `border-style`, and so on, remember that the order of the values is top-right-bottom-left. This can be abbreviated as TRBL, so remembering it will keep you out of TRouBLe.

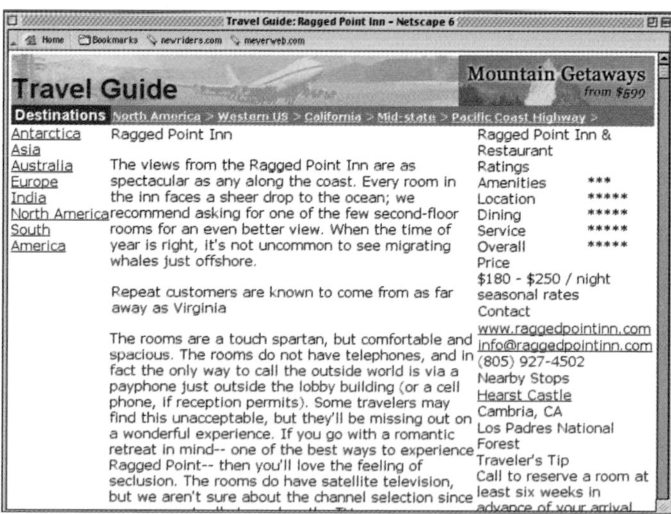

FIGURE 1.8

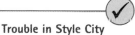

The top of the main content table is looking a lot better.

Styling the Sidebar

With the top of the page in good shape, it's time to tackle that left-hand sidebar. This is the first place where we'll find a dramatic reduction in the amount of markup needed to attain a number of layout effects and where we'll see how that can make a document a lot easier to edit and maintain.

The actual markup from the original all-HTML design is too long to list here, but let's take a look at just the first three rows of the table that contains sidebar links.

```
<td width="120" valign="top" bgcolor="#EBDAC6">
<table width="100%" border="0" cellpadding="0" cellspacing="0">
<tr>
<td><img src="blank.gif" height="3" width="1" alt=""></td>
</tr>
<tr>
<td> <a href="/antarctic/"><font size="-1" face="Verdana, Arial,
  Helvetica, sans-serif">Antarctica</font></a></td>
</tr>
<tr>
<td bgcolor="#A98763"><img src="blank.gif" height="1" width="1"
  alt=""></td>
</tr>
```

By way of contrast, here's what we have for the entire set of links after stripping out the unnecessary HTML, including the table cell that contains this table:

```
<td>
<table cellspacing="0">
<tr><td><a href="/antarctic/">Antarctica</a></td></tr>
<tr><td><a href="/asia/">Asia</a></td></tr>
<tr><td><a href="/austral/">Australia</a></td></tr>
<tr><td><a href="/europe/">Europe</a></td></tr>
<tr><td><a href="/india/">India</a></td></tr>
<tr><td><a href="/northam/">North America</a></td></tr>
<tr><td><a href="/southam/">South America</a></td></tr>
</table>
</td>
```

You probably already know what's coming: We need to `id` an element. In this case, it will be the enclosing `td` element.

```
<td id="leftside">
```

The obvious first step here is to re-create the styles from the original HTML.

```
tr td#crumbs a:visited {color: gray;}
td#leftside {width: 120px; background: #EBDAC6;}
</style>
```

Remember that we don't need to declare `vertical-align: top` because that was already done at the beginning of the style sheet. All we need here is to define the width and background, as we've done.

Next we need to carefully consider what the original design was set up to do. The blank images between the links were inserted so that their cells would be 1 pixel tall and have a medium brown background. The effect is to have thin borders between the links. Now those cells are gone, but the cells that contain the links remain, and we can style those directly (see Figure 1.9).

```
td#leftside {width: 120px; background: #EBDAC6;}
td#leftside td {border-bottom: 1px solid #A98763;}
</style>
```

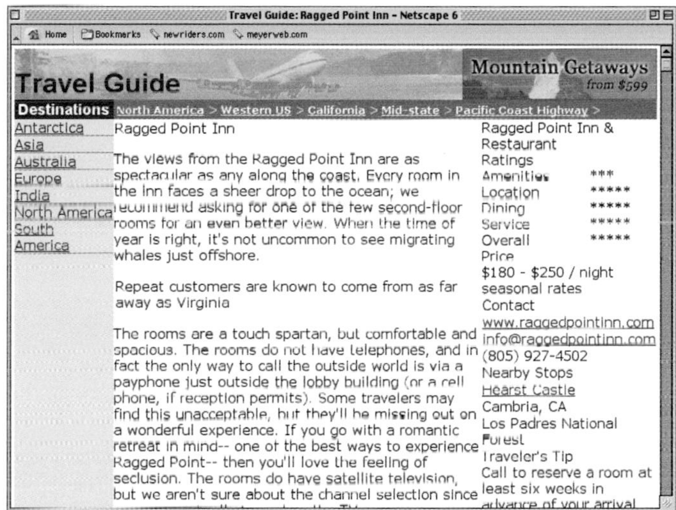

FIGURE 1.9

Simple borders replace complicated image-and-cell combinations.

At this point we're ready to set the font size to match the HTML-based design and throw in a little bit of padding just to make things look nicer.

```
td#leftside td {border-bottom: 1px solid #A98763; font-size: 85%;
  padding: 0 0 1px 0.33em;}
```

There's one thing we still need to do. Remember that the HTML-based design had a cell above the first link with a 3-pixel-tall blank image and no background color. The intent was to push the links downward, separating them from the Destinations box a little bit. So all we really need is a top margin on the table.

```
td#leftside td {border-bottom: 1px solid #A98763; font-size: 85%;
  padding: 0 0 1px 0.33em;}
td#leftside table {margin-top: 3px;}
</style>
```

Padding Instead?

Another way to create that 3-pixel space is to declare `padding-top: 3px` for the `leftside` table cell itself. If we did that and left the `table`'s top margin in place, that would result in a 6-pixel separation because the padding and margin would add up to that distance.

The Content Cell

The main content cell of the page is actually one of the easiest to style, but it contains some interesting challenges nonetheless. Once we give the `td` element an `id` of `content`, we're all set to style away.

The paragraphs are the simplest to take care of:

```
td#leftside table {margin-top: 3px;}
td#content p {font: 85% Arial, Helvetica, Verdana, sans-serif;}
</style>
```

We've styled these paragraphs using a descendant selector just in case we run into paragraphs elsewhere in the design or paragraphs get added in a later overhaul of the site.

We also need to consider the spacing inside this cell that exists in the original design. This space was enforced using a table that started out like this:

```
<table width="100%" border="0" cellspacing="15" cellpadding="0">
<tr>
<td width="10"><img src="blank.gif" height="1" width="10" alt=""></td>
<td>
```

There are two things to consider in this case: the `cellspacing` and the width of the image-only cells. (There's another one after the main content.) Once we figure out the distances, we can come up with the padding we want to set on the `content` cell.

At the top, there will be 15 pixels of space opened up; this is entirely due to the value of `cellspacing`. On the sides, there will be 40 pixels of space: 10 pixels for the blank images and 15 pixels to either side of the cells that contain the blank images. Therefore, we write the following:

```
td#leftside table {margin-top: 3px;}
td#content {padding: 15px 40px;}
td#content p {font: 85% Arial, Helvetica, Verdana, sans-serif;}
```

Our progress is shown in Figure 1.10. We can see from Figure 1.10 that two bits of text didn't get styled here: the page's title and the pullquote. Each one requires some individual attention.

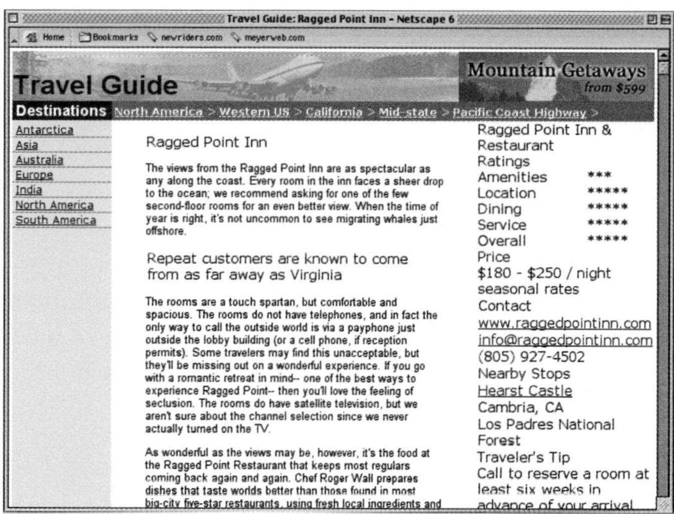

FIGURE 1.10

Styling the paragraphs and padding the cell have a noticeable effect on the layout.

Restoring the Title

In our original design, the title ("Ragged Point Inn") was styled using this HTML table:

```
<table width="100%" border="0" cellpadding="1" cellspacing="1">
<tr>
<td>
<font size="+2" face="Arial, Helvetica, Verdana, sans serif"
  color="#602020"><b>Ragged Point Inn</b></font>
</td>
</tr>
<tr>
<td bgcolor="#804040"><img src="blank.gif" height="1" width="1"
  alt=""></td>
</tr>
</table>
```

We're actually going to replace the whole thing with this very simple construct:

```
<td id="content">
<h1>Ragged Point Inn</h1>
<p>
The views from the Ragged Point Inn are as spectacular as any along the coast.
Every room in the inn faces a sheer drop to the ocean; we recommend asking for
one of the few second-floor rooms for an even better view.  When the time of
year is right, it's not uncommon to see migrating whales just offshore.
</p>
```

A simple `h1` element is all it takes. This lets us re-create the original appearance using some very simple rules. For example, setting the font styles and color is as simple as this:

```
td#content p {font: 85% Arial, Helvetica, Verdana, sans-serif;}
h1 {font: bold 150% Arial, Helvetica, Verdana, sans-serif;
  color: #602020;}
</style>
```

We still have to re-create the thick line underneath the text. Looking back to the all-HTML design, we see that the line was created with an image 1 pixel tall. However, the table's cells also had 1-pixel `cellpadding`, which means the visible height of that cell was actually 3 pixels (one each for the top and bottom cell padding and one for the image height). Therefore:

```
h1 {font: bold 150% Arial, Helvetica, Verdana, sans-serif;
  color: #602020; border-bottom: 3px solid #804040;}
```

Finally, we ought to reproduce the separation between the text and the border beneath it. The cells in the table had 1 pixel of padding, but only the padding in the "Ragged Point Inn" cell should be considered because we've already accounted for the padding in the "border" cell. There was also 1 pixel of cell spacing, so that means 2 pixels of extra space (as we can see in Figure 1.11).

```
h1 {font: bold 150% Arial, Helvetica, Verdana, sans-serif;
  color: #602020; border-bottom: 3px solid #804040;
  padding-bottom: 2px;}
```

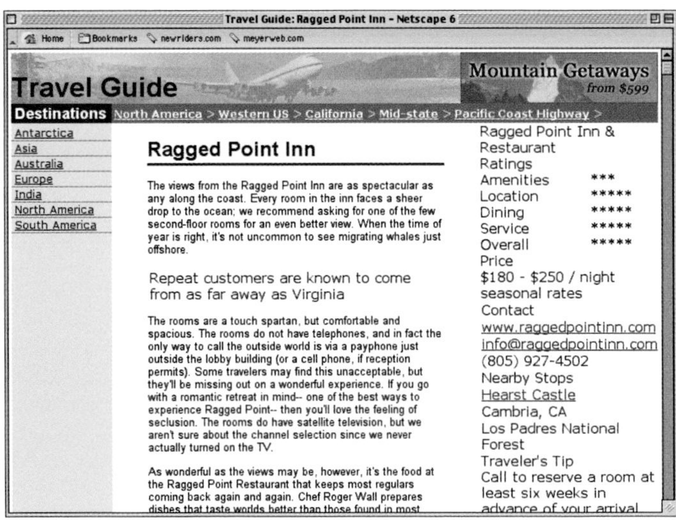

FIGURE 1.11

Styling the page's title with a single element and no table markup.

Styling the Pullquote

In many ways, the pullquote represents the entire `content` cell in miniature in that it has some space to either side enforced by image-only table cells. It's also reminiscent of the title because the lines to the top and bottom are created using images in table cells that have a background color set. Reproducing these effects will be fairly straightforward.

Let's take a look at the original markup for this part of the document:

```
<table width="160" border="0" cellpadding="0" cellspacing="1"
  align="right">
<tr>
<td width="5"><img src="blank.gif" height="1" width="5" alt=""></td>
<td>
<table width="100%" border="0" cellpadding="2" cellspacing="1">
<tr>
<td bgcolor="#908070"><img src="blank.gif" height="3" width="1"
  alt=""></td>
</tr>
<tr>
<td><font color="#A09080" face="Arial, Helvetica, Verdana,
  sans-serif"><b>Repeat customers are known to come from as far away
  as Virginia</b></font></td>
</tr>
<tr>
<td bgcolor="#908070"><img src="blank.gif" height="3" width="1"
  alt=""></td>
</tr>
</table>
</td>
<td width="5"><img src="blank.gif" height="1" width="5" alt=""></td>
</tr>
</table>
```

Pretty ugly. The one major difference here is that the visible part of the pullquote is nested inside another table. This "outer" table's job is to insert some more space around the pullquote and then float it to the right with `align="right"`.

The first thing we're going to do is jettison all of that cruft and replace it with a nice, clean element.

```
<div class="pullquote">
Repeat customers are known to come from as far away as Virginia
</div>
```

That's honestly all we need. Let's kick off this round of styling with some basics, as illustrated in Figure 1.12.

Why a Class This Time?

We've given the pullquote a `class` instead of an `id` because we don't know for sure that all designs will have only one pullquote. If there were ever two or more, the `id` value of `pullquote` wouldn't be unique, as `id` values must be.

```
h1 {font: bold 150% Arial, Helvetica, Verdana, sans-serif;
  color: #602020; border-bottom: 3px solid #804040;
  padding-bottom: 2px;}
div.pullquote {float: right; width: 160px;
   font: bold 1em Arial, Helvetica, Verdana, sans-serif;}
</style>
```

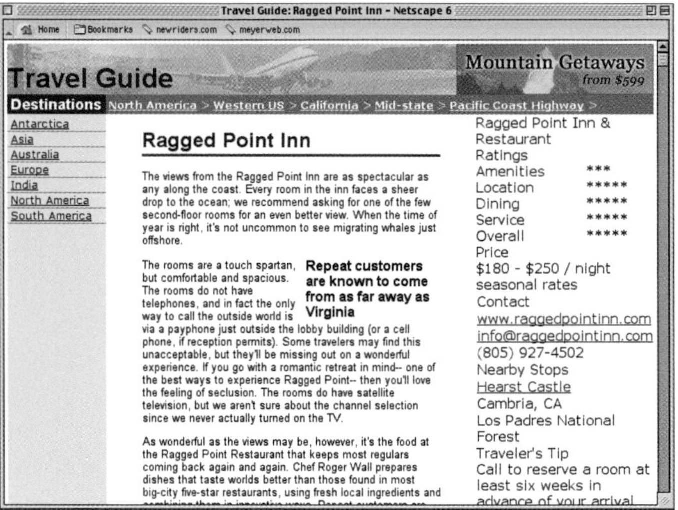

FIGURE 1.12

The beginnings of a well-styled pullquote.

We've set the `font-size` value to `1em` because there was no `size` attribute for the `font` element in the original design, and we listed it at all because `font` requires that its value contain both the size and family, in that order. The `width` value was taken from the `width="160"` from the outer table, but don't get too attached to it yet.

Let's set the color of the text and create the borders. Setting the text color is simple.

```
div.pullquote {float: right; width: 160px; color: #A09080;
  font: bold 1em Arial, Helvetica, Verdana, sans-serif;}
```

The original top and bottom borders were the effect of blank images inside table cells, so once again we need to do some math. The images were both 3 pixels tall, and the cell in which they resided had 2-pixel padding. Adding everything up, we find that 3 + 2 + 2 = 7, so that's how thick our borders should be.

We can't just set the entire border of the pullquote to be a 7-pixel-wide line, though, because the left and right sides don't have any border at all. There are a number of ways to account for this, but in this case, we're going to set the color and style of the border with one declaration and the thickness of the sides with another.

```
div.pullquote {float: right; width: 160px; color: #A09080;
  border: solid #908070; border-width: 7px 0;
  font: bold 1em Arial, Helvetica, Verdana, sans-serif;}
```

Now for the padding and margins. The padding around the text should be 2 pixels to reflect the `cellpadding="2"`, but the top and bottom get an extra pixel to reflect the effects of `cellspacing="1"`.

```
div.pullquote {float: right; width: 160px; color: #A09080;
  border: solid #908070; border-width: 7px 0;
  font: bold 1em Arial, Helvetica, Verdana, sans-serif;
  padding: 3px 2px;}
```

The margins are a reproduction of the effects of the image-only cells in the outer table and the value of `cellspacing` for that same table. (We can ignore `cellpadding` because it was set to `0`.) That leads us to 1 pixel on the top and bottom (based on the spacing) and 7 pixels on the right and left—5 pixels for the images and 1 pixel of spacing to either side of the cells containing those images.

```
div.pullquote {float: right; width: 160px; color: #A09080;
  border: solid #908070; border-width: 7px 0;
  font: bold 1em Arial, Helvetica, Verdana, sans-serif;
  padding: 3px 2px; margin: 1px 7px;}
```

With that in place, we need to make only one more small adjustment. Because the original pullquote was a table inside the outer table, its width will be narrower than `160px`. We need to reduce the value by the total of the left and right margins we just set. Furthermore, the `width` of an element in CSS refers to the width of the contents, not the overall visible width, so we need to subtract out the left and right padding on the element. The math works out to be 160 - 7 - 7 - 2 - 2 = 142. Let's round that down a couple so we have a nice even number. All these changes result in Figure 1.13.

```
div.pullquote {float: right; width: 140px; color: #A09080;
  border: solid #908070; border-width: 7px 0;
  font: bold 1em Arial, Helvetica, Verdana, sans-serif;
  padding: 3px 2px; margin: 1px 7px;}
```

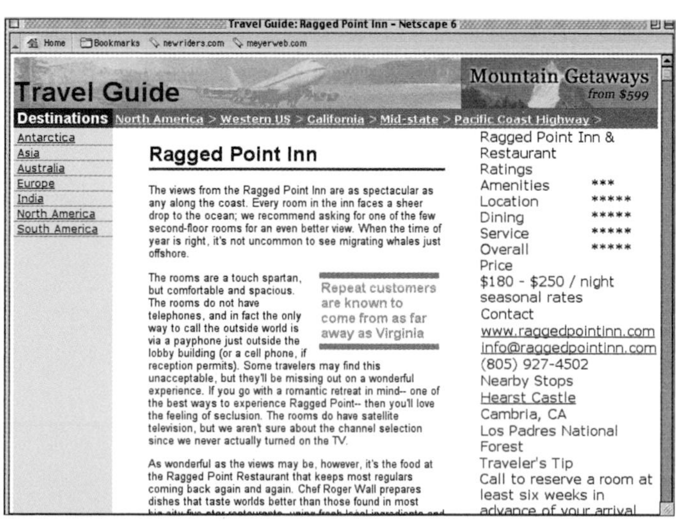

FIGURE 1.13

The pullquote is restored to its former glory in a much leaner way.

The Right Styles for the Right Side

Of all the pieces of the design, the most complicated is probably the right sidebar. A lot of information is being conveyed there, and that information is contained in quite a few elements.

As usual, though, let's handle the basics first. We'll give an `id` to the cell that defines this sidebar.

```
<td id="rightside">
```

Having done that, we can define the width of the cell and the size of the text within it.

```
div.pullquote {float: right; width: 140px; color: #A09080;
   border: solid #908070; border-width: 7px 0;
   font: bold 1em Arial, Helvetica, Verdana, sans-serif;
   padding: 3px 2px; margin: 1px 7px;}
td#rightside {width: 150px;}
td#rightside td {font-size: 66%; padding: 1px;}
</style>
```

The second rule will set the text for all table cells found inside the `rightside` cell to be `66%` normal size. This roughly corresponds to the HTML construct `<font size="-2">`.

We're going to skip ahead just a bit and style the separator heads between each chunk of information in the sidebar. For example, the cell containing the word "Ratings" used to look like this:

```
<tr>
<td colspan="2" align="center" bgcolor="#D6B58C"><font size="-2"
  face="Verdana, Arial, Helvetica,
  sans-serif"><b>Ratings</b></font></td>
</tr>
```

With all of the HTML-based presentation gone, we need to add in a `class` that indicates what kind of information is found in this cell.

```
<tr><td colspan="2" class="head">Ratings</td></tr>
```

Here's another example of the same thing later on in the document:

```
<tr><td class="head">Nearby Stops</td></tr>
```

Once we've classed all four cells that contain separator head text, we can style them in a consistent manner (see Figure 1.14).

```
td#rightside td {font-size: 66%; padding: 1px;}
td.head {background: #D6B58C; text-align: center; font-weight: bold;}
</style>
```

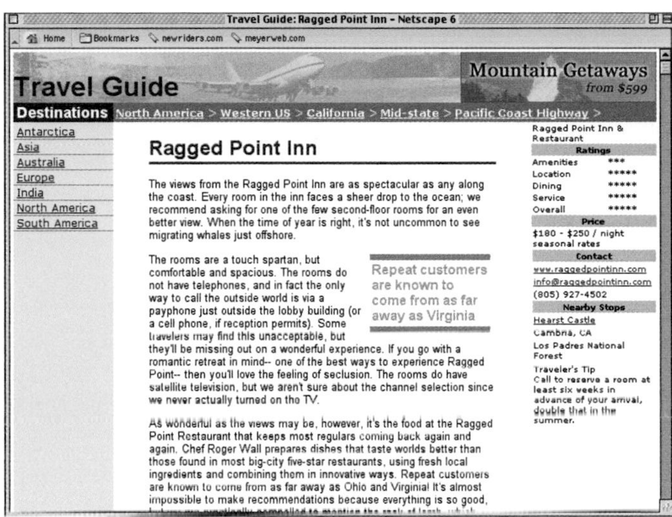

FIGURE 1.14

Styling all four separator heads with a single rule.

At this point, we're actually pretty close to being finished with the right side, at least from a visual standpoint. All we really have to do is style the top of the sidebar, the Ratings table, and the Traveler's Tip at the bottom.

The top of the sidebar will be simple. In this case, rather than attaching another `id` to the cell, we're going to change the nature of the cell.

```
<tr>
<th colspan="2">Ragged Point Inn &amp; Restaurant</th>
</tr>
<tr>
<td colspan="2" class="head">Ratings</td>
</tr>
```

Because the information in the cell is a sort of heading for the entire sidebar, it makes some sense to convert the `td` to a `th`. This also lets us style the entire element in one go.

```
td.head {background: #D6B58C; text-align: center; font-weight: bold;}
td#rightside th {font-size: 85%; padding: 2px;
  background: #774411; color: white; text-align: center;}
</style>
```

It may seem odd that the rule's selector has a `th` following the `td#rightside`, but it's fine. That's because the `th` elements are descended from the right side `td`. They're also descended from the `table` and `tr` elements that contain them. The elements "between" the `td` and the `th` don't prevent the descendant selector from working.

Centering a Table Header

Although most browsers will automatically center the contents of a `th` element, you never know when a new browser will come along that doesn't. That's why we've explicitly defined `text-align` in our `td#rightside th` rule.

Furthermore, because the contents of this `th` cell aren't contained in any other kind of element (such as a link or a `span`), we can get away with just styling the `th` itself. This is illustrated in Figure 1.15.

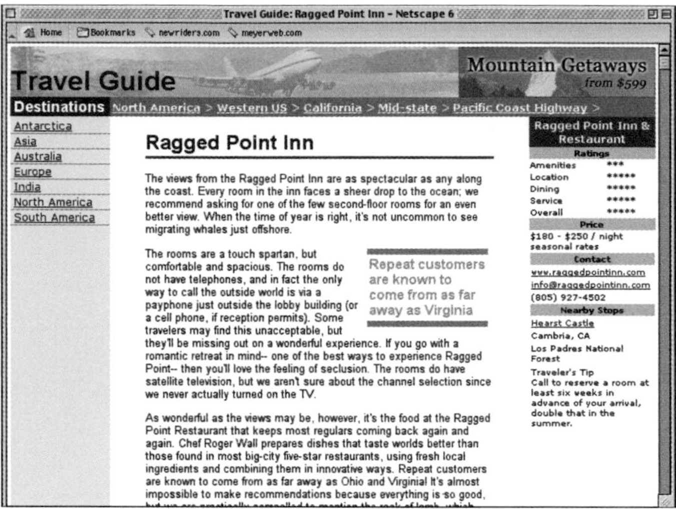

FIGURE 1.15

Giving the top of the right sidebar some style.

Ratings with Style

You might think we're about to convert the ratings to some complex set of elements and CSS, but that's not the case. It makes perfect sense to represent this data in a table, so we're not going to change that aspect of the page.

In the original design, there were different text colors for different numbers of stars. Also, the second and fourth rows were given `bgcolor="#F7F0E7"`, resulting in a nice alternate-row highlighting effect. To reproduce these effects, we'll need to enhance the structure of the table.

For the row highlighting, we could just `class` the rows as being even or odd, depending on which they are. So, for the ratings, it would make sense to class each cell according to the number of stars it contains (that is, the actual rating). So here's what we're going to do to the markup for the ratings:

```
<tr class="odd">
<td>Amenities</td><td class="r3">***</td>
</tr>
<tr class="even">
<td>Location</td><td class="r5">*****</td>
</tr>
<tr class="odd">
<td>Dining</td><td class="r5">*****</td>
</tr>
<tr class="even">
<td>Service</td><td class="r5">*****</td>
</tr>
<tr class="odd">
<td>Overall</td><td class="r5">*****</td>
</tr>
```

Starting with a Letter

We've started the rating `class` names with an "r" because CSS doesn't permit `class` or `id` values to begin with a number (unless you throw in an escape character), and thus some browsers won't recognize a `class` or `id` name that starts with a number.

We started with `odd` because, of course, 1 is an odd number, so the first row is an odd one. With the rows classed in this manner, highlighting every other one is a simple matter. We can also use this rule to set the `width` of the cells to match the original design.

```
td#rightside th {font-size: 85%; padding: 2px;
  background: #774411; color: white;}
tr.even td {background: #F7F0E7; width: 50%;}
</style>
```

We could apply the background color directly to the `tr` element itself, but there's no guarantee that a browser will know how to style an actual table row. Because there is no space between the cells in this table, we can go ahead and style the cells themselves. Their backgrounds will touch each other and thus provide the appearance of a single row style.

Three-Digit Colors

Don't worry; we didn't forget any numbers. If three digits (or letters) are provided for a color value, each one is replicated to fill out the usual six-digit notation. Thus, `#660` is the same as `#666600` and `#060` is equivalent to `#006600`.

Styling the rating cells is just as easy.

```
tr.even td {background: #F7F0E7; width: 50%;}
td.r3 {color: #660;}
td.r5 {color: #060;}
</style>
```

With these styles in place, the Ratings area of the page is ready to go, as we can see in Figure 1.16.

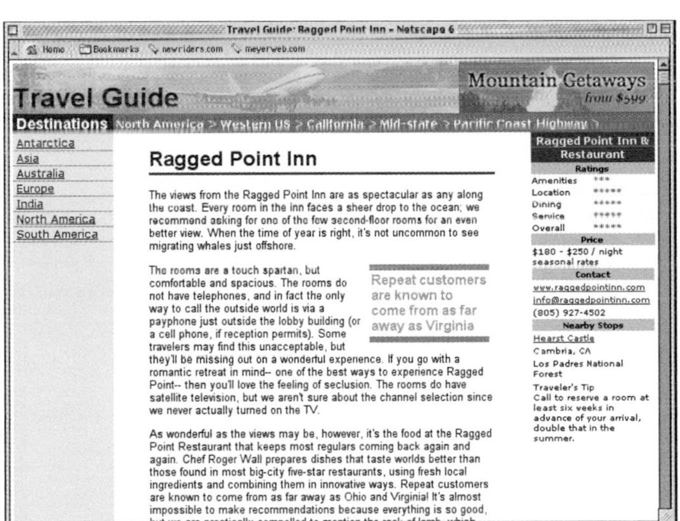

FIGURE 1.16

The ratings regain their old appearance.

A Stylish Tip

We're getting close to the end. All we need to do is style the Traveler's Tip, and we'll be done with the right sidebar. After that, we'll do a quick styling of the footer and be done.

The original markup for the tip should be familiar by now: a table nested inside a table. In this case, however, the point was to draw a thick, dark border around a block of text with a differently colored background. We can re-create that easily enough.

```
<div id="traveltip">
<b>Traveler's Tip</b><br>
Call to reserve a room at least six weeks in advance of your arrival, double
that in the summer.
</div>
```

We're going to leave the `<b>` and `<br>` elements in place because it doesn't really make any sense to pull them out. Sure, we could replace them with an `h5` and style it, but why bother? What we have now will serve well enough.

Once we work through the math of table-cell spacing and padding, we find that the border should be 3 pixels wide and the `div` should have 8 pixels of padding. Furthermore, the text needs to be centered, the background color set, and the entire element given a largish top margin so that it doesn't crowd the bottom of the Nearby Stops area.

Finally, we need to set the text to be the same small size as the rest of the sidebar. We need to do this because the tip is no longer inside a table cell, so the rule `td#rightside td` no longer applies to this element. We'll need to reproduce the value used to style the rest of the sidebar. This leads us to write the following rule (see Figure 1.17):

```
td.r5 {color: #060;}
div#traveltip {border: 3px solid #804040; background: #EBDAC6;
  text-align: center; margin-top: 1.5em; padding: 8px; font-size: 66%;}
</style>
```

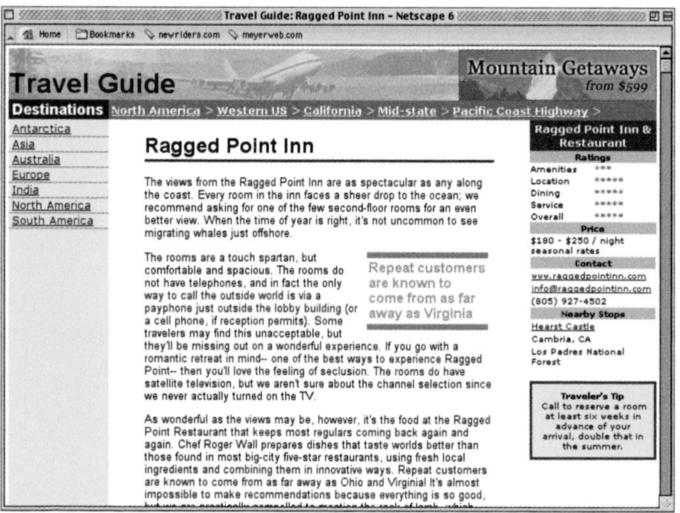

FIGURE 1.17

A beautiful tip that's useful to boot.

Fixing the Footer

As we enter the homestretch, all that remains is to style the footer of the document. In keeping with our new habits, we're going to `id` everything to make styling easier.

```
<tr id="footer">
<td id="feedback"><a href="/feedback.html">Feedback -
  Contact</a></td>
<td id="tg">Travel Guide</td>
<td id="copyright">Copyright 2002</td>
</tr>
```

First let's set the font size, horizontal alignment, and style of the fonts. In the original design, the "Feedback—Contact" text was centered, the "Travel Guide" text was centered and slightly larger than the other two cells, and the copyright was italicized and right justified. In addition, the entire row was set to `valign="middle"`. No problem there, as Figure 1.18 shows.

```
div#traveltip {border: 3px solid #804040; background: #EBDAC6;
  text-align: center; margin-top: 1.5em; padding: 8px; font-size: 66%;}
tr#footer td {vertical-align: middle; font-size: 66%;}
td#feedback {text-align: center; padding: 0.2em;}
tr#footer td#tg {font-size: 85%; text-align: center;}
td#copyright {text-align: right; font-style: italic;}
</style>
```

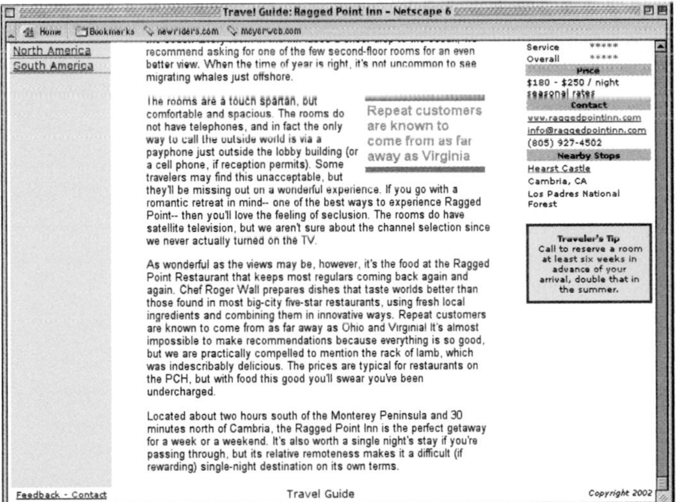

FIGURE 1.18
Bringing the footer mostly in line with its original look.

With these styles in place, all we need to add now is whatever coloration was present in the original. One design feature we can't overlook is the 3-pixel "border" running between the main content and the footer. This was (as you might expect) created with a blank image inside a table cell. However, that cell and image are gone now, so we'll have to replace them with something else, like a border on top of the three cells in the `footer` row.

```
tr#footer td {vertical-align: middle; font-size: 66%;
  border-top: 3px solid #EFE1D1;}
```

Finally, here are the necessary background and foreground colors for the footer:

```
td#feedback {text-align: center; padding: 0.2em;
  background: #EFE1D1;}
tr#footer td#tg {font-size: 85%; text-align: center;}
td#copyright {text-align: right; font-style: italic; color: #999;}
```

These last few changes lead to the result shown in Figure 1.19 and the end of our re-creation of HTML-based presentation in CSS. The complete style sheet is provided in Listing 1.1.

FIGURE 1.19

The footer is returned to its original appearance.

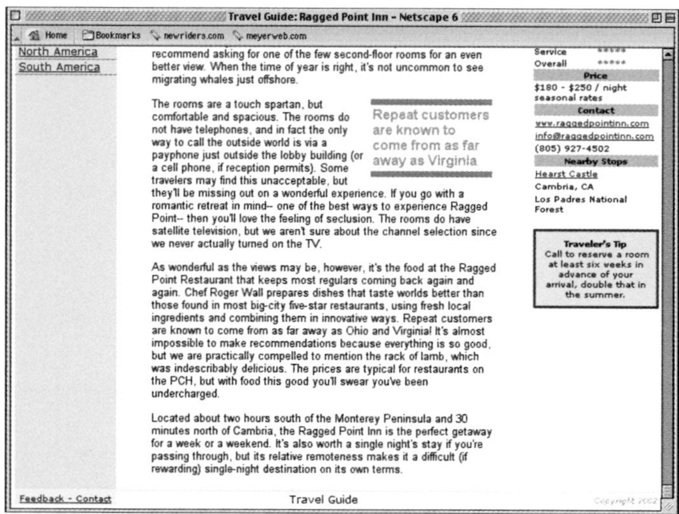

Listing 1.1 The Complete Style Sheet

```
body {margin: 4px; color: black; background: white;}
table {width: 100%; margin: 0;}
table td {padding: 0; border-width: 0; vertical-align: top;
  font-family: Verdana, Arial, Helvetica, sans-serif;}
a:link {color: #990000;}
a:visited {color: #990099;}
td#title {vertical-align: bottom; color: #442200;
   background: transparent url(topbg.gif) top left;
   font: bold 200% Arial, Helvetica, Verdana, sans-serif;}
td#advert {width: 234px;}
#content-top td {vertical-align: middle; color: white;
  font-weight: bold; padding: 0.1em 0.2em 0;}
tr td#sidetop {background: #663300;
  font: bold 115% Arial, Helvetica, Verdana, sans-serif;}
tr td#crumbs {background: #997753; font-size: 85%;}
tr td#crumbs a:link {color: white;}
tr td#crumbs a:visited {color: gray;}
td#leftside {width: 120px; background: #EBDAC6;}
```

```
td#leftside td {border-bottom: 1px solid #A98763; font-size: 85%;
  padding: 0 0 1px 0.33em;}
td#leftside table {margin-top: 3px;}
td#content {padding: 17px 42px;}
td#content p {font: 85% Arial, Helvetica, Verdana, sans-serif;}
h1 {font: bold 150% Arial, Helvetica, Verdana, sans-serif;
  color: #602020; border-bottom: 3px solid #804040;
  padding-bottom: 2px;}
div.pullquote {float: right; width: 140px; color: #A09080;
   border: solid #908070; border-width: 7px 0;
   font: bold 1em Arial, Helvetica, Verdana, sans-serif;
   padding: 3px 2px; margin: 1px 7px;}
td#rightside {width: 150px;}
td#rightside td {font-size: 66%; padding: 1px;}
td.head {background: #D6B58C; text-align: center; font-weight: bold;}
td#rightside th {font-size: 85%; padding: 2px;
  background: #774411; color: white;}
tr.even td {background: #F7F0E7; width: 50%;}
td.r3 {color: #660;}
td.r5 {color: #060;}
div#traveltip {border: 3px solid #804040; background: #EBDAC6;
  text-align: center; margin-top: 1.5em; padding: 8px; font-size: 66%;}
tr#footer td {vertical-align: middle; font-size: 66%;
  border-top: 3px solid #EFE1D1;}
td#feedback {text-align: center; padding: 0.2em;
  background: #EFE1D1;}
tr#footer td#tg {font-size: 85%; text-align: center;}
td#copyright {text-align: right; font-style: italic; color: #999;}
```

The Benefits of All Our Work

It might occur to you to wonder why exactly we've gone to all this effort. After all, there were plenty of places where we had to type more CSS than the HTML represented. There are two good reasons.

First, the document structure is a lot cleaner and thus a lot easier to edit and generally maintain. Let's say you have an unclosed element somewhere in your markup, and it is completely messing up the layout. Would you rather sift through the HTML design, choked as it is with `font` tags and tables nested inside tables, or the relatively clean structure we had at the end of the conversion process? Personally, I'd much prefer the latter.

Second, there is a marked savings in terms of file size. Table 1.1 compares the file sizes, element counts, and server hits that are (or might be) necessary for each of three approaches: the all-HTML design, the converted document with the style sheet embedded, and the converted document with the style sheet made external and `link`ed in.

External Styles

For more information on external style sheets, see Project 2, "Styling a Press Release."

Table 1.1 A Qualitative Comparison of the Three Approaches

Method	Size*	Characters	Server Hits	Images	Tables	Font Tags
All HTML	100%	10,617	4 to 19	18 (16 repeat)	11	49
HTML+CSS	64.2%	6,819	3	2	5	0
HTML with link	44.6%	4,738 + 2,112	3 to 4	2	5	0

*Compared to the all-HTML method; refers to the size of the HTML document only

Even with the style sheet left inside the document, there's a 35% reduction in the size of the file. In addition, thanks to the elimination of all those "blank" images, the number of server hits required to serve up the page actually drops by one at a minimum.

If the style sheet is moved into an external file, the benefits are even more striking. The size of the HTML document drops to less than half its original size, for starters. Even better, the number of server hits is no more than the original document would have been and might drop by one after the first page is loaded from the server. This is because browsers usually cache external style sheets after they're loaded the first time. Thus, the server won't be asked for the external style sheet after the user loads the first page (that uses this style sheet) from the server.

All in all, it seems like a worthwhile effort to undertake, especially when it's so easy to get results like those shown in Figure 1.20.

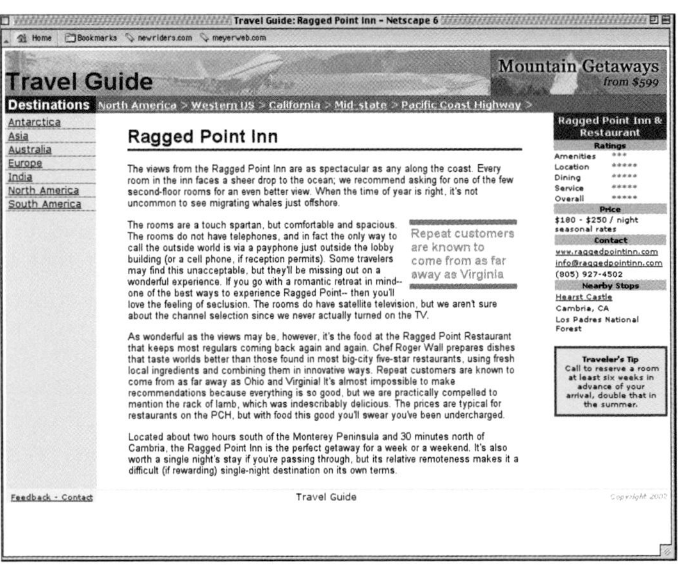

FIGURE 1.20

The complete design, as redone in CSS.

Further Savings

It's worth noting that we didn't pare down the document structure as far as we could have. (Why not? Mostly to keep the project from being longer than it already is.)

For example, many of the foreground and background colors we defined could have been shortened to the three-digit notation instead of using six digits. This would have yielded a small reduction in file size. On the other hand, it might not be worth it if you find the three-digit notation confusing.

More obvious savings could be derived from change to the HTML document itself. The left-side links were left inside a `table` that was nested inside a table cell. We could have replaced this structure with one in which each link was enclosed inside its own `div` element, and we'd still have gotten exactly the same visual layout. This might have shaved another 100 to 200 characters from the file and made it still easier to read.

Even More Link Savings

For that matter, we could have done away with the `table` and not dropped in any `div`s (instead just leaving the links in the cell by themselves), and we'd still have gotten the same visual effect. See Project 5, "How to Skin a Menu," for details.

Similarly, most of the tables on the right side, with the exception of the actual ratings, could have been reduced to heading elements (for example, `h4`) and `div`s. The reduction in file size again would have been relatively small, and this is why we didn't bother. For your own edification, try tearing out as many tables as you can while still maintaining the original appearance. While you're at it, look to the next section for some new challenges.

Branching Out

Starting with the styles we created in this project, try to accomplish the following modifications without changing the document's structure—and notice how easy it is to do this way instead of trying to rewrite the HTML.

1. Eliminate the underlines from the links in the left-hand sidebar and the "breadcrumbs" area but not the right-hand sidebar or the footer. (Hint: The property `text-decoration` will be of use here.) In addition, give the right-hand sidebar links a different default color than the rest of the page. Use the same shade of brown that's set in the background of the `th` element at the top of the right-hand sidebar.

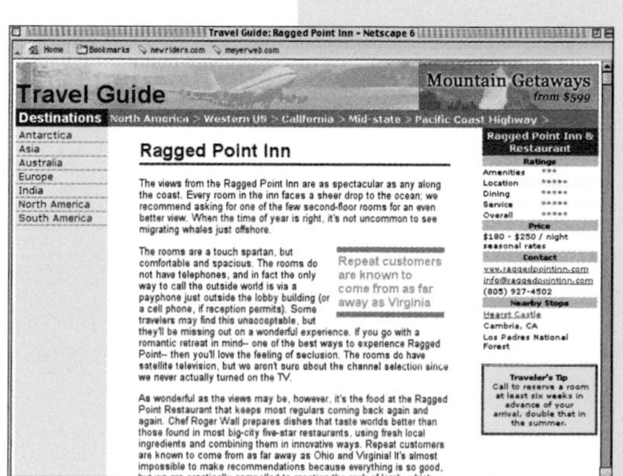

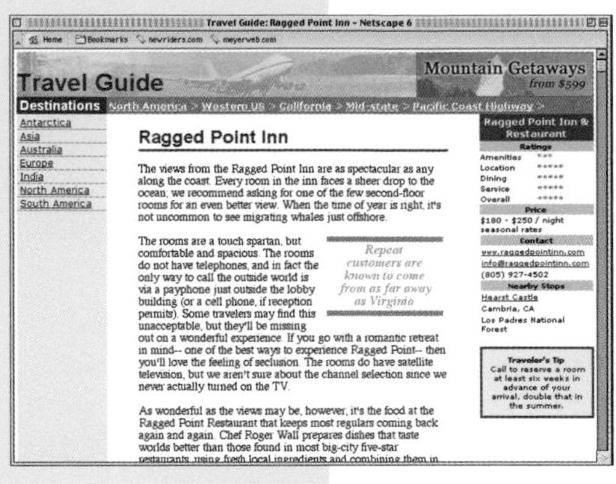

2. Try restyling the pullquote so that it's noticeably different than the design we settled on. For example, it could be given extra side padding so that the top and bottom borders "overhang," and the text could be centered and italicized. For that matter, the font could be changed to a serif font, and the whole element would be given a different color. With that done, change the main-text paragraphs so they use a normal-size serif font like Times.

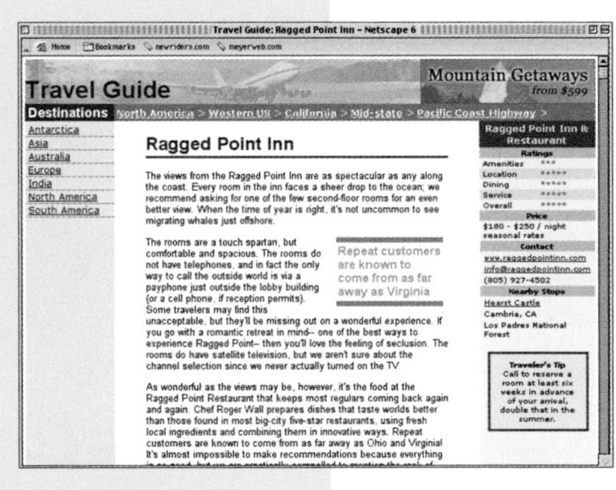

3. Give the right-hand sidebar a background color like the left-hand sidebar, but use the same shade of brown found in the background of the footer. Add some margins to the Traveler's Tip so that it doesn't touch the side of the sidebar any more and add some left padding to the table cells inside the sidebar. Finally, adjust the highlight colors for the Ratings table so they don't clash with the new background.

2

Styling a Press Release

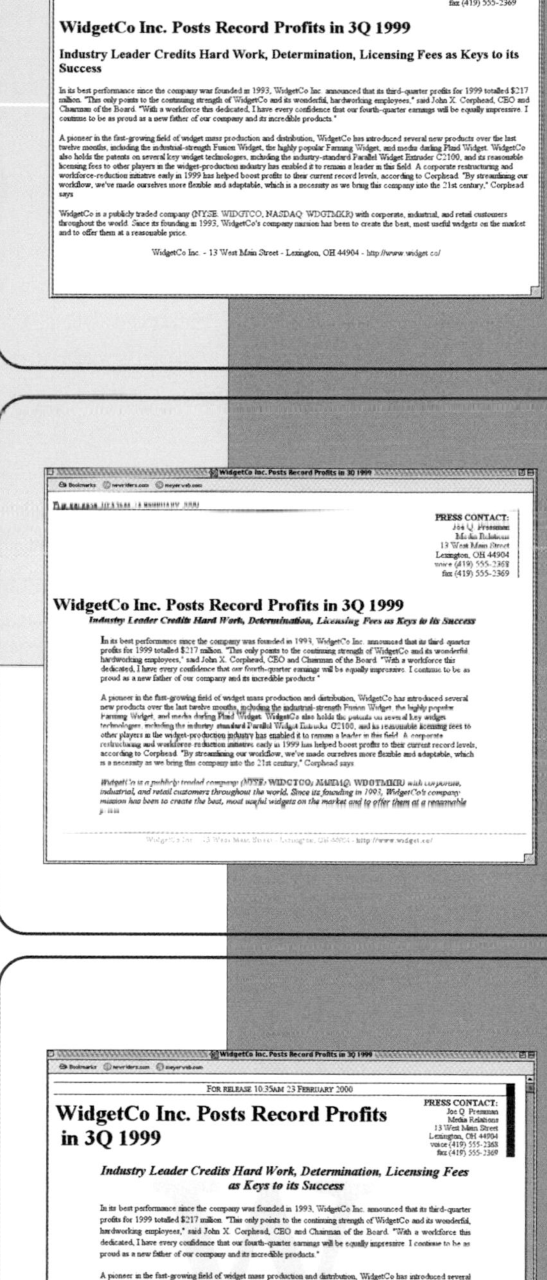

Corporation, n. An ingenious device for obtaining individual profit without individual responsibility.

—*Ambrose Bierce*

In the corporate world, press releases are pretty commonplace, and it's just as common to take those press releases and put them on the Web. In many cases they're posted as raw text files, which is about as boring as you might imagine. Others put up press releases with the thinnest of styling—a font selection maybe and not much else. Wouldn't it be nicer if this information were at least pleasant to the eye, if not always the stomach?

Project Goals

As part of an improved outreach program, our top client, WidgetCo, will be posting all of its press releases to the Web site. Of course, most press releases are pretty dull to look at, so the client hopes that jazzing up its look a bit will help set the company apart as a dynamic, cutting-edge firm. To that end, we'll take a very straightforward press-release template and create a style sheet for it.

Preparation

See the Introduction for instructions on how to download files from the Web site.

Download the files for Project 2 from the book's Web site. If you're planning to play along at home, load the file `ch02proj.html` into the editing program of your choice. This is the file you'll be editing, saving, and reloading as the project progresses.

Laying the Groundwork

First we need to look over the press release with some basic HTML markup (see Figure 2.1). This needs to be fairly simple structural markup, not the nested-table stuff you usually see. We'll add in some `div`s and classes to give ourselves some styling hooks in just a moment.

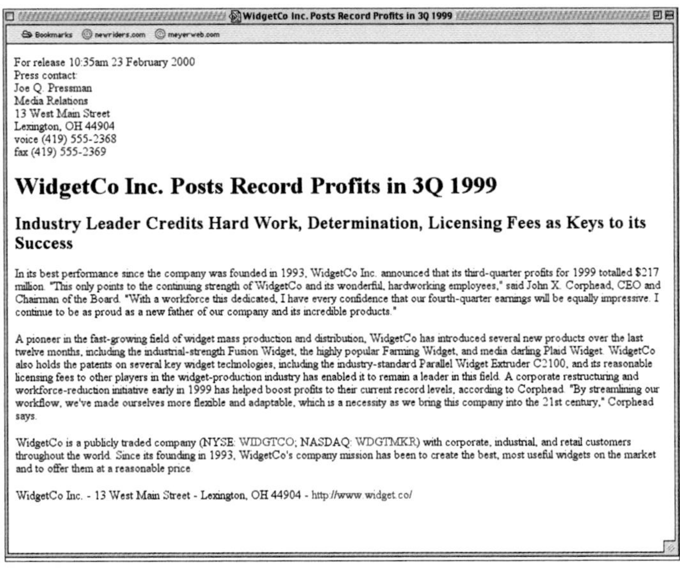

WidgetCo Inc. Posts Record Profits in 3Q 1999

Bookmarks newriders.com meyerweb.com

For release 10:35am 23 February 2000
Press contact:
Joe Q. Pressman
Media Relations
13 West Main Street
Lexington, OH 44904
voice (419) 555-2368
fax (419) 555-2369

WidgetCo Inc. Posts Record Profits in 3Q 1999

Industry Leader Credits Hard Work, Determination, Licensing Fees as Keys to its Success

In its best performance since the company was founded in 1993, WidgetCo Inc. announced that its third-quarter profits for 1999 totalled $217 million. "This only points to the continuing strength of WidgetCo and its wonderful, hardworking employees," said John X. Corphead, CEO and Chairman of the Board. "With a workforce this dedicated, I have every confidence that our fourth-quarter earnings will be equally impressive. I continue to be as proud as a new father of our company and its incredible products."

A pioneer in the fast-growing field of widget mass production and distribution, WidgetCo has introduced several new products over the last twelve months, including the industrial-strength Fusion Widget, the highly popular Farming Widget, and media darling Plaid Widget. WidgetCo also holds the patents on several key widget technologies, including the industry-standard Parallel Widget Extruder C2100, and its reasonable licensing fees to other players in the widget-production industry has enabled it to remain a leader in this field. A corporate restructuring and workforce-reduction initiative early in 1999 has helped boost profits to their current record levels, according to Corphead. "By streamlining our workflow, we've made ourselves more flexible and adaptable, which is a necessity as we bring this company into the 21st century," Corphead says.

WidgetCo is a publicly traded company (NYSE: WIDGTCO; NASDAQ: WDGTMKR) with corporate, industrial, and retail customers throughout the world. Since its founding in 1993, WidgetCo's company mission has been to create the best, most useful widgets on the market and to offer them at a reasonable price.

WidgetCo Inc. - 13 West Main Street - Lexington, OH 44904 - http://www.widget.co/

Figure 2.1

A basic press release, not yet styled with CSS.

Next we want to add a little more structure to the head of the document so that it will be much easier to style later on. We'll separate out the release-date line into its own `div`, like this:

```
<div>
For release 10:35am 23 February 2000
</div>
<div>
Press contact:<br>
```

What Happened to the Break?

The `<br>` was removed from the release `div` because it's no longer needed. The line-break effect of the `<br>` has been replaced by the implicit line break caused by the new `</div>`. `div`, being a block-level element, has the effect of forcing a line break at its end.

Now that we've done that, we need to make each `div` distinct from the other. We're going to use a `class` and an `id` here:

```
<div class="release">
For release 10:35am 23 February 2000
</div>
<div id="contact-info">
Press contact:<br>
```

The release date gets a `class` because it's possible that another release line might be added to the template later, perhaps at the bottom of the file, and we want to give that second release line the same `class` as the first one. The contact information, on the other hand, should appear only once within the press release, so we'll use an `id`.

THE DIFFERENCE BETWEEN `class` AND `id`

A `class` is used whenever the same type of information will be seen more than once in a document. For example, you could class all hyperlinks that point to other Web servers as "external," or if you have a document with lots of examples, you could class every "example" element. An `id` is used to mark information that is unique within a document (for example, a footer or the title of the page). You might have multiple `id`s in a document, but each `id` must have a value that is different from all other `id` values in that document. In addition, `id` values must not be case-insensitive matches; in other words, you shouldn't have `id="page-title"` and `id="Page-Title"` in the same document.

While we're at it, let's `class` and `id` a few more elements in the document. The lead paragraph of the press release might need some special styling later on, so let's give it a `class` of `lead-para`. The third paragraph is a sort of corporate summary, so we'll give it an `id` of `summary`. The last paragraph is a footer of sorts, so we'll convert it to a `div` and give it an appropriate `id`:

Why We Class

Why a `class` instead of an `id`? Because future press releases might have multiple sections—each with its own lead paragraph.

```
<div id="footer">
WidgetCo Inc. - 13 West Main Street - Lexington, OH  44904 - <a
href="http://www.widget.co/">http://www.widget.co/</a>
</div>
```

Finally, let's put the same class on both links to the stock-market Web sites' information about WidgetCo. A class called `stockinfo` seems sensible, so we'll alter the markup like this:

```
WidgetCo is a publicly traded company (NYSE: <a
href="http://www.nyse.sm/show_stock.cgi?WIDGTCO"
class="stockinfo">WIDGTCO</a>; NASDAQ: <a
href="http://www.nasdaq.sm/list/tech/wdgtmkr/"
class="stockinfo">WDGTMKR</a>)
with corporate, industrial, and retail customers throughout the world.
```

With all that done, we're ready to get stylish!

Styling the Document

The first thing we'll do is change the horizontal alignment of a couple of elements—the contact information (right-aligned) and the footer (centered), like this:

```
<style type="text/css">
body {background: white; color: black;}
div#contact-info {text-align: right;}
div#footer {text-align: center;}
</style>
```

We have included a default `body` rule so that we know where we're starting: with black text on a white background. This is the most common browser default, so it's where we're going to start. By explicitly declaring these values, we make sure that any CSS-capable browser is going to start from the same point we did when we wrote our styles.

▸▸ Alignment Myths

The property `text-align` can be used to center the content of block-level elements such as paragraphs, but it is not meant to center the elements themselves. This sets `text-align: center` apart from the deprecated `center` element, which centers everything within it—both content and block-level elements. Modern browsers, such as Netscape 6.x and IE6, understand this distinction. Therefore, trying to use `text-align: center` to replace `center` is strongly discouraged. You'll only get frustrated. On the other hand, older browsers like IE5.x treated `text-align: center` as if it were `center`, so this needs to be taken into account when designing. On the third hand, this problem can be used to overcome certain browser bugs, as we'll see in Project 8, "Creating an Online Greeting Card."

Let's keep styling the contact information and footer.

Old-Time Ignorance

Pre-version 5 browsers don't understand `:first-line`, so they will ignore this style. Although we could add some HTML and extra CSS to compensate for this, it's probably better to just accept the difference in old browsers and move on.

The Contact Info

To highlight the contact information, we want to boldface and uppercase the words "Press contact:" and give the entire element a little bit of a right-hand margin so that it isn't jammed up against the right-hand side of the browser window. Fortunately for us, the words "Press contact:" make up the first line of the `div`, so styling them is simple.

```
div#contact-info {text-align: right;}
div#contact-info:first-line {font-weight: bold;
   text-transform: uppercase;}
div#footer {text-align: center;}
```

To give the contact info a right margin and some padding, add the appropriate style to a rule we already have (see Figure 2.2):

```
div#contact-info {text-align: right;
   margin-right: 1em; padding-right: 1em;}
```

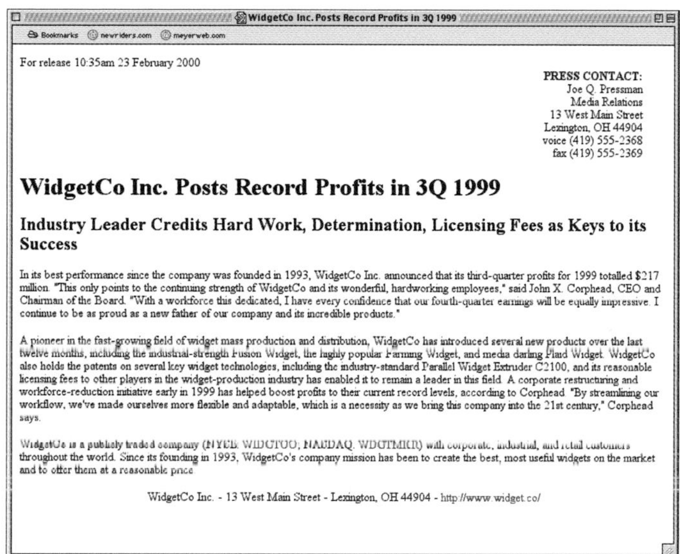

WidgetCo Inc. Posts Record Profits in 3Q 1999

Bookmarks newriders.com meyerweb.com

For release 10:35am 23 February 2000

PRESS CONTACT:
Joe Q. Pressman
Media Relations
13 West Main Street
Lexington, OH 44904
voice (419) 555-2368
fax (419) 555-2369

WidgetCo Inc. Posts Record Profits in 3Q 1999

Industry Leader Credits Hard Work, Determination, Licensing Fees as Keys to its Success

In its best performance since the company was founded in 1993, WidgetCo Inc. announced that its third-quarter profits for 1999 totalled $217 million. "This only points to the continuing strength of WidgetCo and its wonderful, hardworking employees," said John X. Corphead, CEO and Chairman of the Board. "With a workforce this dedicated, I have every confidence that our fourth-quarter earnings will be equally impressive. I continue to be as proud as a new father of our company and its incredible products."

A pioneer in the fast-growing field of widget mass production and distribution, WidgetCo has introduced several new products over the last twelve months, including the industrial-strength Fusion Widget, the highly popular Farming Widget, and media darling Plaid Widget. WidgetCo also holds the patents on several key widget technologies, including the industry-standard Parallel Widget Extruder C2100, and its reasonable licensing fees to other players in the widget-production industry has enabled it to remain a leader in this field. A corporate restructuring and workforce-reduction initiative early in 1999 has helped boost profits to their current record levels, according to Corphead. "By streamlining our workflow, we've made ourselves more flexible and adaptable, which is a necessity as we bring this company into the 21st century," Corphead says.

WidgetCo is a publicly traded company (NYSE: WIDGTCO; NASDAQ: WDGTMKR) with corporate, industrial, and retail customers throughout the world. Since its founding in 1993, WidgetCo's company mission has been to create the best, most useful widgets on the market and to offer them at a reasonable price.

WidgetCo Inc. - 13 West Main Street - Lexington, OH 44904 - http://www.widget.co/

FIGURE 2.2

The release information gets a touch of style.

A little bit later on, we'll see why combining margins and padding is a good idea.

The Page Footer

Let's turn to the footer now. Because it is a footer, we're going to give it a larger top margin, give it a top rule (or line) to set it apart, and make its text look significantly different from the rest of the document. First, let's set it apart from the rest of the document by adding on to our existing rule:

```
div#footer {text-align: center; margin-top: 2.5em;
   border-top: 1px solid gray;}
```

We also want to "fade" the text and have decided to make it smaller than normal (see Figure 2.3). This leads us to the following rule:

```
div#footer {text-align: center; margin-top: 2.5em;
   border-top: 1px solid gray; color: #AAA; font-size: 85%;}
```

There are three things to notice here:

- The text is kind of close to the top border.
- The text looks kind of squished together.
- The hyperlink has not changed color, so it looks a little odd next to the faded text.

FIGURE 2.3

Fading text reduces its impact on page balance.

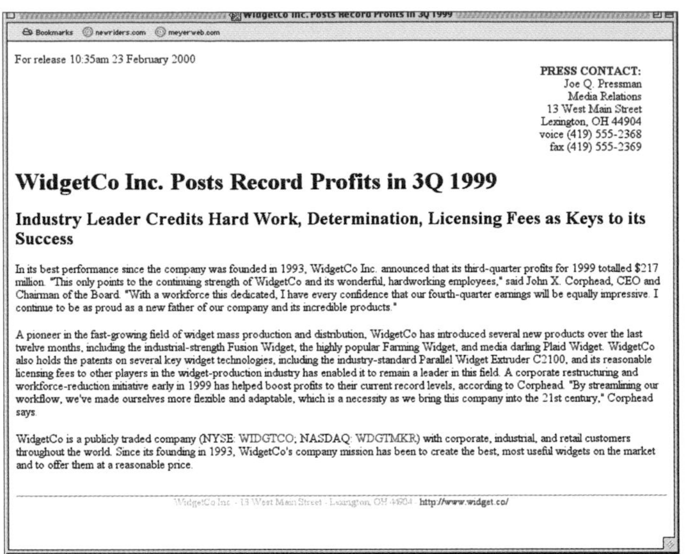

WidgetCo Inc. Posts Record Profits in 3Q 1999

Bookmarks newriders.com meyerweb.com

For release 10:35am 23 February 2000

PRESS CONTACT:
Joe Q. Pressman
Media Relations
13 West Main Street
Lexington, OH 44904
voice (419) 555-2368
fax (419) 555-2369

WidgetCo Inc. Posts Record Profits in 3Q 1999

Industry Leader Credits Hard Work, Determination, Licensing Fees as Keys to its Success

In its best performance since the company was founded in 1993, WidgetCo Inc. announced that its third-quarter profits for 1999 totalled $217 million. "This only points to the continuing strength of WidgetCo and its wonderful, hardworking employees," said John X. Corphead, CEO and Chairman of the Board. "With a workforce this dedicated, I have every confidence that our fourth-quarter earnings will be equally impressive. I continue to be as proud as a new father of our company and its incredible products."

A pioneer in the fast-growing field of widget mass production and distribution, WidgetCo has introduced several new products over the last twelve months, including the industrial-strength Fusion Widget, the highly popular Farming Widget, and media darling Plaid Widget. WidgetCo also holds the patents on several key widget technologies, including the industry-standard Parallel Widget Extruder C2100, and its reasonable licensing fees to other players in the widget-production industry has enabled it to remain a leader in this field. A corporate restructuring and workforce-reduction initiative early in 1999 has helped boost profits to their current record levels, according to Corphead. "By streamlining our workflow, we've made ourselves more flexible and adaptable, which is a necessity as we bring this company into the 21st century," Corphead says.

WidgetCo is a publicly traded company (NYSE: WIDGTCO; NASDAQ: WDGTMKR) with corporate, industrial, and retail customers throughout the world. Since its founding in 1993, WidgetCo's company mission has been to create the best, most useful widgets on the market and to offer them at a reasonable price.

WidgetCo Inc. - 13 West Main Street - Lexington, OH 44904 - http://www.widget.co/

To deal with the first problem, all we need is a little top padding. To handle the second issue, we'll spread out the letters just a little bit:

```
div#footer {text-align: center; margin-top: 2.5em;
   border-top: 1px solid gray; color: #AAA; font-size: 85%;
   padding-top: 0.33em; letter-spacing: 1px;}
```

To change the color of the hyperlink in the footer, we'll need a new rule:

```
div#footer {text-align: center; margin-top: 2.5em;
   border-top: 1px solid gray; color: #AAA; font-size: 85%;
   padding-top: 0.33em; letter-spacing: 1px;}
div#footer a:link {color: #778;}
</style>
```

Making the link a shade of gray darker than the rest of the text—with just a hint of blue—gives it a subtle difference of appearance without unduly drawing the eye. We'll also want to style it in its visited state, using a similarly faded purple (see Figure 2.4):

```
div#footer a:link {color: #778;}
div#footer a:visited {color: #878;}
</style>
```

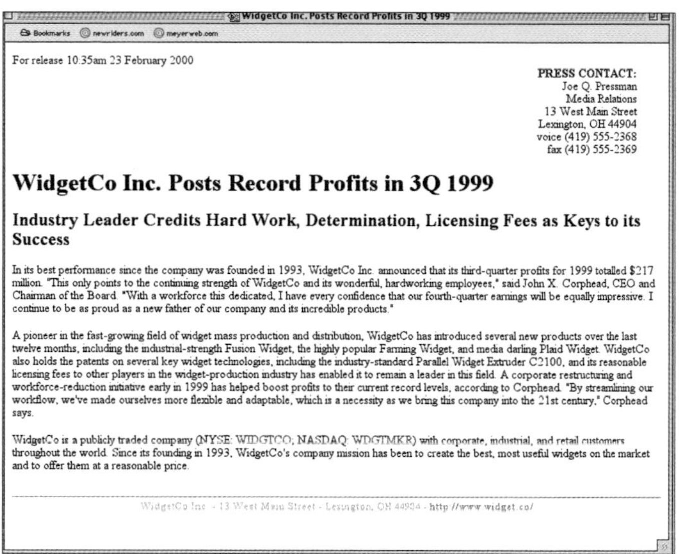

WidgetCo Inc. Posts Record Profits in 3Q 1999

Bookmarks newriders.com meyerweb.com

For release 10:35am 23 February 2000

PRESS CONTACT:
Joe Q. Pressman
Media Relations
13 West Main Street
Lexington, OH 44904
voice (419) 555-2368
fax (419) 555-2369

WidgetCo Inc. Posts Record Profits in 3Q 1999

Industry Leader Credits Hard Work, Determination, Licensing Fees as Keys to its Success

In its best performance since the company was founded in 1993, WidgetCo Inc. announced that its third-quarter profits for 1999 totalled $217 million. "This only points to the continuing strength of WidgetCo and its wonderful, hardworking employees," said John X. Corphead, CEO and Chairman of the Board. "With a workforce this dedicated, I have every confidence that our fourth-quarter earnings will be equally impressive. I continue to be as proud as a new father of our company and its incredible products."

A pioneer in the fast-growing field of widget mass production and distribution, WidgetCo has introduced several new products over the last twelve months, including the industrial-strength Fusion Widget, the highly popular Farming Widget, and media darling Plaid Widget. WidgetCo also holds the patents on several key widget technologies, including the industry-standard Parallel Widget Extruder C2100, and its reasonable licensing fees to other players in the widget-production industry has enabled it to remain a leader in this field. A corporate restructuring and workforce-reduction initiative early in 1999 has helped boost profits to their current record levels, according to Corphead. "By streamlining our workflow, we've made ourselves more flexible and adaptable, which is a necessity as we bring this company into the 21st century," Corphead says.

WidgetCo is a publicly traded company (NYSE: WIDGTCO; NASDAQ: WDGTMKR) with corporate, industrial, and retail customers throughout the world. Since its founding in 1993, WidgetCo's company mission has been to create the best, most useful widgets on the market and to offer them at a reasonable price.

WidgetCo Inc. - 13 West Main Street - Lexington, OH 44904 - http://www.widget.co/

FIGURE 2.4

Keeping links distinctive from their surroundings is an important usability feature.

The Main Text

There are two things to consider in the main body text: the presentation of the paragraphs in general and the styling of the summary paragraph near the end. First we'll work on the general look of all three paragraphs and their width within the browser window. Rather than let the paragraphs run to the edges of the window, we'll add some margins so that there's some separation (see Figure 2.5):

```
body {background: white; color: black;}
p {margin-left: 10%; margin-right: 10%;}
div#contact-info {text-align: right;}
```

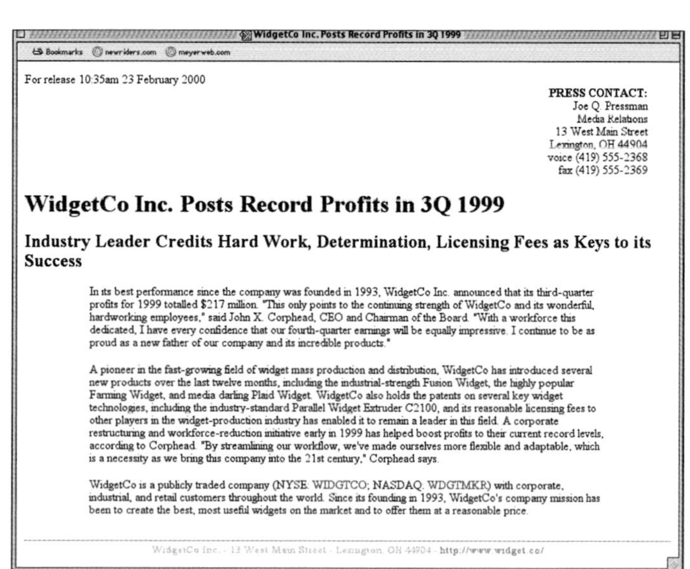

WidgetCo Inc. Posts Record Profits in 3Q 1999

Bookmarks newriders.com meyerweb.com

For release 10:35am 23 February 2000

PRESS CONTACT:
Joe Q. Pressman
Media Relations
13 West Main Street
Lexington, OH 44904
voice (419) 555-2368
fax (419) 555-2369

WidgetCo Inc. Posts Record Profits in 3Q 1999

Industry Leader Credits Hard Work, Determination, Licensing Fees as Keys to its Success

In its best performance since the company was founded in 1993, WidgetCo Inc. announced that its third-quarter profits for 1999 totalled $217 million. "This only points to the continuing strength of WidgetCo and its wonderful, hardworking employees," said John X. Corphead, CEO and Chairman of the Board. "With a workforce this dedicated, I have every confidence that our fourth-quarter earnings will be equally impressive. I continue to be as proud as a new father of our company and its incredible products."

A pioneer in the fast-growing field of widget mass production and distribution, WidgetCo has introduced several new products over the last twelve months, including the industrial-strength Fusion Widget, the highly popular Farming Widget, and media darling Plaid Widget. WidgetCo also holds the patents on several key widget technologies, including the industry-standard Parallel Widget Extruder C2100, and its reasonable licensing fees to other players in the widget-production industry has enabled it to remain a leader in this field. A corporate restructuring and workforce-reduction initiative early in 1999 has helped boost profits to their current record levels, according to Corphead. "By streamlining our workflow, we've made ourselves more flexible and adaptable, which is a necessity as we bring this company into the 21st century," Corphead says.

WidgetCo is a publicly traded company (NYSE: WIDGTCO; NASDAQ: WDGTMKR) with corporate, industrial, and retail customers throughout the world. Since its founding in 1993, WidgetCo's company mission has been to create the best, most useful widgets on the market and to offer them at a reasonable price.

WidgetCo Inc. - 13 West Main Street - Lexington, OH 44904 - http://www.widget.co/

FIGURE 2.5

Pushing the text away from the window edges.

Bigger-Than-Browser Bodies!

It is possible to make the `body` element wider or narrower than the browser window by using the property `width` or by giving it margins, but we won't be doing that in this project. Because we aren't, the width of `body` defaults to very nearly the width of the browser window. (By default, the `body` element has either margins or padding that makes the content area of `body` slightly less than the width of the browser window.)

All of the paragraphs now have left and right margins that are 10% of the width of the parent element; in this particular case, that's the `body` element, which is as wide as the browser window. So the paragraphs will now have margins that are 10% as wide as the browser window. This enables the paragraphs to adapt gracefully to changes in the size of the browser window due to user action, changes in screen resolution, or other factors.

It's a common practice to italicize the summary paragraph of a press release, so that's what we'll do here:

```
p {margin-left: 10%; margin-right: 10%;}
p#summary {font-style: italic;}
div#contact-info {text-align: right;
   margin-right: 1em; padding-right: 1em;}
```

While we're at it, let's style the stock-info hyperlinks within the summary. We don't want to go too far overboard, so we'll just boldface the links and turn off the italics, make them blue-on-white by default, and give them a "reverse" appearance when they're hovered over with the mouse pointer:

```
div#footer a:visited {color: #878;}
a.stockinfo {font-weight: bold; font-style: normal;
   color: blue; background: white;}
a.stockinfo:hover {background: blue; color: white;}
</style>
```

Just for fun, we're going to specially style the first letter of the lead paragraph, making it larger and bolder than the rest of the text (see Figure 2.6):

```
p {margin-left: 10%; margin-right: 10%;}
p.lead-para:first-letter {font-size: 133%; font-weight: bold;}
p#summary {font-style: italic;}
```

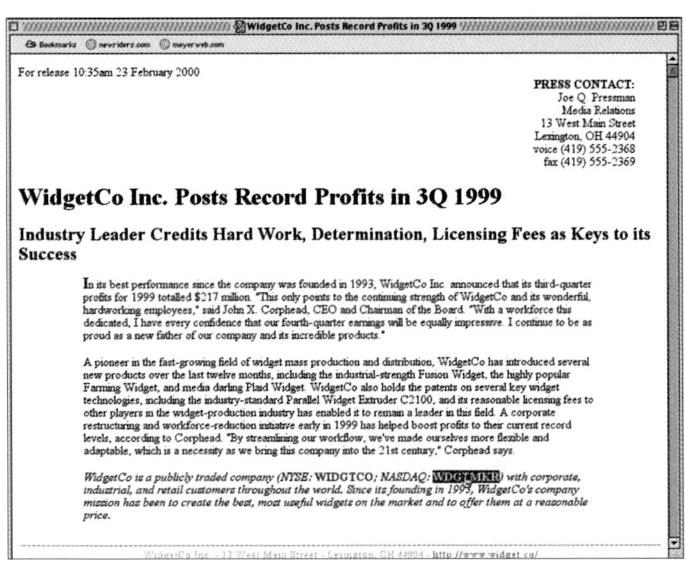

WidgetCo Inc. Posts Record Profits in 3Q 1999

Bookmarks newriders.com meyerweb.com

For release 10:35am 23 February 2000

PRESS CONTACT:
Joe Q. Pressman
Media Relations
13 West Main Street
Lexington, OH 44904
voice (419) 555-2368
fax (419) 555-2369

WidgetCo Inc. Posts Record Profits in 3Q 1999

Industry Leader Credits Hard Work, Determination, Licensing Fees as Keys to its Success

In its best performance since the company was founded in 1993, WidgetCo Inc. announced that its third-quarter profits for 1999 totalled $217 million. "This only points to the continuing strength of WidgetCo and its wonderful, hardworking employees," said John X. Corphead, CEO and Chairman of the Board. "With a workforce this dedicated, I have every confidence that our fourth-quarter earnings will be equally impressive. I continue to be as proud as a new father of our company and its incredible products."

A pioneer in the fast-growing field of widget mass production and distribution, WidgetCo has introduced several new products over the last twelve months, including the industrial-strength Fusion Widget, the highly popular Farming Widget, and media darling Plaid Widget. WidgetCo also holds the patents on several key widget technologies, including the industry-standard Parallel Widget Extruder C2100, and its reasonable licensing fees to other players in the widget-production industry has enabled it to remain a leader in this field. A corporate restructuring and workforce-reduction initiative early in 1999 has helped boost profits to their current record levels, according to Corphead. "By streamlining our workflow, we've made ourselves more flexible and adaptable, which is a necessity as we bring this company into the 21st century," Corphead says.

WidgetCo is a publicly traded company (NYSE: WIDGTCO; *NASDAQ:* WDGTMKR*) with corporate, industrial, and retail customers throughout the world. Since its founding in 1993, WidgetCo's company mission has been to create the best, most useful widgets on the market and to offer them at a reasonable price.*

WidgetCo Inc. - 13 West Main Street - Lexington, OH 44904 - http://www.widget.co/

FIGURE 2.6

The summary text is visually distinct, and the lead letter has more weight.

Styling the First Word

There is nothing in CSS2 that lets you style the first word of an element. You can style the first line or the first letter, but not the first word. If you need to style just the first word of an element, you could wrap it in a `span` element and give that `span` a `class` such as `first-word`.

The Headers

Now we turn to the h1 and h2 elements. These actually don't need a whole lot of work because, by their very nature, they already are what we want them to be: large, bold headlines that announce the basic information in a page. Still, there's nothing so perfect that it can't be improved!

First let's set the margins of the heading elements. We want to get the two headings closer together and indent h2 so that its left edge almost lines up with the left edge of the paragraphs. Thus:

```
a.stockinfo:hover {background: blue; color: white;}
h1 {margin-bottom: 0;}
h2 {margin: 0 5% 0 7.5%;}
</style>
```

Trouble In Mind

The value `0 5% 0 7.5%` sets all four margins of the element at once and in this order: top, right, bottom, left. This is most easily remembered as TRBL, which will keep you out of TRouBLe so long as you keep it in mind.

The h1 element seems a little too close to the contact info, so let's give it a top margin:

```
h1 {margin-bottom: 0; margin-top: 1em;}
```

While we're at it, let's set h2's font size to be a little smaller than it is now. Most browsers make h2 text about 150% the size of normal text, but we'll pull that down to 120% of h2's parent element. While we're at it, we'll also italicize the text (see Figure 2.7):

```
h2 {margin: 0 5% 0 7.5%; font-size: 120%; font-style: italic;}
```

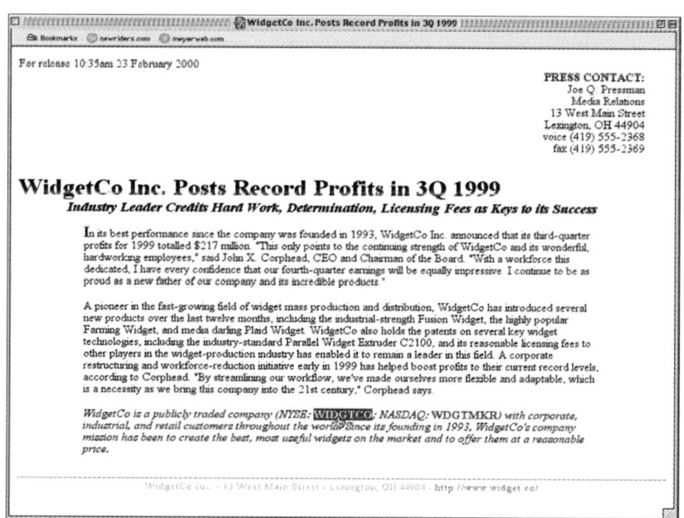

WidgetCo Inc. Posts Record Profits in 3Q 1999

Bookmarks newriders.com meyerweb.com

For release 10:35am 23 February 2000

PRESS CONTACT:
Joe Q. Pressman
Media Relations
13 West Main Street
Lexington, OH 44904
voice (419) 555-2368
fax (419) 555-2369

WidgetCo Inc. Posts Record Profits in 3Q 1999

Industry Leader Credits Hard Work, Determination, Licensing Fees as Keys to its Success

In its best performance since the company was founded in 1993, WidgetCo Inc. announced that its third-quarter profits for 1999 totalled $217 million. "This only points to the continuing strength of WidgetCo and its wonderful, hardworking employees," said John X. Corphead, CEO and Chairman of the Board. "With a workforce this dedicated, I have every confidence that our fourth-quarter earnings will be equally impressive. I continue to be as proud as a new father of our company and its incredible products."

A pioneer in the fast-growing field of widget mass production and distribution, WidgetCo has introduced several new products over the last twelve months, including the industrial-strength Fusion Widget, the highly popular Farming Widget, and media darling Plaid Widget. WidgetCo also holds the patents on several key widget technologies, including the industry-standard Parallel Widget Extruder C2100, and its reasonable licensing fees to other players in the widget-production industry has enabled it to remain a leader in this field. A corporate restructuring and workforce-reduction initiative early in 1999 has helped boost profits to their current record levels, according to Corphead. "By streamlining our workflow, we've made ourselves more flexible and adaptable, which is a necessity as we bring this company into the 21st century," Corphead says.

WidgetCo is a publicly traded company (NYSE: WIDGTCO; NASDAQ: WDGTMKR) with corporate, industrial, and retail customers throughout the world. Since its founding in 1993, WidgetCo's company mission has been to create the best, most useful widgets on the market and to offer them at a reasonable price.

WidgetCo Inc. - 13 West Main Street - Lexington, OH 44904 - http://www.widget.co/

FIGURE 2.7

The headings at the top of the document—new and improved!

Touching Up the Top

With the majority of the document nicely styled, let's revisit the top of the document. We've already styled the contact information, but we never did anything to the release line. It also would be kind of neat to visually tie the release and contact information together using some borders.

Small Caps, Tall Letters

Versions of IE/Win before IE6 make small-caps text all uppercase letters of exactly the same size. This is technically permitted by CSS1, but it might not be quite what the author expects because "small-caps" usually means that the text uses a mix of large and small uppercase letters—It would look SOMETHING LIKE THIS SHORT PIECE OF TEXT.

Just to set it apart a bit, let's change the appearance of the release line by putting it in a small-caps font:

```
p#summary {font-style: italic;}
div.release {font-variant: small-caps;}
div#contact-info {text-align: right;
   margin-right: 1em; padding-right: 1em;}
```

That was simple enough, but the process of visually tying the two together will be a little more complicated. First we'll give the release a bottom border:

```
div.release {font-variant: small-caps; border-bottom: 1px solid black;}
```

Next we'll give the contact information a right-hand border (see Figure 2.8):

```
div#contact-info {text-align: right;
   margin-right: 1em; padding-right: 1em;
   border-right: 1px solid black;}
```

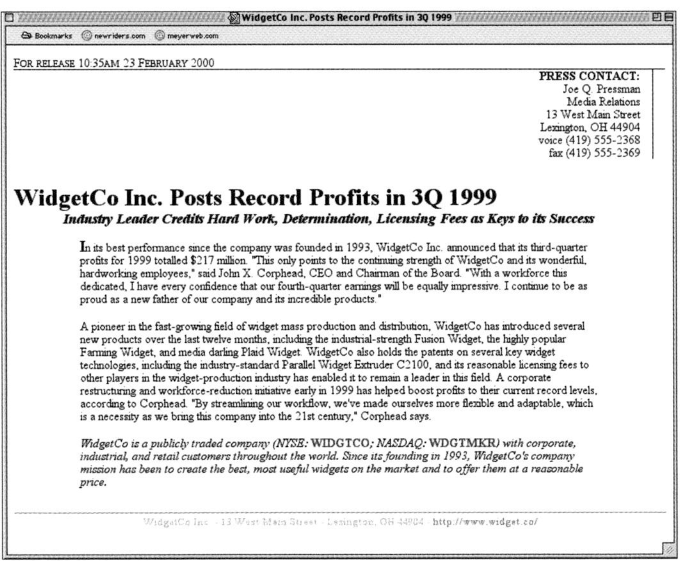

WidgetCo Inc. Posts Record Profits in 3Q 1999

Bookmarks newriders.com meyerweb.com

FOR RELEASE 10:35AM 23 FEBRUARY 2000

PRESS CONTACT:
Joe Q. Pressman
Media Relations
13 West Main Street
Lexington, OH 44904
voice (419) 555-2368
fax (419) 555-2369

WidgetCo Inc. Posts Record Profits in 3Q 1999

Industry Leader Credits Hard Work, Determination, Licensing Fees as Keys to its Success

In its best performance since the company was founded in 1993, WidgetCo Inc. announced that its third-quarter profits for 1999 totalled $217 million. "This only points to the continuing strength of WidgetCo and its wonderful, hardworking employees," said John X. Corphead, CEO and Chairman of the Board. "With a workforce this dedicated, I have every confidence that our fourth-quarter earnings will be equally impressive. I continue to be as proud as a new father of our company and its incredible products."

A pioneer in the fast-growing field of widget mass production and distribution, WidgetCo has introduced several new products over the last twelve months, including the industrial-strength Fusion Widget, the highly popular Farming Widget, and media darling Plaid Widget. WidgetCo also holds the patents on several key widget technologies, including the industry-standard Parallel Widget Extruder C2100, and its reasonable licensing fees to other players in the widget-production industry has enabled it to remain a leader in this field. A corporate restructuring and workforce-reduction initiative early in 1999 has helped boost profits to their current record levels, according to Corphead. "By streamlining our workflow, we've made ourselves more flexible and adaptable, which is a necessity as we bring this company into the 21st century," Corphead says.

WidgetCo is a publicly traded company (NYSE: WIDGTCO*; NASDAQ:* WDGTMKR*) with corporate, industrial, and retail customers throughout the world. Since its founding in 1993, WidgetCo's company mission has been to create the best, most useful widgets on the market and to offer them at a reasonable price.*

WidgetCo Inc · 13 West Main Street · Lexington, OH 44904 · http://www.widget.co/

FIGURE 2.8

Running a line down the right side for that hip look.

As you might remember from earlier in the project, we gave the contact information both padding and margin, and now we see why. Had we used only a margin, the right-hand border we just added would be right up against the contact information. Had we relied solely on padding, the border would be very near the edge of the browser window. By balancing the margin and padding, we get good border placement.

However, the borders don't really "link up" very nicely, so let's fix that. Like the contact information, the release `div` needs a right margin:

```
div.release {font-variant: small-caps; border-bottom: 1px solid black;
   margin-right: 1em;}
```

Just to make things a little more pleasing, let's give the contact information `div` a small amount of top padding to push the text away from the line above it (see Figure 2.9):

```
div#contact-info {text-align: right;
   margin-right: 1em; padding-right: 1em;
   border-right: 1px solid black; padding-top: 0.25em;}
```

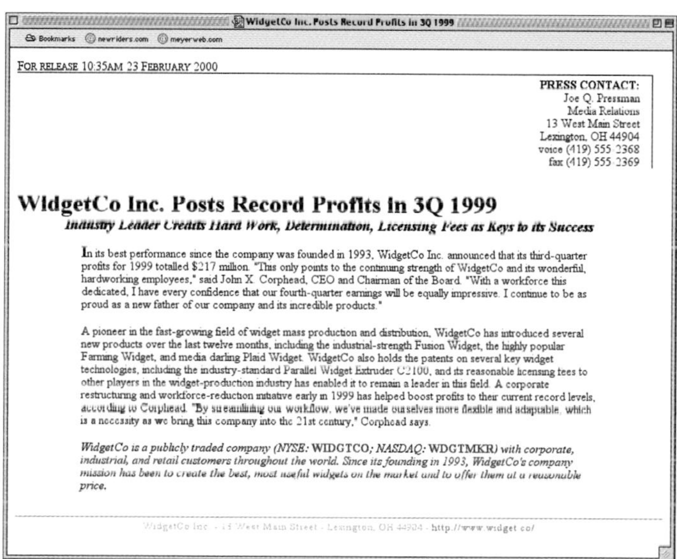

WidgetCo Inc. Posts Record Profits in 3Q 1999

Bookmarks newriders.com meyerweb.com

FOR RELEASE 10:35AM 23 FEBRUARY 2000

PRESS CONTACT:
Joe Q. Pressman
Media Relations
13 West Main Street
Lexington, OH 44904
voice (419) 555-2368
fax (419) 555-2369

WidgetCo Inc. Posts Record Profits in 3Q 1999

Industry Leader Credits Hard Work, Determination, Licensing Fees as Keys to its Success

In its best performance since the company was founded in 1993, WidgetCo Inc. announced that its third-quarter profits for 1999 totalled $217 million. "This only points to the continuing strength of WidgetCo and its wonderful, hardworking employees," said John X. Corphead, CEO and Chairman of the Board. "With a workforce this dedicated, I have every confidence that our fourth-quarter earnings will be equally impressive. I continue to be as proud as a new father of our company and its incredible products."

A pioneer in the fast-growing field of widget mass production and distribution, WidgetCo has introduced several new products over the last twelve months, including the industrial-strength Fusion Widget, the highly popular Farming Widget, and media darling Plaid Widget. WidgetCo also holds the patents on several key widget technologies, including the industry-standard Parallel Widget Extruder C2100, and its reasonable licensing fees to other players in the widget-production industry has enabled it to remain a leader in this field. A corporate restructuring and workforce-reduction initiative early in 1999 has helped boost profits to their current record levels, according to Corphead. "By streamlining our workflow, we've made ourselves more flexible and adaptable, which is a necessity as we bring this company into the 21st century," Corphead says.

WidgetCo is a publicly traded company (NYSE: WIDGTCO; *NASDAQ:* WDGTMKR*) with corporate, industrial, and retail customers throughout the world. Since its founding in 1993, WidgetCo's company mission has been to create the best, most useful widgets on the market and to offer them at a reasonable price.*

WidgetCo Inc. - 13 West Main Street - Lexington, OH 44904 - http://www.widget.co/

FIGURE 2.9

Keeping the text in balance with the lines around it.

ALTERING THE STYLES

Now that we've built up one style sheet, let's create a new and different one. Instead of starting from scratch, though, let's rewrite the one we have so that we can recycle the bits we want to keep and change the bits we don't. We aren't going to mess with the HTML any more. We're just going to change the CSS, and this time we're going to start at the top of the page and work our way down.

The Page Itself

Before we start changing the text, let's change the page itself. A nice touch would be to "watermark" the company logo into the background of the page. To do this, all we need is a graphic file containing the logo—let's assume it's `WidgetCoLogo.gif`—and an alteration to our basic `body` styles:

```
body {background: white url(WidgetCoLogo.gif) center no-repeat;
   color: black;}
```

You can find a copy of `WidgetCoLogo.gif` in the files you downloaded from the book's Web site.

Placement Problems

Netscape Navigator 4.x always puts background images in the top-left corner of the document, regardless of any styles meant to place it else-where. You can try to overcome this by adding whitespace to the top and left sides of a background image, but it's usually better to just use backgrounds that will work in the upper-left corner. The other option is to hide the background image from NN4.x altogether.

See "Tricking Browsers and Hiding Styles" on the Web site for details.

This will place the graphic in the center of the document and prevent it from repeating (tiling). There is a difference between the center of the document and the center of the browser window. The center of the document is the middle of the body element; so, if you have a long document, the logo might initially be placed offscreen and only be revealed as the user scrolls through the document. If you want the logo to always be seen in the center of the browser window, add the keyword `fixed` to your `background` declaration (see Figure 2.10).

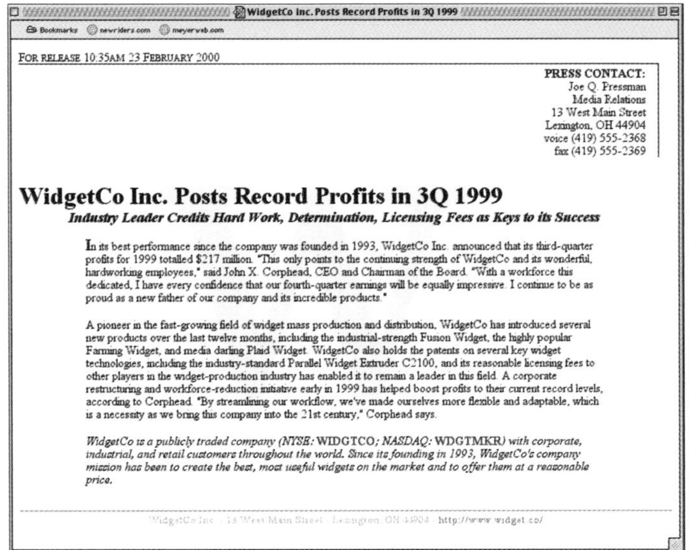

WidgetCo Inc. Posts Record Profits in 3Q 1999

Bookmarks newriders.com meyerweb.com

FOR RELEASE 10:35AM 23 FEBRUARY 2000

PRESS CONTACT:
Joe Q. Pressman
Media Relations
13 West Main Street
Lexington, OH 44904
voice (419) 555-2368
fax (419) 555-2369

WidgetCo Inc. Posts Record Profits in 3Q 1999

Industry Leader Credits Hard Work, Determination, Licensing Fees as Keys to its Success

In its best performance since the company was founded in 1993, WidgetCo Inc. announced that its third-quarter profits for 1999 totalled $217 million. "This only points to the continuing strength of WidgetCo and its wonderful, hardworking employees," said John X. Corphead, CEO and Chairman of the Board. "With a workforce this dedicated, I have every confidence that our fourth-quarter earnings will be equally impressive. I continue to be as proud as a new father of our company and its incredible products."

A pioneer in the fast-growing field of widget mass production and distribution, WidgetCo has introduced several new products over the last twelve months, including the industrial-strength Fusion Widget, the highly popular Farming Widget, and media darling Plaid Widget. WidgetCo also holds the patents on several key widget technologies, including the industry-standard Parallel Widget Extruder C2100, and its reasonable licensing fees to other players in the widget-production industry has enabled it to remain a leader in this field. A corporate restructuring and workforce-reduction initiative early in 1999 has helped boost profits to their current record levels, according to Corphead. "By streamlining our workflow, we've made ourselves more flexible and adaptable, which is a necessity as we bring this company into the 21st century," Corphead says.

WidgetCo is a publicly traded company (NYSE: WIDGTCO; *NASDAQ:* WDGTMKR) *with corporate, industrial, and retail customers throughout the world. Since its founding in 1993, WidgetCo's company mission has been to create the best, most useful widgets on the market and to offer them at a reasonable price.*

WidgetCo Inc · 13 West Main Street · Lexington, OH 44904 · http://www.widget.co/

FIGURE 2.10

"Watermarking" the document with a centered logo graphic.

Of course, putting a logo in the background may or may not be advisable, depending on your company's logo and the content you're presenting.

The Top of the Page

First we'll make the release line stand out even more by giving it a top border to match its bottom border. We'll also center the text and give it a small touch of top and bottom padding.

Marginal Changes

We've changed the right margin from 1em to 10px to avoid a bug in IE5.x/Win later on.

```
div.release {font-variant: small-caps; text-align: center;
   margin-right: 10px; padding: 0.125em 0;
   border: 1px solid black; border-width: 1px 0;}
```

Now, to lend a more contemporary look to the document, we're going to tie the release and contact information together with a thick right border in a different color for each element. The first step is to give the release line a thickened right border (see Figure 2.11):

```
div.release {font-variant: small-caps; text-align: center;
   margin-right: 10px; padding: 0.125em 0;
   border: 1px solid black; border-width: 1px 1em 1px 0;}
```

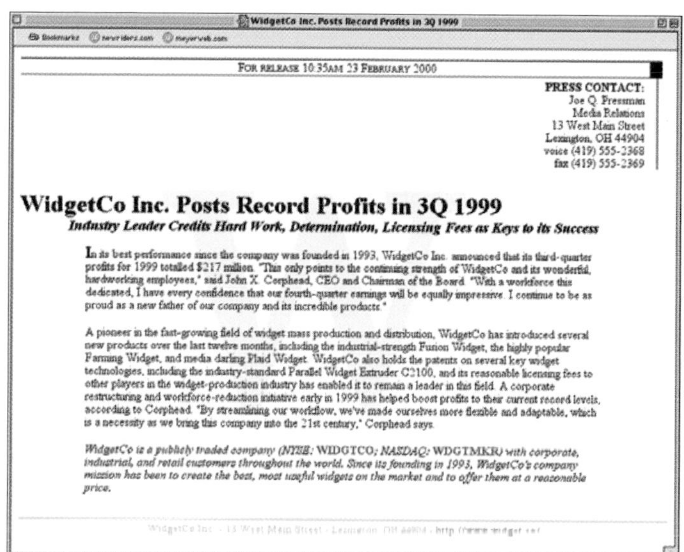

WidgetCo Inc. Posts Record Profits in 3Q 1999

Bookmarks newriders.com meyerweb.com

FOR RELEASE 10:35AM 23 FEBRUARY 2000

PRESS CONTACT:
Joe Q. Pressman
Media Relations
13 West Main Street
Lexington, OH 44904
voice (419) 555-2368
fax (419) 555-2369

WidgetCo Inc. Posts Record Profits in 3Q 1999

Industry Leader Credits Hard Work, Determination, Licensing Fees as Keys to its Success

In its best performance since the company was founded in 1993, WidgetCo Inc. announced that its third-quarter profits for 1999 totalled $217 million. "This only points to the continuing strength of WidgetCo and its wonderful, hardworking employees," said John X. Corphead, CEO and Chairman of the Board. "With a workforce this dedicated, I have every confidence that our fourth-quarter earnings will be equally impressive. I continue to be as proud as a new father of our company and its incredible products."

A pioneer in the fast-growing field of widget mass production and distribution, WidgetCo has introduced several new products over the last twelve months, including the industrial-strength Fusion Widget, the highly popular Farming Widget, and media darling Plaid Widget. WidgetCo also holds the patents on several key widget technologies, including the industry-standard Parallel Widget Extruder C2100, and its reasonable licensing fees to other players in the widget-production industry has enabled it to remain a leader in this field. A corporate restructuring and workforce-reduction initiative early in 1999 has helped boost profits to their current record levels, according to Corphead. "By streamlining our workflow, we've made ourselves more flexible and adaptable, which is a necessity as we bring this company into the 21st century," Corphead says.

WidgetCo is a publicly traded company (NYSE: WIDGTCO; *NASDAQ:* WDGTMKR) *with corporate, industrial, and retail customers throughout the world. Since its founding in 1993, WidgetCo's company mission has been to create the best, most useful widgets on the market and to offer them at a reasonable price.*

FIGURE 2.11

Creating a thicker border.

Now the contact information needs to have its right border set to match the release line's, but at the same time, we want it to be a different color. So, we'll rewrite the `contact-info` styles as follows:

```
div#contact-info {text-align: right;
   margin-right: 1em; padding-right: 1em;
   border-right: 1em solid #446; padding-top: 0.25em;}
```

Now the right borders match up, yet they are still distinct. It's all very contemporary, but we aren't done yet. Let's also tone down the contact information a little bit by lightening up the text and giving it a brownish tinge.

```
div#contact-info {text-align: right;
   margin-right: 1em; padding-right: 1em;
   border-right: 1em solid #446; padding-top: 0.25em;
   color: #321;}
```

Actually, let's make the contact information text a little smaller except for the first line, which we want to keep the normal size. First we'll squeeze down the entire element's text:

```
div#contact-info {text-align: right;
   margin-right: 1em; padding-right: 1em;
   border-right: 1em solid #446; padding-top: 0.25em;
   color: #321; font-size: 90%;}
```

Now we need to raise the first line's size back up to normal, but we have to do it by multiplying the font size by the new size of the `div`, which is 90% normal. The value 90% is the same as 0.9, and 0.9 times 1.111 is roughly equal to 1.0. Therefore, we write the following:

```
div#contact-info {text-align: right;
   margin-right: 1em; padding-right: 1em;
   border-right: 1em solid #446; padding-top: 0.25em;
   color: #321; font-size: 90%;}
div#contact-info:first-line {text-transform: uppercase;
   font-size: 1.111em; font-weight: bold;}
div#footer {text-align: center; margin-top: 2.5em;
   border-top: 1px solid gray; color: #AAA; font-size: 85%;
   padding-top: 0.33em; letter-spacing: 1px;}
```

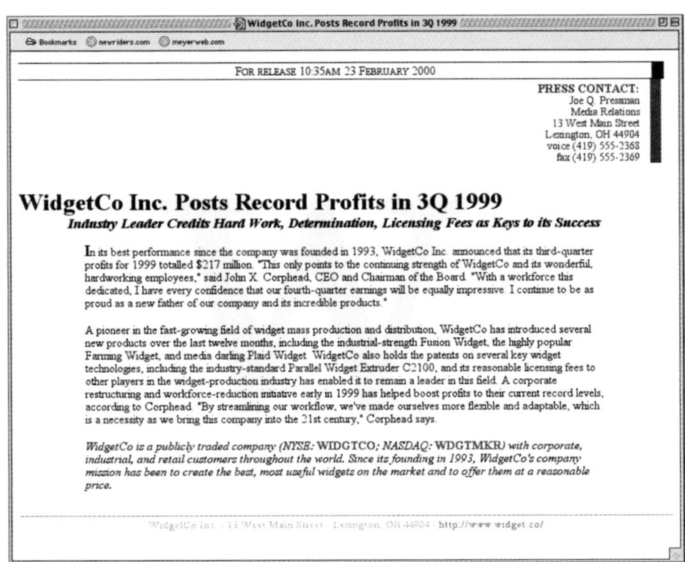

WidgetCo Inc. Posts Record Profits in 3Q 1999

Bookmarks newriders.com meyerweb.com

FOR RELEASE 10:35AM 23 FEBRUARY 2000

PRESS CONTACT:
Joe Q. Pressman
Media Relations
13 West Main Street
Lexington, OH 44904
voice (419) 555-2368
fax (419) 555-2369

WidgetCo Inc. Posts Record Profits in 3Q 1999

Industry Leader Credits Hard Work, Determination, Licensing Fees as Keys to its Success

In its best performance since the company was founded in 1993, WidgetCo Inc. announced that its third-quarter profits for 1999 totalled $217 million. "This only points to the continuing strength of WidgetCo and its wonderful, hardworking employees," said John X. Corphead, CEO and Chairman of the Board. "With a workforce this dedicated, I have every confidence that our fourth-quarter earnings will be equally impressive. I continue to be as proud as a new father of our company and its incredible products."

A pioneer in the fast-growing field of widget mass production and distribution, WidgetCo has introduced several new products over the last twelve months, including the industrial-strength Fusion Widget, the highly popular Farming Widget, and media darling Plaid Widget. WidgetCo also holds the patents on several key widget technologies, including the industry-standard Parallel Widget Extruder C2100, and its reasonable licensing fees to other players in the widget-production industry has enabled it to remain a leader in this field. A corporate restructuring and workforce-reduction initiative early in 1999 has helped boost profits to their current record levels, according to Corphead. "By streamlining our workflow, we've made ourselves more flexible and adaptable, which is a necessity as we bring this company into the 21st century," Corphead says.

WidgetCo is a publicly traded company (NYSE: WIDGTCO; *NASDAQ:* WDGTMKR*) with corporate, industrial, and retail customers throughout the world. Since its founding in 1993, WidgetCo's company mission has been to create the best, most useful widgets on the market and to offer them at a reasonable price.*

WidgetCo Inc. - 13 West Main Street - Lexington, OH 44904 - http://www.widget.co/

FIGURE 2.12

Alterations in the text size make for a better visual impact.

We can also see a shrinking of the right border because it's based on the font size of the element itself. It's also offset just a bit, which ruins the effect. It would be nice if we could stick to ems, but unfortunately, bugs in Explorer for Windows force us to convert the borders to pixel widths. Because of this, both the `release` and `contact-info` borders, as well as the margin on `contact-info`, need to be changed:

```
div.release {font-variant: small-caps; text-align: center;
   margin-right: 10px; padding: 0.125em 0;
   border: 1px solid black; border-width: 1px 15px 1px 0;}
div#contact-info {text-align: right;
   margin-right: 10px; padding-right: 15px;
   border-right: 15px solid #446; padding-top: 0.25em;
   color: #321; font-size: 90%;}
```

With these last changes, we've arrived at a good style sheet, which is shown in its entirety in Listing 2.1.

Listing 2.1 The Complete Style Sheet

```
<style type="text/css">
body {background: white url(WidgetCoLogo.gif) center no-repeat;
   color: black;}
p {margin-left: 10%; margin-right: 10%;}
p.lead-para:first-letter {font-size: 133%; font-weight: bold;}
p#summary {font-style: italic;}
div.release {font-variant: small-caps; text-align: center;
   margin-right: 10px; padding: 0.125em 0;
   border: 1px solid black; border-width: 1px 15px 1px 0;}
div#contact-info {text-align: right;
   margin-right: 10px; padding-right: 1em;
   border-right: 15px solid #446; padding-top: 0.25em;
   color: #321; font-size: 90%;}
div#contact-info:first-line {text-transform: uppercase;
   font-size: 1.111em; font-weight: bold;}
div#contact-info:first-line {font-weight: bold;
   text-transform: uppercase;}
div#footer {text-align: center; margin-top: 2.5em;
   border-top: 1px solid gray; color: #AAA; font-size: 85%;
   padding-top: 0.33em; letter-spacing: 1px;}
div#footer a:link {color: #778;}
div#footer a:visited {color: #878;}
a.stockinfo {font-weight: bold; font-style: normal;
   color: blue; background: white;}
a.stockinfo:hover {background: blue; color: white;}
h1 {margin-bottom: 0; margin-top: 1em;}
h2 {margin: 0 5% 0 7.5%; font-size: 120%; font-style: italic;}
</style>
```

Externalizing Our Style

Because we've been creating a style sheet meant for multiple press releases, now would be a good time to take our style sheet and make it external. This enables us to have one style sheet file that can style multiple press-release documents. The advantage is that if we make a change to the external style sheet, then the changes will be reflected in all of the documents that use that style sheet.

The first step is to take the entire style sheet shown in Listing 2.1 and place it in a text file of its own. After that's done, we need to remove the first and last lines because there can be *no* HTML markup in an external style sheet! So the `<style>` and `</style>` lines have to be deleted.

After you've removed the HTML from your new text file, save the file as `press-rel.css`. The file should be saved as plain text, ASCII text, or whatever your editing program calls raw text files.

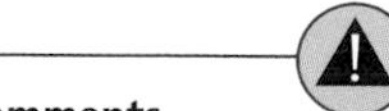

No Comments

When we say "no HTML," we really mean it. Not even HTML comments are allowed inside external style sheets, so if you have `<!--` and `-->` in the style sheet, they'll need to be deleted as well.

Now all we need to do is link the press release to the external style sheet. This is accomplished with the HTML element `link`, which can only be placed inside the `head` element. There are some attributes to the `link` element that need specific values to work:

- The attribute `rel` must have the value `stylesheet`.
- The attribute `type` must have the value `text/css`.
- The attribute `href` must have the URL of the external style sheet. This can be either a relative or absolute URL.

Because we've called our external style sheet `press-rel.css` and have saved it to the same directory as our project files, we can use a relative URL for the `href`. The `head` of our document will look like this:

```
<head>
<title>WidgetCo Inc. Posts Record Profits in 3Q 1999</title>
<link rel="stylesheet" type="text/css" href="press-rel.css">
</head>
```

This tells the browser to get the style sheet and apply its styles to the document (see Figure 2.13).

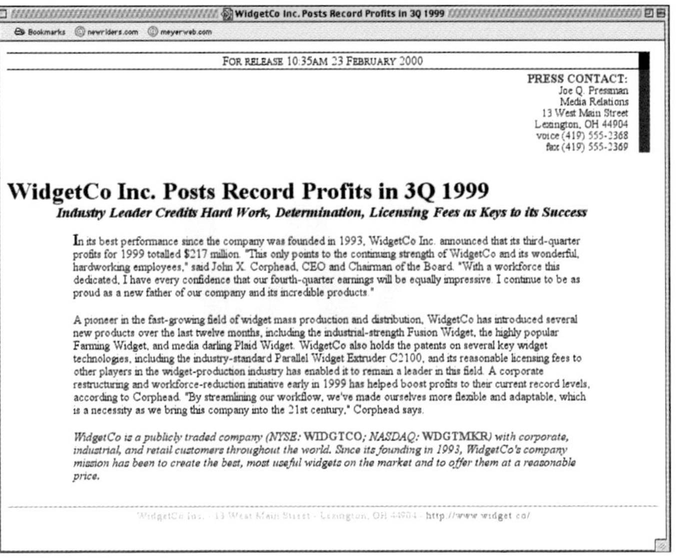

FIGURE 2.13

Styling the press release with an external style sheet.

Multiple style sheets can be linked to a single document. In these cases, the styles from the various external style sheets are combined together.

To finish out the project, let's return to using an embedded style sheet as we make the look of the press release a little more sophisticated. You can always take the end product and make it an external style sheet.

Be On Target

Make sure that all of your `href` values point to actual style sheets. Although most browsers will just ignore a `link` that doesn't load a style sheet, Navigator 4.x will refuse to display a document if any of its `link`ed style sheets don't load.

Adding to the Basic Design

The press release, as it stands, is not a bad little piece of work. It conveys the information in a straightforward fashion and looks professional enough. But is it really as "jazzed up" as the client wanted? No. Let's get a little more creative and see what we can do to make the release look really good.

Back to the Headings

You'll recall that we have all that empty whitespace next to the contact information. How about we put the `h1` into that space? It would look pretty cool and would save some space to boot. However, we'll have to approach this with some caution.

First we need to define the size of the `h1` text. Because it's going into a large empty space, let's make it bigger than usual—say, three times the size of normal text. We'll want to pull it upward so that it doesn't quite reach the bottom border of the release line, and we'll want to make sure it doesn't overlap the contact information. Here's our first try:

```
a.stockinfo:hover {background: blue; color: white;}
h1 {font-size: 250%; margin-top: -3em; margin-right: 3em;}
</style>
```

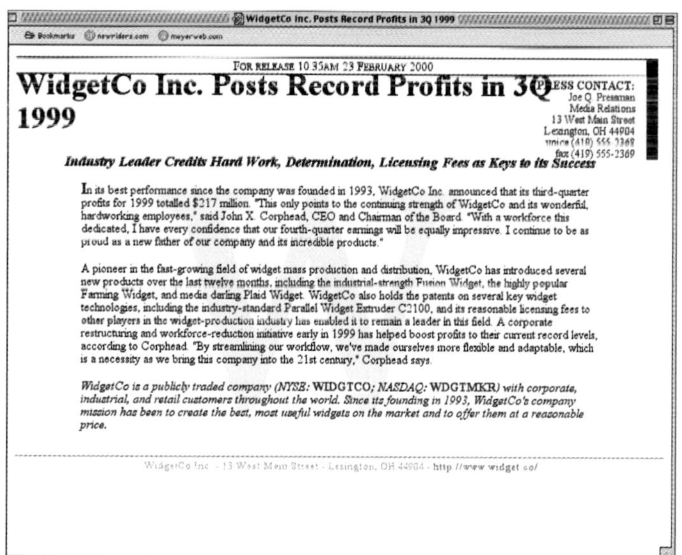

FOR RELEASE 10:35AM 23 FEBRUARY 2000

WidgetCo Inc. Posts Record Profits in 3Q 1999

PRESS CONTACT:
Joe Q. Pressman
Media Relations
13 West Main Street
Lexington, OH 44904
voice (419) 555-2368
fax (419) 555-2369

Industry Leader Credits Hard Work, Determination, Licensing Fees as Keys to its Success

In its best performance since the company was founded in 1993, WidgetCo Inc. announced that its third-quarter profits for 1999 totalled $217 million. "This only points to the continuing strength of WidgetCo and its wonderful, hardworking employees," said John X. Corphead, CEO and Chairman of the Board. "With a workforce this dedicated, I have every confidence that our fourth-quarter earnings will be equally impressive. I continue to be as proud as a new father of our company and its incredible products."

A pioneer in the fast-growing field of widget mass production and distribution, WidgetCo has introduced several new products over the last twelve months, including the industrial-strength Fusion Widget, the highly popular Farming Widget, and media darling Plaid Widget. WidgetCo also holds the patents on several key widget technologies, including the industry-standard Parallel Widget Extruder C2100, and its reasonable licensing fees to other players in the widget-production industry has enabled it to remain a leader in this field. A corporate restructuring and workforce-reduction initiative early in 1999 has helped boost profits to their current record levels, according to Corphead. "By streamlining our workflow, we've made ourselves more flexible and adaptable, which is a necessity as we bring this company into the 21st century," Corphead says.

WidgetCo is a publicly traded company (NYSE: WIDGTCO*; NASDAQ:* WDGTMKR*) with corporate, industrial, and retail customers throughout the world. Since its founding in 1993, WidgetCo's company mission has been to create the best, most useful widgets on the market and to offer them at a reasonable price.*

WidgetCo Inc. - 13 West Main Street - Lexington, OH 44904 - http://www.widget.co/

FIGURE 2.14

Holy overlap! The vertical placement is close to correct, but the length needs a little work.

That isn't too bad, except for the overlap between the title and the contact information and the fact that the text is a little too high (see Figure 2.14). It isn't much, but it's enough to be annoying. In any case, it probably would be best to keep a decent separation between the title and the contact info, so let's bump up the right margin but decrease the top margin. At the same time, we'll alter the indentation of the first line and subsequent lines:

```
h1 {font-size: 250%; margin-top: -2.5em; margin-right: 5em;
   padding-left: 0.33em; text-indent: -0.25em;}
```

By setting a negative text-indent, we've pushed the first line of the `h1` to the left a little bit. The left padding is set so that the first line doesn't get pushed so far that it hangs off the browser window.

Now it's time to alter the `h2` element. Given the new layout, it might be more interesting to center the text, increase the right and left margins, and bump up the font size (see Figure 2.15). To do this, we write:

```
h1 {font-size: 250%; margin-top: -2.5em; margin-right: 5em;
   padding-left: 0.33em; text-indent: -0.25em;}
h2 {font-size: 150%; font-style: italic; text-align: center;
   margin: 0 10%;}
</style>
```

WidgetCo Inc. Posts Record Profits in 3Q 1999

Bookmarks newriders.com meyerweb.com

FOR RELEASE 10:35AM 23 FEBRUARY 2000

PRESS CONTACT:
Joe Q. Pressman
Media Relations
13 West Main Street
Lexington, OH 44904
voice (419) 555-2368
fax (419) 555-2369

WidgetCo Inc. Posts Record Profits in 3Q 1999

Industry Leader Credits Hard Work, Determination, Licensing Fees as Keys to its Success

In its best performance since the company was founded in 1993, WidgetCo Inc. announced that its third-quarter profits for 1999 totalled $217 million. "This only points to the continuing strength of WidgetCo and its wonderful, hardworking employees," said John X. Corphead, CEO and Chairman of the Board. "With a workforce this dedicated, I have every confidence that our fourth-quarter earnings will be equally impressive. I continue to be as proud as a new father of our company and its incredible products."

A pioneer in the fast-growing field of widget mass production and distribution, WidgetCo has introduced several new products over the last twelve months, including the industrial-strength Fusion Widget, the highly popular Farming Widget, and media darling Plaid Widget. WidgetCo also holds the patents on several key widget technologies, including the industry-standard Parallel Widget Extruder C2100, and its reasonable licensing fees to other players in the widget-production industry has enabled it to remain a leader in this field. A corporate restructuring and workforce-reduction initiative early in 1999 has helped boost profits to their current record levels, according to Corphead. "By streamlining our workflow, we've made ourselves more flexible and adaptable, which is a necessity as we bring this company into the 21st century," Corphead says.

WidgetCo is a publicly traded company (NYSE: WIDGTCO*; NASDAQ:* WDGTMKR*) with corporate, industrial, and retail customers throughout the world. Since its founding in 1993, WidgetCo's company mission has been to create the best, most useful widgets on the market and to offer them at a reasonable price.*

WidgetCo Inc. - 13 West Main Street - Lexington, OH 44904 - http://www.widget.co/

FIGURE 2.15

Thanks to some judicious margins, the headlines are much better placed.

The Main Text (Again)

We aren't going to do a whole lot to the main text in this restyle because it looks pretty good as it is. We are just going to remove the lead paragraph's first-letter style because it looks a little odd here. Just delete the entire line, as follows:

```
p.lead-para:first-letter {font-size: 133%; font-weight: bold;}
```

The Usual Height

The default value for `line-height` is somewhere between 1em and 1.2em, depending on the browser. If you feel it's important to have a certain `line-height` to make the design look good, you need to declare it yourself.

To keep the paragraphs from looking too plain, we're going to fully justify the paragraph text. This will cause the ends of the lines to "line up" with each other. We'll also spread the lines apart just a bit by changing their `line-height`:

```
p {margin-left: 10%; margin-right: 10%;
   text-align: justify; line-height: 1.33em;}
```

However, the summary paragraph gets a huge facelift. Not only are we removing the italics, but we're enclosing the whole paragraph in a green box with a very thick left border, a light tan background, and some padding to match. We're also going to take its `line-height` back to the default so that it still looks different from the other paragraphs. Because we're changing the background of the summary paragraph, we also have to change the styling of the `stockinfo` links (see Figure 2.16).

```
p#summary {border: 2px solid #008000; border-width: 2px 2px 2px 2em;
   padding: 0.5em 0.5em 0.5em 1em; background: #FFE;
   line-height: 1em;}
 /* deleted 'font-style: italic' */

a.stockinfo {font-weight: bold; font-style: normal;
   color: blue; background: #FFE;}
```

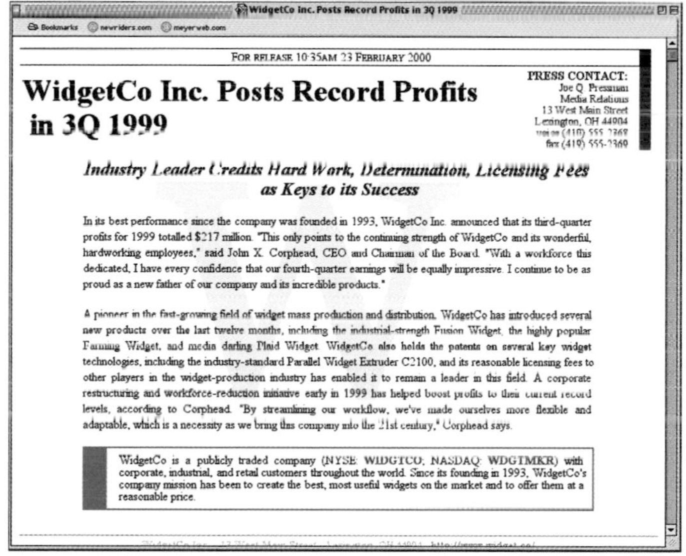

FIGURE 2.16

The summary might be boxed in now, but it's looking better than ever.

This might be a little much for a press release, but it does set the information apart from everything else.

The Footer

Although it's possible to make footers as visually striking as anything else, the tendency in most quarters is to keep them low profile and visually neutral. Accordingly, all we're going to do is italicize the text, remove the letter spacing, and right-align the content (see Figure 2.17):

```
div#footer {text-align: right; margin-top: 2.5em;
   border-top: 1px solid gray; color: #AAA; font-size: 85%;
   padding-top: 0.33em; font-style: italic;}
 /* removed 'letter-spacing: 1px' */
```

That's all it takes! The final style sheet is given in Listing 2.2.

Listing 2.2 The Complete and Improved Style Sheet

```
<style type="text/css">
body {background: white url(WidgetCoLogo.gif) center no-repeat;
   color: black;}
p {margin-left: 10%; margin-right: 10%;}
p#summary {border: 2px solid #008000; border-width: 2px 2px 2px 2em;
   padding: 0.5em 0.5em 0.5em 1em; background: #FFE;
   line-height: 1em;}
div.release {font-variant: small-caps; text-align: center;
   margin-right: 10px; padding: 0.125em 0;
   border: 1px solid black; border-width: 1px 15px 1px 0;}
div#contact-info {text-align: right;
   margin-right: 10px; padding-right: 15px;
   border-right: 15px solid #446; padding-top: 0.25em;
   color: #321; font-size: 90%;}
div#contact-info:first-line {text-transform: uppercase;
   font-size: 1.111em; font-weight: bold;}
div#contact-info:first-line {font-weight: bold;
   text-transform: uppercase;}
div#footer {text-align: right; margin-top: 2.5em;
   border-top: 1px solid gray; color: #AAA; font-size: 85%;
   padding-top: 0.33em; font-style: italic;}
 /* removed 'letter-spacing: 1px' */
div#footer a:link {color: #778;}
div#footer a:visited {color: #878;}
a.stockinfo {font-weight: bold; font-style: normal;
   color: blue; background: #FFE;}
a.stockinfo:hover {background: blue; color: white;}
h1 {font-size: 250%; margin-top: -2.5em; margin-right: 5em;
   padding-left: 0.33em; text-indent: -0.25em;}
h2 {font-size: 150%; font-style: italic; text-align: center;
   margin: 0 10%;}
</style>
```

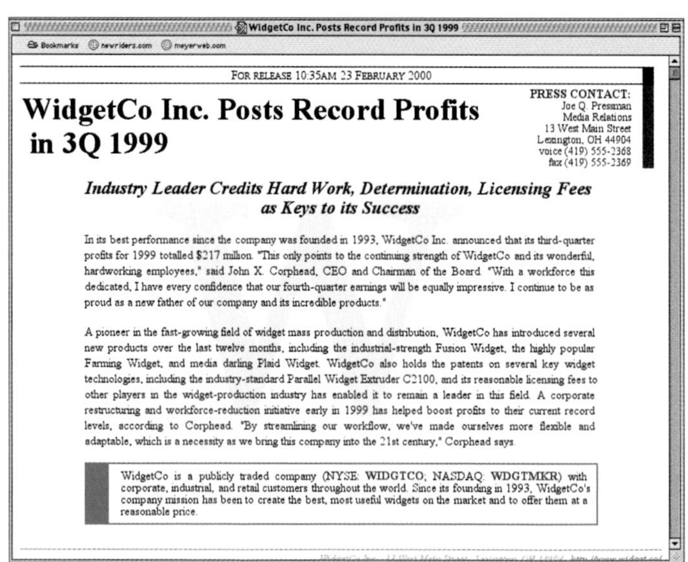

FIGURE 2.17

The finished product.

Branching Out

Starting with the styles we created in this project, it's possible to mix and match them for new effects or to take them in completely new directions. Here are some things to try out:

1. Flip-flop the head of the document by moving the contact info to the left, flipping the borders around to match, and moving the page title's placement to accommodate the change. Also place the company logo in a different spot on the page, such as the lower-right corner or the top center of the browser window.

2. Change the main paragraphs' margins and indentation so that they are no longer separated by a blank line and so that the first line of every paragraph is intended as though a Tab key had been used at the beginning of each paragraph. While you're at it, change the fonts used in various elements. For example, try setting the main text to be a serif font and the headlines to be in sans-serif.

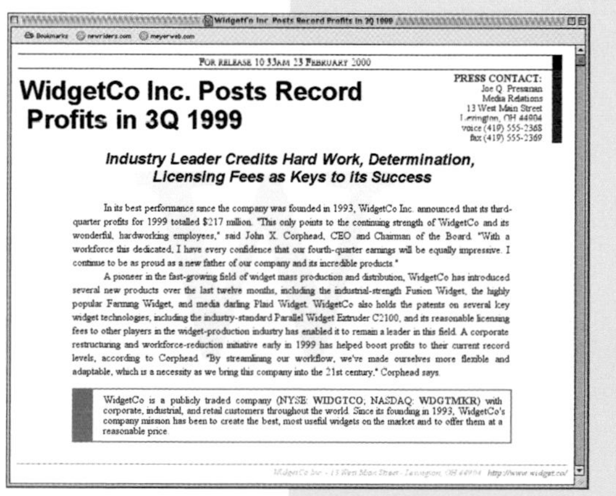

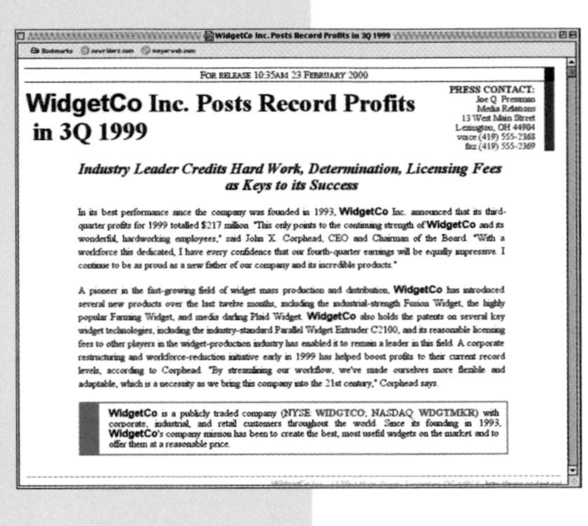

FOR RELEASE 10:35AM 23 FEBRUARY 2000

PRESS CONTACT:
Joe Q. Pressman
Media Relations
13 West Main Street
Lexington, OH 44904
voice (419) 555-2368
fax (419) 555-2369

WidgetCo Inc. Posts Record Profits in 3Q 1999

Industry Leader Credits Hard Work, Determination, Licensing Fees as Keys to its Success

In its best performance since the company was founded in 1993, **WidgetCo** Inc. announced that its third-quarter profits for 1999 totalled $217 million. "This only points to the continuing strength of **WidgetCo** and its wonderful, hardworking employees," said John X. Corphead, CEO and Chairman of the Board. "With a workforce this dedicated, I have every confidence that our fourth-quarter earnings will be equally impressive. I continue to be as proud as a new father of our company and its incredible products."

A pioneer in the fast-growing field of widget mass production and distribution, **WidgetCo** has introduced several new products over the last twelve months, including the industrial-strength Fusion Widget, the highly popular Farming Widget, and media darling Plaid Widget. **WidgetCo** also holds the patents on several key widget technologies, including the industry-standard Parallel Widget Extruder C2100, and its reasonable licensing fees to other players in the widget-production industry has enabled it to remain a leader in this field. A corporate restructuring and workforce-reduction initiative early in 1999 has helped boost profits to their current record levels, according to Corphead. "By streamlining our workflow, we've made ourselves more flexible and adaptable, which is a necessity as we bring this company into the 21st century," Corphead says.

WidgetCo is a publicly traded company (NYSE: WIDGTCO; NASDAQ: WDGTMKR) with corporate, industrial, and retail customers throughout the world. Since its founding in 1993, **WidgetCo**'s company mission has been to create the best, most useful widgets on the market and to offer them at a reasonable price.

3. Try placing `span` elements around various pieces of the document and styling them. For example, you could enclose every instance of the word "WidgetCo" with `<span class="corpname">WidgetCo</span>`. This would let you boldface the company name or make it bigger, a different color, or anything else that strikes your fancy. Some changes could be restricted to certain contexts (such as styling in paragraphs as opposed to headings).

3

Styling an Events Calendar

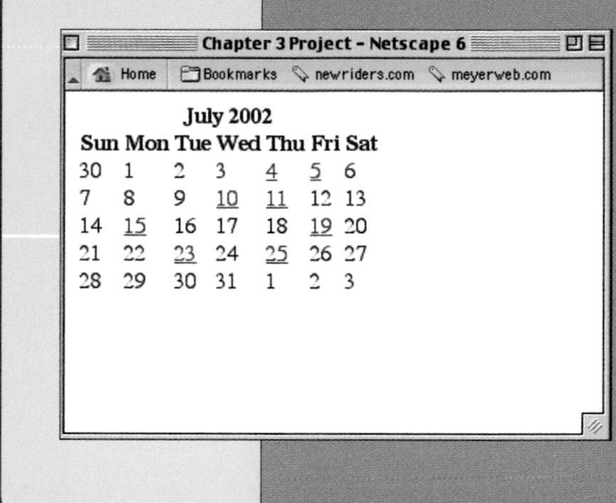

Most modern calendars mar the sweet simplicity of our lives by reminding us that each day that passes is the anniversary of some perfectly uninteresting event.

—Oscar Wilde

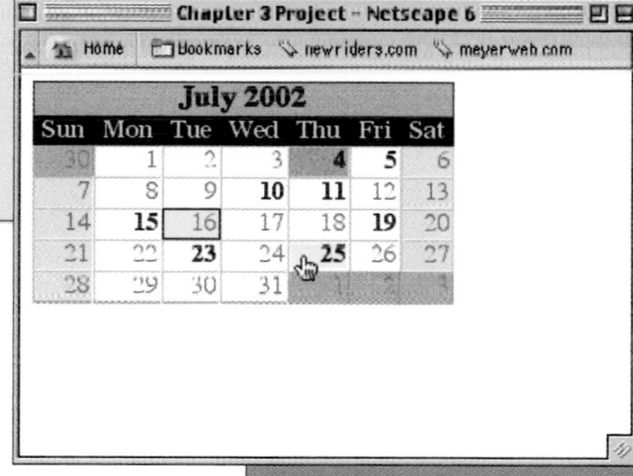

Although they aren't common, it's surprising just how useful events calendars can be on the Web. A personal site might use one to indicate when a web log was updated or to show important dates in history. Even more interesting, an organization or community could use a calendar to publicize upcoming and recurring events.

In this project, we'll look at the basic structure of Web-based calendars, explore ways to set the borders between days, and discuss how the days should be classed and identified to give us the most flexibility for later styling.

Project Goals

This time around, our project is to help a community-events organization of a local government get some useful calendars on the Web. These calendars will be generated by a database on the server, so we don't have to worry about anyone hand-coding the calendar. All we need to do is figure out what markup the scripts should produce based on our styling needs. After that's done, we'll take a small, simple calendar of days and mark it up so that it's easy to style. Then we'll tackle a larger, more detailed version of that calendar, which will force us to deal with text content within a given day.

Preparation

See the Introduction for instructions on how to download files from the Web site.

Download the files for Project 3 from this book's Web site. If you're planning to play along at home, load the file `ch03proj.html` into the editing program of your choice. This is the file you'll be editing, saving, and reloading as the project progresses.

Note that we'll be working with a related project partway through the project. You should also locate the file `ch03proj2.html` so that you know where to get it later on.

Laying the Groundwork

If we load up the bare-bones calendar of days that the database output script is producing, the content is pretty much recognizable as a calendar already. We can also see right off the bat that the content is enclosed in a table (see Figure 3.1).

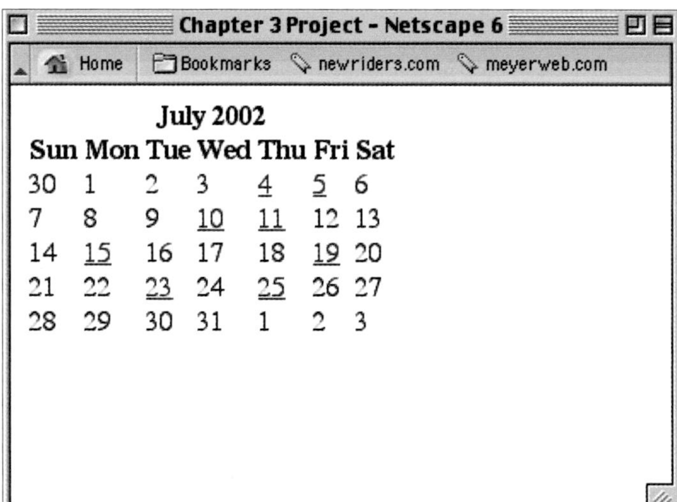

Figure 3.1

The unstyled calendar of days.

We can see that some days are hyperlinked to other pages and some aren't, but what's the table's overall structure? We could just turn on borders, but that might not tell us enough. Instead, let's temporarily insert some styles that will reveal the structure of the table to us (see Figure 3.2):

```
<title>Project 3 Chapter</title>
<style type="text/css">
table {border: 1px solid red;}
th {border: 1px dotted red;}
td {border: 1px dotted gray;}
</style>
</head>
```

FIGURE 3.2

Revealing the structure of the calendar.

So we have two rows of `th` elements, and the rest is made up of `td` elements. We can also quickly see that the calendar's "title" is in a `th` cell that spans all seven columns.

It's also the case that the script is filling in the days before the beginning of the month and after the end of the month. We could probably change the script to not fill in those days, but let's keep things the way they are. Our first order of business should be to class and identify various pieces of the calendar to reflect their nature. Let's start by identifying table rows. The second row is the traditional day-names row, and above that is what we might call a title. So let's identify those rows as well as the calendar itself:

```
<table id="calendar">
<tr id="title">
<th colspan="7">July 2002</th>
</tr>
<tr id="days">
<th>Sun</th>
```

For various reasons, it's probably a good idea to `id` the first and last weeks in the calendar. The reasons for this will become clear later in the project, but for now let's label them according to their nature:

```
</tr>
<tr id="firstweek">
<td>30</td>

</tr>
<tr id="lastweek">
<td>28</td>
```

Now we need to consider how we should label the ordinary `td` cells—the ones that contain the actual days of the month. Every day in the month is also a day of the week; that is, the day will be a Monday, a Thursday, or one of the other days of the week. But if you recall, we have days from three different months. Finally, every day can be uniquely identified as a combination of month and date. So we could label the cell corresponding to Tuesday the 9th of July like this:

```
<td class="jul tue" id="jul09">9</td>
```

Thus, this particular table cell belongs to the classes `jul` and `tue`, and the day's `id` is `jul09`. Labeling all of the days on the calendar in a similar fashion will provide us with a great deal of flexibility later on, so let's do that now. Don't forget that the first day on the calendar is part of June, so its markup should look like this:

```
td class="jun sun" id="jun30">30</td>
```

If you don't want to type in all of those `classes` and `ids`—and who could blame you?—the finished markup can be found in the file `ch0303.html`. If it seems like there's too much markup here, remember this: The calendar will eventually be generated by a script, and you can get your programmer to change the script output to give all of the `classes` and `ids` automatically.

Similarly, the last few days on the grid are part of August, so they should have their `class` and `id` values adjusted accordingly.

While we're at it, we should add day-of-the-week classes to the `th` elements in the day-names row, like this:

```
<tr id="days">
<th class="sun">Sun</th>
<th class="mon">Mon</th>
<th class="tue">Tue</th>
<th class="wed">Wed</th>
<th class="thu">Thu</th>
<th class="fri">Fri</th>
<th class="sat">Sat</th>
</tr>
```

And last but not quite least, we're going to get rid of the separation between table cells so that the table is as compact as we can make it (see Figure 3.3):

```
<table cellspacing="0" id="calendar">
```

July 2002						
Sun	Mon	Tue	Wed	Thu	Fri	Sat
30	1	2	3	4	5	6
7	8	9	10	11	12	13
14	15	16	17	18	19	20
21	22	23	24	25	26	27
28	29	30	31	1	2	3

FIGURE 3.3

The slightly more compact calendar, all marked up.

With that, we're finally done with the markup grind and can get on to the fun part!

On the Use of `cellspacing`

The HTML-based `cellspacing="0"` is used because it's the only widely supported way to control the spacing between table cells. CSS2 does have a mechanism for doing the same thing, but support is minimal. The HTML attributes `cellpadding` and `border` are both unnecessary, on the other hand, because support for the CSS properties `padding` and `border` is very widespread.

STYLING THE DOCUMENT

There are so many possibilities that it's hard to decide what to do first. Still, we have to start somewhere, so let's begin at the top of the calendar and then work on the grid of dates.

Setting the Top Apart

It's probably easiest to set the row of day names apart by reversing the content to be light blue text on a dark blue background. While we're at it, we'll get rid of the table-structure styles:

```
<style type="text/css">
tr#days th {color: #CCE; background-color: #224;
   font-weight: bold; text-align: center;
   padding: 1px 0.33em;}
</style>
```

The padding fills out the labels a little better and thus prevents them from jamming up next to each other. Now would be an excellent time to tie together the row of day names and the title immediately above it. Let's give it a light blue background, center and boldface the text, and put a border on the cell that matches the background color for the row of days. While we're at it, let's bump up the `font-size` just a bit.

```
<style type="text/css">
tr#days th {color: #CCE; background-color: #224;
   font-weight: bold; text-align: center;
   padding: 1px 0.33em;}
tr#title th {background: #AAC; color: black;
   border: 1px solid #224; font-size: 120%;}
</style>
```

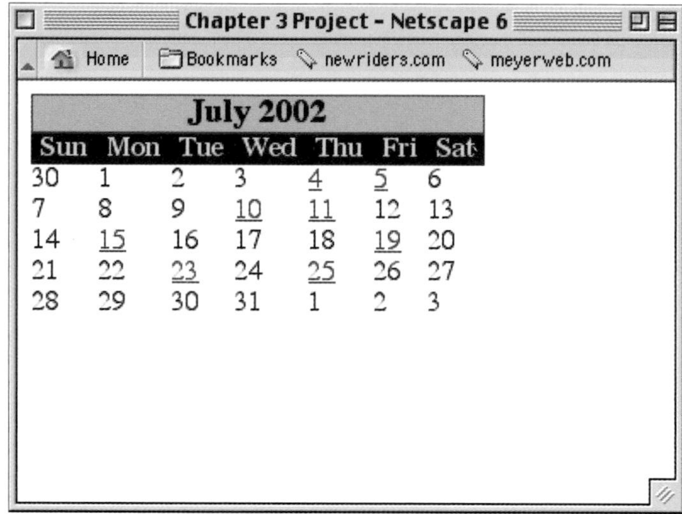

FIGURE 3.4

The calendar now has a well-styled top.

Now we have a calendar top that all fits together (see Figure 3.4). Of course, if you don't like blue, you can always change the color values, but you might want to wait until we're done to decide that.

Centering and Bolding?

In the last two changes, we've reproduced the traditional styles for a `th` element by centering and boldfacing the text. This might seem redundant, but it's actually a very good authoring practice. We could rely on the browser defaults instead of explicitly writing out these styles, but it might be the case that some browsers don't center `th` elements, for example.

Creating the Grid

Even though the main part of the calendar, the grid of days, is part of a table, there aren't any borders between the numbers yet. We can fix that, but it isn't as simple as you might think at first. For example, we could simply give every `td` element a border, but the results aren't likely to be quite what we want (see Figure 3.5):

```
tr#title th {background: #AAC; color: black;
   border: 1px solid #224; font-size: 120%;}
td {border: 1px solid gray;}
</style>
```

Because each cell has four borders of its own, any place two cells adjoin each other, their borders are going to be placed right next to each other. Therefore, inside the table, the borders between cells add up to be 2 pixels thick, whereas the ones along the outside are only 1 pixel thick.

There are two ways to deal with this. One is to only style two borders—say, the right and bottom borders—and make sure the other two borders have no width. The other way is to manipulate the colors of the borders so that the borders all look roughly the same but each cell still has all four borders "turned on." We're going to choose the latter route for reasons that will become obvious later in this project.

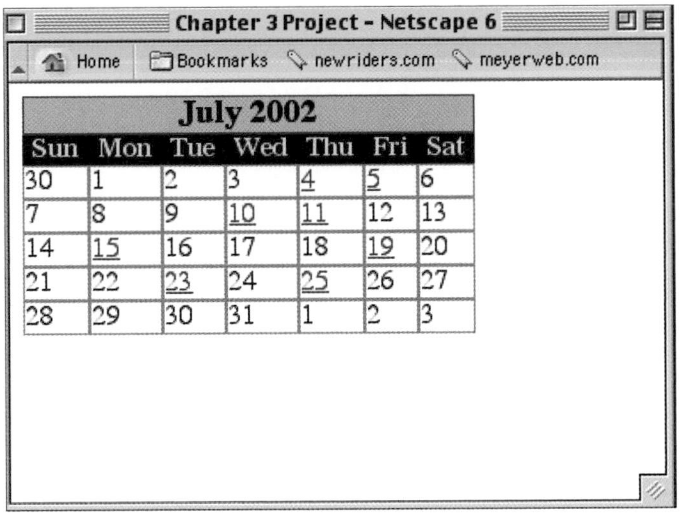

FIGURE 3.5

Borders on table cells don't overlap, so many appear to be doubled in thickness.

```
tr#title th {background: #AAC; color: black;
   border: 1px solid #224; font-size: 120%;}
td {border: 1px solid gray;
   border-color: #DDD #CCC #CCC #DDD;}
</style>
```

We're working in shades of light gray to produce a subtle inset-border effect. Therefore, the top and left borders get a darker shade than the bottom and right borders. (We're assuming that the virtual light source is coming from the top left.) The problem is that the right borders on the last column will be a very light gray, making it look like the calendar grid isn't closed. To fix this, we'll set a different style for the right border of only the cells in that column (see Figure 3.6):

```
td border: 1px solid gray;
   border-color: #BBB #EEE #EEE #BBB;}
td.sat {border-right: 1px solid #BBB;}
</style>
```

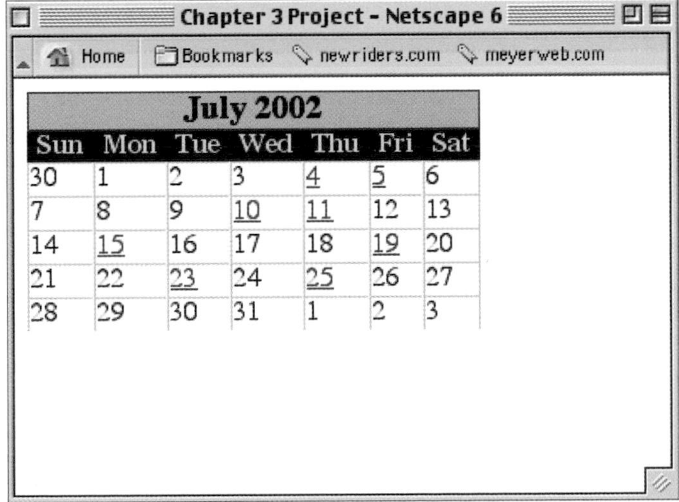

FIGURE 3.6

Subtle color variations make the grid less obtrusive.

What About inset?

Why did we manually create an inset effect instead of just using `border-style: inset`? Because there's no reliable way to control the shading a browser uses for the inset style. By doing things ourselves, we get much more precise control over the look of the borders.

You can see that the cells along the bottom of the grid look sort of "unclosed" because of the light bottom borders. That's how the right side of the calendar would have looked if we hadn't added in the `td.sat` rule. Instead of creating a similar rule for the bottom of the calendar, though, let's move on to other issues and get back to the bottom of the calendar later.

Distinguishing the Months

Now that we have a grid, we should go about making its contents a little more interesting. First on the agenda is a way to make the non-July days look very different so that it's obvious they aren't part of the month in question. Again, there are a multitude of options. For example, we could just set them to be white text on a white background, making them disappear entirely. Instead, let's blue them out, so to speak.

Here's where all that classing and ID'ing really pays off. Because the non-July days are already part of the classes `jun` and `aug`, we can just write styles that apply to those classes (see Figure 3.7):

```
td.sat {border-right: 1px solid #BBB;}
td.jun, td.aug {background: #AAB; color: #889;
   border: 1px solid #AAB; border-right-color: #99A;}
</style>
```

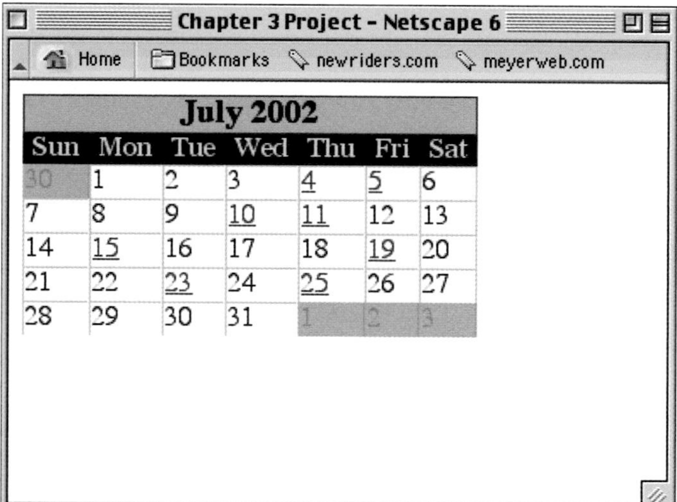

FIGURE 3.7

"Blueing" out the other months helps keep the focus on July.

We're using shades of blue to go along with the styling of the calendar top, of course. By setting the text color and the background color close to each other in terms of brightness, the dates are washed out while still remaining relatively readable.

Now that we've styled the non-July days, we can go ahead and cap off the bottom of the grid. To give it a little more weight, let's set a border that's 2 pixels thick and whose color matches the background of the days in August.

Fortunately, this is very easy to do because we already labeled the last row in the table (see Figure 3.8):

```
td.jun, td.aug {background: #AAB; color: #889;
   border: 1px solid #AAB; border-right-color: #99A;}
tr#lastweek td {border-bottom: 2px solid #AAB;}
</style>
```

FIGURE 3.8

Capping off the calendar with a thickened blue bottom border.

We also could have taken a simpler route and just applied a border to the bottom of the table itself, but that could result in less flexibility later on. In some circumstances, however, applying borders to the table element itself makes a whole lot of sense, so keep it in mind as a potential tool.

Distinguishing the Days

Just for a little extra visual flair, let's set a background on Saturdays and Sundays. Because the month is July and we already have blue and white, how about a nice light red background:

```
td.sat {border-right: 1px solid #BBB;}
td.sat, td.sun {background: #FDD;}
td.jun, td.aug {background: #AAB; color: #889;
   border: 1px solid #AAB; border-right-color: #99A;}
```

Notice that we put that rule *before* the one that washes out the June and August days. If we hadn't, June 30 and August 3 would both have had red backgrounds, thanks to the way our selectors are written.

So now July is nicely red, white, and blue (see Figure 3.9). What about the 4th, which is a national holiday in America? We ought to highlight it. Again, there are two choices. One would be to write a rule with the selector `td#jul04`, and that would work just fine. However, let's go for a more generic solution: We'll add a `holiday` class to that day:

Keeping Rules Ordered

Because `td.sat` and `td.sun` have the same specificity as `td.jun` and `td.aug`, whichever rule comes later will win out in terms of the background color.

FIGURE 3.9

Highlighting the weekends in a patriotic fashion.

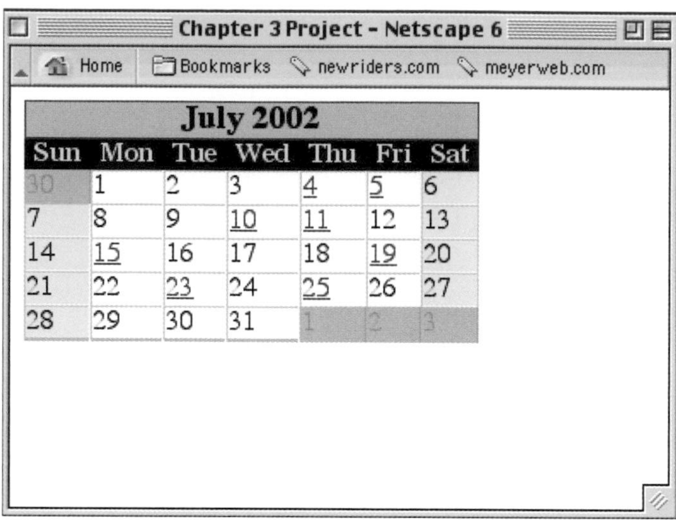


```
<td class="jul thu holiday" id="jul04"><a href="jul04.html">4</a></td>
```

Now we can write a style that will apply to all holidays:

```
tr#lastweek td {border-bottom: 2px solid #AAB;}
td.holiday {background: #FAA;
   border-color: #BBB #FCC #FCC #BBB;}
</style>
```

In addition to the medium-red background, the border colors are set so that the highlighting blends in a little better with the background (see Figure 3.10).

FIGURE 3.10

Making Independence Day stand out.

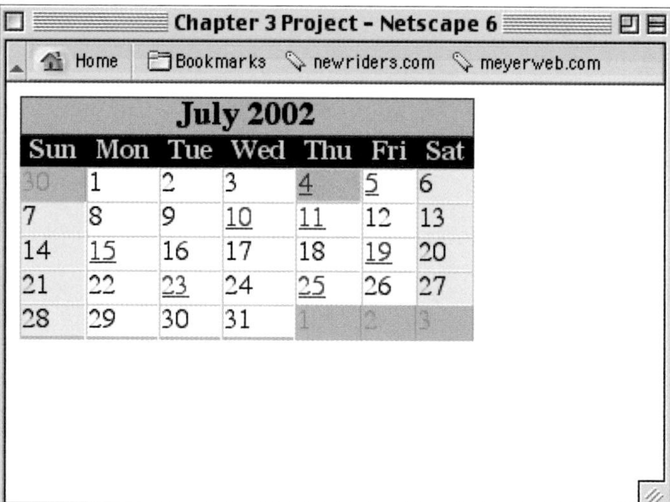

Altering the Days of July

Now might be a good time to step back and look at the calendar as a whole. Are the individual days styled the way we want them? Should we do anything about the links versus normal text? Do we want to keep the underlining of the linked days? Do we want to change the padding of these table cells?

Let's start by assuming we don't want the linked days to be underlined. The rule to remove the underlines is very simple, but let's make sure it applies only to the links in the calendar:

```
<style type="text/css">
table#calendar a {text-decoration: none;}
tr#days th {color: #CCE; background-color: #224;
   font-weight: bold; text-align: center;
   padding: 1px 0.33em;}
```

Goodbye underlines. As a consequence of this decision, we have to come up with a way to make the links stand apart from the days that aren't linked.

There are many ways to handle such a situation, of course, but let's attack it from two directions. First, let's fade out the text of any unlinked days and additionally boldface any linked days. And, just for the heck of it, let's right-align all of the days (see Figure 3.11).

```
td {color: #777; text-align: right;
   border: 1px solid gray;
   border-color: #BBB #EEE #EEE #BBB;}
td.sat {border-right: 1px solid #BBB;}
td a {font-weight: bold;}
td.sat, td.sun {background: #FDD;}
```

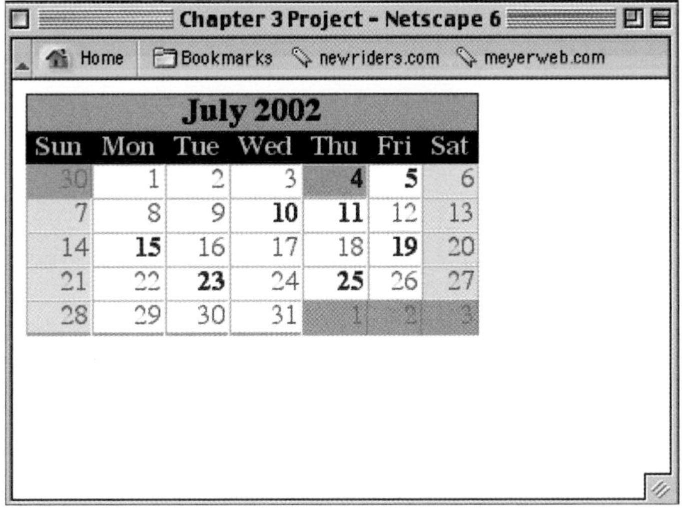

FIGURE 3.11

The linked days now stand out much more clearly, and all the days have shifted to the right.

The links could stand to be even more obvious, so let's change their color. A navy blue would be nice (not to mention would fit in with the rest of the calendar), and we could set visited links to be purple. In addition, let's make the background of the links a medium yellow when the user hovers over a link.

```
td a {font-weight: bold;}
table#calendar a:link {color: navy;}
table#calendar a:visited {color: purple;}
table#calendar a:hover {background: #FF6;}
td.sat, td.sun {background: #FDD;}
```

Unfortunately, the hover effect will only appear behind the actual text of the link, not the entire table cell. There are a number of ways to correct this problem, but most of them use highly complicated JavaScript in an attempt to support Navigator 4.x. Let's use the much simpler CSS way of making the links block-level elements. That way, they'll fill up the whole cell and neatly solve our problem (see Figure 3.12).

```
td.sat {border-right: 1px solid #BBB;}
td a {font-weight: bold; display: block; margin: 0;}
td a:link {color: navy;}
```

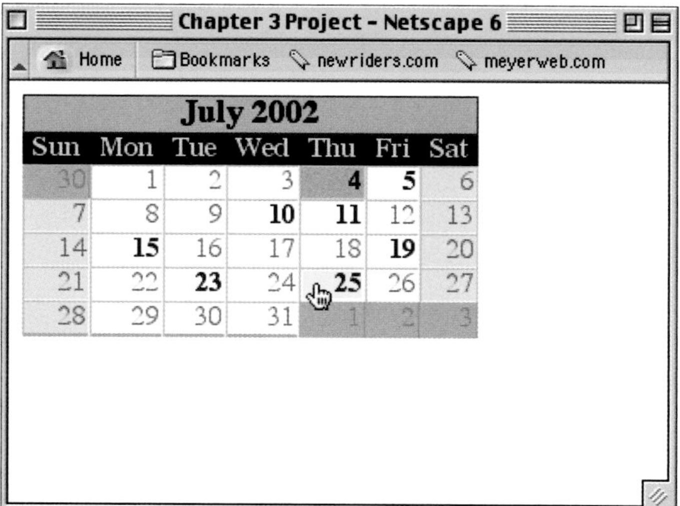

FIGURE 3.12

The linked days now stand out much more clearly.

Making Today a Major Highlight

With everything else basically done, now we just need to highlight the current date. For testing purposes, we'll assume it's July 16. Let's go with a yellow background and a black border to really make today obvious (see Figure 3.13):

```
td.holiday {background: #FAA; border-color: #BBB #FCC #FCC #BBB;}
td#jul16 {background-color: yellow; border: 1px solid black;}
</style>
```

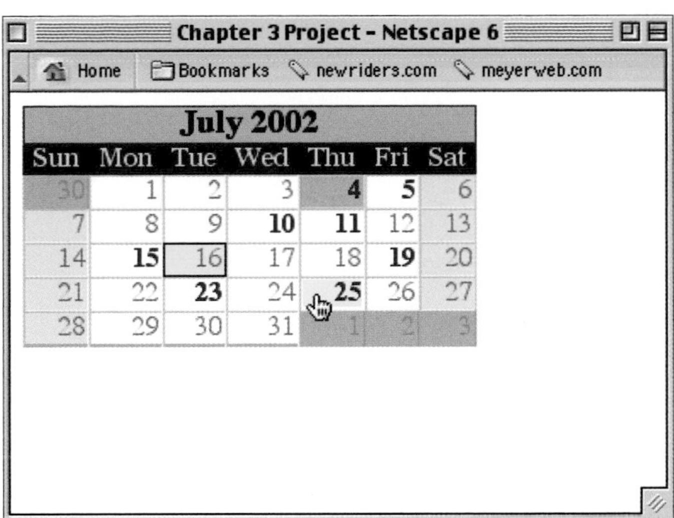

FIGURE 3.13

Highlighting the current date.

Now we see why it was a good idea to set all four borders for every cell. Had we not done so, setting the border on the current date could have thrown off the layout of the table due to our setting all four borders for the current date.

Day-to-Day Changes

Obviously, it won't always be July 16, 2002. Therefore, the "highlight today" rule would need to be changed every day. Rather than doing it by hand, it makes more sense to have the database output script write the rule appropriate to each day. Alternatively, the styles could be written into a `style` attribute on the cell containing the current date. In either case, it's a matter to take up with the script programmer.

Placing the Calendar in an Existing Document

Because we've been styling a document that contains only the calendar, we've been able to get a little lazy about our selectors. Consider the following rule from our style sheet, for example:

```
td {color: #777; text-align: right;
   border: 1px solid gray;
   border-color: #BBB #EEE #EEE #BBB;}
```

This works fine in our test document, but imagine applying the rule to a page that had the calendar placed somewhere on it. We don't want all of the text in every single table cell in the whole page to be grayed out and right aligned!

There is really only one fix, but fortunately it's a simple one. We need to add the string `table#calendar` at the front of any selector that doesn't already contain it. Listing 3.1 shows the changes this causes in the context of the entire style sheet. It's necessary to make all of these changes because, if we don't, the differences in specificity could cause the styles to change as rules begin to override each other in unexpected ways.

Listing 3.1 The Full Style Sheet, Showing Altered Selectors

```
<style type="text/css">
table#calendar a {text-decoration: none;}
table#calendar tr#days th {color: #CCE; background-color: #224;
   font-weight: bold; text-align: center;
   padding: 1px 0.33em;}
table#calendar tr#title th {background: #AAC; color: black;
   border: 1px solid #242; font-size: 120%;}
table#calendar td {color: #777; text-align: right;
   border: 1px solid gray;
   border-color: #BBB #EEE #EEE #BBB;}
table#calendar td.sat {border-right: 1px solid #BBB;}
table#calendar a {font-weight: bold; display: block; margin: 0;}
table#calendar a:link {color: navy;}
table#calendar a:visited {color: purple;}
table#calendar a:hover {background: #FF6;}
table#calendar td.sat, table#calendar td.sun {background: #FDD;}
table#calendar td.jun, table#calendar td.aug {
   background: #AAB; color: #889;
   border: 1px solid #AAB; border-right-color: #99A;}
table#calendar tr#lastweek td {border-bottom: 2px solid #AAB;}
table#calendar td.holiday {background: #FAA;
   border-color: #BBB #FCC #FCC #BBB;}
table#calendar td#jul16 {background-color: yellow;
   border: 1px solid black;}
</style>
```

Looking at the resulting rules, it might have been better to give the table an `id` value of `cal` or maybe `smcal`, just to keep the selectors shorter. Nevertheless, these kinds of selectors are necessary when you're styling just one portion of a document. In this case, the addition of `table#calendar` keeps the calendar styles confined to just that piece of the document.

Working with a More Detailed Calendar

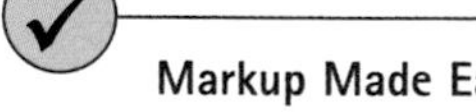

Markup Made Easy

To save time, we'll assume that the programmer for the project has learned from the changes we made to the markup for the smaller calendar and has used similar principles to mark up the information in this new format.

Having shown the resulting calendar to the clients, they've approved it enthusiastically. Now they want us to give the same treatment to their detailed monthly calendar, which lists the events that are happening throughout the month. This will be generated from the same database that produced the smaller calendar. Therefore, the markup will be consistent with what we already know. Let's apply the styles we already wrote to this new calendar and see what we get (see Figure 3.14).

Already it would seem that we have our work cut out for us. Although the larger calendar makes full use of the work we've already done, there is much more information here, and it will have to be styled in a way that makes sense.

FIGURE 3.14

The larger calendar with the styles from Listing 3.1.

Dissecting a Day

Before we start styling the events in this calendar, we have to understand how the information in a given day is structured. We'll look at July 15 because it contains two events, one of which (the Children's Hour) appears to be recurrent:

```
<td class="jul mon">
<div class="date">15</div>
<div class="event recur"><span class="time">2:00pm</span> <span
class="title">Children's Hour</span> <span class="loc">Main Street Public
Library</span></div>
<div class="event"><span class="time">6:00pm</span> <span class="title">City
Council Open Forum</span> <span class="loc">Council Chambers</span></div>
</td>
```

The full markup for the larger calendar can be found in the `cho3proj2.html`.

There are three important things to notice here:

- The date (15) is now enclosed in a `div` with a `class` of `date`.
- Every event is contained in a `div`.
- The pieces of an event—the time, the title, and the location—are all wrapped in appropriately classed `span` elements.

We can use all of these things to our advantage.

Looking over the calendar again, we can see that every day has exactly the same kind of information, so we can assume it's marked up in a similar way. Well, there is one exception: July 4th, which has the text "Independence Day (U.S.)" in the cell. That might be an event, but then again it might not. Let's look:

```
<td class="jul thu holiday">
<div class="date">4</div>
<div class="event"><span class="time">10:00am</span> <span class="title">4th of
July Parade</span> <span class="loc">Main Street</span></div>
<div class="event"><span class="time">9:30pm</span> <span
class="title">Fireworks!</span> <span class="loc">Meadowlands Park</span></div>
<div class="holiday">Independence Day (U.S.)</div>
</td>
```

Ah-ha! The text is contained in a `div` that has a `class` of `holiday`. We'll need to keep that in mind as we go about styling the calendar.

Global Changes

Our first order of business should be to bring consistency to the placement of information in each day. This will mean taking out a few declarations even as we add others.

For example, the declarations that make all table-cell text gray and right–aligned are no longer appropriate. We should also top align all of the content so that the date is always on the top line of the cell. In the old days, this was done with the HTML attribute `valign`, but CSS enables us to do the same thing without having to add an attribute to every row (or cell):

Commenting in CSS

There is only one comment syntax in CSS, as shown in the code block on this page. CSS comments can span multiple lines and contain any text at all, but comments have to start with `/*` and end with `*/`. HTML-style comments are not allowed.

```
table#calendar tr#title th {background: #AAC; color: black;
   border: 1px solid #242; font-size: 120%;}
table#calendar td {vertical-align: top;
   /* we removed "color: #777; text-align: right;" */
   border: 1px solid gray;
   border-color: #BBB #EEE #EEE #BBB;}
table#calendar td.sat {border-right: 1px solid #BBB;}
```

Let's also add some margins to the `div`s so that they don't run together any more. We don't want to add too much space, so half an em is just the right amount (see Figure 3.15):

```
table#calendar td#jul16 {background-color: yellow;
   border: 1px solid black;}
div.event {margin: 0.5em;}
</style>
```

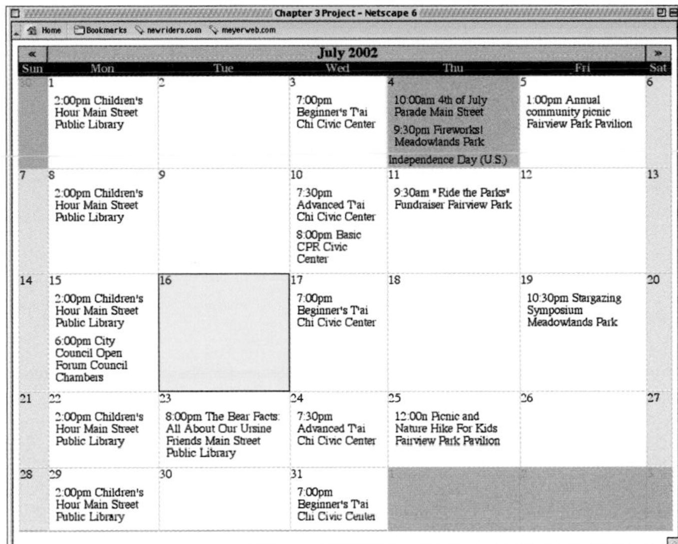

FIGURE 3.15

Just a little bit of margin helps keep the events distinct from each other.

Blocking the Spans

Now that we have the events separate from each other, we ought to make the contents look a little better. Right now the information sort of runs together, and it's hard to tell where one type of information ends and the next begins.

As you might recall, the time, title, and location of each event are enclosed in span elements. The first thing to do is convert these spans into block-level elements so that each one creates a line break at the end of the element.

```
div.event {margin: 0.5em;}
div.event span {display: block;}
</style>
```

Now we can more easily style the time, title, and location. Let's try boldfacing the time and making the location text italicized and dark gray (see Figure 3.16):

```
div.event span {display: block;}
span.time {font-weight: bold;}
span.loc {color: #555; font-style: italic;}
</style>
```

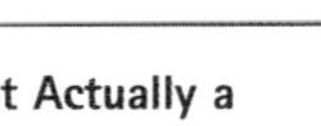

Not Actually a Line Break

Okay, so block-level elements don't generate line breaks. What they do is prevent any other element from appearing next to them (unless the element has been floated or positioned). So, from a text point of view, it's a lot like hitting Return at the end of the element. The difference is in how the element box is drawn; a block-level element generates its own box, whereas inserting a <br> would actually insert a line break without ending the element.

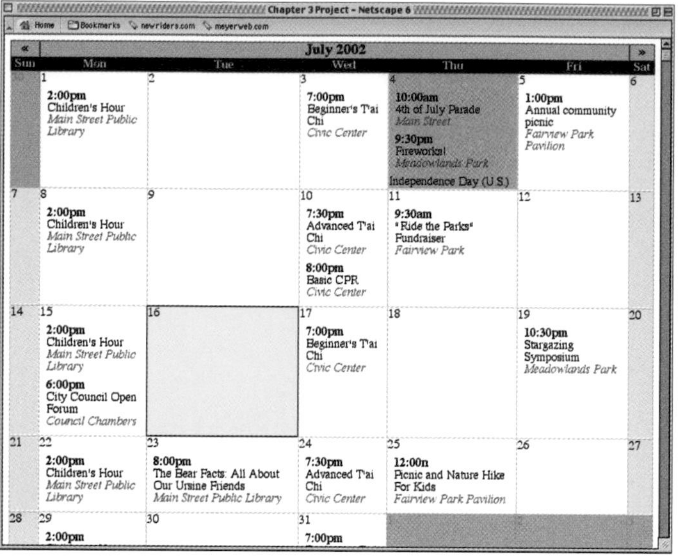

FIGURE 3.16

Events are much easier to understand now that the bits of information are styled in distinct ways.

Cornering Our Dates

Much as it might sound like a social event gone horribly wrong, date cornering is almost required for calendars of this kind. It's expected that the date will be in one of the top corners of the box, with the actual events of the day flowing past the date. Sounds a lot like the date is a floated element, actually. So let's float the dates into the right corner of each date box and give them borders and a background (see Figure 3.17):

```
span.loc {color: #555; font-style: italic;}
div.date {float: right; text-align: center;
   border: 1px solid gray; border-width: 0 0 1px 1px;
   background: #F3F3F3;}
</style>
```

It's a good start, but we can already see things that need to be corrected. The borders are a little too snug against the numbers, for starters. We can beef up the floated date box with `padding` and set the margin to zero in the bargain:

```
span.loc {color: #555; font-style: italic;}
div.date {float: right; text-align: center;
   border: 1px solid gray; border-width: 0 0 1px 1px;
   padding: 0.125em 0.25em 0 0.25em; margin: 0;
   background: #F3F3F3;}
</style>
```

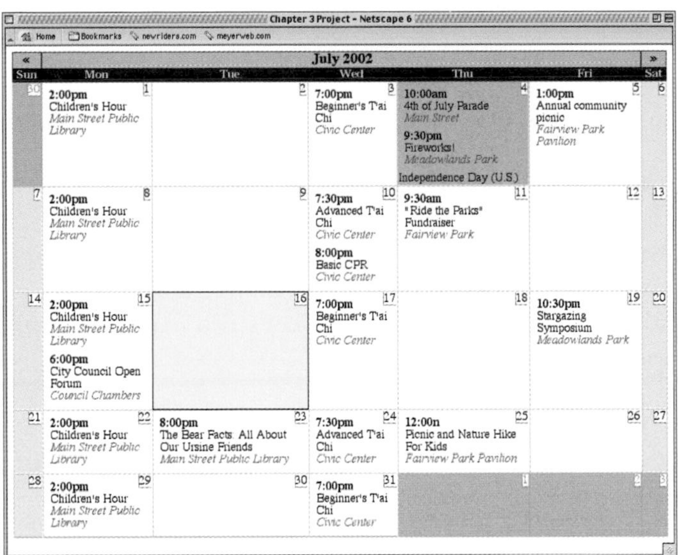

FIGURE 3.17

By floating the dates, we both compact the calendar and make it look more like a print calendar.

A bigger problem is that the date boxes on weekends (and those in June and August) don't match their backgrounds. Plus they don't really need the borders. The most sensible choice is to write rules that override the properties that need to be different (see Figure 3.18):

```
div.date {float: right; text-align: center;
   border: 1px solid gray; border-width: 0 0 1px 1px;
   padding: 0.125em 0.25em 0 0.25em; margin: 0;
   background: #F3F3F3;}
td.sat div.date, td.sun div.date {border-width: 0;
   color: gray; background: transparent;}
td.jun div.date, td.aug div.date {border-width: 0;
   color: gray; background: transparent;}
</style>
```

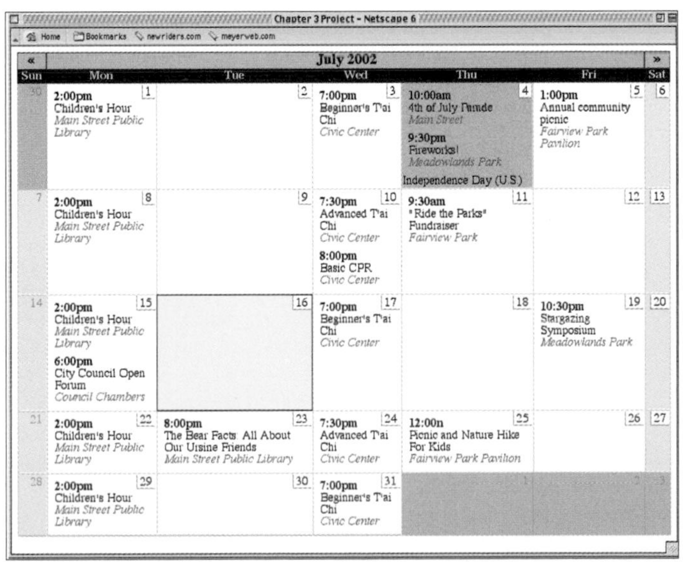

FIGURE 3.18

The date boxes look a lot better with a little padding, and the dates in June and August aren't an eyesore any more.

By setting all of the date-box borders in June and August to have zero width, we effectively turn them off. Making the backgrounds transparent enables the table-cell background color to shine through. This will be useful if, for example, a later revision of the site changes the background colors for weekend days.

Restructuring the Grid

Because the calendar has expanded, the "inset" look to the cell borders seems a little too washed out. Let's change the way they're drawn by going from an all-four-sides border to a two-sides border. Let's also make sure there's no padding on the table cells.

```
table#calendar tr#title th {background: #AAC; color: black;
   border: 1px solid #242; font-size: 120%;}
table#calendar td {vertical-align: top; padding: 0;
   border: 0px solid gray; border-width: 0 0 1px 1px;}
/* we deleted "border: 1px solid gray;
border-color: #BBB #EEE #EEE #BBB;" */
table#calendar td.sat {border-right: 1px solid #BBB;}
```

Now only the left and bottom borders are being drawn for most cells. However, some cells (like holidays and non-July days) still have rules to style all four borders. As a result, we need to change or get rid of the holdovers (see Figure 3.19).

```
table#calendar td {vertical-align: top; padding: 0;
   border: 0px solid gray; border-width: 0 0 1px 1px;}
/* deleted "border: 1px solid gray;
border-color: #BBB #EEE #EEE #BBB;" */

table#calendar td.sat {border-right: 1px solid gray;}
/* changed the color from "#BBB" to "gray" */

table#calendar td.jun, table#calendar td.aug {
   background: #AAB; color: #889;}
/* deleted "border: 1px solid #AAB;
border-right-color: #99A;" */
```

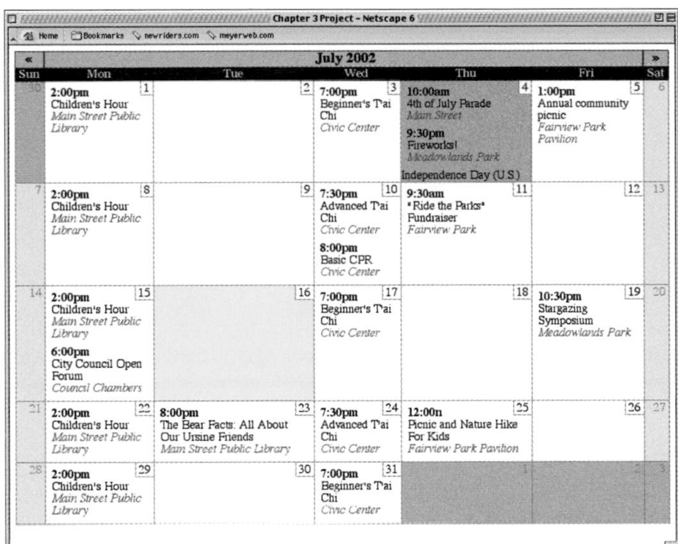

FIGURE 3.19

Tightening up the grid makes the calendar look a lot more cleanly drawn.

A Few Last Touches

Before we close out this phase of the project, let's do a few small things to make the calendar look even better.

Throughout the project, we've ignored the fact that the columns are of varying width. We could leave it that way—after all, one of the strengths of the Web is its fluidity—but let's set regular widths. Because the weekends are always empty, though, we might as well leave them skinny. If we set the Saturday and Sunday columns to each be 5% of the width of the table, that would leave us with 90% to be divided among five columns, which results in 18% each. To keep things simple, we can set the column width by setting the width of the cells in the "days" row:

```
table#calendar a {text-decoration: none;}
tr#days th {width: 18%;}
tr#days th.sat, tr#days th.sun {width: 5%;}
table#calendar tr#days th {color: #CCE; background-color: #224;
   font-weight: bold; text-align: center;
   padding: 1px 0.33em;}
```

Although the current date is fairly well highlighted with its yellow background, let's take it one step further by boldfacing the text and coloring it dark red while also making the background of the date a light yellow:

```
table#calendar td#jul16 {background-color: yellow;}
td#jul16 div.date {color: #C33; font-weight: bold; background: #FFC;}
div.event {margin: 0.5em;}
```

More Daily Changes

Remember that the rules relating to the current day will actually be generated by the same script that produces the calendar markup. You'll need to work with the programmer to make sure he adds this new rule to the script.

More Daily Changes

Remember that the rules relating to the current day will actually be generated by the same script that produces the calendar markup. You'll need to work with the programmer to make sure he adds this new rule to the script.

To conform to widespread calendar conventions, let's italicize the text that names holidays. Thus, the text "Independence Day (U.S.)" will be in italics:

```
div.event span {display: block;}
div.holiday {font-style: italic;}
span.time {font-weight: bold;}
```

Finally, as a dollop of icing on our already well-styled cake, let's add an image of a firecracker to the background of the whole calendar:

```
<style type="text/css">
table#calendar {background: white url(fwork.gif) center no-repeat;}
table#calendar a {text-decoration: none;}
```

We're applying the background image to the table so that it can be centered, more or less, within the grid. We could shift it around by changing the position values, but centering it in the table seems like the best move.

All of these changes, taken together, create the effect of a print calendar on the Web (see Figure 3.20).

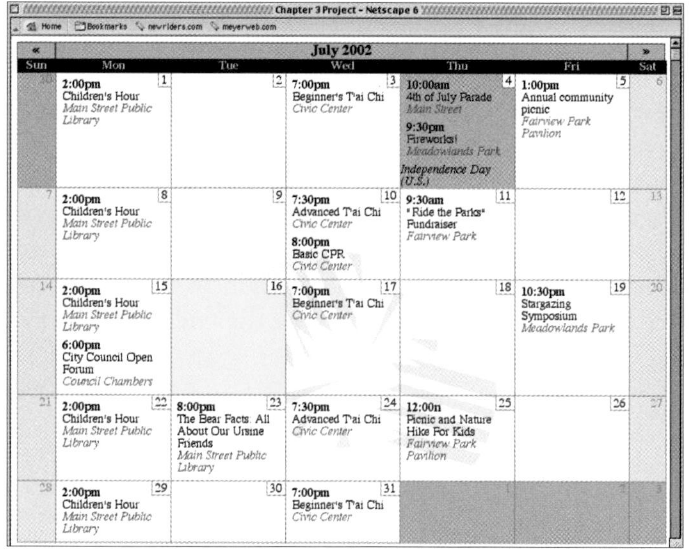

FIGURE 3.20

The columns are more regular, the current date is more obvious, the holiday is labeled in italics, and there's clip art in the background. All is right with the world.

Branching Out

There are many other ways to style a calendar in addition to the methods used in this project. Here are a few suggestions:

1. Another possibility when styling the smaller calendar is to put borders between rows instead of boxing in all the cells and centering the dates within their cells.

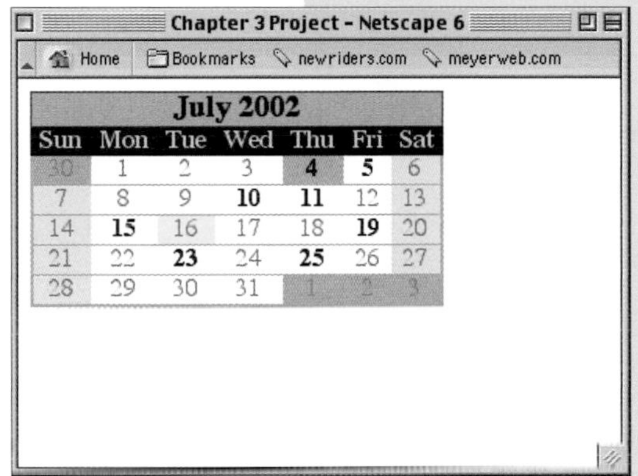

2. You can visually distinguish the recurring events in the larger calendar by giving them a slightly different style than nonrecurring events. Color and font changes are the easiest to implement without upsetting the overall design, but it might also be useful to set a border or background color.

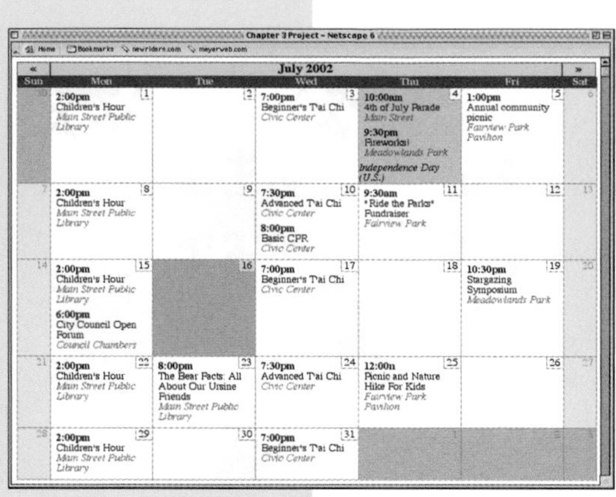

3. Try rewriting the style sheet for the larger calendar to reflect another seasonal or holiday theme. Manipulating the colors and adding in a few appropriate graphics is all that's really necessary. For example, you could create a Halloween theme using orange and brown or a wintry look with snowflakes in the background. Be creative!

4

Bringing Hyperlinks to Life

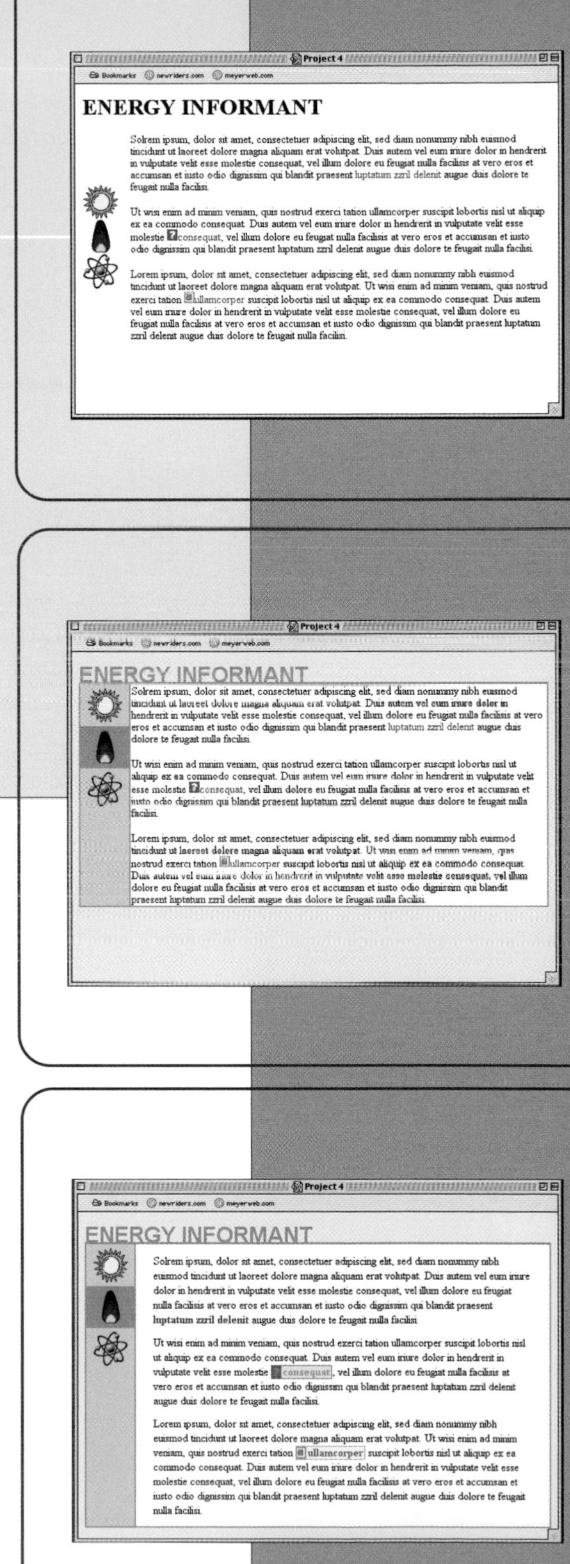

We are strangers to each other
Each one's life a novel no one else has read
Even joined in bonds of love
We're linked to one another by such slender threads…

—Neil Peart

Hyperlinks are what make the Web a web at all. Without them, we'd be forced to manually type in the address of every page we wanted to visit. We probably spend more of our time on the Web searching out the right links and interacting with them than we do anything else. But hyperlinks can be much more than simple text or graphics with the borders removed.

In the course of this project, we'll explore ways to creatively style hyperlinks and see how to base their styles on various link states.

Project Goals

As part of site design for a cutting-edge energy-supply company, we need to create a compact interface to convey information about the three main types of energy sources used by the client: natural gas, nuclear power, and solar power. The name for this interface is "Energy

Informant," a name supplied by the client. The client also insists that some links should look different than a normal text link. "The help-system and press-release links need to really stand out compared to other links," the client said, and the boss agreed.

Preparation

See the Introduction for instructions on how to download the files from the Web site.

Download the files for Project 4 from this book's Web site. If you're planning to play along at home, load the file `ch04proj.html` into the editing program of your choice. This is the file you'll be editing, saving, and reloading as the project progresses.

Laying the Groundwork

First let's take a peek at the basic file the design department produced for the client's preapproval (see Figure 4.1). This file uses some HTML-based presentation attributes such as `valign` and `bgcolor`, and we'll remove them as we create the overall design.

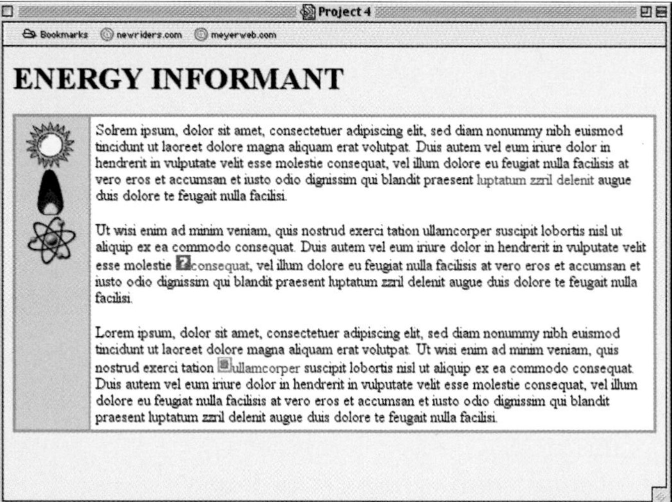

Figure 4.1

The basic design template, not yet styled with CSS.

In addition to this general design template, a few comments from the design people came along with it:

- The icon corresponding to the current page should be highlighted in some fashion that fits in with the overall look of the page.
- The title needs to be much closer to the table containing the icons and general information and needs to fit in better with the overall design. Suggestions include changing the color and font and eliminating the space between the text and the table.

- The help and press-release links (the ones with the icons) need to be improved dramatically but still make use of the icons. One suggestion is to draw a box around the link whose color matches the icon background.

Overall, the goals are fairly straightforward. The links are going to require the most work, especially because we have two very different kinds of links to worry about: the icons on the left side of the page and the icon links in the main text.

Let's get the markup more to our liking before we proceed. First let's strip out the HTML styling and throw in some IDs and classes. The table gets an `id` of `inform` so that we can style it specifically if we need to. We'll identify the left-side cell as `navbuttons` and the content area as `main`. We also need to identify each of the left-side icons according to their type.

```
<table cellspacing="0" id="inform">
<tr>
<td id="navbuttons">
<a href="sun.html"><img src="sun.gif" id="sun"></a>
<a href="gas.html"><img src="gas.gif" id="gas"></a>
<a href="atom.html"><img src="atom.gif" id="atom"></a>
</td>
<td id="main">
```

Finally, we'll add classes of `help` and `pr` (for "press release") to the appropriate links. Having done all this, we can see that the document is now laid bare and ready for our styling (see Figure 4.2).

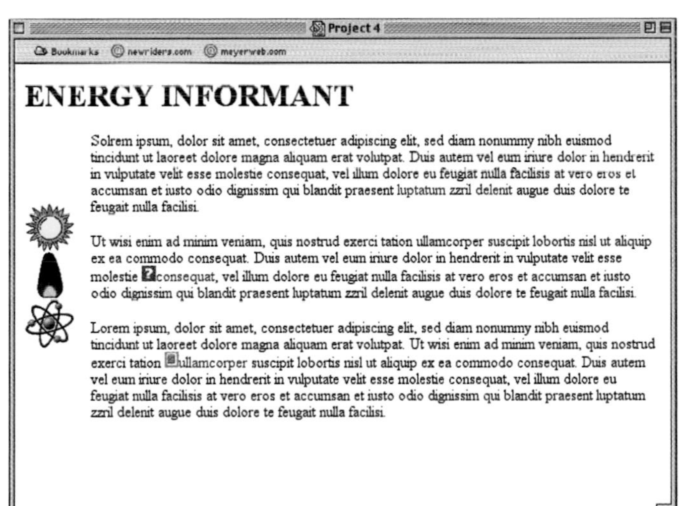

FIGURE 4.2

Having stripped out the HTML-based presentation and dropped in some `ids`, we're ready to begin styling.

There's something worth noting for later on: The icons are partially transparent. The nonicon parts of the images are transparent pixels, allowing the background to show through. That will be very useful.

Styling the Document

Basically, we have two main tasks ahead of us:

- To make the page look like it did when it relied on HTML-based presentation
- To push the icons to a new level of visual effect by applying some creative CSS to them

Getting Back to Square One

Before we get down 'n' dirty with the links, let's quickly reproduce the original basic design look in CSS. Because we have the HTML file to guide us, we can just rewrite the styles to match what we had before (see Figure 4.3).

```
<style type="text/css">
body {background: #CEC; color: black;}
td#navbuttons {background: #ACA; padding: 0;
   border: 2px solid #797;}
td#main {background: #FFD; color: black;
   border: 2px solid #797;}
</style>
```

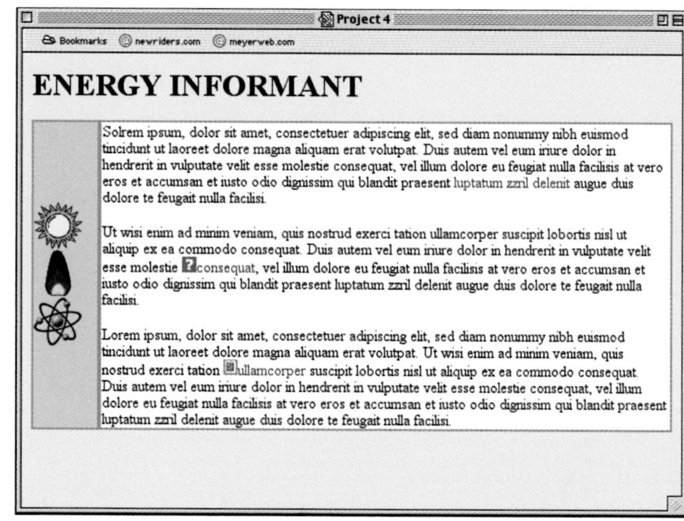

Figure 4.3

The first step in re-creating the basic design.

Alternate Border Effects

We also could have created the borders around the cells by setting a background color for the `table` itself and then setting a value (such as 2) for the `cellspacing` attribute. Although this approach works in some cases, it also tends to rob the designer of flexibility because it enforces a single padding on all cells instead of allowing different amounts of padding on different cells. That's why we're avoiding it here.

The space between the two cells is now 4 pixels thick, thanks to the fact that there are two adjacent borders and each is `2px` thick. We need to reduce one of them to zero or both to be 1 pixel wide. Let's try the latter:

```
td#navbuttons {background: #ACA; padding: 0;
   border: 2px solid #797; border-width: 2px 1px 2px 2px;}
td#main {background: #FFD; color: black;
   border: 2px solid #797; border-width: 2px 2px 2px 1px;}
```

We should also set the vertical and horizontal alignment of the content within the cells. We know that both the icons and the text should be aligned to the top of their table cells, and the icons ought to be center aligned within their cells (see Figure 4.4). Thus:

```
body {background: #CEC; color: black;}
table#inform td {vertical-align: top;}
td#navbuttons {background: #ACA; padding: 0;
   border: 2px solid #797; border-width: 2px 1px 2px 2px;
   text-align: center;}
```

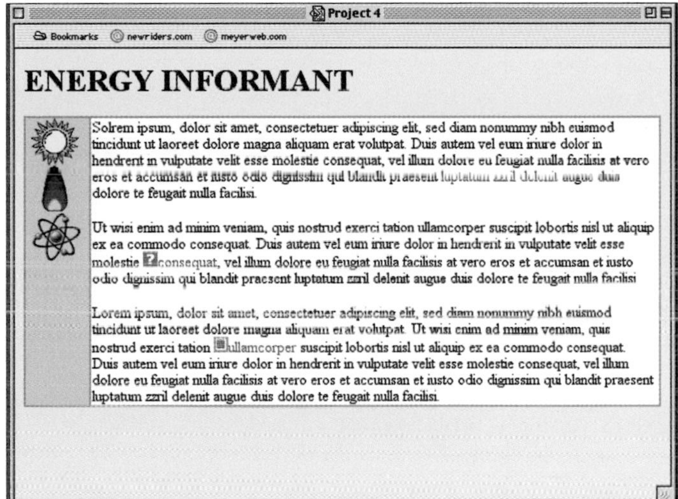

FIGURE 4.4

Everything's back (more or less) to where we started.

The only thing left to do would be to reproduce the effect of the attribute `cellpadding="5"` in the original file. We could do that with `padding`, but we're going to put it off until later when we have a better idea of how the layout might be affected by padding on the cells.

Upgrading the Title

Before we get to the links, we need to make the title fit in with the rest of the design. The design department, you might recall, suggested that we eliminate the space between the text and the table (see Figure 4.5). They probably meant that we should set the bottom margin to zero, but let's take them literally at their word:

```
body {background: #CEC; color: black;}
h1 {margin-bottom: -0.25em;}
table#inform td {vertical-align: top;}
```

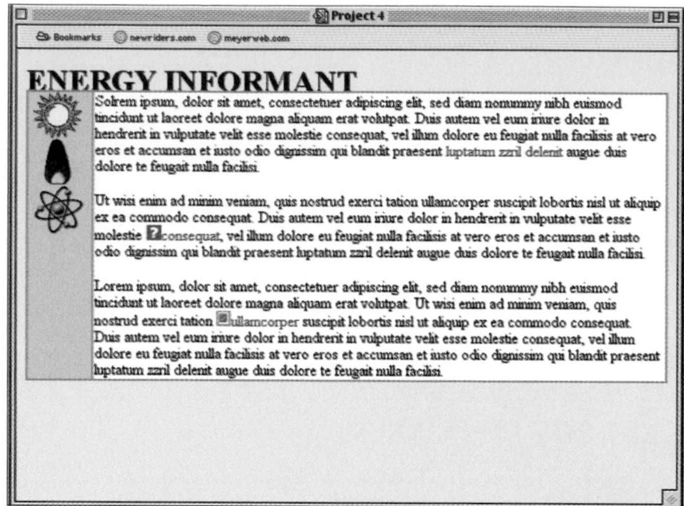

FIGURE 4.5

Get rid of the space between text and table? You got it!

It still doesn't fit in too well, so let's change the color to match the medium-green borders and also switch it to be a sans-serif font. While we're in the area, we'll also boldface it and make sure it's twice the normal text size.

```
body {background: #CEC; color: black;}
h1 {margin-bottom: -0.25em;
   font: bold 200% Arial, sans-serif; color: #797;}
table#inform td {vertical-align: top;}
```

There's one more thing that would make this work even better, and that's a thicker top border on the table. Let's make it easy and just add the border to the table itself instead of messing with the table cells (see Figure 4.6).

```
h1 {margin-bottom: -0.25em;
   font: bold 200% Arial, sans-serif; color: #797;}
table#inform td {vertical-align: top; border-top: 3px solid #797;}
```

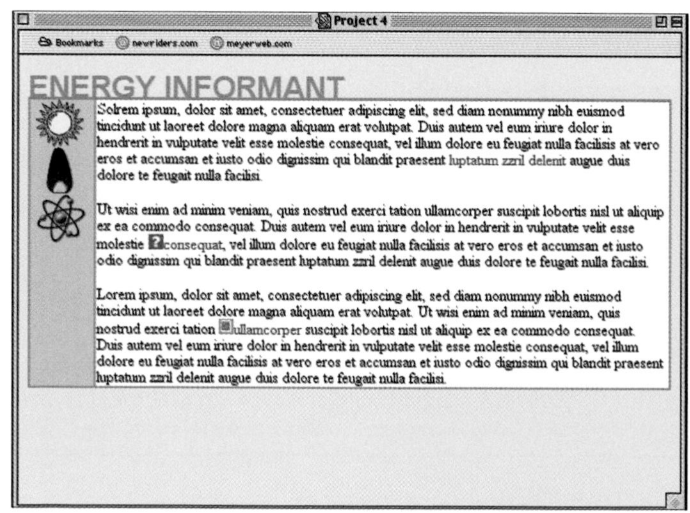

FIGURE 4.6

Making the title part of the organic whole.

Now it looks like the title is rising from the border itself or maybe was carved out of the same stuff. Whatever visual metaphor it invokes, it's an interesting effect. We'll keep it and see what the client thinks.

The Icons

The relatively simple nature of the icons (each is a single image alone in a link element) makes them easier to work with. We'll tackle the left-side icons first. We know that each icon is 50×50 pixels. We also know that we want them to sit in the left-side panel with no extra space around them, so we need to convert them to block-level elements with no margin. But we need to be careful about what we convert!

```
td#main {background: #FFD; color: black;
   border: 2px solid #797; border-width: 2px 2px 2px 1px;}
td#navbuttons a {display: block; margin: 0;}
td#navbuttons img {display: block; height: 50px; width: 50px;}
</style>
```

This won't have any immediate visual impact, but it avoids trouble in the next step. We want to increase the amount of space around each image, but rather than doing it with margins, let's do it with borders that exactly match the background color of the cell. We'll also set the background color of the images to be transparent so that the cell background remains visible around each icon.

```
td#navbuttons a {display: block; margin: 0;}
td#navbuttons img {display: block; height: 50px; width: 50px;
   border: 1px solid #ACA; border-width: 5px 10px;
   background: transparent;}
</style>
```

Visitation Styles

We'll skip writing a "visited" style for the icons, although we could create one easily enough. As an example, we could have written `td#navbutton a:visited {border-color: gray;}`.

Okay, so besides adding some apparently empty space around the icons, what good did this do? Plenty. Assume that the current page is the Natural Gas page. We can highlight the icon by adding a rule that makes the border and background the same color as the intracell borders (see Figure 4.7).

```
td#navbuttons a {display: block; margin: 0;}
td#navbuttons img {display: block; height: 50px; width: 50px;
   border: 1px solid #ACA; border-width: 5px 10px;
   background: transparent;}
td#navbuttons img#gas {border-color: #797; background: #797;}
</style>
```

The big win we get here is not just that we can easily indicate the current page, but also make the background and border colors change when the link is hovered over by the mouse pointer or when the icon is clicked.

FIGURE 4.7

Highlighting an icon with borders and background.

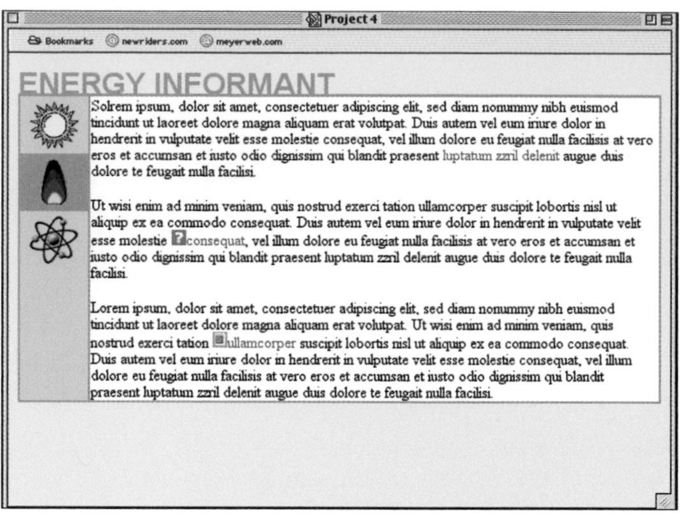

Two Blocks?

Yes, we've set both the hyperlinks and the images to be block-level elements. By making both elements blocks, we can be assured that they'll behave in a predictable way—sort of like one `div` inside another. If we left the images alone, they would default to being inline elements, which can cause unexpected space to appear in recent browsers.

```
td#navbuttons img#gas {border-color: #797; background: #797;}
td#navbuttons a:hover {background: yellow;}
td#navbuttons a:hover img { border-color: yellow;}
td#navbuttons a:active img {border-color: #FC0;
   border-style: inset;}
</style>
```

Now any link (other than the one for the current page) will get a yellow background when hovered over. If an icon is clicked, its border will turn orange, thus framing the link for a moment in a thick orange box with the yellow background still visible inside (see Figure 4.8).

FIGURE 4.8

Combining hover and active styles can lead to interesting effects.

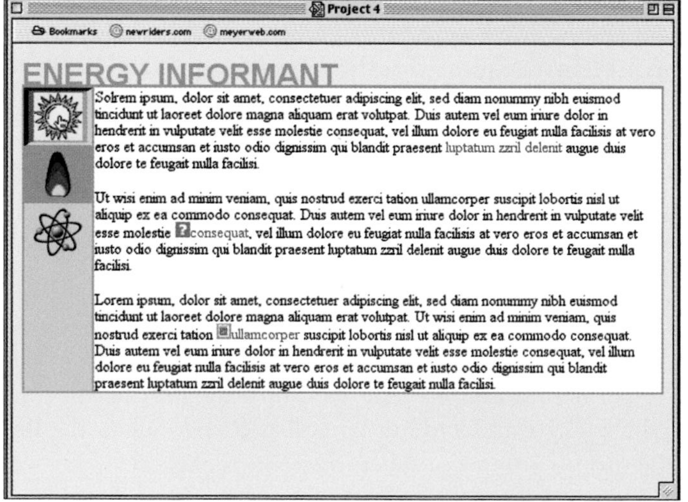

It's worth spending a moment on the selectors. Take, for example, `td#navbuttons a:hover img`. It's written this way because we want to give a yellow highlight to any image that's descended from a link being hovered over—both of which are contained within a `td` element with an `id` of `navbuttons`. Ditto for the "active" rule.

It's worth asking, though, why we set the background color on the hyperlink instead of for the image itself. It turns out that IE5.x for Windows mostly ignores background styles on images that are part of hovered links. This failure is very odd because it will change the border color, but there you have it. Because IE5.x *will* set the background color of the hyperlink, we can sneak around this bug in the manner shown. If you're developing for a situation in which IE5.x isn't an issue, you could just style the background of the image and not mess with the link's background at all.

No Hover for the "Current" Icon

So why doesn't the icon for the current page (the gas flame) take on the hover or active styles? Because the specificity of its selector (`td#navbuttons img#gas`) outweighs the selectors for the hover and active states, so its values for the border and background colors win out.

Altering the Main-Text Links

With the left-side icons working the way we'd like, let's give the text links a makeover. Our first order of business is to define a "baseline" for the text links. Typically, designers will change the color of a link in its various states, and sometimes they'll forcibly remove the underlines.

In this case, we're just going to change the colors but leave the underlines alone. That way, the user's preference setting regarding link underlining will hold sway, which will help them recognize links for what they are. Because the blue doesn't really work with our green-and-sand color scheme, though, we're going to make the links a dark green when unvisited and dusky purple when visited. Just to make sure the links stand out, let's boldface them as well.

```
td#navbuttons a:active img {border-color: #FC0;
   border-style: inset;}
a:link, a:visited {background-color: transparent; font-weight: bold;}
a:link {color: #171;}
a:visited {color: #747;}
</style>
```

Splitting Up the Styles

We split the styles between the `a:link, a:visited` rule and the `a:link` and `a:visited` rules to keep them as simple as possible. Otherwise, we would have been duplicating the `background-color` and `font-weight` styles for both link states, which doesn't make much sense.

Now we need a good hover style. Actually, we need two good hover styles: one for unvisited links and one for visited links:

```
a:visited {color: #747;}
a:visited:hover {color: #FFD; background-color: #747;}
a:link:hover {color: #FFD; background-color: #797;}
</style>
```

Now we get a reverse-text effect on all our links. In CSS2-aware browsers, we'll get yellow-on-green for hovered unvisited links and yellow-on-purple for hovered visited links (see Figure 4.9). It doesn't matter what order these rules come in because they can never conflict with each other. That's because a link can't be both visited and unvisited.

▸▸ Dealing with Explorer

If you use the form of "chained" selector shown for your hover styles, make sure you put the default second—that is, whichever hover style you'd prefer to be applied to all links in a document, visited or otherwise. Explorer doesn't understand this syntax, so it will treat all such rules as if they're simple `a:hover` *rules.*

Another problem you might encounter in Explorer is that it thinks the last link that was clicked is still active. Therefore, if you click a link and then hit the Back button, the page will come up with the link still in the active state even though it isn't active. Given this fact, you might want to avoid writing `a:active` *styles if Explorer users will make up a big portion of your audience.*

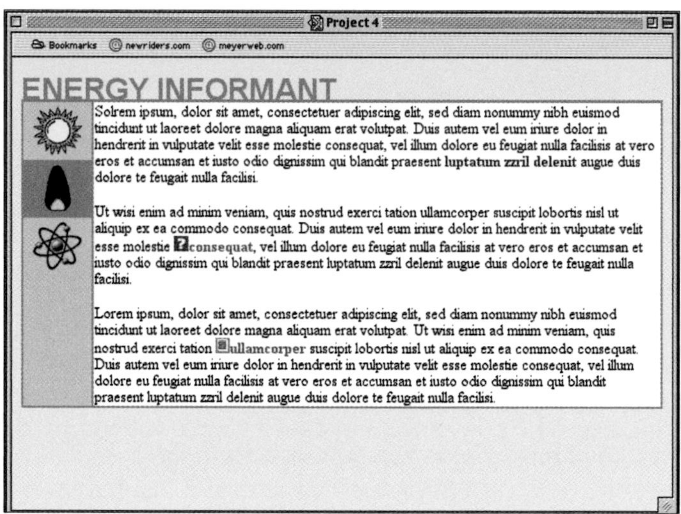

FIGURE 4.9

When changing the appearance of links, it's best to make sure they still stand out.

Help! A Press Release!

Now that we've done the basic style work on text links, let's jazz up the help and press-release links. The icons are cute enough, but we can do something a lot more interesting than having these graphics embedded in the page itself.

"Taller" images already exist in the files you downloaded from the Web site: `help-icon.gif` and `pr-icon.gif`.

The first thing we need to do is remove the icons from the HTML and create taller versions—say, 32 pixels high instead of 16. The important thing is that the icons should be an even number of pixels tall.

Now let's put a border around the help link, place the icon in the background, position it on the left side and centered vertically, set padding to keep the text from overlapping the icons, and also change the text and background colors to go along with it (see Figure 4.10). Oh, and just for the heck of it, we'll eliminate the underline, too.

```
a:link:hover {color: #FFD; background-color: #797;}
a.help:link, a.help:visited {padding: 0 2px 1px 16px;
   background: #FDD url(help-icon.gif) left center no-repeat;
   color: #733; border: 1px solid #C66;
   text-decoration: none;}
</style>
```

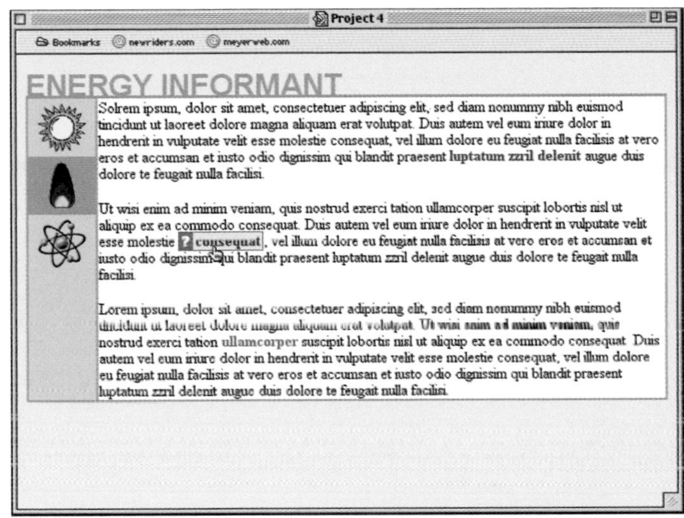

FIGURE 4.10

Taking a text link from "blah" to "boo-yah!"

By aligning the background image with the left centerpoint of the link (using the keywords `left center`), we can make it look like it's inline. As for the padding, it helps keep the borders pushed a little bit away from the text and opens up enough space on the left to show the background image. It's easy enough to adjust the padding as necessary (for example, to close up the space between the edge of the icon and the text).

Removing the Images

Remember to remove the `img` elements from the help and press-release links in the HTML document itself. If they're left in, they will obscure the background images we're inserting and greatly interfere with the intended effect.

It looks like the icon is still part of the document, and that's exactly what we want. The advantage of putting it in the background of the link, of course, is that we can easily change it later without having to touch the document source. We might decide to put the icon on the right side of the hyperlink, for example. Doing that would be a simple matter of changing the values for `padding` and `background`—nothing more.

Let's give the same treatment to the press-release link, using its icon and colors to match:

```
a.help:link, a.help:visited {padding: 0 2px 1px 16px;
   background: #FDD url(help-icon.gif) left center no-repeat;
   color: #733; border: 1px solid #C66;
   text-decoration: none;}
a.pr:link, a.pr:visited {padding: 0 2px 1px 16px;
   background: #EEC url(pr-icon.gif) left center no-repeat;
   color: #171; border: 1px solid #797;
   text-decoration: none;}
</style>
```

The only real differences are in the colors and the image; otherwise, everything's the same. Now all we need are some good hover effects for the links, and we'll be golden (see Figure 4.11):

```
a.pr:link, a.pr:visited {padding: 0 2px 1px 16px;
   background: #EEC url(pr-icon.gif) left center no-repeat;
   color: #171; border: 1px solid #797;
   text-decoration: none;}
a.help:hover {color: #FFD; background-color: #C66;}
a.pr:hover {color: #FFD; background-color: #797;}
</style>
```

FIGURE 4.11

Now there are two way-cool links for our viewing pleasure.

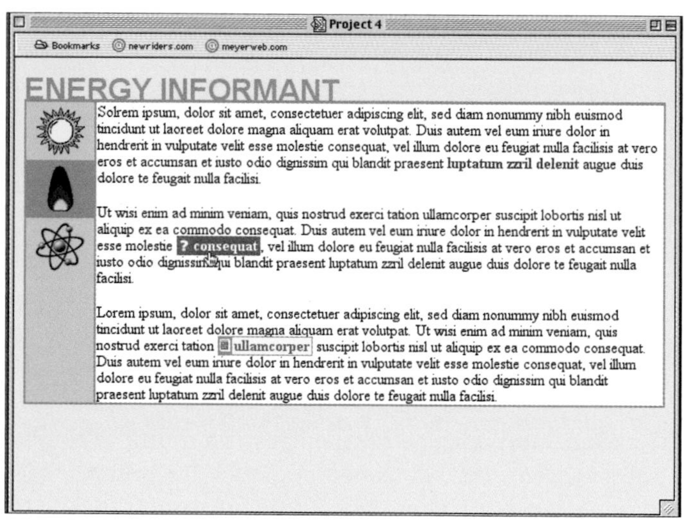

Changes on Hover

In theory, you could also change the background image in the hover state, but Explorer 5.x for Windows doesn't handle hover-based changes very gracefully. Its usual behavior is to change the background image when you hover over a link and then keep the hover image after the mouse moves off the link. Sadly, there doesn't seem to be a CSS-based way around this bug.

Look for the files `help-vicon.gif` and `pr-vicon.gif` in the files you downloaded from the Web site. These are the washed-out versions of the link icons we've been using (see Figure 4.12).

Now let's create some "visited" styles for our way-cool links. We could do the usual and change the various colors, but let's take it a step further and display a different background image—thus, changing the icon for visited links.

The basic need here is for new images. We'll go with ones that look "washed out" because they're the easiest to produce. Then all we need to do is create the styles to drop them into place when a link's been visited, as well as some color shifts.

```
a.pr:link, a.pr:visited {padding: 0 2px 1px 16px;
   background: #EEC url(pr-icon.gif) left center no-repeat;
   color: #171; border: 1px solid #797;
   text-decoration: none;}
a.help:visited {color: #A88; background-color: #EDD;
   background-image: url(help-vicon.gif);}
a.pr:visited {color: #797; background-color: #DDC;
   background-image: url(pr-vicon.gif);}
a.help:hover {color: #FFD; background-color: #C66;}
```

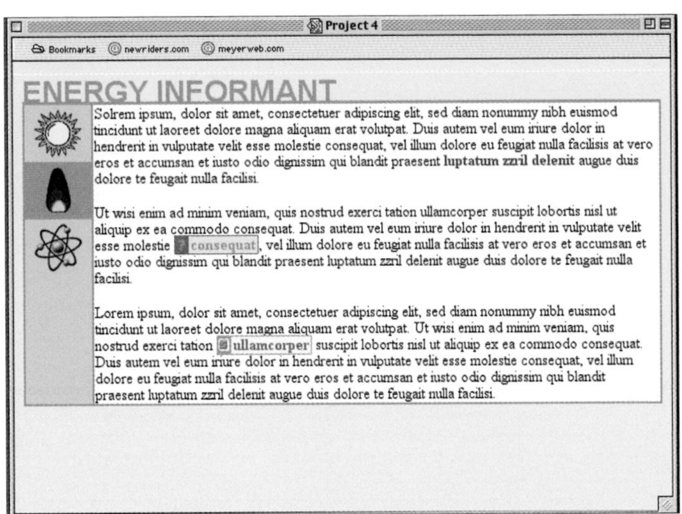

FIGURE 4.12

Visitation changes: Washing out a link after it's been visited helps users remember where they've been.

Of course, we could have used any icon at all—one with a little "X" over the icon, maybe an inverse image in which the colors are all reversed, or really anything. The only limitation is what you can fit into the space.

Order in the Link States

We've added the various link states in a specific order in this project: link, visited, hover, active. In general, maintaining this order is critical because changing it causes link styles to stop working. The order of LVHA has a few mnemonics you can use: "LoVe-HA!" and "Like Various Hairy Apes" are two particularly memorable ones.

A Touch of Cleanup

If you look closely at the text above and below the jazzed-up links, you can see that it comes very close to the borders of the links. This is because when you set a border on an inline element (such as a hyperlink) and then give it some top and bottom padding, the border will get pushed into other lines of text. The lines won't get pushed apart. If you set the padding large enough, the box will start overlapping other lines or being overlapped by them.

Given this fact, and also seeing that the paragraphs are snuggling up to the edges of the table cell, let's give it some margins and increase the height of the text lines:

```
td#main {background: #FFD; color: black;
   border: 2px solid #797; border-width: 2px 2px 2px 1px;}
td#main p {margin: 0.75em 1.5em; line-height: 1.33em;}
td#navbuttons a {display: block; margin: 0;}
td#navbuttons img {display: block; height: 50px; width: 50px;
   border: 1px solid #ACA; border-width: 5px 10px;
   background: transparent;}
```

With this last change, we're ready to dazzle the client with our new design! The complete style sheet is shown in Listing 4.1, and the result is shown in Figure 4.13.

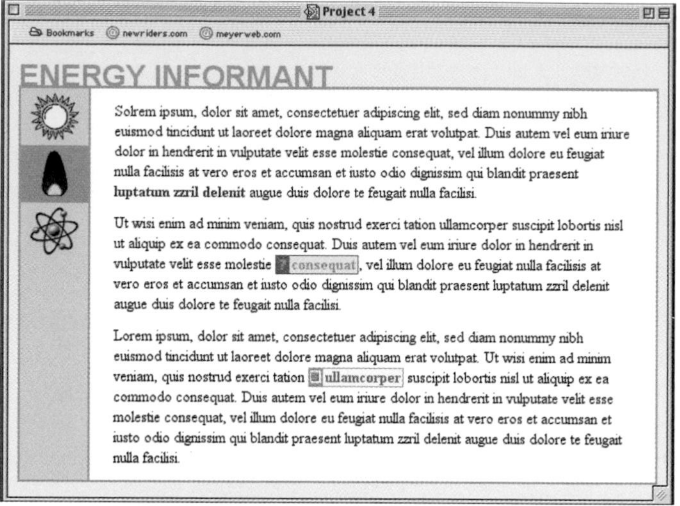

Figure 4.13 *Making the text a little easier on the eyes.*

Listing 4.1 The Complete Style Sheet

```
<style type="text/css">
body {background: #CEC; color: black;}
h1 {margin-bottom: -0.25em;
   font: bold 200% Arial, sans-serif; color: #797;}
table#inform td {vertical-align: top; border-top: 3px solid #797;}
td#navbuttons {background: #ACA; padding: 0;
   border: 2px solid #797; border-width: 2px 1px 2px 2px;
   text-align: center;}
td#main {background: #FFD; color: black;
   border: 2px solid #797; border-width: 2px 2px 2px 1px;}
td#main p {margin: 0.75em 1.5em; line-height: 1.33em;}
td#navbuttons a {display: block; margin: 0;}
td#navbuttons img {display: block; height: 50px; width: 50px;
   border: 1px solid #ACA; border-width: 5px 10px;
   background: transparent;}
td#navbuttons img#gas {border-color: #797; background: #797;}
td#navbuttons a:hover {background-color: yellow;}
td#navbuttons a:hover img {border-color: yellow;}
td#navbuttons a:active img {border-color: #FC3;
   border-style: inset;}
a:link, a:visited {background-color: transparent; font-weight: bold;}
a:link {color: #171;}
a:visited {color: #747;}
a:visited:hover {color: #FFD; background-color: #747;}
a:link:hover {color: #FFD; background-color: #797;}
a.help:link, a.help:visited {padding: 0 2px 1px 16px;
   background: #FDD url(help-icon.gif) left center no-repeat;
   color: #733; border: 1px solid #C66;
   text-decoration: none;}
a.pr:link, a.pr:visited {padding: 0 2px 1px 16px;
   background: #EEC url(pr-icon.gif) left center no-repeat;
   color: #171; border: 1px solid #797;
   text-decoration: none;}
a.help:visited {color: #A88; background-color: #EDD;
```

```
   background-image: url(help-vicon.gif);}
a.pr:visited {color: #797; background-color: #DDC;
   background-image: url(pr-vicon.gif);}
a.help:hover {color: #FFD; background-color: #C66;}
a.pr:hover {color: #FFD; background-color: #797;}
</style>
```

Branching Out

There are a ton of things you can do differently with this design, from the color choices down to the way the links are set up. Here are just a few to try out:

1. Try making the icons look and act like physical buttons by using the border styles `outset` and `inset`.

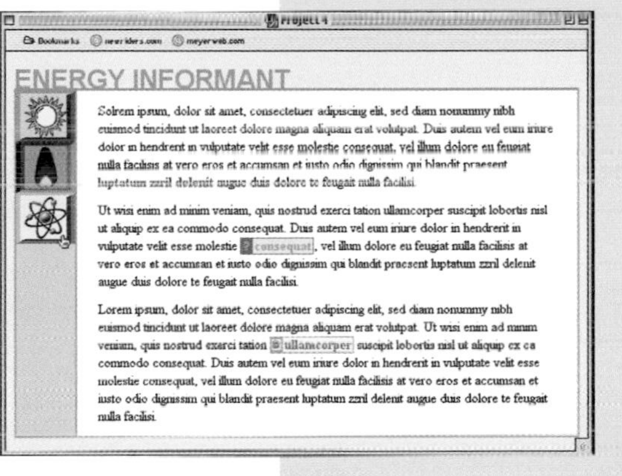

2. Switch the icons from the left side of the help and press-release links to the right. Then write styles to change the side on which the icon appears based on whether or not the link has been visited.

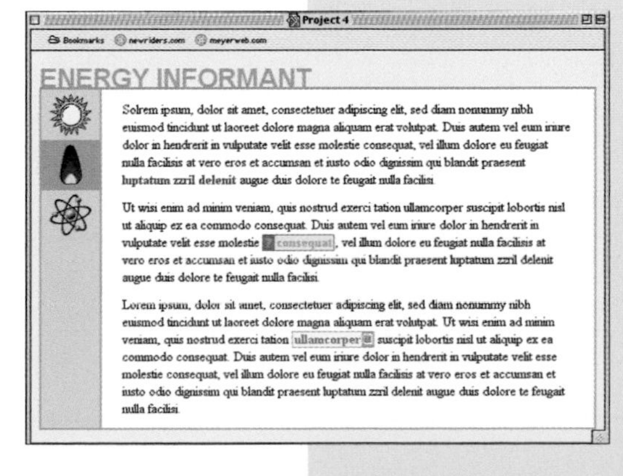

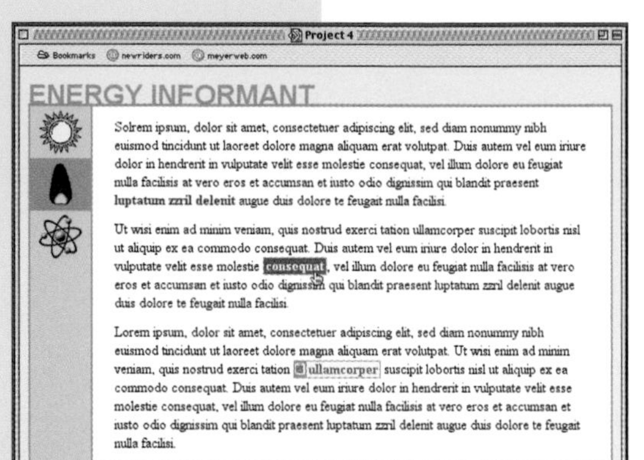

3. Completely remove the background image from any `help` or `pr` link that has been visited and adjust the padding to close up the icon's space. Remember that this might lead to a reflow of the document because the link won't consume as much space without the icon as it did with it.

5

How to Skin a Menu

Choices are like connecting highways. They all take you to the same place. Some just take longer to get there.

DREAM FOR AN INSOMNIAC (1998)

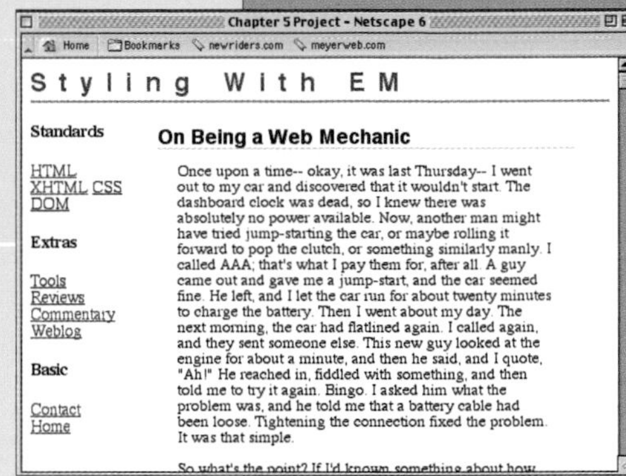

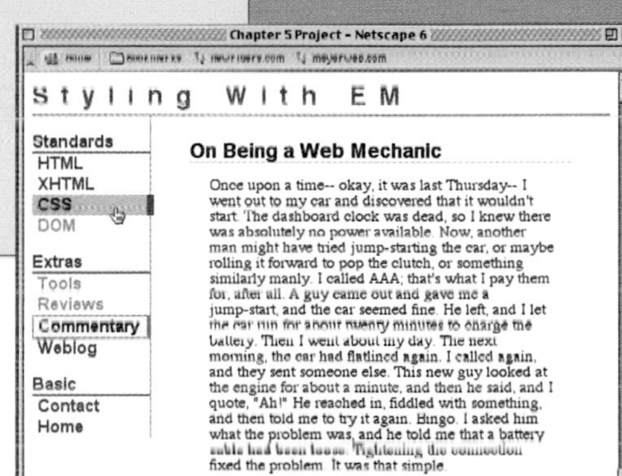

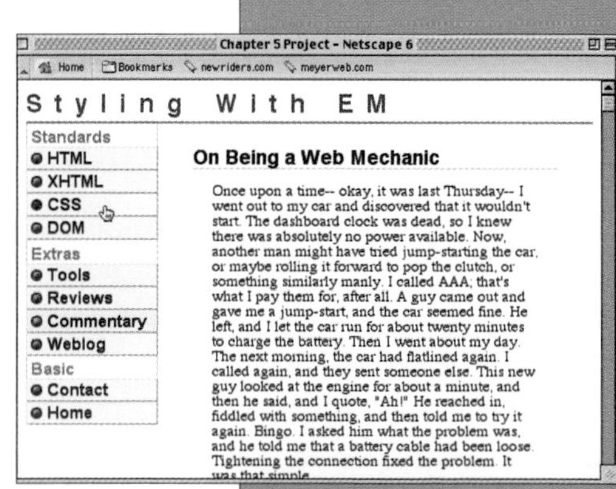

ALMOST EVERY WEB SITE that offers up more than a few pages sports a menu of navigation links. Sometimes they're across the top of the page, but the most popular setup is to put this navigational menu along the left side of the page. This helps make the links visible as soon as a page loads, yet it doesn't push the main page content downward. It also seems that users are much more comfortable with a one-link-per-line layout for navigational menus instead of having all the links in a single line across the top of the page.

Because a left-side menu is usually nothing more complicated than a series of hyperlinks, it's rich with styling possibilities. Just by manipulating the type of element that a hyperlink is, we can do some fascinating things to menu links. In this project, we'll use some of the concepts explored in Project 4, "Bringing Hyperlinks to Life," as well as new ways to style hyperlinks.

Project Goals

In creating a layout for a Web design advice and commentary site, we've come to the point where we need to style the links that run down the left side of the page. At the moment, these are just a bunch of `a` elements broken up into three groups by some `h4` elements.

To make the menu usable and attractive, we'll aim for the following:

- There should be one link per line, which after all is only traditional.
- The links should be visually separated from the main body of the text.
- The menu should visually tie into the site's banner.
- Each link should assume a different style when being hovered.
- The link representing the area in which the current piece is located should be styled in a different way. For example, if the user is reading a commentary piece, the "Commentary" link should be given a unique style.
- Each section should be separated from the others by a small amount of blank space.

As a final personal challenge, this should be done (if at all possible) without changing the HTML in any way. The idea here is that if the menu is generated by a server script and we can't change the markup, the styles should still work.

Before the project is complete, we'll actually devise two different sets of menu styles. That way, we can compare them and pick the one we like better.

Preparation

See the Introduction for instructions on how to download files from the Web site.

Download the files for Project 5 from this book's Web site. If you're planning to play along at home, load the file `ch05proj.html` into the editing program of your choice. This is the file you'll be editing, saving, and reloading as the project progresses.

Laying the Groundwork

The site's design is laid out using a very simple table, with each major component of the design placed in its own cell. Each of these cells has an `id` that makes it easy to apply styles to the contents of a given cell.

As it happens, we already have an overall style sheet for the page. (Pretend we're partway through a design, and we've only just now hit the menu stage.) The styles are a little basic, but they're good enough for now. Of more importance is the menu itself, which we haven't tackled yet. Figure 5.1 shows where we are at this point, and Listing 5.1 provides the style sheet that's giving us what we have.

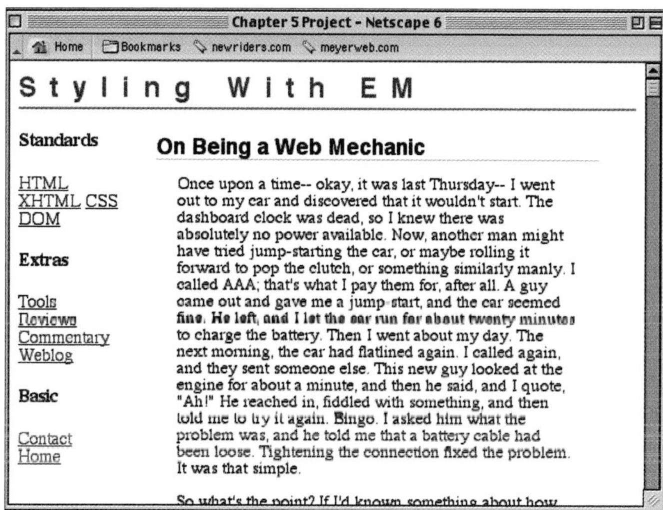

FIGURE 5.1

Where things stand at the moment

Listing 5.1 The Preexisting Style Sheet

```
<style type="text/css">
body {background-color: rgb(100%,98%,96%); color: black;}
td {border-width: 0; padding: 0;}
td#banner {border-bottom: 2px solid rgb(60%,50%,40%);}
td#banner h1 {color: rgb(40%,30%,20%);
   margin: 0; padding: 0.25em 0 0.125em 0;
   font: bold 150% sans-serif; letter-spacing: 0.5em;}
td#main {background-color: transparent; color: black;
   padding: 1em; font: 95% Times, serif;}
td#main h2 {font: bold 125% sans-serif;
   margin: 0.5em 1em; padding: 0;
   border-bottom: 1px solid rgb(80%,75%,70%);}
td#main p {margin: 1em 2.5em;}
td#sidelinks {vertical-align: top;}
td#footer {background-color: transparent; color: rgb(70%,60%,50%);
   border-top: 1px solid rgb(60%,50%,40%);
   text-align: right; font-size: 85%;
   padding-top: 0.33em; font-style: italic;}
</style>
```

As we can see, the style sheet is mostly centered around making the colors come out okay and getting some basic separation styles into place (for example, the `padding` defined for `td#main`). So far, the only menu style that exists aligns the sidebar's content with the top of the cell.

Before we get started, let's examine the markup of the sidelinks, as shown in Listing 5.2.

Excessive id

Why all the id attributes in the links? We'll get to that later in this project, but here's a clue: Think about the design goal that has us styling a link uniquely based on the user's place in the site's structure.

Listing 5.2 The Menu Markup

```
<td id="sidelinks">
<h4>Standards</h4>
<a href="html.html" id="html">HTML</a>
<a href="xhtml.html" id="xhtml">XHTML</a>
<a href="css.html" id="css">CSS</a>
<a href="dom.html" id="dom">DOM</a>
<h4>Extras</h4>
<a href="tools.html" id="tools">Tools</a>
<a href="review.html" id="reviews">Reviews</a>
<a href="comment.html" id="comment">Commentary</a>
<a href="weblog.html" id="weblog">Weblog</a>
<h4>Basic</h4>
<a href="contact.html" id="contact">Contact</a>
<a href="index.html" id="home">Home</a>
</td>
```

It couldn't be much simpler—some h4 elements to title each group of links, and the links themselves, all wrapped in a table cell. As they sometimes say, from humble acorns grow mighty oak trees. With only this very straightforward markup to guide us, we're going to create some very sophisticated menu styles.

Styling the Menu

To raise our mighty oak, we'll need to get familiar with some basic concepts. The first stop in that process is an alteration of the fundamental nature of the links themselves. With that established, we'll move on to defining the appearance of the links in various situations. Then we'll back out some of our styles and create new ones to give the menu a different look.

Blocking Out the Links

The first step is as crucial as it is simple: We're going to create a new style sheet to go with the old one, and in it we'll place a rule to make our hyperlinks into block-level elements.

```
</style>
<style type="text/css">
/* menu styles */
td#sidelinks a {display: block;}
</style>
</head>
```

It's nothing more complicated than that. What good does this do us? Frankly, it does us a world of good.

By making our sidebar link into block-level elements, we've done something very similar to wrapping each link in its own `div`. Imagine for a moment the effects of this purely hypothetical markup:

```
<h4>Standards</h4>
<div><a href="html.html" id="html">HTML</a></div>
<div><a href="xhtml.html" id="xhtml">XHTML</a></div>
<div><a href="css.html" id="css">CSS</a></div>
<div><a href="dom.html" id="dom">DOM</a></div>
```

Don't Edit!

Don't start inserting `div`s into the project file! This is just an example to illustrate a concept. Remember, we're trying to not change the HTML at all. Although the `div` element is often very useful, in this particular case it would just be superfluous markup.

This would indeed have the effect of putting each link on a line of its own because each link is enclosed in its own block-level element. Rather than wrap the links in a block-level element like `div`, though, we're changing the hyperlinks *themselves* into block-level elements. There are two major advantages to doing this:

- We don't have to add in any extra markup just to create the effect we want.
- We can style the links just as we would any block-level element.

Just to make the effect of "blocking" our hyperlinks more obvious—and to illustrate the point about styling block-level links—let's give them a temporary margin. This will lead to the layout shown in Figure 5.2.

```
/* menu styles */
td#sidelinks a {display: block; margin: 0.66em;}
</style>
```

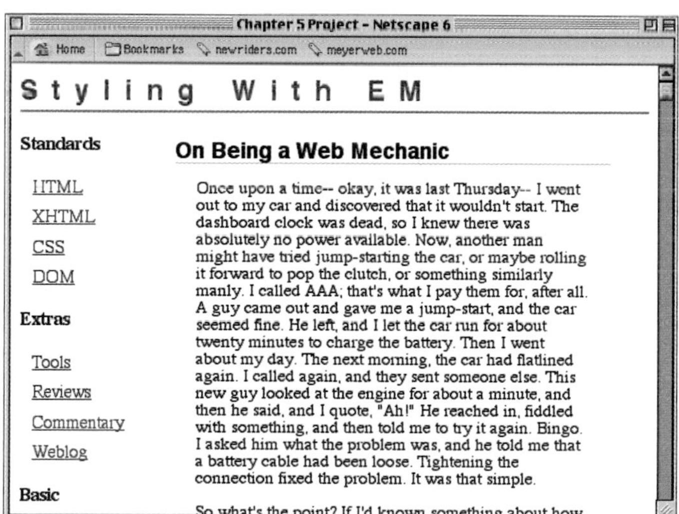

FIGURE 5.2

Block-level hyperlinks with margins (for clarity).

Notice how the links are not only spread apart but also pushed inward a bit. That's because every link in the sidebar now has a 0.66em margin all the way around, and they're being laid out like any other block-level element with the same style. But they're still links and are still clickable and highly adaptable.

Padding The Links

Another advantage to using padding instead of margins is that the padding can help define the clickable area of the link, whereas margins would not. (Assuming the browser doesn't restrict the clickable area to the text of the link itself.)

Setting Font and Initial Spacing

Although we could leave the links all spread out like that, some very interesting effects are possible if the links aren't separated from each other, so we'll eliminate these margins. However, we don't want the link text too close together, so we'll give the links some padding. Instead of the usual ems, we'll actually be using pixels this time.

```
td#sidelinks a {display: block;
   margin: 0; padding: 1px;}
```

We want the `h4` elements to have similar styles, and we especially want to make sure they have no margin to keep the various menu pieces from having any space between them. To get the separation between the groups of links, we'll need to set a large top padding for each `h4` (and no padding on the sides or bottom). Just for flavor, we'll also make the `h4` text the same dark brown that's seen elsewhere in the design.

```
td#sidelinks a {display: block;
   margin: 0; padding: 1px;}
td#sidelinks h4 {background-color: transparent; color: rgb(30%,20%,10%);
   margin: 0; padding: 1em 0 0;}
</style>
```

Now we face a choice: Should the menu font match the site banner or the main body text? It seems a much better choice to make the navigation fit with the site banner, as illustrated in Figure 5.3. Otherwise, there's a risk that the menu and the main text could become visually jumbled.

```
td#sidelinks a {display: block;
   margin: 0; padding: 1px;
   font: bold 100% Arial, Verdana, sans-serif;}
td#sidelinks h4 {background-color: transparent; color: rgb(30%,20%,10%);
   margin: 0; padding: 1em 0 0;
   font: bold 100% Arial, Verdana, sans-serif;}
```

It might also be a good idea to remove the underlines from the hyperlinks. Usually it's better to leave that up to the user's browser, but in this case, the underlines might get in the way of some styling we'd like to do later on.

```
td#sidelinks a {display: block;
   text-decoration: none;
   margin: 0; padding: 1px;
   font: bold 100% Arial, Verdana, sans-serif;}
```

We'll probably revisit the padding values for the links, but this will do for now. The next step is to tie all of these elements together and visually separate them from the main content.

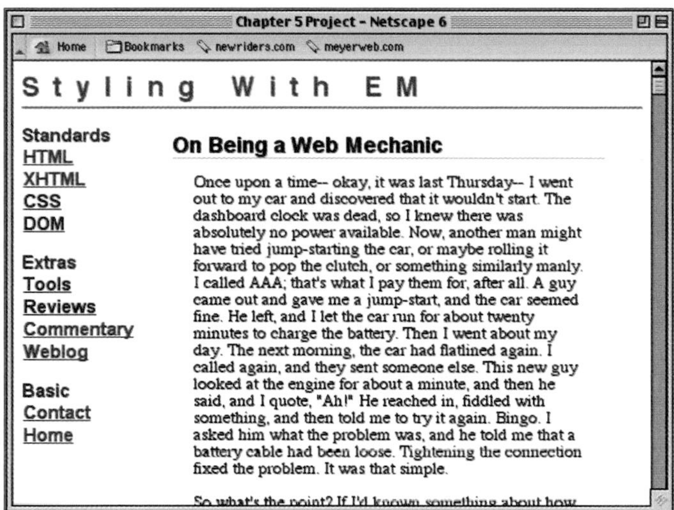

FIGURE 5.3

Matching the menu text to the top banner.

Bordering the Sidebar

The usual way to create visual separation is with a different background color or by drawing a line between two pieces of a design. How many times have you created a 1-pixel-wide (or tall) table cell with an invisible GIF and a background color? Fortunately, CSS doesn't require us to do that. We could just set a border on the right side of the sidebar cell and be done.

That isn't what we're going to do, though. Instead, we're going to set a border on the right side of the links themselves, with the result seen in Figure 5.4.

```
td#sidelinks a {display: block;
   text-decoration: none;
   margin: 0; padding: 1px;
   font: bold 100% Arial, Verdana, sans-serif;
   border-right: 1px solid rgb(60%,50%,40%);}
```

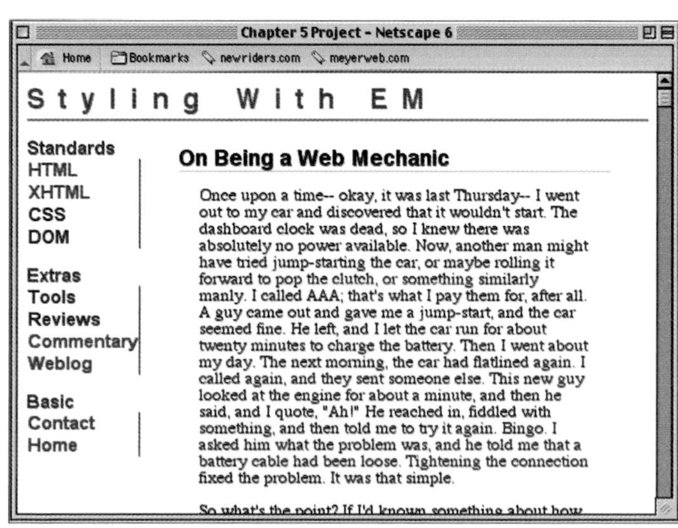

FIGURE 5.4

Link borders create visual separation.

Links with the Light Brown Border

The border color we've chosen here matches the color of the border underneath the site's banner.

Because the links don't have any top or bottom margins, their right-side borders touch and appear to form continuous lines. It's really a collection of several small lines, but that isn't obvious.

On the other hand, we do have gaps in the separator at every `h4` element because they haven't been given borders yet. Let's give them the same right border as we did the links and also a thicker and darker bottom border.

```
td#sidelinks h4 {background-color: transparent; color: rgb(30%,20%,10%);
   margin: 0; padding: 1em 0 0;
   font: bold 100% Arial, Verdana, sans-serif;
   border-right: 1px solid rgb(60%,50%,40%);
   border-bottom: 2px solid rgb(50%,40%,30%);}
```

Now that we've put a separating border on the menu, it should be pushed a little bit away from the text within the links. This is partly for aesthetic reasons, but it's also because, with a little extra room to work, we can do some very interesting things.

```
td#sidelinks a {display: block;
   margin: 0; padding: 1px 10px 1px 5px;
   text-decoration: none;
   font: bold 100% Arial, Verdana, sans-serif;
   border-right: 1px solid rgb(60%,50%,40%);}
```

Now we've balanced the top and bottom padding, made the left padding 5 pixels wide, and set the right padding to 10 pixels wide. This will push the text over a little bit to the right and will push the link borders outward so that they're at least 10 pixels away from the text. We can see all this in Figure 5.5.

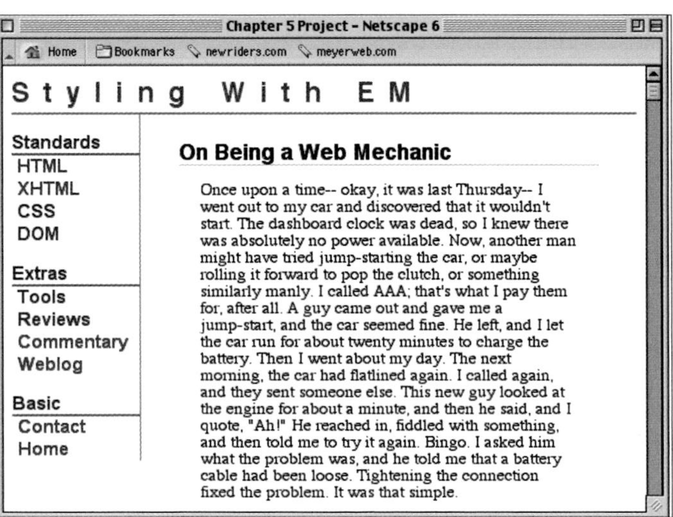

FIGURE 5.5

A little padding goes a long way toward good design.

Highlighting the Current Section

The menu is now basically styled, but it needs more work to meet all of the design goals. If you recall, one of them was to visually distinguish the current section link from the other links. The particular page we're working on is a commentary piece, so we need to write a style to highlight the "Commentary" link.

The obvious way to highlight a link is to give it a different background color. In this case, we'll make it a little darker than the page background, and we'll also make the text black so that it doesn't look like a link.

```
td#sidelinks h4 {background-color: transparent; color: rgb(30%,20%,10%);
   margin: 0; padding: 1em 0 0;
   font: bold 100% Arial, Verdana, sans-serif;
   border-right: 1px solid rgb(60%,50%,40%);
   border-bottom: 2px solid rgb(50%,40%,30%);}
td#sidelinks a#comment {
   background-color: rgb(100%,92%,90%); color: black;}
</style>
```

That's good as far as it goes, but it doesn't really make the link stand out. Let's give it a border that goes all the way around the link.

```
td#sidelinks a#comment {
   background-color: rgb(100%,92%,90%); color: black;
   border: 1px solid rgb(60%,50%,40%);}
```

That's better but still not quite enough. For an extra little touch, let's make the right-side border thicker. In so doing, we need to reduce the padding on that side. This leads to the result seen in Figure 5.6.

```
td#sidelinks a#comment {
   background-color: rgb(100%,92%,90%); color: black;
   border: 1px solid rgb(60%,50%,40%);
   border-right-width: 4px; padding-right: 7px;}
```

How did we get a right padding of 7 pixels? We used to have a right border of `1px` and a right padding of `10px`. Because we increased the border's thickness by 3 pixels, the padding needed to be reduced by the same amount.

You might be wondering why we changed the padding at all. By doing so, we prevented the current link from making the sidebar wider than it was before. If we'd just made the border wider without adjusting the padding, it would have increased the width of the sidebar by 3 pixels. This might not seem like such a big deal, but in general, it's better to keep things consistent. To see why, let's move on to the next part of the project.

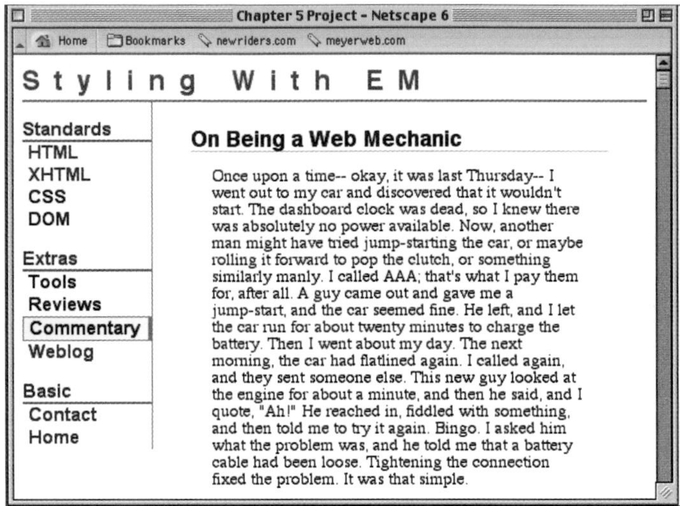

FIGURE 5.6

Making the current section's link stand out.

Hovering the Menu

In addition to highlighting the current section, we also need to define hover styles so that the user gets immediate visual feedback regarding which link will be selected if he or she clicks the mouse button.

As in the last section, let's start with a change in background color.

```
td#sidelinks h4 {background-color: transparent; color: rgb(30%,20%,10%);
   margin: 0; padding: 1em 0 0;
   font: bold 100% Arial, Verdana, sans-serif;
   border-right: 1px solid rgb(60%,50%,40%);
   border-bottom: 2px solid rgb(50%,40%,30%);}
td#sidelinks a:hover {background-color: rgb(100%,70%,70%);}
td#sidelinks a#comment {
   background-color: rgb(100%,92%,90%); color: black;
   border: 1px solid rgb(60%,50%,40%);
   border-right-width: 4px; padding-right: 7px;}
```

That in itself might be enough, but it's not enough for us. Let's make the border red and thicker when we hover, a move that practically requires us to reduce the padding on that side. This will have the effect seen in Figure 5.7.

```
td#sidelinks a:hover {background-color: rgb(100%,70%,70%);
   border-right: 4px solid rgb(80%,30%,20%);
   padding-right: 7px;}
```

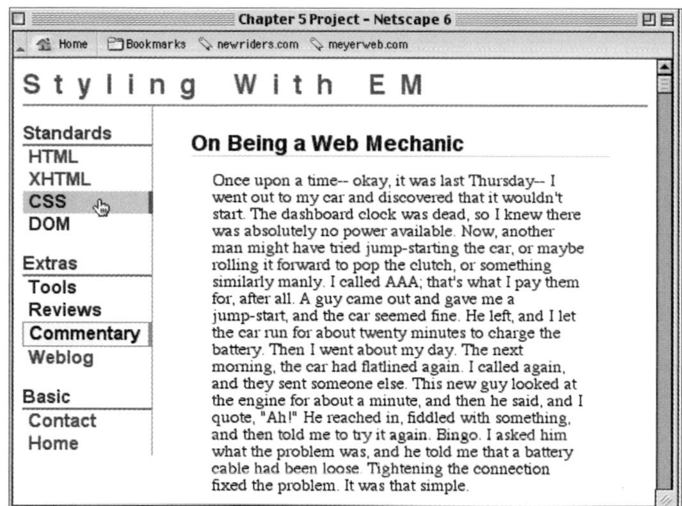

FIGURE 5.7

Giving the menu links some basic hover styles.

Try loading the file `ch0507.html` and removing the `padding-right` property or redefining its value to be `10px` (which it was before). Then try moving the mouse on and off the links and see what happens.

Again, we've reduced the padding by 3 pixels because the border was increased by 3 pixels. In this case, doing so prevents the sidebar from jumping between two different widths as the mouse pointer moves on and off the links.

Now we have some fairly respectable hover styles for our menu. It stands to reason, though, that if we can increase the border width and manipulate the padding, we could increase it further and play around with the margins of the links. If we did that, the border would actually straddle the dividing line between the menu and the main content. We'd have to be careful in how we go about it.

It ought to be possible for us to make the border thicker and actually assign a negative margin to the hovered link. That would pull the right side of the link further out, actually increasing the width of the element. This doesn't work in IE5.x/Win and earlier, so sadly the idea is out. We can set the links to have a margin by default, however, and then zero it out when the link is hovered.

We'll begin by adding a right margin to the links and the `h4` elements because we still want the dividing line to look coherent.

```
td#sidelinks a {display: block;
   margin: 0 3px 0 0; padding: 1px 10px 1px 5px;
   text-decoration: none;
   font: bold 100% Arial, Verdana, sans-serif;
   border-right: 1px solid rgb(60%,50%,40%);}
td#sidelinks h4 {background-color: transparent; color: rgb(30%,20%,10%);
   margin: 0 3px 0 0; padding: 1em 0 0;
   font: bold 100% Arial, Verdana, sans-serif;
   border-right: 1px solid rgb(60%,50%,40%);
   border-bottom: 2px solid rgb(50%,40%,30%);}
```

This won't have much effect on the layout except that it will push open 3 pixels of space between the borders of the links (and h4s) and the edge of the table cell in which they reside. This will probably make the main-content table cell 3 pixels more narrow, but it's no big deal. Now we need to bump up the border width of the hover styles and set the right margin to zero. We can see the effect in Figure 5.8.

```
td#sidelinks a:hover {background-color: rgb(100%,70%,70%);
   border-right: 7px solid rgb(80%,30%,20%);
   padding-right: 7px; margin-right: 0;}
```

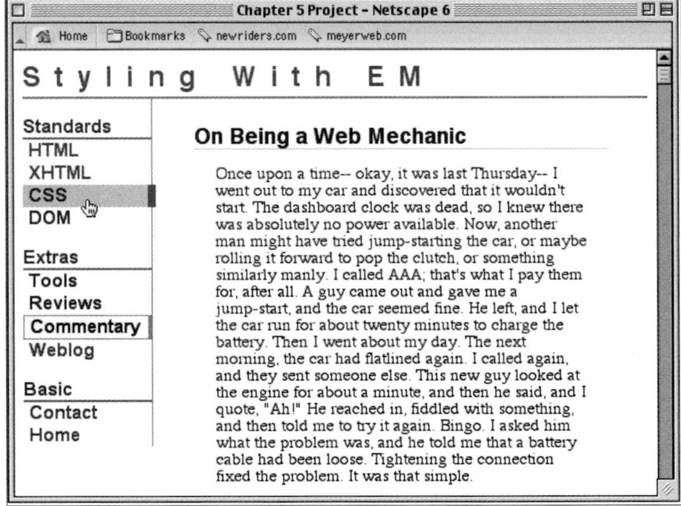

FIGURE 5.8

Protruding borders on hovered elements—pretty cool.

The Border Remains the Same

The border's width is changed to `7px` by the hover styles because the selector `td#sidelinks a#comment` has a higher specificity than the rule for `td#sidelinks a:hover`, and both rules set the width of the right border. Until this change, though, the hover rule set the margin to zero, and the comment rule didn't define a margin value. This is why the hover rule was able to change it.

There's one thing we still have to do to make this effect perfect: Define a right margin for the current link. If we don't, the `:hover` styles will cause its margin to be reset to zero without a corresponding increase in border thickness, and that would cause some strange effects. (For example, making the rest of the document bounce back and forth, as would happen with our current styles.)

```
td#sidelinks a#comment {
   background-color: rgb(100%,92%,90%); color: black;
   border: 1px solid rgb(60%,50%,40%);
   border-right-width: 4px; padding-right: 7px;
   margin-right: 3px;}
```

Instead of preventing the current link's margin from being set to zero, we could instead set it to zero and make the right border `7px` wide. That would cause the current-link border to always straddle the dividing line. You can certainly try that if you like, but let's move on to smoothing out the menu colors just a tad.

▶▶ Non-hovered Selection

The mouse is the most common way to surf the Web, but it isn't the only way. It's possible to use the keyboard to select links in many modern Web browsers. If you want to create styles for that type of input, the keyboard-navigation equivalent of `:hover` *is* `:focus`*. For example:*

```
td#sidelinks a:hover, td#sidelinks a:focus {
   background-color: rgb(100%,70%,70%);
   border-right: 7px solid rgb(80%,30%,20%);
   padding-right: 7px; margin-right: 0;}
```

This would apply the same styles to the links when they're either hovered with a mouse pointer or focused using the keyboard. In many browsers this can be done using the Tab key on the keyboard, but check your browser's Help files to be sure.

A Little Extra Coloring

Because the rest of the design features fairly muted colors, the blue of the links seems to stick out a little too much. The solution is to use a slightly "cooler" blue. It would help to show which sections the user has visited, so we'll define a grayed-out color for any such links.

```
td#sidelinks a {display: block;
   margin: 0 3px 0 0; padding: 1px 10px 1px 5px;
   text-decoration: none;
   font: bold 100% Arial, Verdana, sans-serif;
   border-right: 1px solid rgb(60%,50%,40%);
   color: rgb(30%,30%,60%); background: transparent;}
td#sidelinks a:visited {color: rgb(55%,55%,60%);}
```

Just one more thing, as Columbo would say. Let's make the text of hovered links a nice, rich red. We can see the effects of these various styles in Figure 5.9.

```
td#sidelinks a:hover {background-color: rgb(100%,70%,70%);
   color: rgb(50%,0%,0%);
   border-right: 7px solid rgb(80%,30%,20%);
   padding-right: 7px; margin-right: 0;}
```

These last few changes represent the final changes we'll make to the style sheet, which is shown in Listing 5.3. (Remember that the page also uses the style sheet shown in Listing 5.1.)

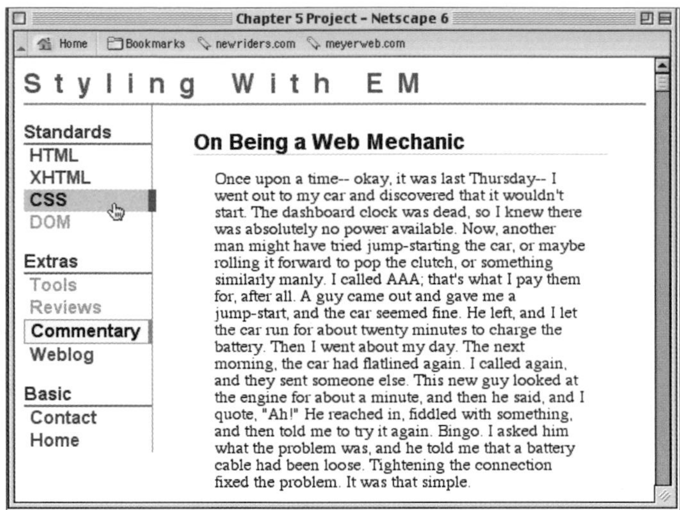

FIGURE 5.9

Subtly altering the link colors makes them less strident.

Listing 5.3 The Complete Menu Style Sheet

```
<style type="text/css">
/* menu styles */
td#sidelinks a {display: block;
   margin: 0 3px 0 0; padding: 1px 10px 1px 5px;
   text-decoration: none;
   font: bold 100% Arial, Verdana, sans-serif;
   border-right: 1px solid rgb(60%,50%,40%);
   color: rgb(30%,30%,60%); background: transparent;}
td#sidelinks a:visited {color: rgb(55%,55%,60%);}
td#sidelinks h4 {background-color: transparent; color: rgb(30%,20%,10%);
   margin: 0 3px 0 0; padding: 1em 0 0;
   font: bold 100% Arial, Verdana, sans-serif;
   border-right: 1px solid rgb(60%,50%,40%);
   border-bottom: 2px solid rgb(50%,40%,30%);}
td#sidelinks a:hover {background-color: rgb(100%,70%,70%);
   color: rgb(50%,0%,0%);
   border-right: 7px solid rgb(80%,30%,20%);
   padding-right: 7px; margin-right: 0;}
td#sidelinks a#comment {
   background-color: rgb(100%,92%,90%); color: black;
   border: 1px solid rgb(60%,50%,40%);
   border-right-width: 4px; padding-right: 7px;
   margin-right: 3px;}
</style>
```

▸▸ Regrouping the Styles

If we look at the style sheet in Listing 5.3 a little more closely, we can see a lot of repetition. For example, the `a` *and* `h4` *elements have the same font styles, margins, and right borders. Rather than keep these scattered throughout various rules, we could group common declarations together. Here's an example of such a regrouping:*

```
<style type="text/css">
/* menu styles */
td#sidelinks a, td#sidelinks h4 {
   margin: 0 3px 0 0;
   font: bold 100% Arial, Verdana, sans-serif;
   border-right: 1px solid rgb(60%,50%,40%);
   background: transparent;}
td#sidelinks a {display: block;
   padding: 1px 10px 1px 5px;
   text-decoration: none;
   color: rgb(30%,30%,60%);}
td#sidelinks a:visited {color: rgb(55%,55%,60%);}
td#sidelinks h4 {color: rgb(30%,20%,10%);
   padding: 1em 0 0;
   border-bottom: 2px solid rgb(50%,40%,30%);}
td#sidelinks a:hover {background-color: rgb(100%,70%,70%);
   color: rgb(50%,0%,0%);
   border-right: 7px solid rgb(80%,30%,20%);
   padding-right: 7px; margin-right: 0;}
td#sidelinks a#comment {
   background-color: rgb(100%,92%,90%); color: black;
   border: 1px solid rgb(60%,50%,40%);
   border-right-width: 4px; padding-right: 7px;
   margin-right: 3px;}
</style>
```

Although it doesn't necessarily make the style sheet any shorter, it does reduce the chance of making mistakes when altering (for example) the right margins of the menu elements.

Reskinning the Menu

Now that we've come this far, let's throw out most of the styles and try a new approach. We're getting rid of the majority of the styles already created and starting with a very basic set, as seen in Listing 5.4.

Listing 5.4 Starting Over

```
<style type="text/css">
/* menu styles */
td#sidelinks a {display: block;}
td#sidelinks h4 {padding: 1em 0 0;}
td#sidelinks a, td#sidelinks h4 {margin: 0;
   font: bold 100% Arial, Verdana, sans-serif;}
</style>
```

The styles we've left in place create a foundation on which to build. The links are made block-level; the h4 elements given some top padding but no other. Finally, both the links and h4 elements are given no margin and set to a consistent font weight, size, and family.

Where do we go from here? Let's make the menu links into buttons, complete with indicator lights.

Buttoning Up

Instead of having links hanging in space, let's make each menu entry look like an actual button. There are many ways to accomplish this. Although the easiest way is to just give them a border style of outset, this leaves a lot of coloration in the hands of the browser. We're better off defining a solid border and setting the colors how we want them.

If they're too thick, though, the buttons will look flat. We're going for a subtle effect here, so let's just make them single-pixel borders (see Figure 5.10).

```
td#sidelinks a {display: block;
   border: 1px solid gray;
   border-color: rgb(90%,85%,80%) rgb(80%,75%,70%)
     rgb(80%,75%,70%) rgb(90%,85%,80%);}
```

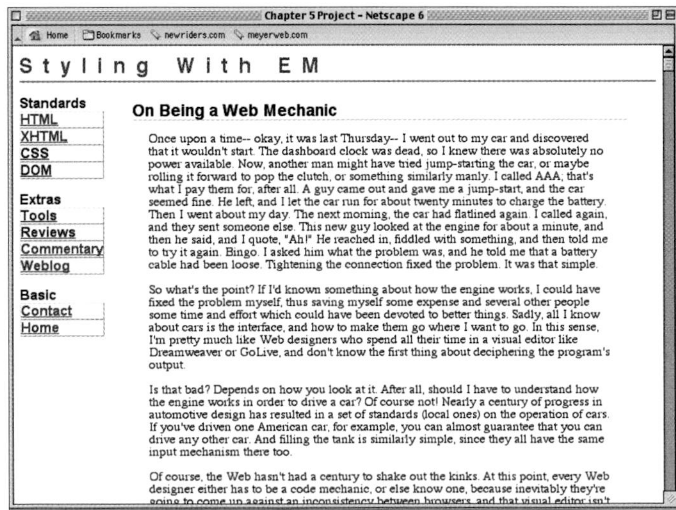

FIGURE 5.10

Making basic buttons out of hyperlinks.

Now we have links as buttons, but it's obvious they could use a little work. For example:

- The underlines need to go away.
- The button backgrounds should be a little darker (or at least in some way different) than the page background.
- The gaps between the button groups need to be filled in with something.
- The buttons themselves need some padding and some color manipulation.

We can quickly deal with the first three points.

```
td#sidelinks a {display: block; text-decoration: none;
   border: 1px solid gray;
   border-color: rgb(90%,85%,80%) rgb(60%,55%,50%)
     rgb(60%,55%,50%) rgb(90%,85%,80%);
   background: rgb(92%,91%,90%);}
td#sidelinks h4 {padding: 1em 0.25em 0;
   border: 1px solid silver; border-width: 0 1px;
   background: rgb(96%,95%,94%);}
```

The background will now extend throughout the buttons and the heading gaps, with some light gray (silver) borders on the left and right sides of the `h4` elements. We're also rid of the underlines on the button text, and the buttons have a slightly darker background than the gaps between them. Now let's give the buttons some padding and change the color of the text. The results are shown in Figure 5.11.

```
td#sidelinks a {display: block; text-decoration: none;
   border: 1px solid gray;
   border-color: rgb(90%,85%,80%) rgb(60%,55%,50%)
     rgb(60%,55%,50%) rgb(90%,85%,80%); color: navy;
   background: rgb(92%,91%,90%);
   padding: 2px 10px 1px 20px;}
```

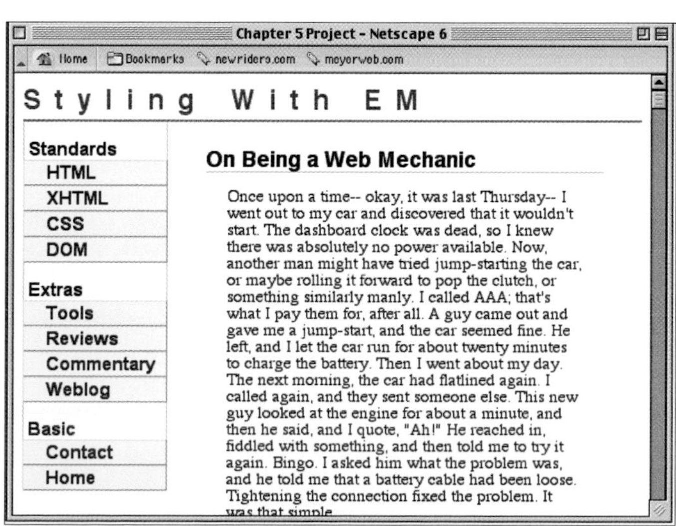

FIGURE 5.11
The buttons start to look more like buttons.

Despite the nice indentation effect that the button padding has created, you might be wondering why we made the values so uneven. Why do we need 20 pixels of padding on the left side? Quite simply, we're holding that space for something else to occupy. If you've already read Project 4, you're probably able to guess what we'll be doing in the next section.

Iconic Buttons

Let's fill in the left-side padding with little icons that will make the buttons even more like buttons. We'll need three icons: one for ordinary links, one for hovered links, and one for the current link. (You didn't forget about the style for the current section, right?)

First we'll fill in the basic link icon.

The GIF files used in this section (for example, `link-base.gif`) are among the files you can download from the Web site.

```
td#sidelinks a {display: block; text-decoration: none;
   border: 1px solid gray;
   border-color: rgb(90%,85%,80%) rgb(60%,55%,50%)
     rgb(60%,55%,50%) rgb(90%,85%,80%); color: navy;
   background: rgb(92%,91%,90%) url(link-base.gif)
     3px 50% no-repeat;
   padding: 2px 10px 1px 20px;}
```

In addition to adding the URL of an image to be placed in the background, we've placed it 3 pixels over from the left edge of the link's left border and vertically centered within the button. Because we only want one icon, we've prevented it from repeating (tiling) as well. The result is shown in Figure 5.12.

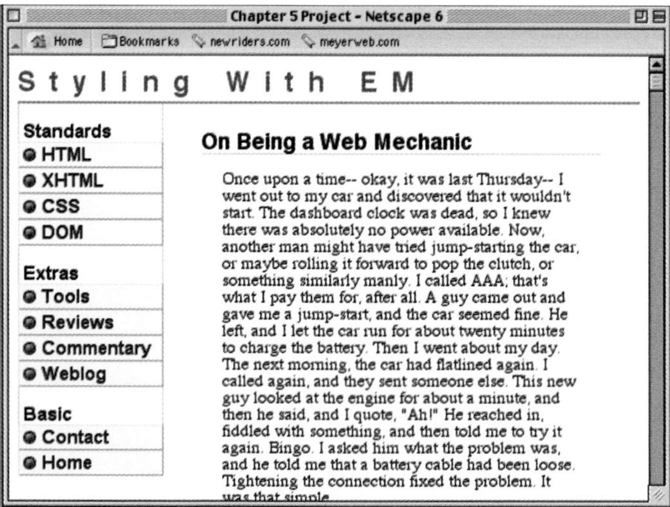

FIGURE 5.12

Adding icons to our buttons.

Next we add in styles to change that icon for a hovered link. Because the `td#sidelinks a` rule already places the icon for us, all we have to do is change the image reference, which means providing a new value for `background-image`.

```
td#sidelinks a {display: block; text-decoration: none;
   border: 1px solid gray;
   border-color: rgb(90%,85%,80%) rgb(60%,55%,50%)
     rgb(60%,55%,50%) rgb(90%,85%,80%); color: navy;
   background: rgb(92%,91%,90%) url(link-base.gif)
     3px 50% no-repeat;
   padding: 2px 10px 1px 20px;}
td#sidelinks a:hover {background-image: url(link-hover.gif);}
td#sidelinks h4 {padding: 1em 0.25em 0;
   border: 1px solid silver; border-width: 0 1px;
   background: rgb(96%,95%,94%);}
```

The only thing left to do is style the current link. Again, all we really need to do is change the image location, but let's color the background a little differently while we're at it and set the text to be black (see Figure 5.13).

```
td#sidelinks a:hover {background-image: url(link-hover.gif);}
td#sidelinks a#comment {background-image: url(link-now.gif);
   background-color: rgb(90%,93%,87%); color: black;}
td#sidelinks h4 {padding: 1em 0.25em 0;
   border: 1px solid silver; border-width: 0 1px;
   background: rgb(96%,95%,94%);}
```

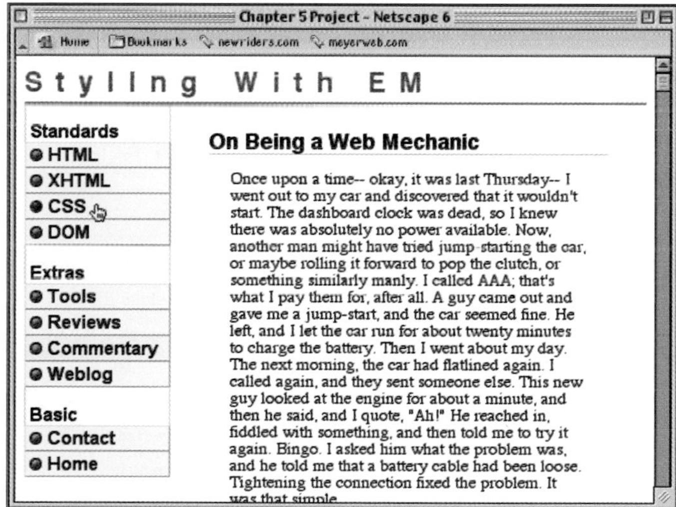

FIGURE 5.13

Styling the current section and hovered links.

Cleaning Up

About the only thing we have left to do here is to reduce the gaps between button groups and make the group headings (the `h4` elements) less obtrusive. All we need to do is reduce the top padding and wash out the text color.

```
td#sidelinks h4 {padding: 0.33em 0.25em 0;
   border: 1px solid silver; border-width: 0 1px;
   background: rgb(96%,95%,94%); color: rgb(46%,45%,44%);}
```

With that, we've arrived at our second menu design. The menu style sheet is provided in Listing 5.5, and the result is shown in Figure 5.14.

Listing 5.5 The Second Complete Menu Style Sheet

```
<style type="text/css">
/* menu styles */
td#sidelinks a {display: block; text-decoration: none;
   border: 1px solid gray;
   border-color: rgb(90%,85%,80%) rgb(60%,55%,50%)
     rgb(60%,55%,50%) rgb(90%,85%,80%); color: navy;
   background: rgb(92%,91%,90%) url(link-base.gif)
     3px 50% no-repeat;
   padding: 2px 10px 1px 20px;}
td#sidelinks a:hover {background-image: url(link-hover.gif);}
td#sidelinks a#comment {background-image: url(link-now.gif);
   background-color: rgb(85%,93%,90%); color: black;}
td#sidelinks h4 {padding: 0.33em 0.25em 0;
   border: 1px solid silver; border-width: 0 1px;
   background: rgb(96%,95%,94%); color: rgb(46%,45%,44%);}
td#sidelinks a, td#sidelinks h4 {margin: 0;
   font: bold 100% Arial, Verdana, sans-serif;}
</style>
```

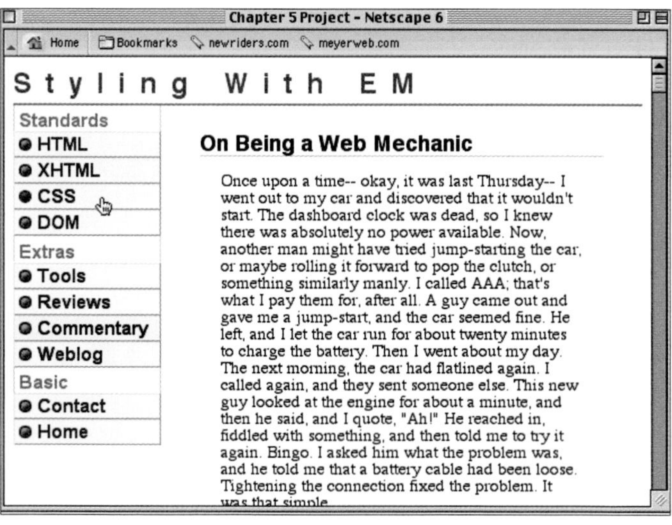

FIGURE 5.14

The second finished menu design

▶▶ Applying the Current Style

Because not every page will be in the "Commentary" section, we obviously can't include that in a site-wide style sheet. The solution is to remove the style from the generic menu styles and put it into its own style sheet. This special style sheet would only be used on pages in the "Commentary" section of the Web site. For example, you could save it to a file called `comment-current.css` *and then, in the* `head` *of every commentary piece, include the following:*

```
<link rel="stylesheet" type="text/css"
   href="http://www.my.site/comment/comment-current.css">
```

In the `head` *of pages that are part of the CSS section of the site, you'd include a* `link` *element like this:*

```
<link rel="stylesheet" type="text/css"
   href="http://www.my.site/css/css-current.css">
```

The file `css-current.css` *would contain this single rule:*

```
td#sidelinks a#css {background-image: url(link-now.gif);
   background-color: rgb(85%,93%,90%); color: black;}
```

In this way, you can control the current style from a series of central style sheets.

Branching Out

There are a ton of things you can do differently with this design, from the color choices to the way the links are set up. Here are just a few to try out:

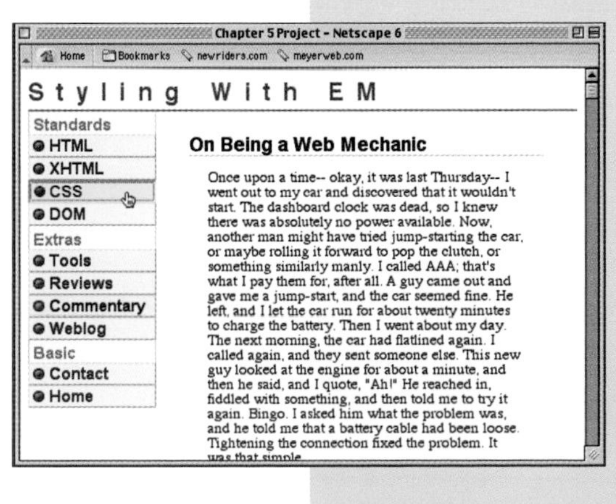

1. Create "active" styles for the menu links. You don't necessarily need to insert new icons or set new borders for the active state, although you could certainly do either (or both). One possibility with the second design is to invert the border colors so that the button appears to have been pressed inward.

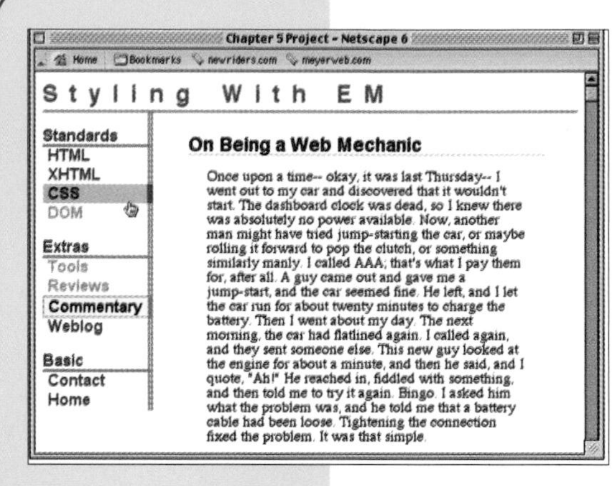

2. Experiment with different border styles for the first menu design. For example, you could make the separator line a double border and then set the border to solid when hovered. This could be accomplished with or without altering the padding and margins.

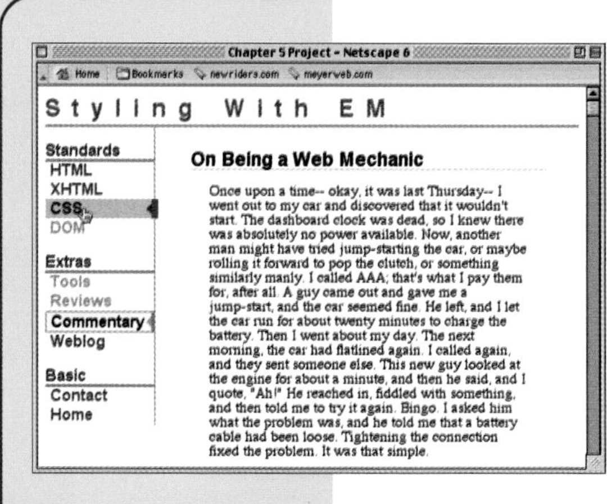

3. Combine techniques and give the links in the first design a background image when they're hovered. Then add a variant image to the current link. This could be an icon, an arrow, or anything else your imagination can devise.

6

Styling for Print

Print is dead.

—*Ghostbusters* (1986)

Even though the biggest portion of our jobs involves electrons and digital bits, there is still a large role in this world for printed material. There are times when a resource is better comprehended, more comfortable, or just better suited to being on paper. After all, you're reading a paper book, aren't you?

The authors of CSS recognized this, and the advent of CSS2 introduced the capability to apply styles to various media, chief among them print. The interesting thing about print styles is that they're almost never the first styles to be written for a Web document. It's almost always the screen styles first and then the print styles second. To that end, we'll spend this project looking at ways to quickly style existing documents.

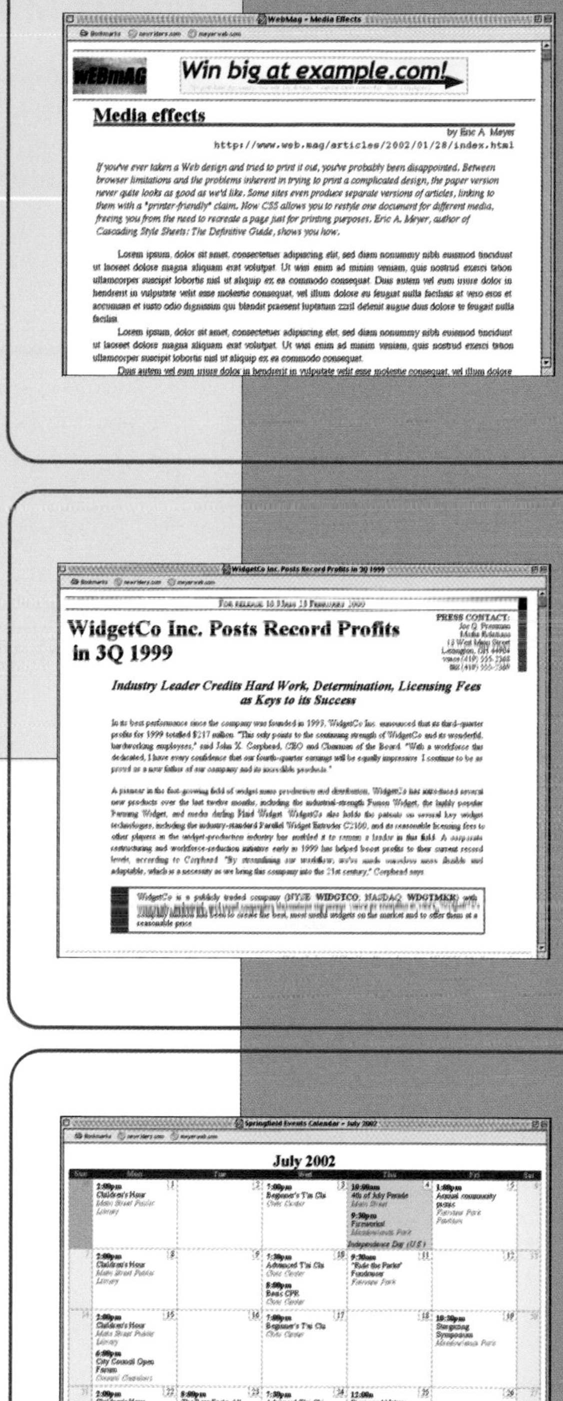

Project Goals

This will actually be a threefold project. In the first part, we'll take an existing Web magazine article design and create a print style sheet for it. With such a style sheet in place, we won't have to create "Click here for printer-friendly version" views of the page. Here are some of the goals we will consider:

- Change the article's font to be serif, which many studies claim is easier to read on a page.
- Restyle the site's masthead so that it doesn't have a background and instead borders along the top and bottom. The site's logo and the top banner ad should also appear. (That way the ad sponsor can be charged for more page views.)
- Prevent the navigation links on the left side of the page from printing.
- Prevent the smaller ads on the right side of the page from printing.
- Expand the article text's column to be nearly, but not quite, as wide as the page.
- Cause the URL of the page to appear in the printed version of the article but not show up in a Web browser.

After we've created print styles for this article, we'll turn to other projects in this book and quickly restyle them for print (the press release from Project 2, "Styling a Press Release," and the larger calendar from Project 3, "Styling an Events Calendar"). Although the specific goals for these projects won't be exactly the same as the ones above, they'll still follow the same broad goal, which is to create a decent version of the screen presentation. We'll get into the specifics as we turn to each.

Preparation

See the Introduction for instructions on how to download the files from the Web site.

Download the files for Project 6 from this book's Web site. If you're planning to play along at home, load the file `ch06proj.html` into the editing program of your choice. This is the file you'll be editing, saving, and reloading as the project progresses.

Laying the Groundwork

Let's take a look at the page design and determine how we can use the markup structure to achieve our goals (see Figure 6.1).

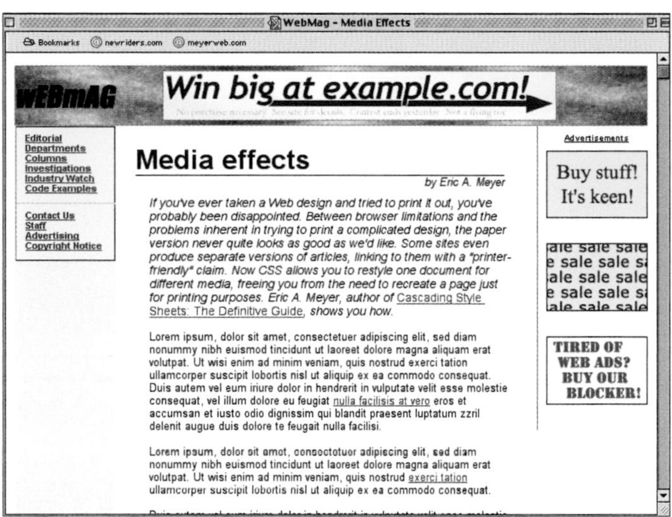

FIGURE 6.1 *The article as it appears in a Web browser.*

The key to most of our design goals will be an effective leveraging of the document's structure, so we need to get a clear picture of what's there. Listing 6.1 shows a simplified version of the document, with the various pieces of text replaced with placeholders.

Listing 6.1 The Simplified Document Structure

```
<table cellspacing="0">
<tr>
<td colspan="3" class="pagetop">
  [logo and banner]
</td>
</tr>
<tr>
<td class="leftside">
  <div class="left1">[links]</div>
  <div class="left2">[links]</div>
</td>
<td class="main">
  <h1>[title]</h1>
  <div class="credit">[credit]</div>
  <div class="abstract">[abstract]</div>
  [article text]
</td>
<td class="rightside">
  <div>[ad images]</div>
</td>
</tr>
<tr>
<td colspan="3" class="footer">
  <div>[footer]</div>
</td>
</tr>
</table>
```

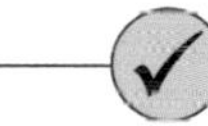

On the Use of `cellspacing`

The HTML-based `cellspacing="0"` is used because it's the only widely supported way to control spacing between cells of a table.

The most obvious feature of the structure is that we're using a table to lay out the page—a simple table, perhaps, but a table nonetheless. This will complicate matters when it comes to "turning off" parts of the page when printing, but we can work around that.

Styling the Document for Print

Probably the easiest way to create a print style sheet is to create the print design you want onscreen and then simply mark the finished product so that it only applies to print media. When creating the print styles, it will be necessary to "zero out" the screen style sheet that already exists. This keeps it from getting mixed up with the print styles by mistake.

Suppressing Styles

Because we're working with an existing design, the document already has a screen style sheet. What we need to do is prevent those styles from showing up onscreen while we work on the print styles. Why? Because the screen styles won't be applied to the printed version of the document. If we mix the two style sheets onscreen and then prevent one of them from applying to print media, we could end up with a broken print style sheet. (Turn it around: Would you want the print styles to be visible when you were designing a screen style sheet?)

The easiest thing to do is to change the value of the `media` attribute on the screen style sheet. We could set it to `print`, but that might be a bit confusing. Instead, let's pick another value, one that we know doesn't apply either onscreen or in print.

```
<style type="text/css" media="aural">
```

Restoring the Medium

Remember that the change in media is only a temporary convenience. At the end of the project, we'll change `aural` back to `screen`.

With this change, the entire style sheet will disappear from our screen and leave us with an unstyled document.

Starting from Scratch

Now that we've cleared the style palette, let's add in a very simple style sheet that will outline the table's structure for us and keep the sidebar content where we can see it. The borders are the important part because they help us see the effects that our styles have on the page's layout, as shown in Figure 6.2.

```
</style>
<style type="text/css" media="screen">
td {vertical-align: top; border: 1px dotted silver;}
</style>
</head>
```

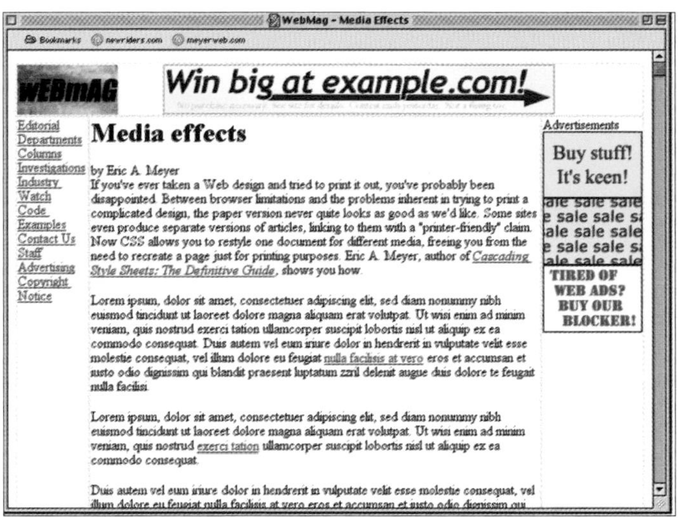

FIGURE 6.2

Applying a dirt-simple style sheet to start out.

Print Screening

Because we're designing for screen right now, we use the `media` value `screen` so that we can see what we're doing. It will be changed to `print` when we're done, thus applying our styles in the print medium, where we want them.

The first and easiest thing to do is to style the main table cell so that the text will be in a serif font. We'll also set a font size and a line height.

```
td {vertical-align: top; border: 1px dotted silver;}
td.main {font: 12pt Times, serif; line-height: 16pt;}
</style>
```

By styling the table cell, we also style its contents because all of these styles will be inherited by the descendant elements. Let's style the `h1` element containing the title of the piece so that it stands out as it did in the Web design. We'll set the title to use the serif font Times (or any other serif font if Times isn't available). We'll also give it a bottom border with a little visual interest, as in Figure 6.3.

```
td.main {font: 12pt Times, serif; line-height: 16pt;}
h1 {font: bold 200% Times, serif;
   margin-top: 0.5em; margin-bottom: 0;
   border-bottom: 4px double black;}
</style>
```

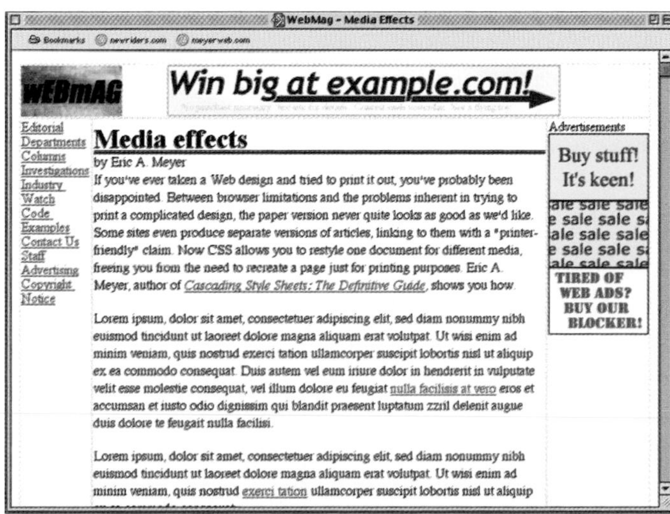

FIGURE 6.3

Styling the title and text of the article.

▸▸On Using Points

If you've read more than a few articles about fonts and CSS, you've probably been admonished to avoid points like the plague. Points are an exceedingly poor choice for Web design, you've been told. You know what? They are. The difference is that we're not doing Web design here; we're doing print design, and that's a whole different fettle of kitsch.

Points are real-world measures, like inches or meters. There are 72 points to an inch, which makes 12 points one-sixth of an inch. It's a fairly standard text measure in print, and we're working in print now. Print, being a physical medium, is an excellent place to use physical measures like centimeters, picas, or points. That's how points suddenly become useful—and, by implication, how pixels suddenly become a whole lot less useful.

That's because there's no clearly defined mapping between pixels and the physical world. How many pixels should there be per inch? Some claim it should be 72ppi, but others hold out for 90ppi, 75ppi, or some other number. So when we go to print, which is a physical medium, pixels become a lot less useful than they are onscreen.

When you're writing print styles, remember that points can be your friend. If you're in the screen medium, you need to once again eschew points in favor of some other sizing method, whether that's pixels, ems, or percentages.

Killing the Sidebars

A few more things will need to be done to the article text, but we're going to put those off for the moment in favor of tackling the sidebars. You'll recall that a design goal was to not print out the contents of either sidebar.

If we carefully examine the contents of the two sidebar cells, we see that all of the content is enclosed in `div` elements. Therefore, if we prevent the `div`s from appearing, we prevent the contents from being seen as well, as Figure 6.4 shows (or doesn't, if you catch my drift).

```
h1 {font: bold 200% Times, serif ;
   margin-top: 0.5em; margin-bottom: 0;
   border-bottom: 4px double black;}
td.leftside div,td.rightside div {display: none;}
</style>
```

We're doing this instead of just setting the cells themselves to `display: none;` because browsers don't always react well to having cells suddenly disappear from a table. Imagine a more complicated table with `colspan` cells in which some cells were set to `display: none;`. Not a pretty picture. Therefore, when trying to suppress the display of content in a table cell, you should always style the content, not the cell itself.

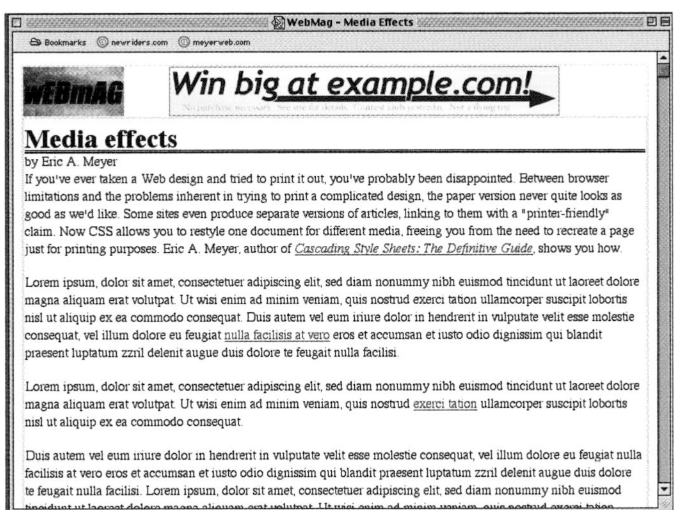

FIGURE 6.4

Making the sidebars disappear.

Of course, we might not always have everything wrapped in `div` elements. Let's adopt a more generic way of accomplishing this effect.

```
td.leftside *, td.rightside * {display: none;}
```

Now we're preventing the display of any element that's descended from either of the sidebar cells. This will have the same effect on our current design as was seen in Figure 6.4, but it's less prone to failure in the event of future changes to the markup.

We can also see that the sidebar cells have collapsed to no width at all. This has happened because they have no visual content, and that's generally a good thing. We can use them to achieve another design goal, though: that of making the article text not quite as wide as the page. We'll do this by declaring explicit widths for the cells themselves, with the result demonstrated in Figure 6.5.

```
td.leftside *, td.rightside * {display: none;}
td.leftside, td.rightside {width: 2em;}
</style>
```

Remember that the dotted gray borders are temporary and not a permanent fixture of the design. Let's style the article text a bit more and then get rid of the borders.

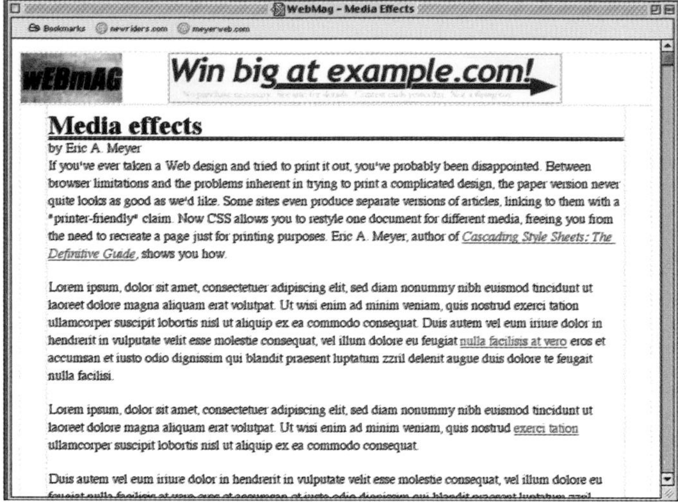

FIGURE 6.5

Using the sidebar cells to narrow the article text a bit

More Article Styling

The article text and title are styled about the way we want already, but the article credit (or byline) and the abstract aren't. We're going to re-create simplified versions of the screen-media styles here by right-aligning the credit and italicizing the abstract—but nothing more than that.

```
td.leftside *, td.rightside * {width: 2em;}
div.credit {text-align: right;}
div.abstract {font-style: italic;}
</style>
```

Just for fun, let's use CSS to reproduce the English-text convention of indenting the first line of each paragraph, fully justifying the text, and not having any extra space between paragraphs.

```
h1 {font: bold 200% Times, serif ;
   margin-top: 0.5em; margin-bottom: 0;
   border-bottom: 4px double black;}
p {margin: 0; text-indent: 2.5em; text-align: justify;}
td.leftside *, td.rightside * {display: none;}
```

The changes that this causes can be seen in Figure 6.6.

The one thing we're really missing is some margins to separate the abstract from the rest of the article, so let's add those in. We'll add a little bit of left and right margin to indent the abstract, and we'll add "one-line" margins to the top and bottom.

```
div.abstract {font-style: italic; margin: 1em 0.33em;}
```

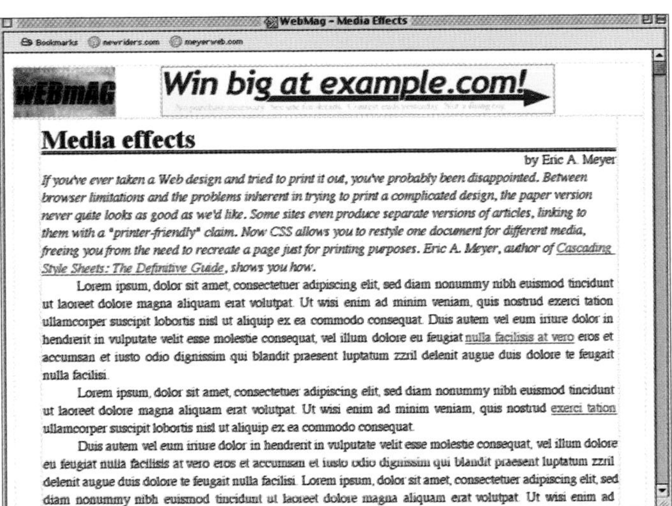

FIGURE 6.6

Improved text styling.

Now we'll show the URL of the article in the article itself. The URL doesn't actually appear in the article's text—we'll insert it ourselves, right beneath the credit.

```
<div class="credit">by Eric A. Meyer</div>
<div class="url">http://www.web.mag/articles/2001/09/07/index.html</div>
<div class="abstract">If you've ever taken a Web design and tried to
```

Now all we need is to style the URL to be right justified and in a monospace font. The effect can be seen in Figure 6.7.

```
div.credit {text-align: right;}
div.url {font-family: Courier, monospace; text-align: right;}
div.abstract {font-style: italic; margin: 1em 0.33em;}
```

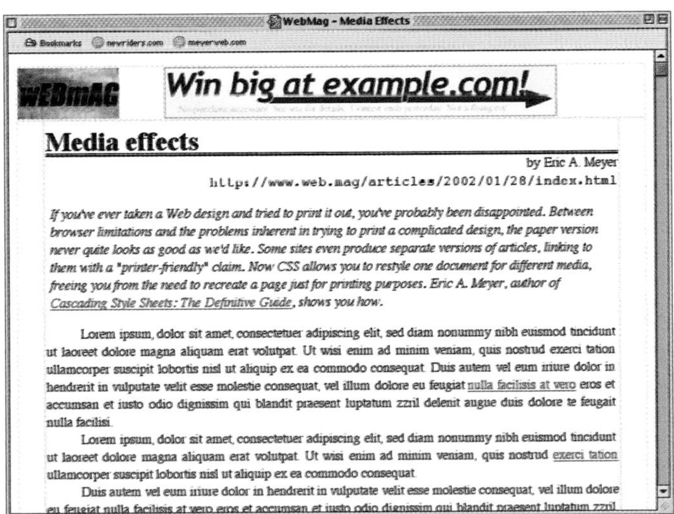

FIGURE 6.7

Displaying the URL and new margins on the abstract.

We'll come back to the URL in a little while, but first let's turn our attention to the end of the document.

The Footer

With all of this top-heavy design focus, it's easy to forget about the end of the document. Still, the page does have a footer, and we need to style it. Otherwise, we could end up with a blob of text that looks like it fell out of the main article.

We'll try the usual footer-type styles: some space on top to separate it from the main text, a smaller font size, a top border, and right-aligning the text. This will have the result shown in Figure 6.8.

```
div.abstract {font-style: italic; margin: 1em 0.33em;}
td.footer div {margin-top: 24pt; font-size: 9pt;
   border-top: 2px solid gray; text-align: right;}
</style>
```

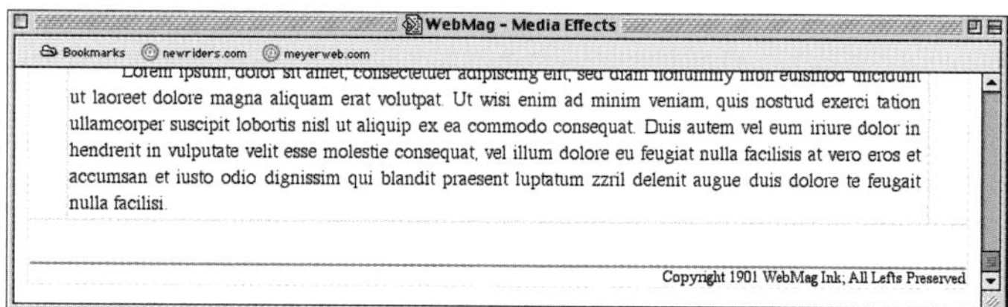

FIGURE 6.8

The page's footer.

Here is one place where it's especially important to remember the difference between screen and print media. On the screen, the footer appears at the very bottom of the "page," or the scrollable area of this document. In other words, we scroll all the way to the bottom of the document, and there's the footer.

In print, the footer will appear wherever it happens to fall on a page. That could be near the bottom, right in the middle, or up near the top—there's really no way to know ahead of time. CSS doesn't provide a way to force the footer to the bottom of the last page, so we have to take our chances. Of course, this is no different than how Web pages have always printed.

Cleaning Up

Just a few more steps and we should be done. The first thing to do is remove the `border` declaration from the `td` rule.

```
<style type="text/css" media="screen">
td {vertical-align: top;}
td.main {font: 12pt Times, serif; line-height: 16pt;}
```

Having done this, it becomes clear that we neglected one of our design goals because now there are no borders on the masthead containing the logo and banner ad. Let's add those in and give the masthead just a bit of padding.

```
td {vertical-align: top;}
td.pagetop {border: 1px solid black; border-width: 1px 0;
   padding: 10px 0;}
td.main {font: 12pt Times, serif; line-height: 16pt;}
```

Finally, we really ought to do something about the hyperlinks. On the page, they obviously aren't going to function as links, so we might as well make them blend in with the rest of the text. Instead of forcing a certain color and removing underlining, we'll let the links pull their styles from their parents.

```
p {margin: 0; text-indent: 2.5em; text-align: justify;}
td.main a {text-decoration: inherit; color: inherit;}
td.leftside *, td.rightside * {display: none;}
```

In using the value `inherit`, we're telling the browser to take whatever value is set for the given property and apply that same value to the link. Thus, if a link appears in an element that's overlined and gray, the link will be overlined and gray. If, as is more often case, the link is part of a paragraph that has no text decoration and is black in color, the links will be undecorated and black. We can see this happening in Figure 6.9.

Is "Unlinking" the Best Choice?

Depending on your feelings, you might decide to leave some or all of the hyperlink styling intact. By so doing, you indicate to a reader of the printout that there are links in the original Web document, potentially enticing the person to investigate the online version. Ultimately, this choice is up to you.

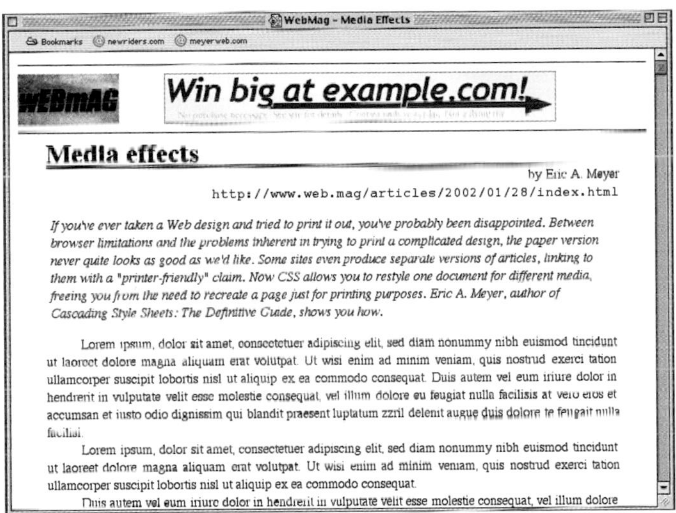

FIGURE 6.9

The links have been "unstyled," and the masthead gains some separation.

This brings us almost to the end of the process. Now that we have a print style sheet, we need to actually apply it to print and bring the screen style sheet back to the screen. All it takes is a couple of quick edits. Replace the `media` value `screen` with `print`, replace `aural` with `screen`, and we're all set! The print style sheet is shown in Listing 6.2.

Listing 6.2 The Complete Print Style Sheet

```
<style type="text/css" media="print">
td {vertical-align: top;}
td.pagetop {border: 1px solid black; border-width: 1px 0;
   padding: 10px 0;}
td.main {font: 12pt Times, serif; line-height: 16pt;}
h1 {font: bold 200% Times, serif ;
   margin-top: 0.5em; margin-bottom: 0;
```

continues

Listing 6.2 Continued

```
   border-bottom: 4px double black;}
p {margin: 0; text-indent: 2.5em; text-align: justify;}
td.main a {text-decoration: none; color: inherit;}
td.leftside *, td.rightside * {display: none;}
td.leftside, td.rightside {width: 2em;}
div.credit {text-align: right;}
div.url {font-family: Courier, monospace; text-align: right;}
div.abstract {font-style: italic; margin: 1em 0.33em;}
td.footer div {margin-top: 24pt; font-size: 9pt;
   border-top: 2px solid gray; text-align: right;}
</style>
```

Suppressing the URL

It might seem a little odd, but we need to turn off display of the article's URL—and after we went to all that trouble to add it, too. We aren't suppressing it in the print styles, though; we're suppressing it in the screen style sheet. Remember that we only want it to appear in the print styles. As things stand now, it will appear in a Web browser totally unstyled because all of its styles are now safely ensconced in the print style sheet.

Fortunately, all we have to do is add one simple little rule to the end of the screen styles.

```
td.footer div {font: bold 10px sans-serif; color: gray;
   text-align: center; padding: 0.5em 0 0;
   border-top: 1px solid navy; margin-top: 10px;}
div.url {display: none;}
</style>
```

That's it. Now the article really is ready for prime time.

Print Styles for a Press Release

If there's one kind of Web page that is likely to be printed out, it's a press release. If you've been through Project 2, you know we've already created a press release style for the Web. In this section, we'll take the end result of that project and modify the screen style sheet for print.

Checking Our Status

A quick check of the end result of Project 2 (see Figure 6.10) shows us that what we have is already fairly close to a print style sheet. The main point of concern here is that the design uses colors and a background image, as we can see in Listing 6.3.

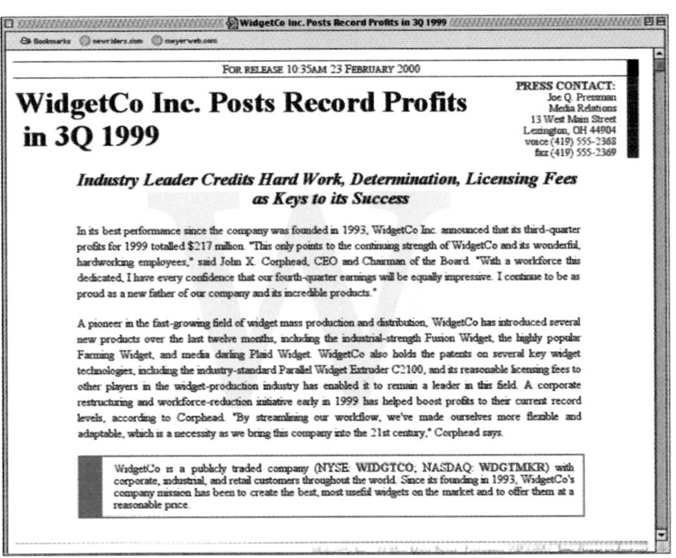

WidgetCo Inc. Posts Record Profits in 3Q 1999

Bookmarks newriders.com meyerweb.com

FOR RELEASE 10:35AM 23 FEBRUARY 2000

WidgetCo Inc. Posts Record Profits in 3Q 1999

PRESS CONTACT:
Joe Q. Pressman
Media Relations
13 West Main Street
Lexington, OH 44904
voice (419) 555-2368
fax (419) 555-2369

Industry Leader Credits Hard Work, Determination, Licensing Fees as Keys to its Success

In its best performance since the company was founded in 1993, WidgetCo Inc. announced that its third-quarter profits for 1999 totalled $217 million. "This only points to the continuing strength of WidgetCo and its wonderful, hardworking employees," said John X. Corphead, CEO and Chairman of the Board. "With a workforce this dedicated, I have every confidence that our fourth-quarter earnings will be equally impressive. I continue to be as proud as a new father of our company and its incredible products."

A pioneer in the fast-growing field of widget mass production and distribution, WidgetCo has introduced several new products over the last twelve months, including the industrial-strength Fusion Widget, the highly popular Farming Widget, and media darling Plaid Widget. WidgetCo also holds the patents on several key widget technologies, including the industry-standard Parallel Widget Extruder C2100, and its reasonable licensing fees to other players in the widget-production industry has enabled it to remain a leader in this field. A corporate restructuring and workforce-reduction initiative early in 1999 has helped boost profits to their current record levels, according to Corphead. "By streamlining our workflow, we've made ourselves more flexible and adaptable, which is a necessity as we bring this company into the 21st century," Corphead says.

WidgetCo is a publicly traded company (NYSE: WIDGTCO; NASDAQ: WDGTMKR) with corporate, industrial, and retail customers throughout the world. Since its founding in 1993, WidgetCo's company mission has been to create the best, most useful widgets on the market and to offer them at a reasonable price.

FIGURE 6.10

The press release as styled for the screen.

Listing 6.3 The Press Release's Stylesheet

```
<style type="text/css">
body {background: white url(WidgetCoLogo.gif) center no-repeat;
   color: black;}
p {margin-left: 10%; margin-right: 10%;
   text-align: justify; line-height: 1.33em;}
p#summary {border: 2px solid #008000; border-width: 2px 2px 2px 2em;
   padding: 0.5em 0.5em 0.5em 1em; background: #FFE;
   line-height: 1em;}
div.release {font-variant: small-caps; text-align: center;
   margin-right: 10px; padding: 0.125em 0;
   border: 1px solid black; border-width: 1px 15px 1px 0;}
div#contact-info {text-align: right;
   margin-right: 10px; padding-right: 15px;
   border-right: 15px solid #446; padding-top: 0.25em;
   color: #321; font-size: 90%;}
div#contact-info:first-line {text-transform: uppercase;
   font-size: 1.111em; font-weight: bold;}
div#contact-info:first-line {font-weight: bold;
   text-transform: uppercase;}
div#footer {text-align: right; margin-top: 2.5em;
   border-top: 1px solid gray; color: #AAA; font-size: 85%;
   padding-top: 0.33em; font-style: italic;}
 /* removed 'letter-spacing: 1px' */
div#footer a:link {color: #778;}
div#footer a:visited {color: #878;}
a.stockinfo {font-weight: bold; font-style: normal;
   color: blue; background: #FFE;}
a.stockinfo:hover {background: blue; color: white;}
h1 {font-size: 250%; margin-top: -2.5em; margin-right: 5em;
   padding-left: 0.33em; text-indent: -0.25em;}
h2 {font-size: 150%; font-style: italic; text-align: center;
   margin: 0 10%;}
</style>
```

Why should we care about color and backgrounds? For these two reasons:

- Color printers, while growing in popularity, are still a minority. Color ink is also a tad expensive, so people tend not to print in color if they can help it. Therefore, it generally makes the most sense to convert your print-style colors to shades of gray.
- Background images usually aren't printed by browsers because that's how most browsers are configured. Because you as the author can't force the background image to be printed, you have to make sure the print styles don't somehow depend on the presence of a background image.

So all we really need to do is get rid of the background image on the `body` element and shift the color to grayscale. That should be pretty simple.

Eliminating the Background

Faded Backgrounds

If your design uses a faded (or "washed-out") background image, one that's specifically designed not to clash with the text, it's okay to leave it in. In fact, we probably could have left this one in—we're removing it mostly for the practice.

To get rid of the background image, we just need to cut down the `body` rule so that it sets a background color and nothing more.

```
<style type="text/css">
body {background: white; color: black;}
p {margin-left: 10%; margin-right: 10%;
   text-align: justify; line-height: 1.33em;}
```

The real change is that we've dropped the values relating to the background image and its position, retaining only the background color. That's all it takes.

Converting to Grayscale

The process of converting colors to grayscale can be a little trickier. Of course, what you could do is take a screenshot of the page, load it into Photoshop or a similar program, set the colors to grayscale, and find out what gray values you get. That's hard to do in a book about CSS, so we'll do it the old-fashioned way. We'll guess.

Hexadecimal Notation

Computer scientists use hexadecimal notation a lot, and it was the first numeric method of representing color on the Web, introduced as part of HTML 3.2. We will not undertake a discussion of hexadecimal notation here, partly because it's long and boring but mostly because there are plenty of free color-picker programs that will output hex values available on the Web.

The first element in the style sheet that has color styles is the summary paragraph near the bottom of the document. Here's how it's being styled now:

```
p#summary {border: 2px solid #008000; border-width: 2px 2px 2px 2em;
   padding: 0.5em 0.5em 0.5em 1em; background: #FFE;
   line-height: 1em;}
```

For the border color, we need a hexadecimal between `00` and `80`. Four is halfway between zero and eight, so we'll just use it in all three slots, giving us `#444`.

The value `#FFE` is equivalent to `#FFFFEE`, so we need a grayscale that smoothes that out. We could try calculating the exact midpoint between `EE` and `FF` in hexadecimal, but instead let's just pick something between the two and see if it will do. `F0` is between `EE` and `FF`, so we'll try it.

```
p#summary {border: 2px solid #444; border-width: 2px 2px 2px 2em;
   padding: 0.5em 0.5em 0.5em 1em; background: #F0F0F0;
   line-height: 1em;}
```

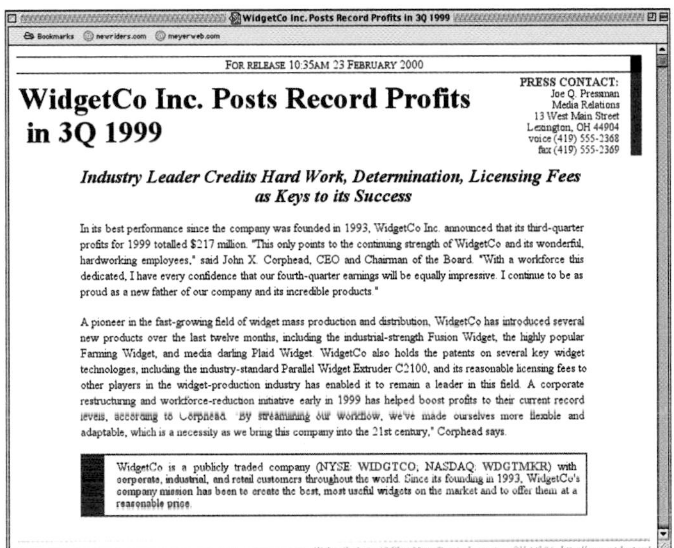

WidgetCo Inc. Posts Record Profits in 3Q 1999

Bookmarks newriders.com meyerweb.com

FOR RELEASE 10:35AM 23 FEBRUARY 2000

WidgetCo Inc. Posts Record Profits in 3Q 1999

PRESS CONTACT:
Joe Q. Pressman
Media Relations
13 West Main Street
Lexington, OH 44904
voice (419) 555-2368
fax (419) 555-2369

Industry Leader Credits Hard Work, Determination, Licensing Fees as Keys to its Success

In its best performance since the company was founded in 1993, WidgetCo Inc. announced that its third-quarter profits for 1999 totalled $217 million. "This only points to the continuing strength of WidgetCo and its wonderful, hardworking employees," said John X. Corphead, CEO and Chairman of the Board. "With a workforce this dedicated, I have every confidence that our fourth-quarter earnings will be equally impressive. I continue to be as proud as a new father of our company and its incredible products."

A pioneer in the fast-growing field of widget mass production and distribution, WidgetCo has introduced several new products over the last twelve months, including the industrial-strength Fusion Widget, the highly popular Farming Widget, and media darling Plaid Widget. WidgetCo also holds the patents on several key widget technologies, including the industry-standard Parallel Widget Extruder C2100, and its reasonable licensing fees to other players in the widget-production industry has enabled it to remain a leader in this field. A corporate restructuring and workforce-reduction initiative early in 1999 has helped boost profits to their current record levels, according to Corphead. "By streamlining our workflow, we've made ourselves more flexible and adaptable, which is a necessity as we bring this company into the 21st century," Corphead says.

WidgetCo is a publicly traded company (NYSE: WIDGTCO; NASDAQ: WDGTMKR) with corporate, industrial, and retail customers throughout the world. Since its founding in 1993, WidgetCo's company mission has been to create the best, most useful widgets on the market and to offer them at a reasonable price.

FIGURE 6.11

Graying out the summary paragraph.

We now turn our attention to the top of the press release. Here we have a dark blue border color (`#446`) and some very dark brown text (`#321`). These are easy to convert. Just split the difference between `4` and `6` to get `5` and average out `#321` to get `#222`.

```
div#contact-info {text-align: right;
   margin-right: 10px; padding-right: 15px;
   border-right: 15px solid #555; padding-top: 0.25em;
   color: #222; font-size: 90%;}
```

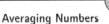

Averaging Numbers

Color enthusiasts and longtime print designers would probably cringe at the approach we're taking here. Properly converting color to grayscale involves considering the hue, lightness, and saturation level of a color. Because CSS doesn't have a way to express those kinds of colors, we're basically making crude guesses as to the proper grayscale conversions. It isn't precise, but it does work relatively well.

The last bits of color to wash out are the hyperlinks in the document. Let's deal with the links in the summary paragraph. We've already set the background of the summary to be `#F0F0F0`, so the link backgrounds will need to match that. As for the text color, let's just make it black and call it done. Then there are the hover styles. We could just dump them because hovering doesn't work in print, but we'll leave them in and replace `blue` with `black` for consistency's sake. Since the rule is irrelevant in this medium, we could as easily remove it, but by the same token it does no harm to leave it in.

```
a.stockinfo {font-weight: bold; font-style: normal;
   color: black; background: #F0F0F0;}
a.stockinfo:hover {background: black; color: white;}
```

For the last touch, we turn to the footer. Its text is already set to the gray color `#AAA`, so we don't have to do anything to change it. The footer's unvisited- and visited-link colors are `#778` and `#878`, respectively, which are really close to being grayscale as it is. Let's just make them both `#888`.

```
div#footer a:link {color: #888;}
div#footer a:visited {color: #888;}
```

With that, we have the press release shown in Figure 6.12.

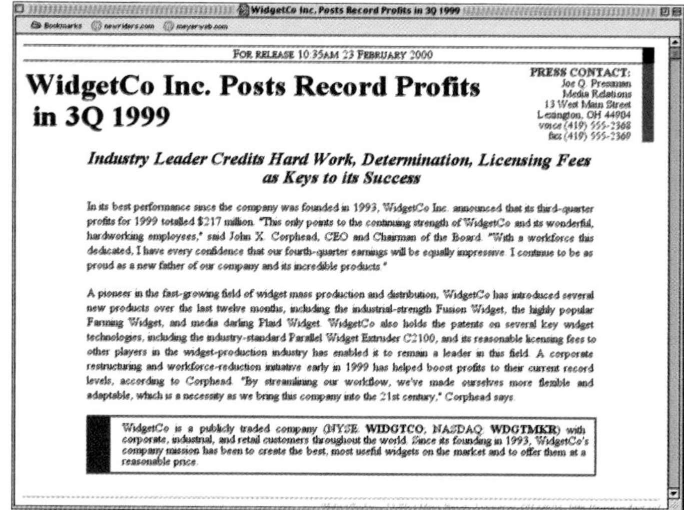

WidgetCo Inc. Posts Record Profits in 3Q 1999

Bookmarks newriders.com meyerweb.com

FOR RELEASE 10:35AM 23 FEBRUARY 2000

PRESS CONTACT:
Joe Q. Pressman
Media Relations
13 West Main Street
Lexington, OH 44904
voice (419) 555-2368
fax (419) 555-2369

WidgetCo Inc. Posts Record Profits in 3Q 1999

Industry Leader Credits Hard Work, Determination, Licensing Fees as Keys to its Success

In its best performance since the company was founded in 1993, WidgetCo Inc. announced that its third-quarter profits for 1999 totalled $217 million. "This only points to the continuing strength of WidgetCo and its wonderful, hardworking employees," said John X. Corphead, CEO and Chairman of the Board. "With a workforce this dedicated, I have every confidence that our fourth-quarter earnings will be equally impressive. I continue to be as proud as a new father of our company and its incredible products."

A pioneer in the fast-growing field of widget mass production and distribution, WidgetCo has introduced several new products over the last twelve months, including the industrial-strength Fusion Widget, the highly popular Fanning Widget, and media darling Plaid Widget. WidgetCo also holds the patents on several key widget technologies, including the industry-standard Parallel Widget Extruder C2100, and its reasonable licensing fees to other players in the widget-production industry has enabled it to remain a leader in this field. A corporate restructuring and workforce-reduction initiative early in 1999 has helped boost profits to their current record levels, according to Corphead. "By streamlining our workflow, we've made ourselves more flexible and adaptable, which is a necessity as we bring this company into the 21st century," Corphead says.

WidgetCo is a publicly traded company (NYSE: **WIDGTCO**, NASDAQ: **WDGTMKR**) with corporate, industrial, and retail customers throughout the world. Since its founding in 1993, WidgetCo's company mission has been to create the best, most useful widgets on the market and to offer them at a reasonable price.

FIGURE 6.12

The press release is now ready for printing.

Remember, though, that you'll need to make this style sheet a print style sheet by using the `media` value `print`. In this case, we'll take the whole style sheet and save it into an external file called `pr-print.css`. Then we'll `link` to this style sheet with the following bit of markup:

```
<link rel="stylesheet" type="text/css" href="pr-print.css"
   media="print">
```

Now we can bring back the screen-media styles from the end of Project 2, but this time restrict them to the `screen` medium.

```
<title>WidgetCo Inc. Posts Record Profits in 3Q 1999</title>
<link rel="stylesheet" type="text/css" href="pr-print.css"
   media="print">
<style type="text/css" media="screen">
body {background: white url(WidgetCoLogo.gif) center no-repeat;
   color: black;}
```

These changes give us a press release that has its own unique styles for both screen and print.

It might have occurred to you that it would have been easier to let the original styles apply to both screen and print media and then just write new rules to override the color values. That's exactly what we'll be doing in the next section.

Styling a Calendar for Printing

Almost as likely as press releases to be printed are events calendars. By the end of Project 3, we'd created a full-month events calendar for a small community. In this section, we'll take the end result of that project and create a new style sheet just for print.

Getting Up-to-Date

Let's take another look at the large events calendar from the end of Project 3 (see Figure 6.13 and Listing 6.4). As in the preceding section, we're going to convert the colors we see to rough grayscale equivalents. This time, however, we'll do it by adding a completely new style sheet to the document. The rules in this second style sheet will include only what we need to replace the colors in the existing style sheet with more appropriate shades of gray.

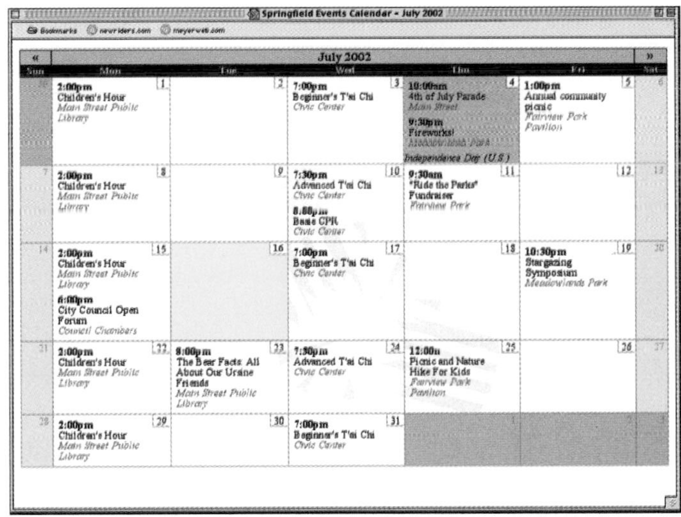

Figure 6.13

The fully styled large events calendar.

Listing 6.4 The Calendar's Stylesheet

```
<style type="text/css">
table#calendar {background: white url(fwork.gif) center no-repeat;}
table#calendar a {text-decoration: none;}
tr#days th {width: 18%;}
tr#days th.sat, tr#days th.sun {width: 5%;}
table#calendar tr#days th {color: #CCE; background-color: #224;
   font-weight: bold; text-align: center;
```

continues

Listing 6.4 Continued

```
   padding: 1px 0.33em;}
table#calendar tr#title th {background: #AAC; color: black;
   border: 1px solid #242; font-size: 120%;}
table#calendar td {vertical-align: top; padding: 0;
   border: 0px solid gray; border-width: 0 0 1px 1px;}
table#calendar td.sat {border-right: 1px solid gray;}
table#calendar a {font-weight: bold; display: block; margin: 0;}
table#calendar a:link {color: navy;}
table#calendar a:visited {color: purple;}
table#calendar a:hover {background: #FF6;}
table#calendar td.sat, table#calendar td.sun {background: #FDD;}
table#calendar td.jun, table#calendar td.aug {
   background: #AAB; color: #889;}
table#calendar tr#lastweek td {border-bottom: 2px solid #AAB;}
table#calendar td.holiday {background: #FAA;}
table#calendar td#jul16 {background-color: yellow;}
td#jul16 div.date {color: #C33; font-weight: bold; background: #FFC;}
div.event {margin: 0.5em;}
div.event span {display: block;}
div.holiday {font-style: italic;}
span.time {font-weight: bold;}
span.loc {color: #555; font-style: italic;}
div.date {float: right; text-align: center;
   border: 1px solid gray; border-width: 0 0 1px 1px;
   padding: 0.125em 0.25em 0 0.25em; margin: 0;
   background: #F3F3F3;}
td.sat div.date, td.sun div.date {border-width: 0;
   color: gray; background: transparent;}
td.jun div.date, td.aug div.date {border-width: 0;
   color: gray; background: transparent;}
</style>
```

Getting Started

Multiple Media

Another possibility would be to give the existing style sheet a `media` attribute and assign it a value of `screen, print`. This would restrict the styles to those two media. More options could be added with another comma, as in `screen, print, projection`.

The important thing about the existing style sheet is that it doesn't have a `media` attribute. That means the styles will apply in all media—screen, print, project, aural, you name it. We could add a `media` attribute, but because we'd just end up giving it a value of `all`, there's no real point. So we'll leave the existing style sheet exactly as it is.

To keep from getting too confused, let's just work our way down the existing style sheet. As we come to rules that have colors, we can add color-replacement rules to our new style sheet. At the top of the style sheet, we find the rules for the top of the calendar.

```
table#calendar tr#days th {color: #CCE; background-color: #224;
   font-weight: bold; text-align: center;
   padding: 1px 0.33em;}
table#calendar tr#title th {background: #AAC; color: black;
   border: 1px solid #242; font-size: 120%;}
```

Remember that we only want to replace the colors with grays, so we can effectively ignore the font- and text-related declarations. Let's add our new style sheet (with `media="screen"` as usual) and two new rules.

```
td.jun div.date, td.aug div.date {border-width: 0;
   color: gray; background: transparent;}
</style>
<style type="text/css" media="screen">
table#calendar tr#days th {color: #DDD; background: #333;}
table#calendar tr#title th {background: #BBB; color: black;
   border-color: #333;}
</style>
</head>
<body>
```

Because we're using the exact same selectors as in the first style sheet and because this new style sheet comes later in the document, the given values override those in the first style sheet. Thus `#DDD` replaces `#CCE`, `#BBB` replaces `#AAC`, and so forth. The other declarations (such as `font-weight: bold`) are not affected and will still apply, as seen in Figure 6.14.

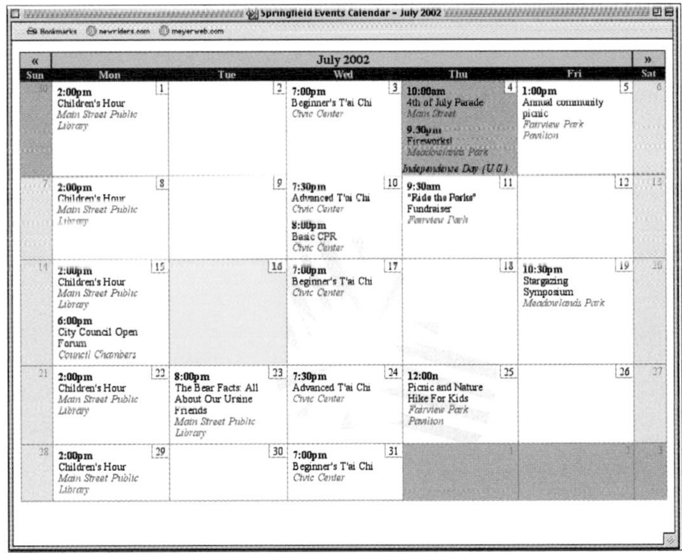

FIGURE 6.14

Bringing grayness to the top of the calendar.

One thing to note is that for the `table#calendar tr#title th` rule, we're included a `border-color` declaration. In the original styles, there was no such declaration. Instead, there was a full `border` declaration, which set the style, width, and color of the border. Rather than try to replace or rewrite that whole rule, we've just used `border-color` to replace the color value while leaving the width and style values alone. In the end, the effect is the same as if we'd said `border: 1px_solid #333`. The advantage to our current approach is that if the screen styles are later altered to be a dashed line or to be `3px` thick, we don't have to adjust the print styles as well.

Grayed-Out Links

Moving on, we see the next two rules also contain color values.

```
table#calendar td {vertical-align: top; padding: 0;
   border: 0px solid gray; border-width: 0 0 1px 1px;}
table#calendar td.sat {border-right: 1px solid gray;}
```

Because they're already calling for `gray`, however, we'll just leave them alone. Let's consider the link styles.

```
table#calendar a:link {color: navy;}
table#calendar a:visited {color: purple;}
table#calendar a:hover {background: #FF6;}
```

This deserves some careful thought. The named color `navy` is equivalent to `rgb(0%,0%,50%)` and `purple` to `rgb(100%,0%,100%)`, but that's not really important. Because links don't do any good in print and because it certainly doesn't matter if a link's been visited or not when you're holding a piece of paper, we should just make them the same shade of gray. As for the hover style, that also won't have any effect in print, but let's include it anyway.

```
table#calendar tr#title th {background: #BBB; color: black;
   border-color: #333;}
table#calendar a:link, table#calendar a:visited,
  table#calendar a:hover {background: transparent; color: #444;}
</style>
```

By grouping the three selectors together, we can efficiently bring unity to the style of any link on the printed page.

Washing Out the Days

Now we're getting into the styling of the actual days in the calendar grid. In our original style sheet, we have a group of four rules that are concerned with color.

```
table#calendar td.sat, table#calendar td.sun {background: #FDD;}
table#calendar td.jun, table#calendar td.aug {
   background: #AAB; color: #889;}
table#calendar tr#lastweek td {border-bottom: 2px solid #AAB;}
table#calendar td.holiday {background: #FAA;}
```

As before, we need only to reproduce the color-related declarations and replace color with grayscale, as shown in Figure 6.15. The change is fairly dramatic.

Replacing the Border Color

Once again, we've used `border-color` to reset the color of a border without affecting its style or width.

```
table#calendar a:link, table#calendar a:visited,
  table#calendar a:hover {background: transparent; color: #444;}
table#calendar td.sat, table#calendar td.sun {background: #E0E0E0;}
table#calendar td.jun, table#calendar td.aug {
   background: #AAA; color: #999;}
table#calendar tr#lastweek td {border-color: #AAA;}
table#calendar td.holiday {background: #CCC;}
</style>
```

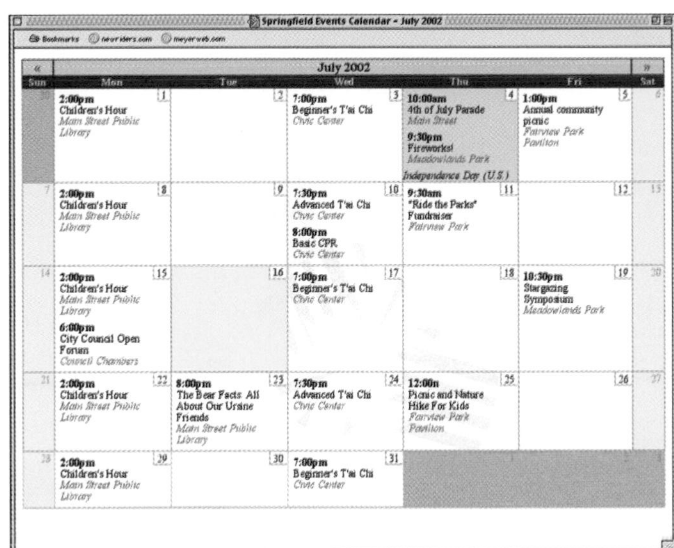

FIGURE 6.15

Washing out the grid of days.

No Styles for Today

Now that we've grayed out most of the calendar, we have only one more day to worry about: today (which in this example is July 16th). We need to get rid of that yellow background and red text.

The key here is that we don't want to convert yellow to a grayscale equivalent because that would still make July 16th look different than other days. We want the printed calendar to be useful throughout the month, so we need to make July 16th look the same as other days. We'll remove the background color altogether and make the date styles the same as other dates.

```
table#calendar td.holiday {background: #CCC;}
table#calendar td#jul16 {background-color: transparent;}
td#jul16 div.date {color: black; background: #F3F3F3;}
</style>
```

Why `transparent` instead of `white`? Because we might decide later that the whole calendar should have a light gray background, for example. More importantly, every other day is based on a `td` that doesn't have a `background-color` set, which means they all have transparent backgrounds, too. Similarly, because all the other dates are black on a light gray (`#F3F3F3`) background, we did the same for July 16th. We can see the results in Figure 6.16.

It looks like we forgot one thing: the boldfacing of today's date. We'll have to add a declaration to get rid of that.

```
td#jul16 div.date {color: black; background: #F3F3F3;
  font-weight: normal;}
```

With that addition, we'll be sure to have an ordinary day today.

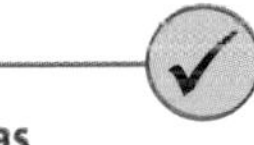

What Day Was Today?

As mentioned in Project 3, the styles for today will be automatically generated. We're just pretending that today is July 16th for testing purposes. When the calendar is actually put online, the script that creates the calendar will also write the rule for today. See Project 3 for more information.

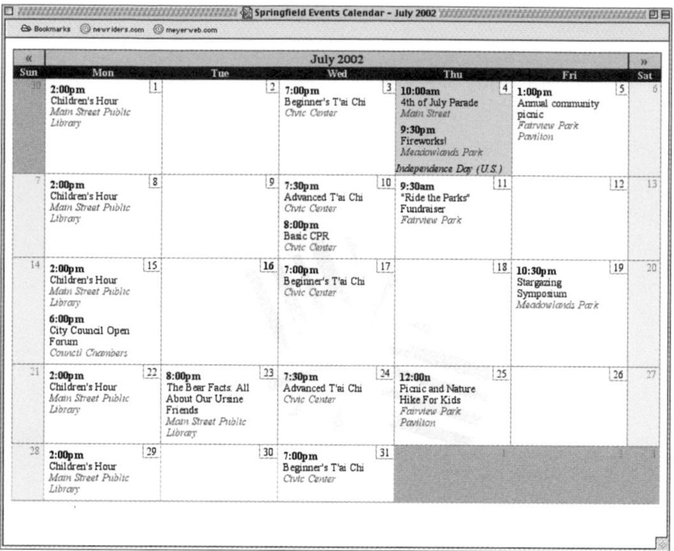

FIGURE 6.16

Making today a day like any other day.

Finishing Up

At this point, all we really need to do is get rid of the firecracker image in the table's background. As we discussed with the press release, we're removing the background image because many browsers are configured to not print backgrounds, so we need to be sure our styles are legible without the background image.

```
<style type="text/css" media="screen">
table#calendar {background-image: none;}
table#calendar tr#days th {color: #DDD; background: #333;}
```

Looking over the calendar again, the top of it seems a little strange. The arrows don't have any meaning in print, and the boxes are a little odd. Plus, the month doesn't seem to stand out as much as it might. Let's rewrite the styles for the title row and add a new rule.

```
table#calendar tr#title th {background: transparent; color: black;
  border-width: 0; font-size: 200%;}
table#calendar th a {display: none;}
table#calendar a:link, table#calendar a:visited,
  table#calendar a:hover {background: transparent; color: #444;}
```

What did we change? The background has gone from a light gray to transparent. The border color has been replaced with a declaration that effectively removes the borders of the `th` elements in the row by setting them to have no width. Finally, we made the text twice as big as its parent element.

In addition to all this, we added a rule to turn off display of the links in that row, which means the backward and forward arrows will disappear. The end result of all these changes—which also happens to be the end result of this section—is shown in Figure 6.17.

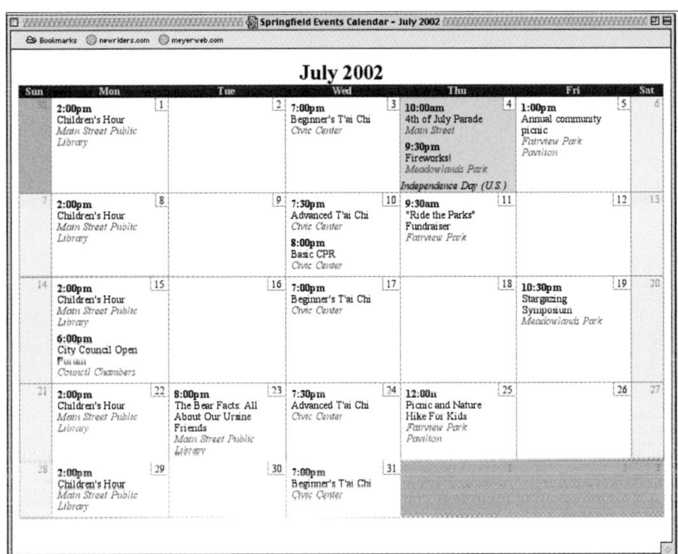

FIGURE 6.17

The print-ready calendar.

Now all we have to do is change our new style sheet's `media` value from `screen` to `print`, and we'll have the style sheet shown in Listing 6.5.

Listing 6.5 The Calendar's Print Style Sheet

```
<style type="text/css" media="print">
table#calendar {background-image: none;}
table#calendar tr#days th {color: #DDD; background: #333;}
table#calendar tr#title th {background: transparent; color: black;
  border-width: 0; font-size: 200%;}
table#calendar th a {display: none;}
table#calendar a:link, table#calendar a:visited,
  table#calendar a:hover {background: transparent; color: #444;}
table#calendar td.sat, table#calendar td.sun {background: #E0E0E0;}
table#calendar td.jun, table#calendar td.aug {
   background: #AAA; color: #999;}
table#calendar tr#lastweek td {border-color: #AAA;}
table#calendar td.holiday {background: #CCC;}
table#calendar td#jul16 {background-color: transparent;}
td#jul16 div.date {color: black; background: #F3F3F3;
  font-weight: normal;}
</style>
```

Branching Out

With three different print-style projects at our disposal, there are practically an infinite number of new things to try. Here are a paltry few suggestions.

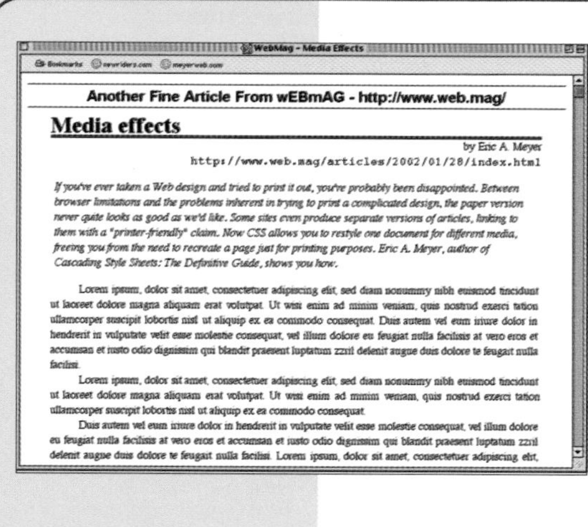

1. In the magazine article, get rid of the ad banner and magazine logo when printing and replace them with a text element that names the magazine and gives its URL. Note that this will require you to add a little extra markup to the document itself before writing the styles. Also remember to prevent the new element from appearing onscreen.

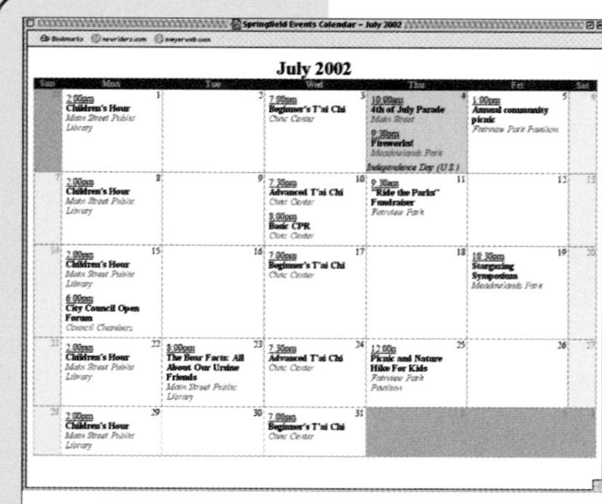

2. Restyle the calendar boxes so that the dates are not boxed in or backed in light gray and are pushed further into their corners. Also rearrange the styling of the text within the date boxes to underline the time and boldface the event.

3. Completely redo the calendar so that it prints in corporate "open inverted L" style for the days. This will involve altering the value of `cellspacing` for the `table` itself. This will also mean that nonweekday, non-July days will have to be set apart using text color instead of background color. Of course, we could also alter the border colors…

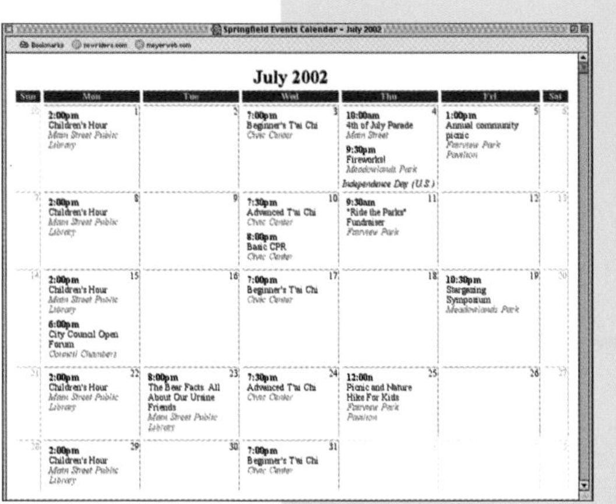

7

Making an Input Form Look Good

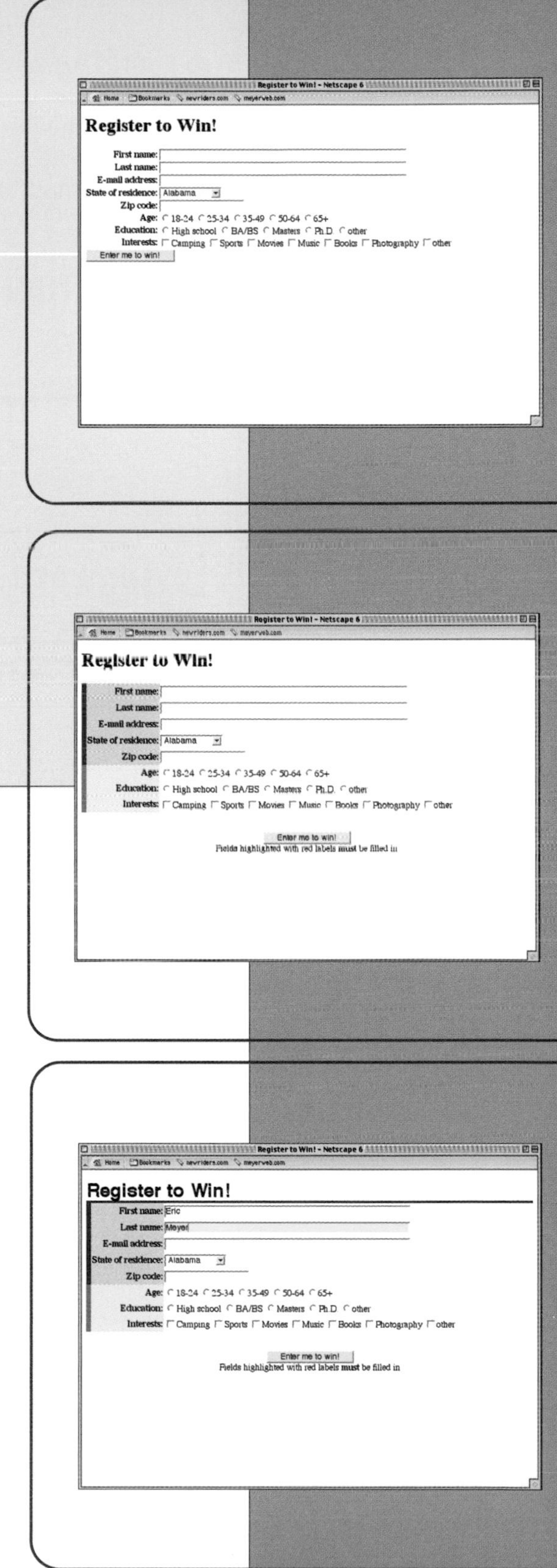

I came into this game for the action, the excitement. Go anywhere, travel light, get in, get out, wherever there's trouble, a man alone. Now they got the whole country sectioned off; you can't make a move without a form.

—*Brazil* (1985)

We can skip around the Web all day long, clicking from page to page, but when you get right down to it, the engine of expansion on the Web is forms. Without them, people couldn't input their personal information to let them buy stuff—let alone actually tell an e-commerce server what they want to buy.

To get a better feel for forms and the issues involved with styling them, we're going to try our hand at pepping up a simple survey form for both screen and print.

Project Goals

A client has decided to run a sweepstakes to gather some basic customer data, such as the area of residence and personal interests of each contest entrant. Although management wants the data to be collected over the Web, state law requires that all contests allow mail-in entries. To kill two birds with one stone, we'll style the entry form so that it can be presented acceptably both on the Web and in print. That way, we don't have to create a whole new "print this page" document and then worry about keeping its contents updated if the entry form changes in the future. In this project, we'll go through the process of styling the form for the Web, then we'll style it for print, and finally we'll balance out the demands of both screen and print.

Preparation

See the Introduction for instructions on how to download files from the Web site.

Download the files for Project 7 from the book's Web site. If you're planning to play along at home, load the file `ch07proj.html` into the editing program of your choice. This is the file you'll be editing, saving, and reloading as the project progresses.

Laying the Groundwork

As always, it's time to take a look at the document in its unstyled state and compare what we have to the project requirements.

Register to Win! - Netscape 6

Home | Bookmarks | newriders.com | meyerweb.com

Register to Win!

First name:
Last name:
E-mail address:
State of residence: Alabama
Zip code:
Age: 18-24 25-34 35-49 50-64 65+
Education: High school BA/BS Masters Ph.D. other
Interests: Camping Sports Movies Music Books Photography other
Enter me to win!

FIGURE 7.1

The unstyled form.

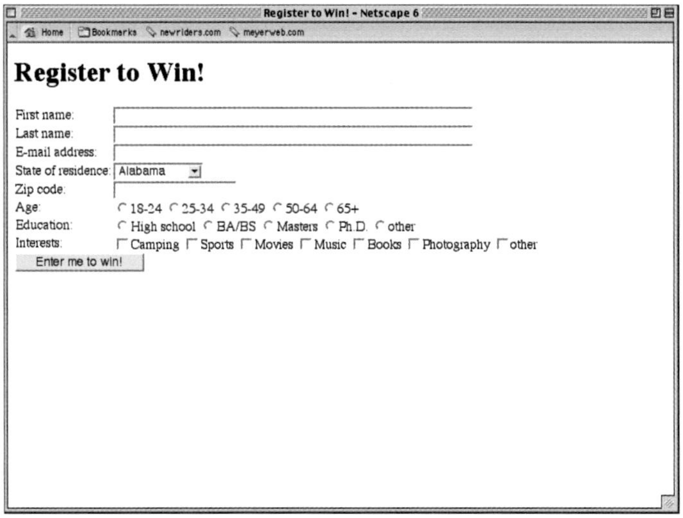

What we have is a pretty simple form, and as with most forms on the Web, it's been laid out with a table. We're going to leave the table in place and use it to our advantage rather than try to re-create the table structure in some other convoluted way. With that in mind, let's review the specific project requirements that have been handed to us from on high:

- The first five fields are required information and should be highlighted in some fashion; the last three are optional and do not need to be highlighted.

- There should be some sort of text explaining the highlighting and what it means.
- The various input labels (First name, Last name, and so on) should be right-aligned and boldfaced.
- When printed, the form should have fill-in-the-blank lines instead of input boxes for the first five entry fields, including the state selection box.
- No colors should be employed when printing. This should prevent users with grayscale printers from being confused by any directions.
- The printed version of the form should have a U.S. mail address on it, but the onscreen version should not; similarly, the submit button should only appear onscreen, not in print.

These are, in broad strokes, the directives we need to fulfill with our styles.

To get our form properly styled, we'll need to put some structural hooks into the document. We know that the first five rows are special (they hold required information), so we'll probably want to style them in a group. The same is true of the input labels. Therefore, we'll need to give them classes that will help us style them later on.

First we'll class the first five rows. Each row contains required information, so let's add a class of `required` to each `tr` element. For example:

```
<table cellspacing="0">
<tr class="required">
<td>First name:</td>
<td><input type="text" name="userFName" size="60" maxlength="100"></td>
</tr>
```

The same thing should be done to each of the first five rows in the table—the last of which is the row that contains the zip code entry.

Next we need to class the labels in each row. While we're at it, let's also class each cell that contains form inputs so that we have the hook there to use if necessary. To avoid potential confusion, we'll use the class names `lbl` and `inp` instead of the names `label` and `input`, which are also the names of HTML elements.

```
<table cellspacing="0">
<tr class="required">
<td class="lbl">First name:</td>
<td class="inp"><input type="text" name="userFName" size="60"
maxlength="100"></td>
</tr>
```

Now we just need to add those classes for the cells in every row of the table (not just the first five). It's a little repetitive, but the effort will pay off in spades later on.

On the Use of `cellspacing`

The HTML-based `cellspacing="0"` is used because it's the only widely supported way to control the spacing between table cells. CSS2 does have a mechanism for doing the same thing, but support is minimal. The HTML attributes `cellpadding` and `border`, on the other hand, are both unnecessary because support for the CSS properties `padding` and `border` is very widespread.

Now that we have these hooks in, let's start styling the document. We might need to add in more classes or IDs later on, but what we've done so far is a good foundation for getting started.

Styling the Document

To make the process as smooth as possible, we'll create the screen styles first and then switch over to create the print styles. This will enable us to arrive at a look we like and then create print styles that echo it as much as is feasible.

Label Styles

The simplest style to accomplish is to right-align and boldface the input labels, so let's start there (see Figure 7.2).

```
<title>Register to Win!</title>
<style type="text/css" media="screen">
td.lbl {font-weight: bold; text-align: right;}
</style>
</head>
```

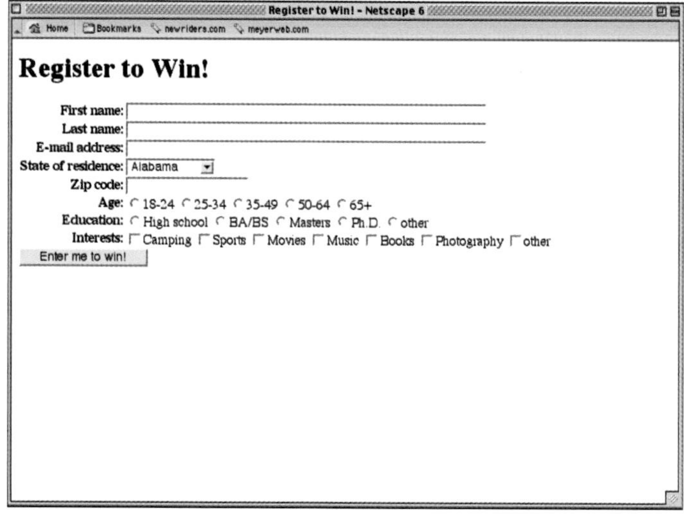

FIGURE 7.2

Styling the labels makes the form a little more professional.

Why Start with screen?

We're setting up the screen styles first because it's easier to style for the screen, then set up print styles, and then determine which styles should be applied in both screen and print media.

Spreading Out the Lines

The form seems a bit crowded at the moment, so let's spread it out a bit. We can do this in a number of ways, but the most robust solution is to add some padding to all of the table cells. This enables us to establish a consistent spacing throughout the form. It's usually easier on the eyes to spread things out vertically, so we'll make the top and bottom padding larger than the right and left.

```
<style type="text/css" media="screen">
td {padding: 0.25em 1px;}
td.lbl {font-weight: bold; text-align: right;}
```

The spacing between each line of text is now, at a minimum, half the `font-size` of the text in the form. The one-pixel left and right padding throws in a just a hint of separation without actually pushing things too far apart (see Figure 7.3).

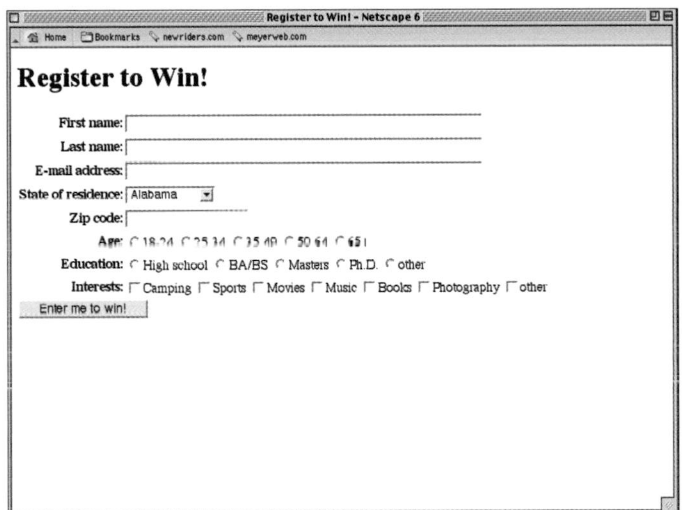

FIGURE 7.3

Increased padding pushes the lines of text apart.

Padding and NN4.x

Applying padding to table cells can lead to major layout problems in Netscape Navigator 4.x. For example, padded cells have been known to become as wide as the browser window, forcing the rest of the table offscreen.

Required Information

For the required fields, we have a wide range of choices. We could color the labels, highlight the rows by filling in the background, italicize the label text, or any number of things. Let's try highlighting the rows themselves by filling in the backgrounds of the table cells with a light red color (see Figure 7.4).

```
td.lbl {font-weight: bold; text-align: right;}
tr.required td {background: #FCC;}   /* a light red */
</style>
```

This seems like a good idea at first, but it looks a little weird with the white form elements embedded in a large block of red. Let's pull back the highlighting so that it only appears behind the labels themselves.

```
td.lbl {font-weight: bold; text-align: right;}
tr.required td.lbl {background: #FCC;}   /* a light red */
</style>
```

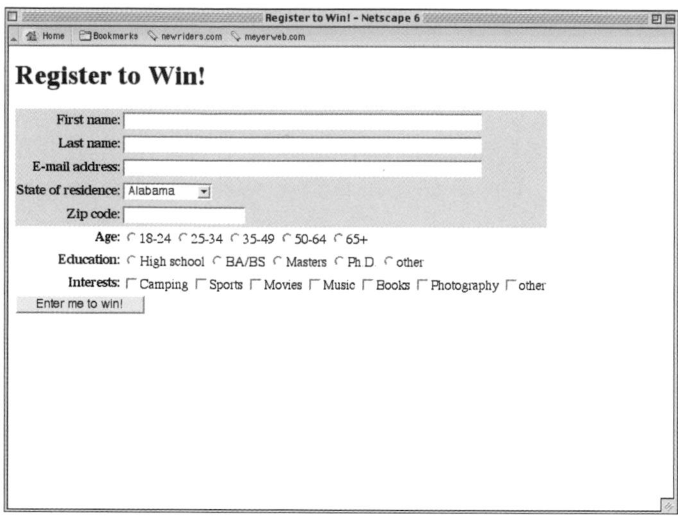

FIGURE 7.4

Giving the required information a red highlight.

Now we have the light red backing restricted to only the “label” cells within the “required” rows. This seems a bit too subtle, though, so let’s punch up the visual effect by adding a bright red border down the left side of the labels (see Figure 7.5).

```
tr.required td.lbl {background: #FCC; border-left: 0.5em solid red;}
</style>
```

FIGURE 7.5

Styling the labels works out a little better.

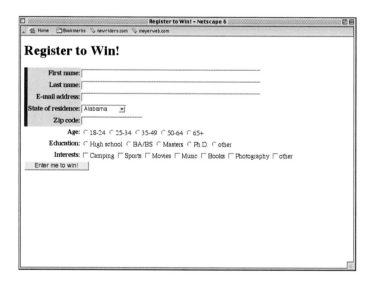

That’s pretty good, but now the optional labels look kind of odd with no styling at all. We can’t give them the same highlight, but we can use a variant—green instead of red, let’s say.

```
tr.required td.lbl {background: #FCC; border-left: 0.5em solid red;}
td.lbl {background: #CFC; border-left: 0.5em solid green;}
</style>
```

This rule applies a light green background and bright green left border to all cells with a class of `lbl`. Thanks to the greater specificity of the required rule, its values will win out over the `td.lbl` rule, so the required rows will still use red.

Because we now have some indication of which fields are required, we need to add some text explaining this so that users know what the red means. Let's just insert some text below the submit button because users are pretty certain to look in that area before they submit the form.

```
</table>
<input type="submit" value="Enter me to win!"><br>
Fields highlighted with red labels <strong>must</strong> be filled in
</form>
```

Another Approach

We could accomplish the same visual effect for the required rows by replacing `border-left: 0.5em solid red;` with `border-color: red;`. This approach works by letting the border style and width be set by the `td.lbl` rule and simply changing the border's color. See the file `ch0706-alt.html` for an illustration of this approach.

The Submit Area

Having the warning text and submit button jammed up against the form and the left margin doesn't look so good, so let's change that. First we need a structural hook in the form of a `div` with an `id`.

```
</table>
<div id="submitArea">
<input type="submit" value="Enter me to win!"><br>
Fields highlighted with red <strong>must</strong> be filled in
</div>
</form>
```

Now we center the text and button and push it downward so that it's visually distinct from the rest of the form (see Figure 7.6).

```
td.lbl {background: #CFC; border-left: 0.5em solid green;}
div#submitArea {text-align: center; margin-top: 1em;
   padding-top: 1em;}
</style>
```

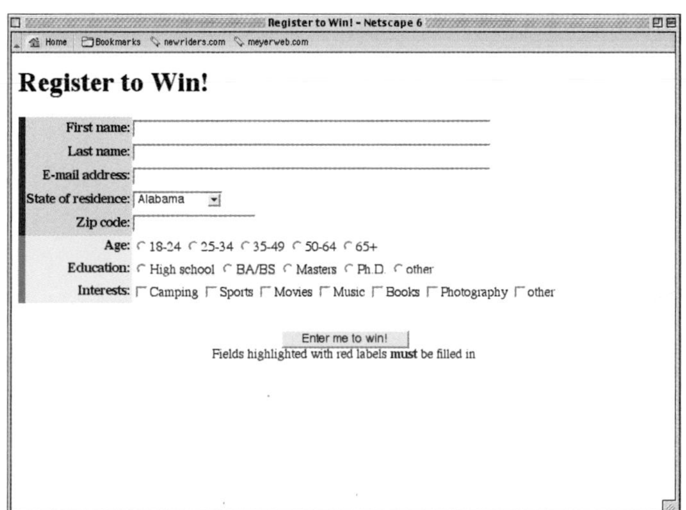

FIGURE 7.6

Styling the advisory text and centering the content at the bottom of the form, and more label styles.

Styling the Title

Now that we have a consistent style for the labels, this would be a good time to tie in the title "Register to Win!" Let's give it a red border along the bottom to make it consistent with the labels, and eliminate its bottom margin in the process.

Margins and Padding

We used both padding and margin in case we later want to put a top border on this `div`. See Project 3, "Styling an Events Calendar," for examples of why this is a good idea.

```
<style type="text/css" media="screen">
h1 {font-family: sans-serif; border-bottom: 0.1em solid #F33;
   margin-bottom: 0;}
td {padding: 0.25em 1px;}
```

The result is, at least to most eyes, a title that doesn't stick out like such a sore thumb compared to the rest of the form.

Focus Styles

Before we leave screen styling, let's set up a rule that changes the look of form elements when they have focus. The element that's currently ready to accept input is the one with focus (for example, whichever form element will take the user's keyboard input). Perhaps a nice bright yellow?

```
div#submitArea {text-align: center; margin-top: 1em; padding-top: 1em;}
input:focus {background: yellow;}
</style>
```

This new rule will give a `yellow` background to whatever `input` element is currently the focus of user input (see Figure 7.7). That means the rule will skip the `select` element, so our drop-down list won't have a yellow background while we use it—but that's probably for the best anyway.

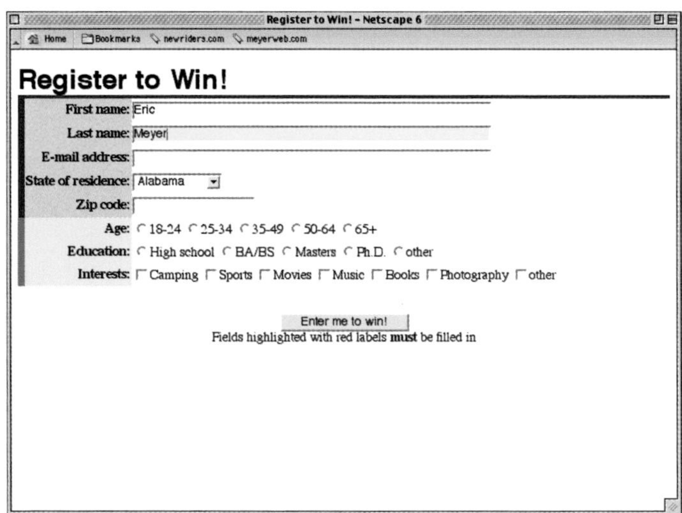

FIGURE 7.7

Giving a yellow background to the current input.

With that, we've finished our screen-media styling. Listing 7.1 shows the complete style sheet for the screen.

Styling All `input` Elements

The new rule will also style radio buttons, check boxes, and even the submit button because they're all different kinds of `input` element. This might not be so bad if not for the inconsistencies browsers have with styling radio buttons and check boxes. A little later in this project we'll run into a similar problem, work around it, and at that point come back to correct the `input:focus` rule so that it applies only to the text input fields.

Listing 7.1 The Screen-Media Style Sheet

```
<style type="text/css" media="screen">
h1 {font-family: sans-serif; border-bottom: 0.125em solid #F33;
   margin-bottom: 0;}
td {padding: 0.25em 1px;}
td.lbl {font-weight: bold; text-align: right;}
tr.required td.lbl {background: #FCC; border-left: 0.5em solid red;}
td.lbl {background: #CFC; border-left: 0.5em solid green;}
div#submitArea {text-align: center; margin-top: 1em; padding-top: 1em;}
input:focus {background: yellow;}
</style>
```

Print Styles

Now it's time to get the page styled for print media. As always, the first step is to hide the screen styles by temporarily setting them to apply to some other medium. This time we'll pick `tty` just for the heck of it.

```
<style type="text/css" media="tty">
h1 {font-family: sans-serif; border-bottom: 0.125em solid #F33;
   margin-bottom: 0;}
```

This will prevent the screen-media styles from appearing while we work on the print styles. It also returns the page to its initial, unstyled state. (See Figure 7.1 for a reminder of what it looks like.) This is exactly what we want; things would get too confusing if we didn't do it this way.

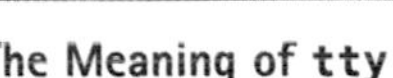

The Meaning of `tty`

The value `tty` refers to teletype media, which no browser supports. By setting a style sheet to this media, we're effectively hiding it from the browser. This is a convenient way to clear our style palate, so to speak, while we work on the print styles.

Now we set up two new style sheets: one for all media and the other (temporarily) for screen media. It's the latter that will eventually become our print style sheet. We're making it a screen-media style sheet purely so that we can see what we're doing onscreen. Otherwise, we'd have to do something silly like print a new copy of the document at every step or at least open the print preview (in those browsers that even have one) just to check our work. Hitting Reload to see the changes is a lot simpler.

```
<style type="text/css" media="all">
</style>
<style type="text/css" media="screen">
</style>
<style type="text/css" media="tty">
```

The all-media style sheet immediately gets a rule: the boldfaced, right-aligned label rule, which should apply no matter what media we're using. In this case, we'll move the entire rule from our old screen style sheet into the all-media style sheet (see Figure 7.8).

```
<style type="text/css" media="all">
td.lbl {font-weight: bold; text-align: right;}
</style>
<style type="text/css" media="screen">
</style>
<style type="text/css" media="tty">
h1 {font-family: sans-serif; border-bottom: 0.125em solid #F33;
   margin-bottom: 0;}
td {padding: 0.25em 1px;}
/* the 'td.lbl {...}' rule used to be here */
tr.required td.lbl {background: #FCC; border-left: 0.5em solid red;}
```

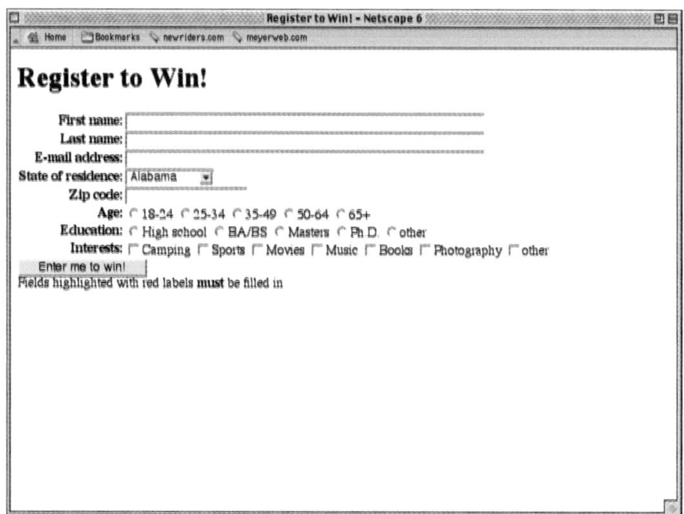

FIGURE 7.8

Reproducing the label styles with an all-media style sheet.

Okay, we're really starting over here…but it won't last long. Let's put off spreading the lines apart and instead turn the text inputs and the drop-down list into blanks to be filled.

Filling Out the Blanks

With the labels done, it's time to concentrate on the `input` elements and how they're presented in print. The key here is to realize that the beveled edges of text inputs and drop-down menus are just borders. Therefore, all we have to do is turn off the top, left, and right borders and then set the bottom border to be a 1-pixel solid black line (see Figure 7.9).

```
<style type="text/css" media="screen">
input, select {border-width: 0; border-bottom: 1px solid black;}
</style>
```

FIGURE 7.9

Making the input blanks into "write here" lines.

Two things should jump out at you. First, the word "Alabama" is already sitting there, which is great if you live there but not so useful if you happen to reside in any of the 49 other states. Second, all of the radio buttons and check boxes (and even the submit button) are being affected by our new rule. We need to change that posthaste, so let's do it right away.

Because the only inputs that need to become blanks are in the "required" rows, we could construct a rule targeted that way, but we might later have input boxes in optional rows, and it's better to plan for such things now. Therefore, we'll add a class to each input that needs to be "written in" by the pen-and-paper user.

```
<td class="inp"><input type="text" class="writein" name="userFName" size="60"
maxlength="100"></td>
```

Adding this new class to the four text inputs and the select element lets us mark the elements that should be turned into write-in blanks. Then we change our CSS to make use of this hook.

```
<style type="text/css" media="screen">
.writein {border-width: 0; border-bottom: 1px solid black;}
</style>
```

While we're at it, remember from earlier in this project that the yellow-background focus style will be applied to all `input` elements, including check boxes and radio buttons. We can take advantage of the change we just made to prevent this from happening. All we have to do is go back into the `tty` style sheet and add the class name `writein` to a single rule.

```
div#submitArea {text-align: center; margin-top: 1em; padding-top: 1em;}
input.writein:focus {background: yellow;}
</style>
```

This will keep the yellow highlighting out of the radio buttons and check boxes.

Submitting to Win!

In this case, our submit button has been labeled "Enter Me to Win!" using the `value` attribute. If you've never seen this done before, check the source code for any of this project's example files.

What's the Problem?

If you try to set the background of radio buttons, some browsers will color in not only the small circle, but will also create a sort of "box" around the outside of the circle. This is why we've taken the step of restricting our focus style so that it only applies to a few form elements.

Now let's deal with the word "Alabama" showing up in the printed form. The simplest course is to simply make the text white (see Figure 7.10).

```
.writein {border-width: 0; border-bottom: 1px solid black;}
select.writein {color: white;}
</style>
```

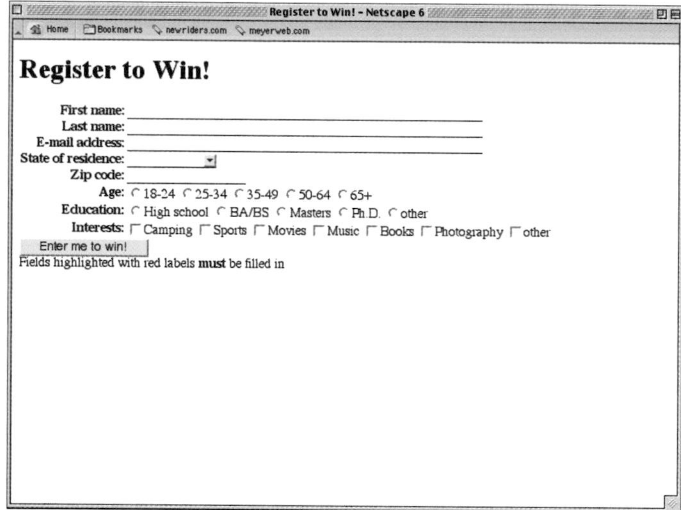

FIGURE 7.10

Blanking out the drop-down (mostly).

This blanks out the text, but it doesn't necessarily get rid of the drop-down arrow. If that's too bothersome to allow, the next section looks at ways to get around it.

Another Approach to `select`

The previous solution (setting the `select` text to be white) works relatively well because, when printed, anything white won't appear. However, we have the remains of the drop-down to consider: In IE5.x for Windows, the drop-down arrow doesn't disappear with the text. There is another way to replace the entire element with a blank line, although it does require some structural hacking.

The first thing to do is insert an empty `span` into the document.

```
</select>
<span id="stateBlank"> </span>
</td>
```

This will be the element that turns into a write-in blank, thanks to the CSS we're about to write. The first step, though, is to prevent the `select` from appearing at all.

```
.writein {border-width: 0; border-bottom: 1px solid black;}
select.writein {display: none;}
</style>
```

Now we need to get the span to appear (see Figure 7.11). This involves promoting it to block-level status. Why? Because only block-level elements can be given a width or a height, and we'll need to do both.

```
select.writein {display: none;}
span#stateBlank {display: block; width: 10em; height: 1em;
   border-bottom: 1px solid black;}
</style>
```

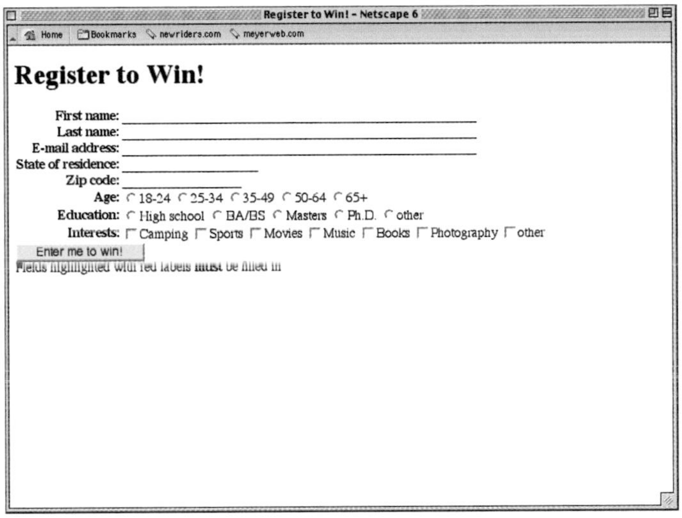

FIGURE 7.11

Using a span *to create a "write here" line for the printed version.*

The width value stretches out the span so that it looks like a blank. Any length or percentage would do, really, but 10em seems like a good value for these circumstances. The height value makes the span the same height as the surrounding text—by default, a block-level element will be as short as possible, which could lead to weird misalignments. This might happen anyway: HTML and CSS don't equal the precision of Postscript or PDF. The big advantage here is that it's really easy to change the size and placement of the blank, if necessary.

Although using the span isn't the best solution in terms of keeping the document structure clean, it does give us more influence over how the blank will be rendered, so we'll hang on to it.

Opening Up Some Space

Now would be an excellent time to push the entry lines apart, as we did for the screen display earlier in the project. As it is, things are rather cramped, and we should provide extra room to accommodate people's writing styles. Once again, we'll accomplish this by adding some padding to the table cells (see Figure 7.12).

```
<style type="text/css" media="screen">
td {padding: 0.5em 0.125em;}
.writein {border-width: 0; border-bottom: 1px solid black;}
```

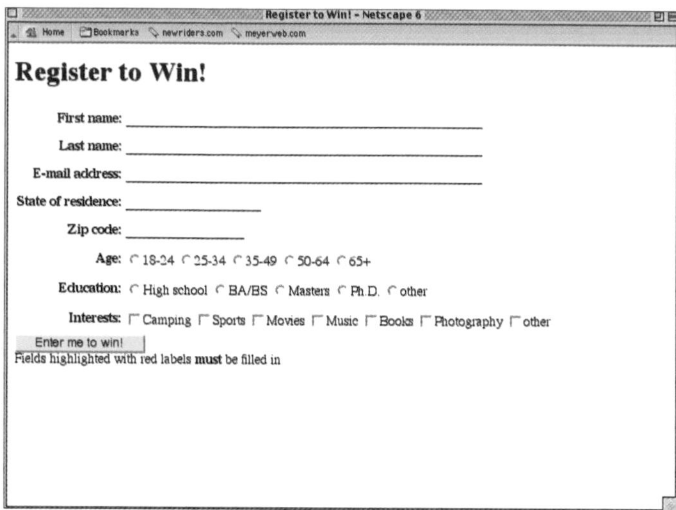

FIGURE 7.12

Opening up the line spacing using padding.

Rather than just duplicate the values we used for screen media, here we've used font-based spaces (thanks to the unit `em`) to push the lines apart. Because one-half em has been added to the top and bottom of every table cell, there is at least one em of space between each entry line. This effectively gives us a full "blank line" between the content of each row.

The Submit Area (Again)

In keeping with the project directives, we need to get rid of the submit button when printing. We should also turn off the "required fields in red" message because it won't apply in the printed version of the form. As you may recall, we already wrapped this section of the document in a `div`.

```
<div id="submitArea">
<input type="submit" value="Enter me to win!"><br>
(Fields highlighted with red labels <strong>must</strong> be filled in)
</div>
```

Now all we have to do it turn off display of the entire `div` (see Figure 7.13).

```
span#stateBlank {display: block; width: 10em; height: 1em;
   border-bottom: 1px solid black;}
div#submitArea {display: none;}
</style>
```

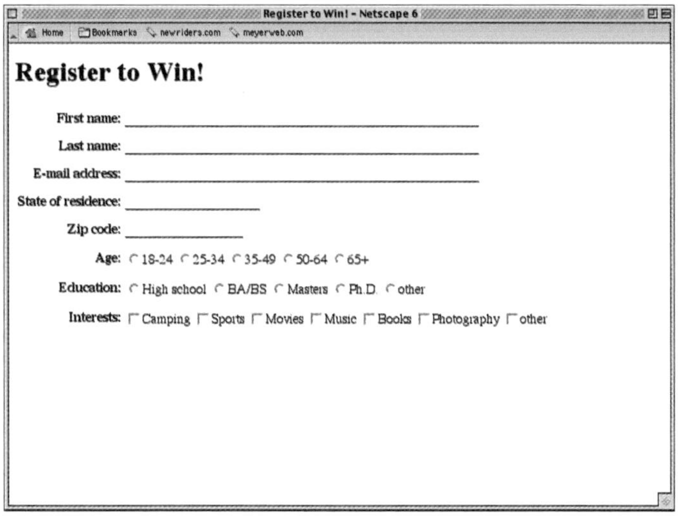

FIGURE 7.13

Turning off the screen-related submit and advisory text.

Having done this, we need to insert information regarding where to send the printed form.

Adding the Address

Because the original form doesn't have U.S. mail information, we'll have to add it ourselves, right before the end of the entire form element.

```
</div>
<div id="mailArea">
<p>
Mail to:<br>
Make Me A Winner Inc.<br>
4141 West 42nd St.<br>
Old York, OK 00100-1010<br>
</p>
</div>
</form>
```

To keep some consistency, let's give this `div` the same basic styles we gave to the "submit area" `div`, in which we centered the text and added some top padding and margin. Rather than reproduce the same styles in this style sheet, let's give both the "mail area" and "submit area" `divs` a common class.

```
<div id="submitArea" class="formEnd">
<input type="submit" value="Enter me to win!"><br>
(Fields highlighted with red labels <strong>must</strong> be filled in)
</div>
<div id="mailArea" class="formEnd">
<p>
Mail to:<br>
```

Now we can move the `submitArea` rule into the all-media style sheet and rename it so that it applies to any `div` with a `class` of `formEnd`. Now the end-of-form information will be consistently styled in both screen and print media (see Figure 7.14).

```
<style type="text/css" media="all">
td.lbl {text-align: right; font-weight: bold;}
div.formEnd {text-align: center; padding-top: 1em; margin-top: 1em;}
</style>
<style type="text/css" media="tty">
h1 {font-family: sans-serif; border-bottom: 0.125em solid #F33;
   margin-bottom: 0;}
tr.required td.lbl {border-left: 0.5em solid red; background: #FCC;}
td.lbl {border-left: 0.5em solid green; background: #CFC;}
/* the 'div#submitArea' rule used to be here */
input.writein:focus {background: yellow;}
```

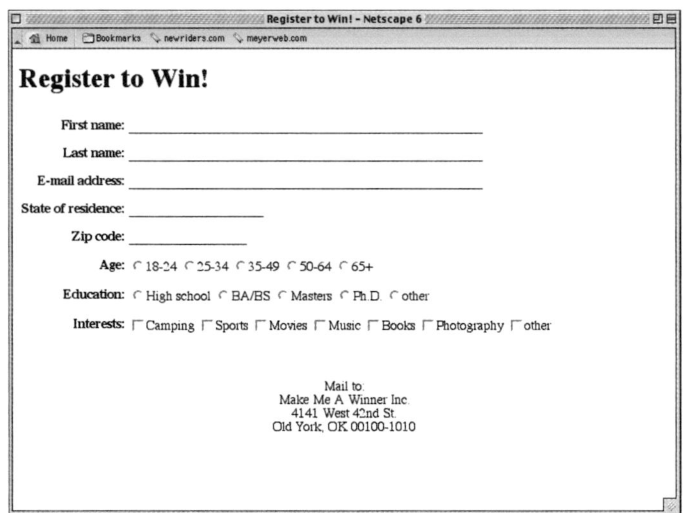

FIGURE 7.14

Bringing cross-media consistency to the end of the form.

Indicating Required Data

We still haven't written print styles to indicate that certain information is required. A common effect is to boldface the labels of required fields, but we've already boldfaced all of the labels, so that won't work. Instead we could italicize the text, for example, or underline the labels. Let's do the latter.

```
td {padding: 0.5em 0.125em;}
tr.required td.lbl {text-decoration: underline;}
.writein {border-width: 0; border-bottom: 1px solid black;}
```

We also ought to put in a note explaining what the underlining means.

```
<div id="mailArea" class="formEnd">
Underlined fields <strong>must</strong> be filled in
<p>
Mail to:<br>
```

One More Print Style

Before we finish, let's add in one more style just for fun. To make it stand out a little better, let's boldface the phrase "Mail to:" at the end of the form. In many circumstances, it would be necessary to place an element around the words, like a `span` or even a `strong`, but we don't have to do that here. Instead, all we need is a simple rule (see Figure 7.15).

```
div#submitArea {display: none;}
div#mailArea p:first-line {font-weight: bold;}
</style>
```

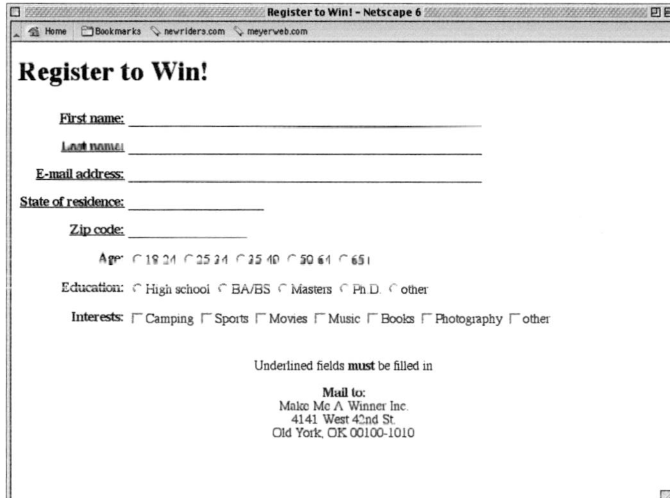

FIGURE 7.15

Boldfacing the first line of the advisory text.

We can get away with this because there is only one paragraph inside the `mailArea` and it's the one containing the address. Because the words we want to boldface are the first line of that paragraph, the new rule has the desired effect. Had there been other paragraphs in the `div`, we might have had to place an `id` on the "Mail to:" paragraph, but because of the way we set up our document structure, that wasn't necessary here. (It's almost like it was planned that way…)

Finishing Up

Now that we have the print styles finished, let's switch the media values back so that the styles actually apply to the media for which they're intended (see Figure 7.16).

```
<style type="text/css" media="screen">
h1 {font-family: sans-serif; border-bottom: 0.125em solid #F33;
   margin-bottom: 0;}
tr.required td.lbl {border-left: 0.5em solid red; background: #FCC;}
td.lbl {border-left: 0.5em solid green; background: #CFC;}
div#mailArea {display: none;}
input.writein:focus {background: yellow;}
</style>
<style type="text/css" media="print">
td {padding: 0.5em 0.125em;}
```

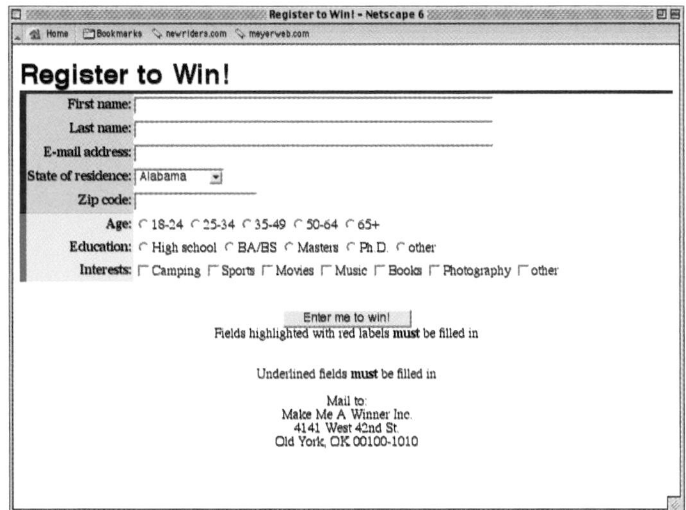

FIGURE 7.16

Returning to the screen styles, we discover a problem.

As you can see, the U.S. mail address we added for printing appears onscreen, and we don't want to see it here. You probably already know what's coming.

```
td.lbl {border-left: 0.5em solid green; background: #CFC;}
div#mailArea {display: none;}
input.writein:focus {background: yellow;}
```

So now we have three style sheets in total—one for all media and one each for screen and print media—all participating in the display of the form. Listing 7.2 presents the complete CSS for this form, and we can compare shots of the screen (see Figure 7.17) and print (see Figure 7.18) versions of the page.

Listing 7.2 The Complete Set of Style Sheets

```
<style type="text/css" media="all">
td.lbl {font-weight: bold; text-align: right;}
div.formEnd {text-align: center; padding-top: 1em; margin-top: 1em;}
</style>
<style type="text/css" media="print">
td {padding: 0.5em 0.125em;}
tr.required td.lbl {text-decoration: underline;}
.writein {border-width: 0; border-bottom: 1px solid black;}
select.writein {display: none;}
```

```
span#stateBlank {display: block; width: 10em; height: 1em;
   border-bottom: 1px solid black;}
div#submitArea {display: none;}
div#mailArea p:first-line {font-weight: bold;}
</style>
<style type="text/css" media="screen">
h1 {font-family: sans-serif; border-bottom: 0.125em solid #F33;
   margin-bottom: 0;}
td {padding: 0.25em 1px;}
tr.required td.lbl {background: #FCC; border-left: 0.5em solid red; }
td.lbl {background: #CFC; border-left: 0.5em solid green;}
div#mailArea {display: none;}
input.writein:focus {background: yellow;}
</style>
```

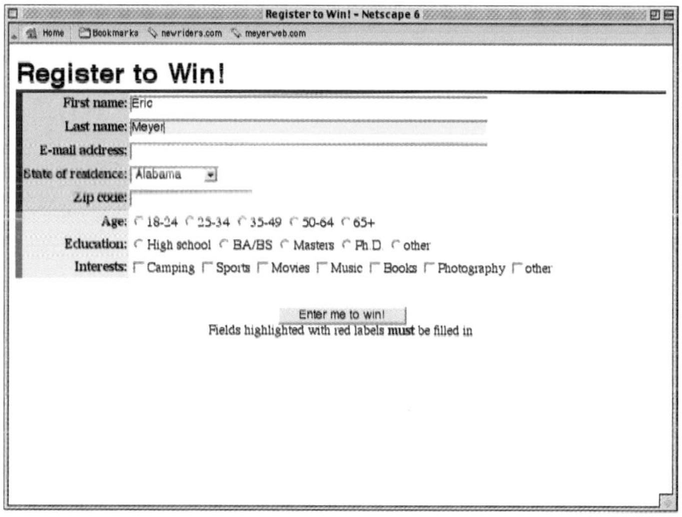

FIGURE 7.17

The final form in the screen medium.

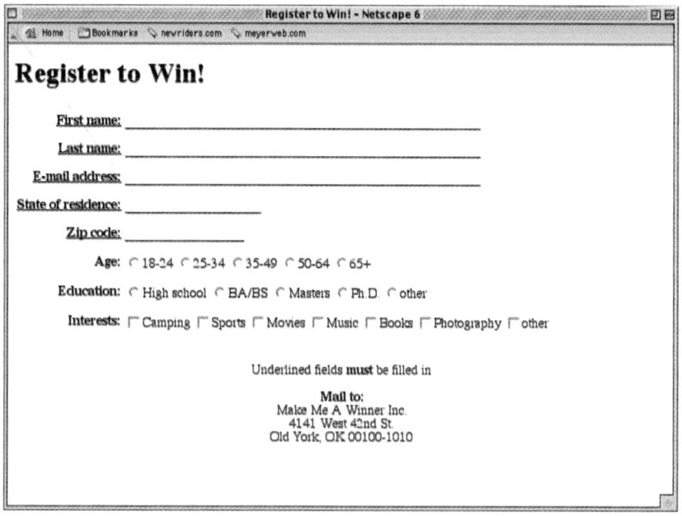

FIGURE 7.18

The final form in the print medium.

Branching Out

There are many other ways to style a form like the one we worked with in this project. Here are a few suggestions:

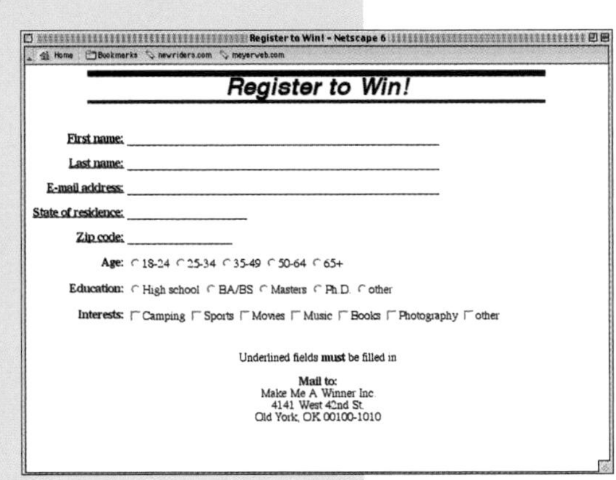

1. The `h1` element was intentionally left unstyled in the print style sheet. Try giving it one set of styles that helps it blend in both screen and print media and then try styling it very differently for each medium. In print, for example, it could be centered and have a noticeable bottom margin with no border or be given its own top and bottom borders to add some visual pizzazz.

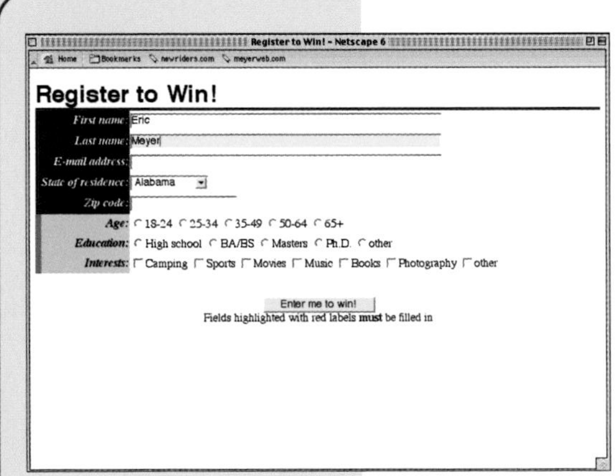

2. Indicate the required fields by setting the labels in reverse text—that is, white text on a dark background. You could even italicize the text at the same time to really get the point across or carry that style through to all of the labels. Try it in either medium!

3. Try setting the width of the `writein input` elements using CSS instead of HTML. You could also give the fields a subtle background color so that they stand out a little bit from the white page background, or you could boldface the text in the input that has focus.

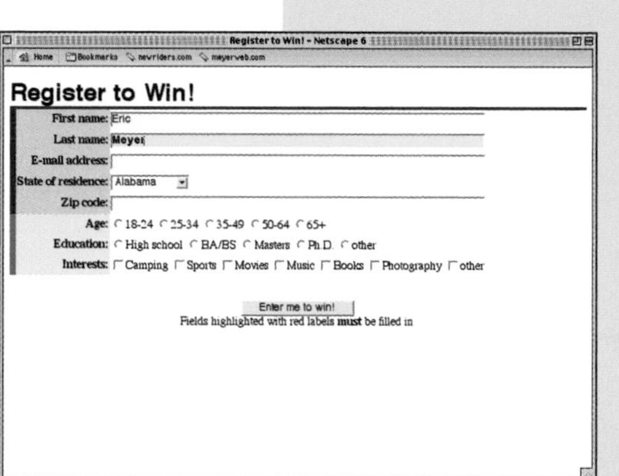

8

Creating an Online Greeting Card

You have to put up with about four years of disgrace when you receive Christmas cards and do not send them, but after that, you know that the people who send you Christmas cards are doing it to please you and that they don't expect a reply.

—*Quentin Crisp* (as quoted by Jon Winokur)

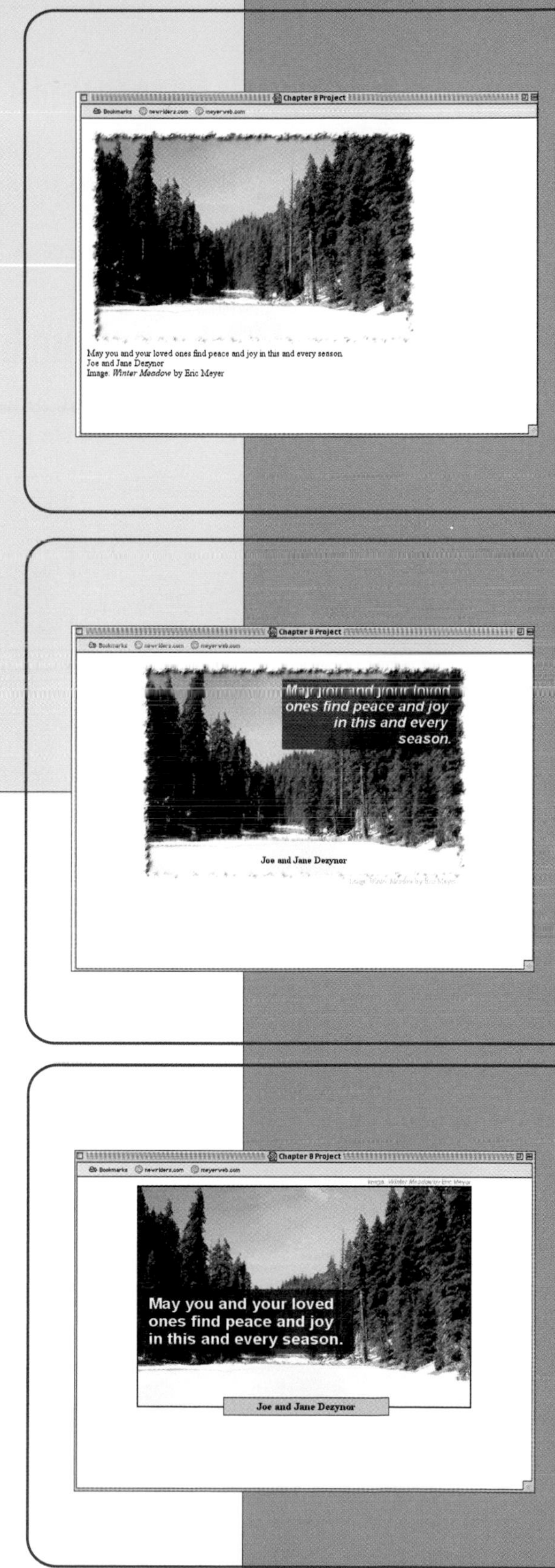

Chapter 8 Project
May you and your loved ones find peace and joy in this and every season.
Joe and Jane Dezynor
Image: Winter Meadow by Eric Meyer
Chapter 8 Project
May you and your loved ones find peace and joy in this and every season.
Joe and Jane Dezynor
Chapter 8 Project
May you and your loved ones find peace and joy in this and every season.
Joe and Jane Dezynor

If you're reading this book, it stands to reason that you probably spend a good deal of time online. It further stands to reason that you probably know a number of people—friends, colleagues, clients, and so on—who are also online. So, in the true digital spirit, why not send them a handcrafted online holiday greeting card? It can be a very merry electric Christmas (or other end-of-year holiday of your choice) for everyone!

Project Goals

Our primary goal here is to create a visually pleasing card to send out to friends and colleagues. We'll accomplish this by using basic positioning to place text over an image, and we'll look at ways to keep the text from fading into parts of the image that are a close color match. Then we'll create alternate card looks by repositioning the text elements with respect to the base image. By the end, we'll have three different layouts for this card.

Preparation

See the Introduction for instructions on how to download the files from the Web site.

Download the files for Project 8 from this book's Web site. If you're planning to play along at home, load the file `ch08proj.html` into the editing program of your choice. This is the file you'll be editing, saving, and reloading as the project progresses.

Laying the Groundwork

First we need an image and a sentiment appropriate to the season. Figure 8.1 shows what we have to start with.

Figure 8.1

The basic greeting card, not yet styled with CSS.

To allow for effective styling, we need to add to the page structure. In this case, we're going to want maximum flexibility, so we'll enclose each line in its own `div` and wrap the whole thing in an overarching `div`. Along the way, we'll knock out all of the `<br>` elements because we won't need them any more. The block-level nature of the `div` elements will take care of the line breaking for us. Listing 8.1 shows the changes.

Listing 8.1 The Document with its New `divs`.

```
<!DOCTYPE HTML PUBLIC "-//W3C//DTD HTML 4.0 Transitional//EN"
                      "http://www.w3.org/TR/REC-html40/loose.dtd">
<html>
<head>
<title>Chapter 8 Project</title>
</head>
<body>
<div id="card">
<img src="card-image.jpg" alt="A winter meadow scene" id="image">
<div id="sentiment">
```

```
May you and your loved ones find peace and joy in this and every season.
</div>
<div id="signature">
Joe and Jane Dezynor
</div>
<div id="credit">
Image: <cite>Winter Meadow</cite> by Eric Meyer
</div>
</div>
</body>
</html>
```

The element `<div id="card">` might seem unnecessary, since it doesn't do much besides sit between the `body` and the contents. In fact, without that element to tie everything together, we'd have a much harder time with our styles to come.

Styling the Document

One of the most important things to know when styling this card is the size of the base image. In this case, it's 575 pixels wide by 384 pixels tall. In Web design, usually the width is more important than the height because elements tend to be made as tall as they need to be to contain their own content. This means that authors rarely have to worry about the height of an element, and they spend much more time worrying about how wide or narrow an element will be. We'll soon see that when it comes to positioning, height can play an important role in our thinking as well.

Centering the Card

To make our digital card a little more, well...card-like, we're going to center the content horizontally.

The best way to center the content is to set an explicit `width` value for the over-arching `div` and then give its right and left margins values of `auto`. When a block-level element like a `div` is given an explicit `width` and `auto` left and right margins, the margins are automatically set to equal widths, thus centering the element.

```
<style type="text/css" media="screen">
div#card {width: 575px; margin-left: auto; margin-right: auto;}
</style>
```

The problem is that the first version of Explorer to support this fairly simple operation is IE6, and even then it does so only when it's in "strict rendering" mode. Fortunately, there's a workaround that IE5.x/Win understands and that won't overly upset the layout we're trying to create.

A Choice of Media

We will be restricting this project's style sheet to the `screen` medium because the designs we're about to create aren't likely to print very well. Designs based on positioning often run into printing problems, and since we're also going to put text over images, that will make the printing even more problematic. Because these styles will be restricted to the screen, any printout will be the "unstyled" look with the text following the main image. This prevents any problems due to an over-lapping element.

Strict and Loose Rendering

When it comes to positioning and other advanced CSS topics, it is often important to know which rendering mode the browser is using. In modern browsers, the choice of rendering mode is controlled by the `DOCTYPE` at the top of the document.

See "Picking a Rendering Mode" on the Web site for details on this process.

In older versions of Explorer, the browser believed that if you set `text-align` to `center`, it would center not only text but also block-level elements like `divs`. This isn't how CSS is supposed to work, but that's what Explorer did. Thus, if we style the `body` element, we'll center the outer `div` in Explorer 5.x for Windows and earlier (not to mention IE6 in "loose rendering" mode).

```
<style type="text/css" media="screen">
body {text-align: center;}     /* IE5.x workaround */
div#card {width: 575px; margin-left: auto; margin-right: auto;}
```

With this extra rule working to overcome browser bugs, we've centered the card. We've also centered the text within the card, which isn't really what we were after, but it's all right for now. We can change that later on without much fuss.

To keep everything clear while we work with the card, let's add some borders to the `divs`. This will let us see where the browser is placing the elements (see Figure 8.2).

```
<style type="text/css" media="screen">
div {border: 1px dotted gray;}   /* temporary borders */
body {text-align: center;}       /* IE5.x workaround */
```

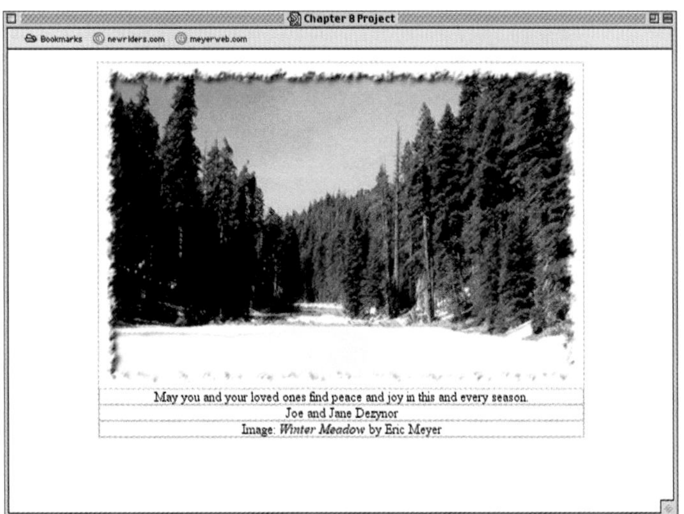

FIGURE 8.2

A centered card with centered text and elements bordered for clarity.

So now we have the card centered and the `div` borders set to aid us. That isn't really positioning, though—it's more a reformatting of normal content. To get into some real positioning, we'll need to lay down a foundation.

Establishing a Context

To be able to position elements, we first have to create a context. After all, you only position something in relation to something else. CSS terms this context a *containing block*, and by definition, any absolutely positioned element has a containing block. The only question is this: What constitutes that containing block?

The containing block for any absolutely positioned element is defined to be the closest ancestor element that has been positioned. In other words, if one of the absolutely positioned element's ancestors were also positioned in some way, then that's the containing block.

If there is no such positioned ancestor, however, then the containing block becomes the "root element," which is taken by browsers to be either the `body` or the `html` element. Thus, if we simply positioned our sentiment, its containing block would be the root element (see Figure 8.3).

```
div#card {width: 575px; margin-left: auto; margin-right: auto;}
div#sentiment {position: absolute; top: 0; right: 0; text-align: right;}
</style>
```

The Meaning of Absolute

There is a tendency to assume that an absolutely positioned element acts like a frame and doesn't scroll with the document. That's actually a good description of fixed-position elements. An absolutely positioned element is placed with respect to its containing block, and if the containing block scrolls with the document, so will the absolutely positioned element.

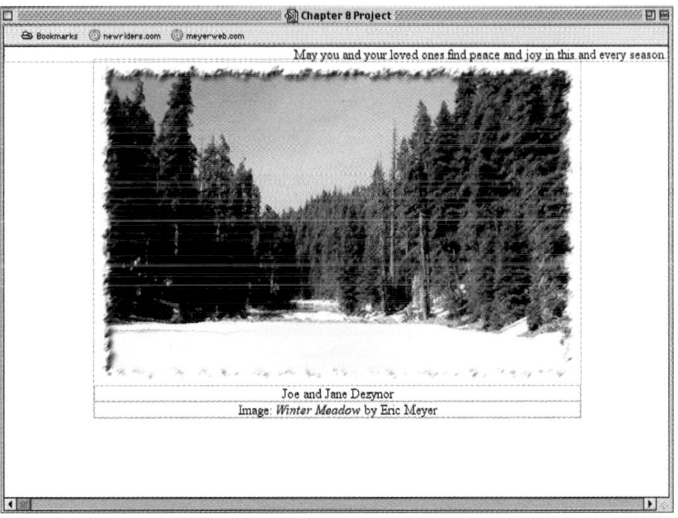
Chapter 8 Project
Bookmarks
newriders.com
meyerweb.com
May you and your loved ones find peace and joy in this and every season.
Joe and Jane Dezynor
Image: Winter Meadow by Eric Meyer

FIGURE 8.3

Positioning an element in the upper-right root element.

With this latest rule, we've managed to put the sentiment into the top right corner of the document, not the card. Because we want the sentiment to look like it's a part of the card, it would be a lot more convenient to have the containing block actually be the card itself. Fortunately, this will be very easy because we already have an element in the right place. All we have to do is position it.

```
body {text-align: center;}        /* IE5.x workaround */
div#card {width: 575px; margin-left: auto; margin-right: auto;
   position: relative;}
div#sentiment {position: absolute; top: 0; right: 0; text-align: right;}
```

Leaving the Normal Flow

Note that when we positioned the sentiment, its space in the normal document flow was "closed up." Check Figure 8.3 again, and you'll see that there is no space between the bottom of the image and the "Joe and Jane Dezynor" `div`. This is what should happen.

With this one simple addition, we've made the outermost `div` the containing block (positioning context) for all of the content within the card. Thus, if we absolutely position any of the `div`s within the card or even the image itself, the context in which we position will be the `div` with an `id` of `card`. Thus, the sentiment will now be positioned in the upper-right corner of the card, not the document.

This works because we've relatively positioned the outermost `div`, but we've done it without any offsets. Thus, the relatively positioned `div` stays exactly where it would have been if it hadn't been positioned at all, so visually there is no change. Despite this lack of movement, this `div` still establishes a containing block for all of its descendants and, thus, a context in which to absolutely position our signature, sentiment, and so on.

Preserving Legibility

If we're going to position text over an image, we need to take steps to ensure that it remains legible. We can make it larger, change its color, and so forth, but there's still the danger that the image's color and brightness will vary so that part of the message will be legible and part won't. Consider the effects of the following styles, in which we move the text down and leftward a bit, whiten it, and make it much larger (see Figure 8.4).

```
div#card {width: 575px; margin-left: auto; margin-right: auto;
   position: relative;}
div#sentiment {position: absolute; top: 30px; right: 25px; width: 50%;
   text-align: right; font: italic bold 25px Arial, sans-serif;
   color: white; }
</style>
```

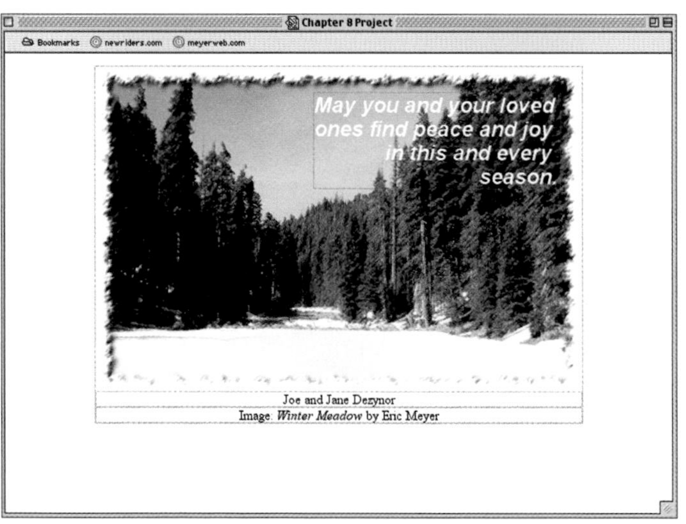

FIGURE 8.4

Placing text over an image can result in contrast problems.

A Pixel-Sized Font?

In most cases, fonts should not be sized using pixels because this can lead to accessibility problems. In this case, the pure visual nature of the design argues for the use of pixels. Even if we had used ems or percentages, though, the design would have survived fairly well.

By setting `top` to `30px` and `right` to `25px`, we've moved the element downward by 30 pixels and leftward by 25 pixels. This moves the text so that it isn't overlapping the ragged-edge border that decorates the base image. These two properties (along with `bottom` and `left`) define offsets from the edges of the containing block. Thus, we've set the top outer edge of the sentiment to be 30 pixels below the top edge of the containing block and its right outer edge 25 pixels to the left of the left edge of the containing block.

Offset Properties

Because their values define an offset distance between the edge of a positioned element and its containing block, `top`, `right`, `bottom`, and `left` are often referred to as the *offset properties*.

Although at this point the text is fairly legible, it's still hard on the eyes as we try to read it, and we move from a light background to a dark background and back again. We need to smooth out the contrast between the text and the image.

To accomplish this, we're going to give the sentiment a background image but not just any old image. Using a trick learned from Todd Fahrner, a Web design veteran and highly respected CSS expert, what we're going to apply to the sentiment is what's called a *halfscreen* image. Basically, it's a checkerboard pattern of colored and transparent pixels (see Figure 8.5).

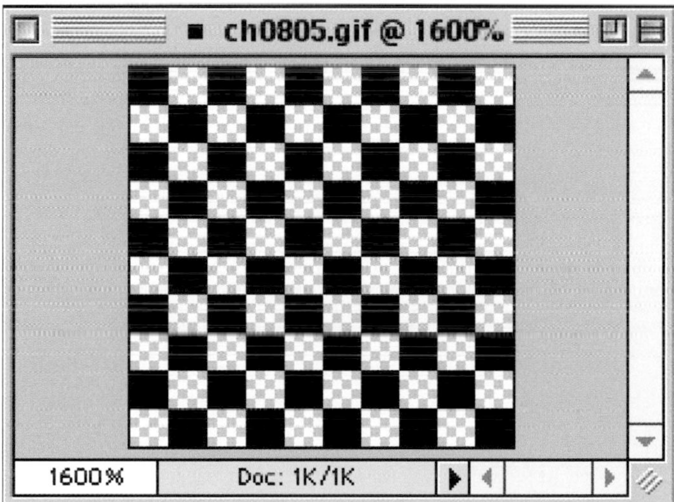

FIGURE 8.5

A halfscreen background image at 1600% normal size, as seen in Photoshop.

Every black pixel seen in this expanded view will be drawn onscreen, but the other pixels are transparent and will allow whatever is behind them to show through. When we add this background image—along with a little padding—to our sentiment, we get a much more legible block of text (see Figure 8.6).

```
div#sentiment {position: absolute; top: 30px; right: 25px; width: 50%;
   text-align: right; font: italic bold 25px Arial, sans-serif;
   color: white; padding: 5px;
   background: transparent url(halfscreen-black.gif) center repeat;}
</style>
```

FIGURE 8.6

The sentiment is now much easier to read, yet it still allows the card's image to show through.

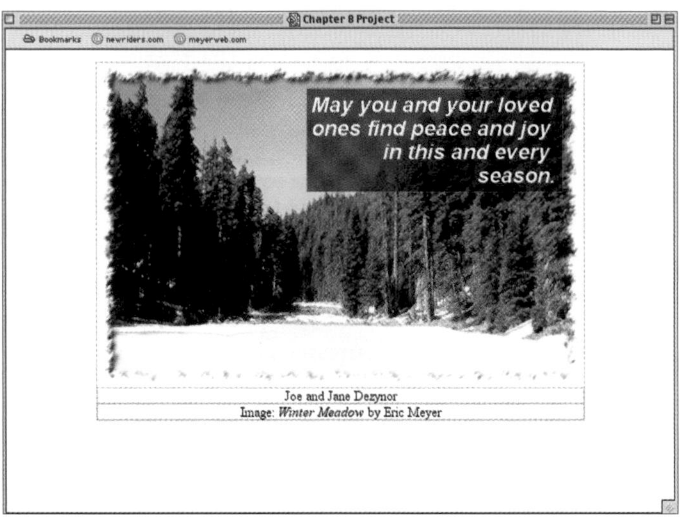

Chapter 8 Project
May you and your loved ones find peace and joy in this and every season.
Joe and Jane Dezynor
Image: Winter Meadow by Eric Meyer

Temporary Borders

Remember that the border around the sentiment is a relic of our "show me all the `divs`" rule, and it will go away before we're done with the project.

Note that the halfscreen we're using is a 10×10 image. It would be possible to go as small as 2×2, but trying to tile so small a background image can significantly slow down browsers when they try to render the card. Because the download time between a 2×2 image and a 10×10 image is practically the same (even over a modem), we're using the larger version to make browsers a little happier.

Signing the Card

Now let's place the signature within the context of the card. Let's center and boldface the text and place it near the bottom of the image. The simplest way to handle this is to set an offset from the top of the containing block and add a style for boldfacing.

```
div#sentiment {position: absolute; top: 30px; right: 25px; width: 50%;
   text-align: right; font: italic bold 25px Arial, sans-serif;
   color: white; padding: 5px;
   background: transparent url(halfscreen-black.gif) center repeat;}
div#signature {position: absolute; top: 335px; left: 0; right: 0;
   width: 100%; font-weight: bold;}
</style>
```

Left, Right, and Width

We've given explicit values to `left` and `right` as well as `width` to dodge positioning bugs in Explorer. Omitting one or more of these values, even though it should be possible to do so, can lead to misaligned or even missing elements in IE5.x.

Now that we've positioned the signature, its space is also closed up so that the credit is now just beneath the image. The signature has been placed so that its top edge is 335 pixels from the top edge of the containing block (see Figure 8.7).

The text is centered because the `text-align` value `center` has been inherited from our IE5.x workaround, which is rather convenient. We've set the `width` to `100%` because it ensures that browsers will keep the `div`'s block as wide as the overall card, and thus put the text in the center of the card.

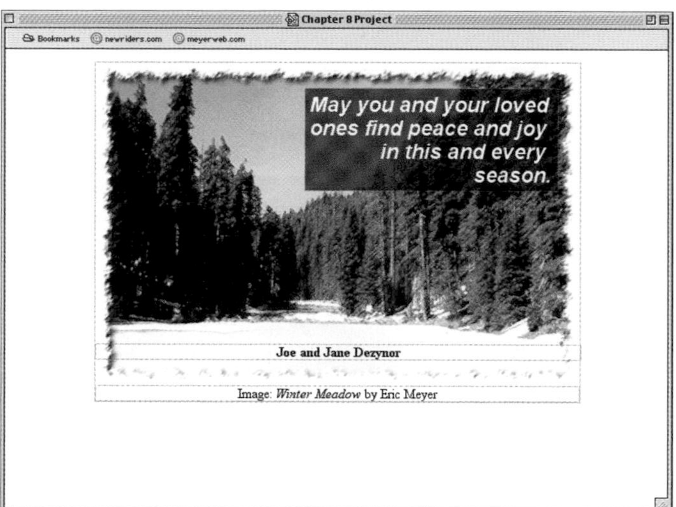

FIGURE 8.7

The signature is placed, relying on inherited as well as newly assigned styles.

Styling the Credit

The last major component we have to tackle is the credit at the bottom of the image. We don't want it to detract too much from the card as a whole, so we'll just reduce the font size and set the text to be a light gray and right aligned. Furthermore, we'll shift it upward a few pixels so that it's overlapping the very bottom of the image a bit (see Figure 8.8).

```
div#signature {position: absolute; top: 335px; left: 0; right: 0;
   width: 100%; font-weight: bold;}
div#credit {color: silver; font-size: 80%; text-align: right;
   position: relative; top: -10px;}
</style>
```

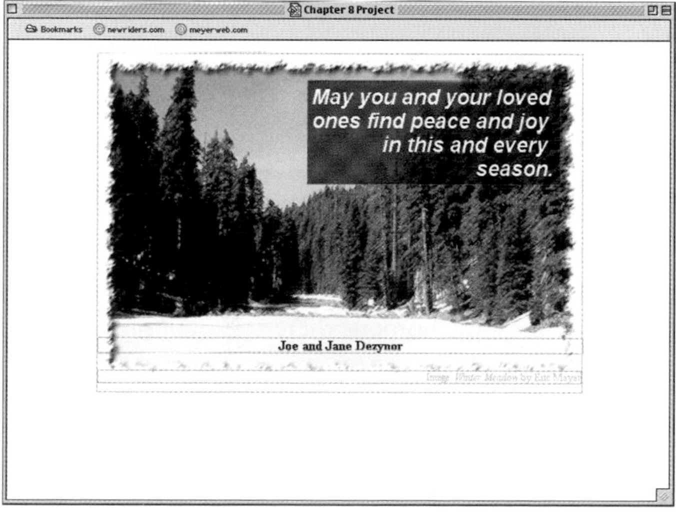

FIGURE 8.8

The credit line now takes up less space and is less obvious.

This time, we've relatively positioned the `div` and can see the result: The credit `div` has been moved upward. Notice, however, that there's some space below its bottom and the bottom of the outermost `div`. When an element is relatively positioned, its space is *not* closed up. Instead, the document is laid out as if the element were not positioned, and the relatively positioned element is shifted according to the values of its offset properties (`top`, `left`, and so on). As we can see in Figure 8.8, this means the credit has been moved upward by 10 pixels.

It seems a little ugly to have the text hanging out past the right edge of the image's ragged border, doesn't it? We need to shift the text back to the left a bit. There are three ways we could do this:

- Set `right` to `25px`.
- Set `margin-right` to `25px`.
- Set `padding-right` to `25px`.

In this particular case, any of these would have the same visual effect. Remember, though, that increasing the padding will increase the distance between the content and any borders that might be set. Therefore, it's generally better to set this sort of offset using either `right` or `margin-right`. Just to be different, let's use the latter.

```
div#credit {color: silver; font-size: 80%; text-align: right;
   position: relative; top: -10px; margin-right: 25px;}
</style>
```

This will move the content (as well as the borders) over to the right, but remember that the value of `right` is still `0`. Margins, just like everything else about an element, are measured relative to the points defined by the offset properties.

The Finished Product

With our card elements positioned, we can at last remove the "show me the borders" rule so that our card looks as beautiful as we always imagined it might (see Figure 8.9).

```
<style type="text/css" media="screen">
/* border-rule deleted */
body {text-align: center;}       /* IE5.x workaround */
```

Note that when we remove the borders, there are some slight shifts in the placement of the elements. This is because the borders take up space as well and pushed the content areas a little further from the points defined by the offset properties. This is a minor effect and one that didn't really upset the design after we removed them, but it's worth remembering in more complex positioning situations.

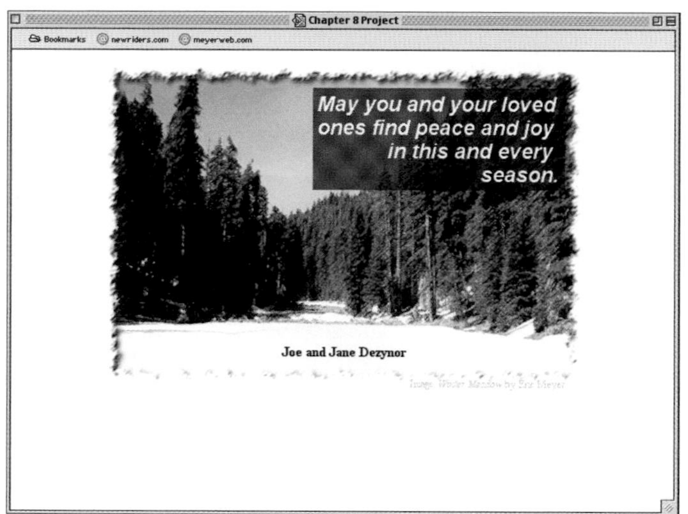
Chapter 8 Project
Bookmarks
newriders.com
meyerweb.com
May you and your loved ones find peace and joy in this and every season.
Joe and Jane Dezynor

FIGURE 8.9

The finished digital greeting card.

With just these few fairly simple steps, we've come to the style sheet shown in Listing 8.2. But let's not stop there!

Listing 8.2 The Complete Style Sheet

```
<style type="text/css" media="all">
body {text-align: center;}        /* IE5.x workaround */
div#card {width: 575px; margin-left: auto; margin-right: auto;
   position: relative;}
div#sentiment {position: absolute; top: 30px; right: 25px; width: 50%;
   text-align: right; font: italic bold 25px Arial, sans-serif;
   color: white; padding: 5px;
   background: transparent url(halfscreen-black.gif) center repeat;}
div#signature {position: absolute; top: 335px; left: 0; right: 0;
   width: 100%; font-weight: bold;}
div#credit {color: silver; font-size: 80%; text-align: right;
   position: relative; top: -10px; margin-right: 25px;}
</style>
```

A Variant Look

Let's assume that, after some consideration, we've decided that the ragged-edge look is a little too rustic for our intended recipients. Maybe we'd prefer something a little more modern and angular for all our hip friends.

To accomplish this, we need to go back to the basic markup and styles as they stood in Figure 8.2 and then style a 2-pixel black border around the image. To account for this, we have to adjust the `width` of the outermost `div` because the image (575 pixels wide) plus the border (2 pixels on each side) equals 579 pixels in width, not 575.

A New Image

We're changing the image as well: `card-image.jpg` has been changed to `card-image2.jpg`. Check the source of `ch08prog10.html` to verify this.

```
<style type="text/css" media="screen">
body {text-align: center;}        /* IE5.x workaround */
div#card {width: 579px; margin-left: auto; margin-right: auto;
   position: relative;}
div#card img {border: 2px solid black;}
div#sentiment {position: absolute; top: 30px; right: 25px; width: 50%;
   text-align: right; font: italic bold 25px Arial, sans-serif;
   color: white; padding: 5px;
   background: transparent url(halfscreen-black.gif) center repeat;}
</style>
```

Note that we've kept our IE5 workaround (because we still want the card to be centered) and the styling of the sentiment, but everything else has been thrown out. Rounding out the changes, the card's width has been adjusted, and we've added a border to the image.

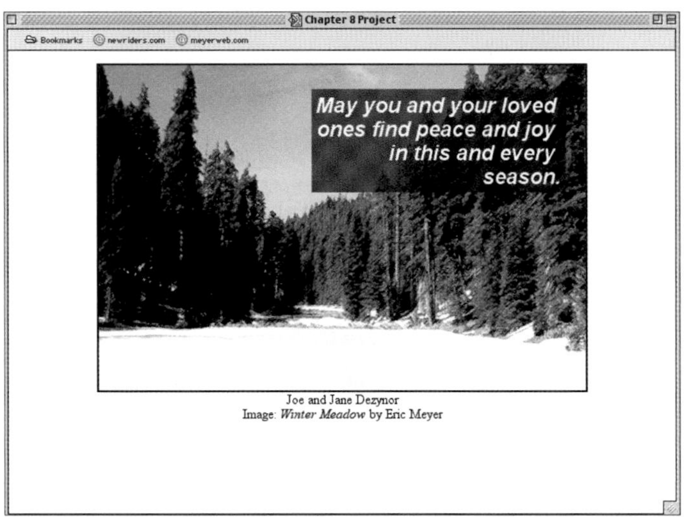
Chapter 8 Project
Bookmarks
newriders.com
meyerweb.com
May you and your loved ones find peace and joy in this and every season.
Joe and Jane Dezynor
Image: Winter Meadow by Eric Meyer

FIGURE 8.10

With a slightly different image in hand, we start again.

We could have kept the rest of the styles from before, and that would have been interesting, but let's see if we can create a look that's distinctive in its own right. Glancing over Figure 8.10, we can see three things that need to be improved:

- The signature needs to be placed in an interesting fashion.
- The credit is also in need of some styling.
- The sentiment could be placed closer to the edges of the image.

Let's tackle those problems in order.

Re-Placing the Signature

Because it's the thought that counts, let's make sure our recipients know who had the thought. We can do this by making the signature a little more obvious than it was in the previous design. It would be fairly nifty to create a hanging-nameplate sort of effect in which the signature is placed in a box that's bisected by the image's border.

Our first steps are to pick styles for the font, background, and border of the signature. After we do that (see Figure 8.11), we can set about positioning the signature.

```
div#sentiment {position: absolute; top: 30px; right: 25px; width: 50%;
   text-align: right; font: italic bold 25px Arial, sans-serif;
   color: white; padding: 5px;
   background: transparent url(halfscreen-black.gif) center repeat;}
div#signature {font-weight: bold; font-size: 18px;
   border: 1px solid black; background: silver;
   width: 275px; margin: 0 auto; padding: 0.25em;}
</style>
```

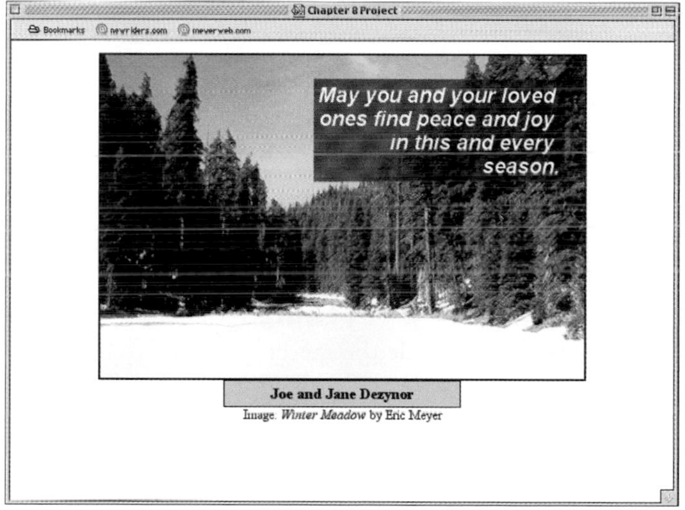
Chapter 8 Project
Bookmarks
newriders.com
meyerweb.com
May you and your loved ones find peace and joy in this and every season.
Joe and Jane Dezynor
Image: Winter Meadow by Eric Meyer

FIGURE 8.11

The signature is looking more like a nameplate now, but it's a little out of position.

With these styles ready to go, we now need to decide how we're going to get the signature to half overlap the bottom of the image. One possibility is to relatively position the signature with an upward offset, but we already did that with the credit in the last design. Let's absolutely position it with respect to the card (which is still the containing block, you'll recall).

It's a good plan, but we need to proceed carefully. We could try to position the signature using a negative bottom offset, but that would offset it relative to the bottom of the card, not the bottom of the base image. We definitely want the signature placed in relation to the image. Fortunately, the top of the card and the top of the image are in the same place, so we'll define a `top` offset instead.

```
div#signature {font-weight: bold; font-size: 18px;
   border: 1px solid black; background: silver;
   width: 275px; margin: 0 auto; padding: 0.25em;
   position: absolute; top: 370px; left: 152px; right: 152px;}
</style>
```

Note that we've provided values for `left` and `right`, which helps avoid bugs in Explorer. We know that the image is 384 pixels tall, so giving a `top` value of `370px` puts the signature just about where we want it (see Figure 8.12).

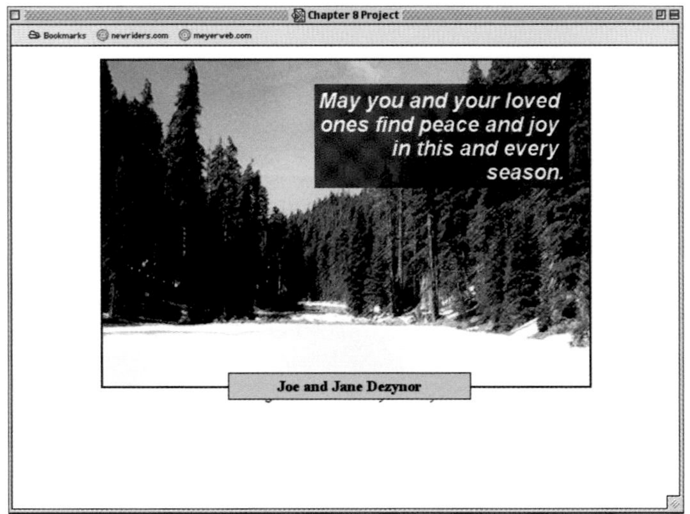
Chapter 8 Project
Bookmarks
newriders.com
meyerweb.com
May you and your loved ones find peace and joy in this and every season.
Joe and Jane Dezynor

FIGURE 8.12

Using a top offset, we can place the signature very precisely, but the credit gets obscured in the process.

Whoops—what happened to the credit? We can just see the bottom of it peeking out from behind the signature in Figure 8.12. It slid underneath the signature because the signature no longer is part of the normal flow of the document. So unless we want to hide the credit entirely, we need to position it so that it's visible.

Credit Where It's Viewed

The way we styled the credit in the last design wasn't too bad, but rather than putting the image credit at the bottom of the card, why not put it right along the top of the image? In fact, how about putting it just above the image?

```
div#signature {font-weight: bold; font-size: 18px;
   border: 1px solid black; background: silver;
   width: 275px; margin: 0 auto; padding: 0.25em;
   position: absolute; top: 370px; left: 150px; right: 150px;}
div#credit {font: 11px Arial, sans-serif; text-align: right;
   position: absolute; top: -13px; left: 0; right: 0; width: 100%;
   color: #999;}
</style>
```

There isn't much new here really. We made the text a light gray and right-aligned it. We set values for `left`, `right`, and `width` so that Explorer will behave. We set a font size and family. The only real difference is that we made the value of `top` negative, and that caused the element to be positioned outside its containing block (see Figure 8.13).

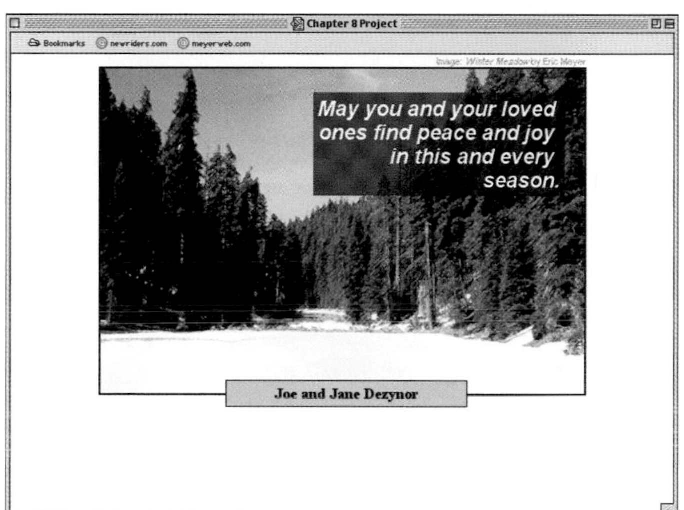
Chapter 8 Project
Bookmarks
newriders.com
meyerweb.com
May you and your loved ones find peace and joy in this and every season.
Joe and Jane Dezynor

FIGURE 8.13

Placing the credit above the image means positioning it outside its containing block.

This isn't a bug; it's exactly what's supposed to happen. Basically, we just said that the offset between the top of the credit `div` and the top edge of the containing block should be `-13px`. Because positive offsets create a positive distance between the two edges, thus pushing positioned elements toward the center of their containing block, it stands to reason that negative values would pull positioned elements outward.

Other Offsets

In a similar vein, we could have placed the credit to the right of the image by using a negative value for `right`.

Getting Sentimental Again

Now that we've made the signature more prominent, we need to do something to make the sentiment stand out on its own terms. This could be as simple as increasing the font size of the element, so we'll do that, but let's also bring its background up against the border surrounding the image. As a result of this change, we'll also want to increase the padding of the sentiment. Then, as a result of *that* change, let's put a 1-pixel black border around the sentiment.

```
div#card img {border: 2px solid black;}
div#sentiment {position: absolute; top: 0; right: 0; width: 33%;
   text-align: right; font: italic bold 28px Arial, sans-serif;
   color: white; padding: 20px; border: 1px solid black;
   background: transparent url(halfscreen-black.gif) center repeat;}
```

FIGURE 8.14

Moving the sentiment up against the image border leads to a few other changes.

Chapter 8 Project
Bookmarks
newriders.com
meyerweb.com
May you and your loved ones find peace and joy in this and every season.
Joe and Jane Dezynor

Width Variance

Note that although IE5/Mac and Netscape 6.x agree with CSS and treat `padding` as a value separate from `width` (and `height`), Explorer 4.x, 5.x, and 6.x in loose rendering mode all treat `padding` as though it were part of the `width` (and `height`) of an element. IE6 in strict rendering mode, on the other hand, agrees with CSS.

See "Tricking Browsers and Hiding Styles" on the Web site for a way to work around the width variance problem.

We could have just as easily set a pixel-based `width` value for the sentiment, but using a percentage is a little more interesting. (If you're feeling ambitious, calculate the resulting width yourself!) The border helps define the sentiment's region without being overly heavy, preventing the subtle ragged-edge effect to the sentiment we had before. The modernism just keeps increasing!

With these changes, we've come up with a pretty good variant of our first design. Listing 8.3 shows the complete style sheet for this design.

Listing 8.3 The Complete Variant Style Sheet

```
<style type="text/css" media="screen">
body {text-align: center;}       /* IE5.x workaround */
div#card {width: 579px; margin-left: auto; margin-right: auto;
   position: relative;}
div#card img {border: 2px solid black;}
div#sentiment {position: absolute; top: 0; right: 0; width: 33%;
   text-align: right; font: italic bold 28px Arial, sans-serif;
   color: white; padding: 20px;
   background: transparent url(halfscreen-black.gif) center repeat;}
div#signature {font-weight: bold; font-size: 18px;
   border: 1px solid black; background: silver;
   width: 275px; margin: 0 auto; padding: 0.25em;
   position: absolute; top: 370px; left: 150px; right: 150px;}
div#credit {font: 11px Arial, sans-serif; text-align: right;
   position: absolute; top: -13px; left: 0; right: 0; width: 100%;
   color: #999;}
</style>
```

One More Variant

Being the inveterate tinkers that we are, it's impossible to resist one more small set of changes to the design. This will involve just a couple of minor changes. First let's flip the sentiment over to the left side and adjust its styles accordingly. This will involve moving it down a bit and also widening the sentiment's box.

Note that in this variant, we've removed the black border from the sentiment (see Figure 8.15).

```
div#card img {border: 2px solid black;}
div#sentiment { position: absolute; top: 180px; left: 0; width: 350px;
   text-align: left; font: bold 28px Arial, sans-serif;
   color: white; padding: 10px 5px 10px 20px;
   background: transparent url(halfscreen-black.gif) center repeat;}
```

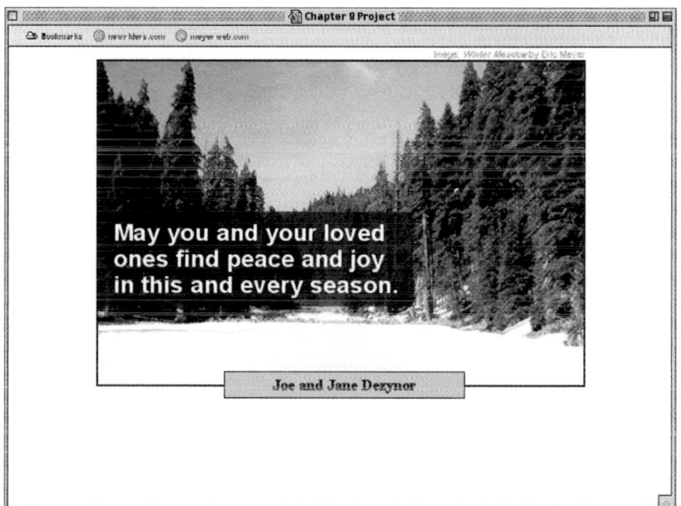
Chapter 8 Project
May you and your loved
ones find peace and joy
in this and every season.
Joe and Jane Dezynor

FIGURE 8.15

Another styling of the sentiment.

As you can see, it's easy to move a positioned element from one place to another with just a few adjustments to the styles. The added advantage is that if a user visits with an older browser that doesn't support positioning, he or she will still be able to read the text just fine.

Unpositioned Cheer

Try removing just the positioning styles to see what the card looks like—you might be surprised at how good it looks. Simulating an unstyled version of the card doesn't require anything more complicated than checking out Figure 8.1, of course.

Branching Out

There are many other ways to style a form like the one we worked with in this project. Here are a few suggestions:

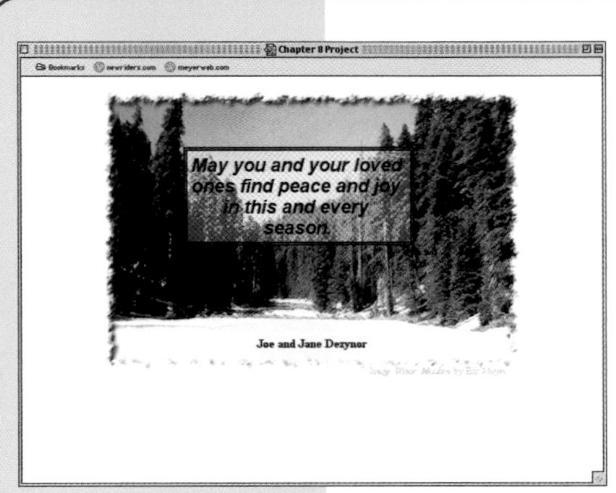
Chapter 8 Project
May you and your loved ones find peace and joy in this and every season.
Joe and Jane Dezynor

1. Try centering the sentiment from the first design and giving it a white halfscreen image for a background. Doing this will likely require you to change the color of the text to something dark, and a border might be nice here. Maybe a nice thick double border would be just the thing…

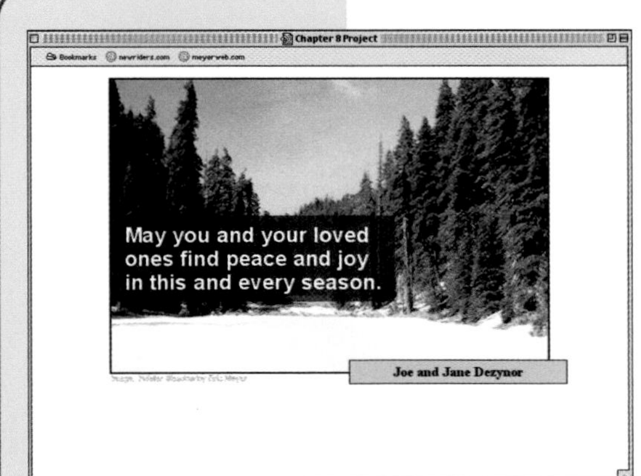
Chapter 8 Project
May you and your loved ones find peace and joy in this and every season.
Joe and Jane Dezynor

2. Shift the variant signature far enough to the right for it to hang off the edge of the image. Doing this should give you enough space to position the credit at the bottom-left corner of the image, which would be a fairly efficient use of space.

3. For an extra challenge, try using a medium gray halfscreen on the sentiment, a white halfscreen for the signature, and a dark halfscreen with medium gray text for the credit, all arranged on top of the card image and none of them overlapping. Using either card image would be interesting, but you get bonus points for using the ragged-edge version of the image.

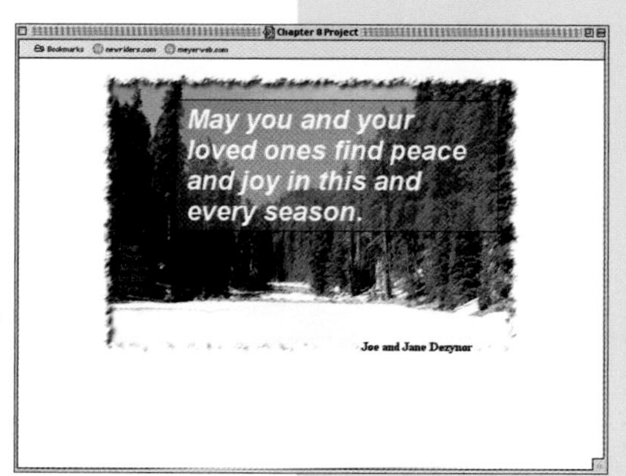
Chapter 8 Project
May you and your loved ones find peace and joy in this and every season.
Joe and Jane Dezynor

9

Multicolumn Layout

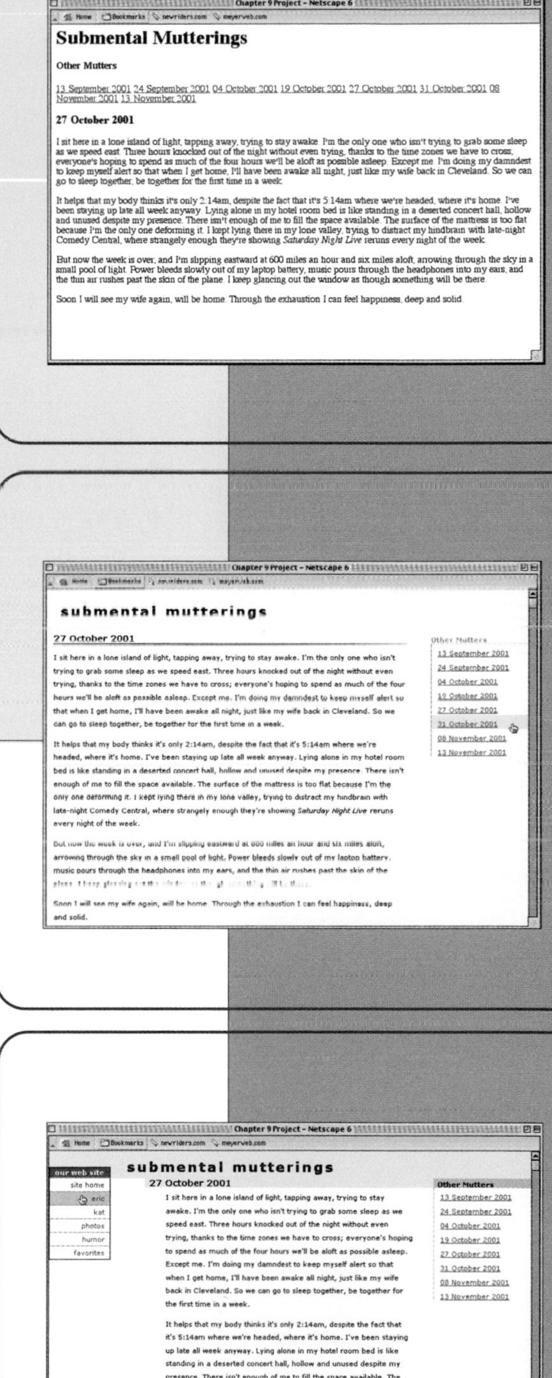

And stand together, and yet not too near together. For even the pillars of the temple must stand apart; and the oak tree and the cypress will not grow in each other's shadow.

—*Khalil Gibran*

After a lifetime of reading newspapers and magazines, we're used to seeing text laid out in multiple columns. It's one of the most common conventions in Western typography, so of course it's one of the most requested features of Web layout. And yet multiple columns of text in a Web page isn't always a good idea. Because of the nature of the Web, a user faced with a multiple-column page might have to scroll downward to read the first column, scroll back up to the top of the second, and so on for every new column.

On the other hand, multicolumn layout corresponds to a very common Web design technique: putting links next to the main text of a page. Traditionally, this has been done with a table that has the main body of the page in one cell and the sidebar links in another. We can do the same thing with CSS and keep the markup a lot simpler in the process.

Project Goals

With all of the client projects and other work we've been doing lately, it seems like a good time to take a break and work on a personal project for a change. To that end, we'll come up with a sparse yet flexible design for a personal journal. This will require a column for the journal entry and another for links to other entries in the same journal.

Let's lay down some basic design directions and see where they take us.

- The page should have a sort of papery look to it, ideally by using a light tan background.
- The paragraph text should be a smallish sans-serif font and spread apart a bit.
- The headings should also be sans serif and appropriately sized.
- The sidebar should be to the right and separated from the journal entry text by a moderately sized gap.
- The sidebar links should be enclosed in a half-box; that is, there should be a border along the top and left sides of the links to set them apart from the rest of the document.

With these goals in mind, it's time to get set up and start styling!

Preparation

See the Introduction for instructions on how to download files from the Web site.

Download the files for Project 9 from this book's Web site. If you're planning to play along at home, load the file `ch09proj.html` into the editing program of your choice. This is the file you'll be editing, saving, and reloading as the project progresses.

Laying the Groundwork

The first thing we need is a properly structured file. Fortunately, we already have it. Listing 9.1 provides the top part of the file's `body`, and Figure 9.1 shows it in its raw, unstyled glory.

Listing 9.1 A Portion of the Document Markup

```
<body>
<h1>Submental Mutterings</h1>
<div id="sidebar">
<h4>Other Mutters</h4>
<a href="mutter01.html">13 September 2001</a>
<a href="mutter02.html">24 September 2001</a>
<a href="mutter03.html">04 October 2001</a>
<a href="mutter04.html">19 October 2001</a>
<a href="mutter05.html">27 October 2001</a>
<a href="mutter06.html">31 October 2001</a>
<a href="mutter07.html">08 November 2001</a>
<a href="mutter08.html">13 November 2001</a>
</div>

<div id="entry">
<h3>27 October 2001</h3>
<p>
I sit here in a lone island of light, tapping away, trying to stay
awake.  I'm the only one who isn't trying to grab some sleep as we
speed east.  Three hours knocked out of the night without even trying,
thanks to the time zones we have to cross; everyone's hoping to spend
as much of the four hours we'll be aloft as possible asleep.  Except me. I'm
doing my damndest to keep myself alert so that when I get home, I'll have been
awake all night, just like my wife back in Cleveland.  So we can go to sleep
together, be together for the first time in a week.
</p>
```

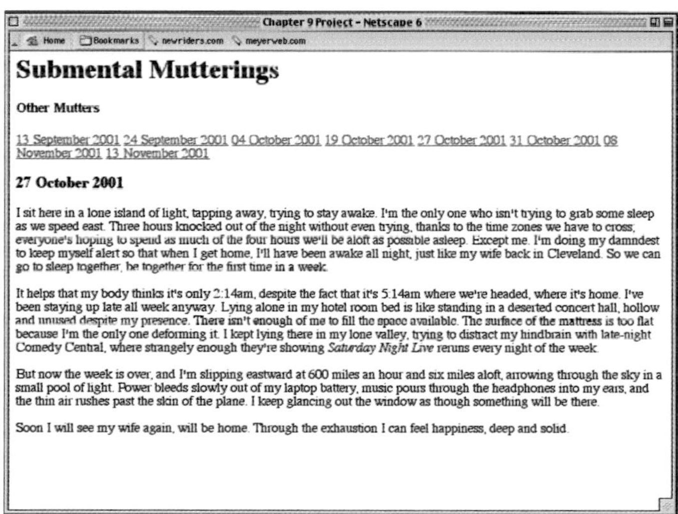

FIGURE 9.1
An unstyled journal page.

In the interest of getting to the good stuff quickly, we're skipping past the usual "here's how you alter the markup" step. Pretend we already went through all that. The markup we have now is all we need to set up a good two-column layout, so let's get stylish!

Styling the Document

This will actually be the first of several passes at styling this document. The first run will use a simple floating method, whereas the second will use a slightly more complicated positioning approach. Then we'll add a third column to the mix and look at different ways to style that type of document.

Defining the Basic Look

The first step is to lay down the basic font rules and the general look of the headings. While we're at it, let's also give the paragraphs an increased `line-height` so that the lines are spread apart a bit. Looking at Figure 9.2, the results of these rules might seem a little bizarre, but hang in there. This will all make sense in a moment.

Padding as Well

When it comes to layouts like we're doing in this project, it's better to always define both margin and padding explicitly. This prevents any unexpected surprises coming from the browsers' default styles.

```
<style type="text/css">
html {margin: 0; padding: 0;}
body {font: 11px Verdana, Arial, Helvetica, sans-serif;
   margin: 0; padding: 0;
   background: rgb(95%,95%,80%); color: black;}
h1 {font-size: 200%; text-transform: lowercase; letter-spacing: 3px;}
h3 {font-size: 133%; margin: 0; padding: 0;
   border-bottom: 1px solid black;}
h4 {font-size: 100%; margin: 0; padding: 0;
   border-bottom: 1px solid gray; color: gray;}
p {line-height: 1.66;}
</style>
```

Figure 9.2

The first steps of styling our journal entry.

Let's consider Figure 9.2 for a second. Obviously, we need to get the text pushed away from the edges of the browser window. While we're at it, we should put the sidebar over to the right.

Floating the Sidebar

To accomplish these tasks, we need to style exactly three elements: the `h1` and both `div` elements. These are just to get us started; we'll be revisiting these values before the project is done. Take a look at Figure 9.3 to see just how much difference these few values have made.

```
h1 {font-size: 200%; text-transform: lowercase; letter-spacing: 3px;
 margin: 1em; padding: 0;}
h3 {font-size: 133%; margin: 0; padding: 0;
   border-bottom: 1px solid black;}
h4 {font-size: 100%; margin: 0; padding: 0;
   border-bottom: 1px solid gray; color: gray;}
p {line-height: 1.66;}
div#entry {margin: 0 1em; padding: 0;}
div#sidebar {margin: 0; padding: 0; float: right; width: 20%;}
</style>
```

Defining the Width

Floated text elements should *always* have an explicitly defined width. Floated images have an intrinsic width and therefore don't need an explicit width value, although it certainly doesn't hurt to give them one.

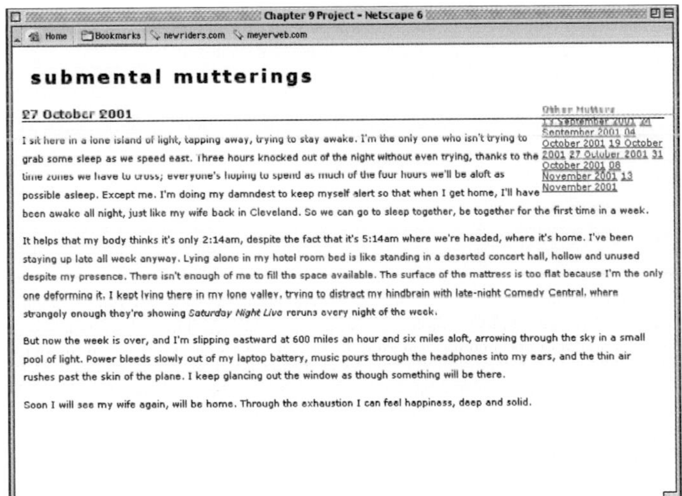

FIGURE 9.3

The floating has begun.

While the page is now marginally more readable, there are still obvious problems. The most obvious is that the border on the entry date is cutting straight through the sidebar, and the borders of the entry date and the Other Mutters sidebar don't line up. A more subtle problem is that this isn't a two-column layout. It's more like a single column with a floated element inside it. Although this might be a desirable layout effect in other circumstances, we're after something different here.

We could float the entry text to the left in some sort of matching-float effort, but that's an unnecessarily complicated way to handle this. Instead, we're just going to give the entry a wide enough right margin to avoid overlapping the sidebar and to appear as its own column.

```
div#entry {margin: 0 25% 1em 1em; padding: 0;}
```

Padding the Sidebar

Instead of adding padding to the top of the h4, we could have set the top padding for the sidebar div to be 0.33em. Either choice will have the same visual effect because the div has neither a border nor a background set.

We should also get the borders to line up. We know that the two div elements have no top margin, and the same is true of the h3 and h4 elements. We also know that the h3 is 133% normal size, whereas the h4 is 100% normal size. These are equivalent to 1.33em and 1em, so there's a 0.33em difference in their heights. We'll add that much padding to the top of the h4 and make sure the bottom padding stays at zero.

```
h4 {font-size: 100%; margin: 0; padding: 0.33em 0 0;
   border-bottom: 1px solid gray; color: gray;}
```

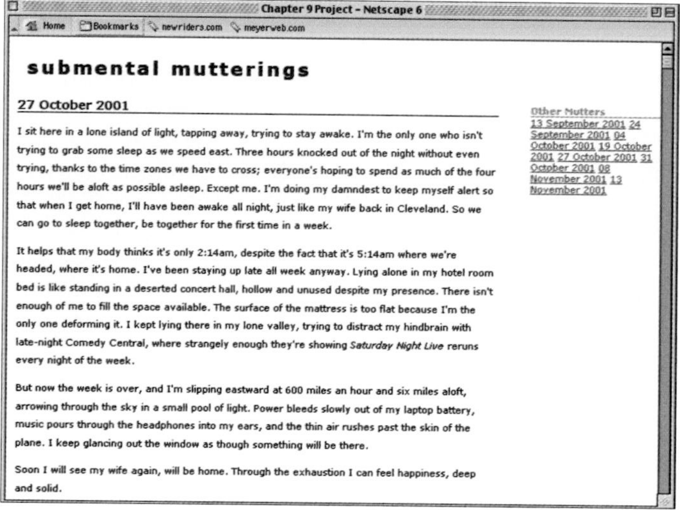

FIGURE 9.4

Bringing the pieces in line with each other.

Improving the Sidebar

Block-Level Links

See Project 5, "How to Skin a Menu," for a detailed exploration of making links block-level elements to achieve useful layout effects.

Despite the small number of styles we've written so far, we're most of the way done with the design. The biggest sore spot right now is the sidebar's content, which is still mashed together and not very usable. We'll use what I sometimes call the classic block-level hyperlink trick to fix that.

Because the design goals call for a border down the left side of the links, we'll create that by adding the border to the links themselves. It would be nice to have some sort of highlighting effect for these links, so let's add that in as well. The results are shown in Figure 9.5.

```
div#sidebar {margin: 0; padding: 0; float: right; width: 20%;}
div#sidebar a {display: block; padding: 8px 0 2px 10px; margin: 0;
   border-left: 1px solid gray;}
div#sidebar a:hover {background: rgb(85%,85%,70%);}
</style>
```

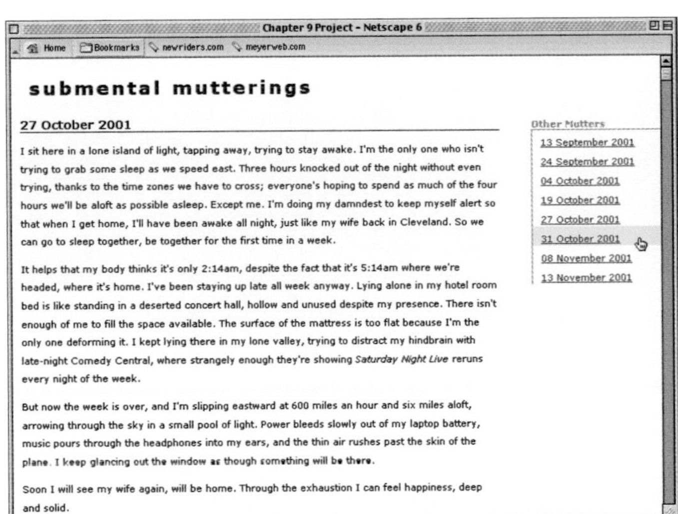

FIGURE 9.5

The sidebar links are a lot more useful now.

At this point, about the only thing left to do is make the entry column and `h1` element flow a little better. Let's actually narrow the entry column a bit by pushing it away from the left edge of the browser window. We should also adjust the paragraph margins so that the first margin gets up a little closer to the date and they're all pushed inward. This will give the date a "hanging indent" look.

```
h4 {font-size: 100%; margin: 0; padding: 0.33em 0 0;
   border-bottom: 1px solid gray; color: gray;}
p {line-height: 1.66; margin: 0.5em 0 1em 3em;}
div#entry {margin: 0 25% 1em 8%; padding: 0;}
div#sidebar {margin: 0; padding: 0; float: right; width: 20%;}
```

Tweaking the Layout

As we make these changes, it's getting a little hard to tell exactly where the two `div`s are being placed. Let's give them temporary backgrounds so that we can visualize the layout a little better. We'll put these in separate rules so that they're easier to remove later on, and we'll use variants of the page's background color so that they don't clash too horribly. Figure 9.6 shows us the results.

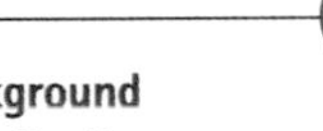

Background Visualization

We're using background colors instead of borders because the borders, even if temporary, could throw off our layout in small but misleading ways. It's much easier to understand the layout if you use a background color.

```
div#sidebar a:hover {background: rgb(85%,85%,70%);}
div#entry {background-color: rgb(95%,85%,85%);}
div#sidebar {background-color: rgb(85%,85%,95%);}
</style>
```

After looking at these styles, it feels like the two columns might be a little too close together. It might be nice to make the sidebar a little wider, given that the link text comes a bit close to the edge of the browser window in a few cases. We need only alter a very few values to change that.

```
div#entry {margin: 0 33% 1em 7%; padding: 0;}
div#sidebar {margin: 0; padding: 0; float: right; width: 25%;}
```

FIGURE 9.6

Visualizing layout with temporary backgrounds.

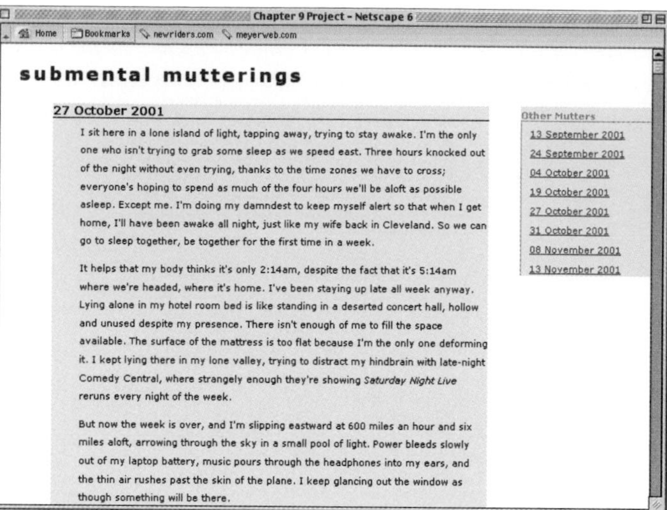

Percentage Margins

The big advantage to setting right and left margins (as well as widths) as percentage values is that they'll flex with the browser window. As the window gets narrower or wider, the percentage margins will scale to match. This is the basis of "liquid" or "fluid" design.

We can also see from Figure 9.6 that the `h1` is taking up a lot of space all by itself. Although we want it to be a bit apart from the rest of the page, we could tighten things up just a bit.

```
h1 {font-size: 200%; text-transform: lowercase; letter-spacing: 3px;
   margin: 0.66em 0 0.33em 3%; padding: 0;}
```

▸▸ Widths, Margins, and Browsers

It's the sad truth that different browsers treat values for `width` *differently. Although* `width` *is supposed to define the width of an element's content area, Internet Explorer 4.x and 5.x for Windows treat it as though it defines the width of the content area, the right and left padding, and the right and left borders. Because IE4.x/Win and 5.x/Win don't agree with the specification—let alone IE5.x/Mac, Netscape 6.x, and Opera—authors have a real dilemma. How can we size elements without having the design break down in one or more browsers? The answer is fairly simple, and it's the approach we'll been using here: Use* `div`*s that have no padding and, if possible, no borders. To create an offset between the edges of the* `div` *and its content, set margins on whatever elements are found within.*

The simplest case is that of a small note that contains a single paragraph of text. Instead of just using a `div` *containing text, wrap the text in a* `p` *element. This enables you to place and size the* `div` *without padding it, which makes its size consistent across browsers. By defining margins (or padding) for the* `p` *element within the* `div`*, you sidestep the whole issue and regain consistent positioning.*

For situations in which you can't use the kind of approach described in this aside, you can still use some interesting parser tricks to get the needed values to different browsers. (Refer to "Tricking Browsers and Hiding Styles" on the Web site for details.)

It's also the case that you need to be careful about letting columns get too close to each other. If you set two columns to `width: 50%` *and then give both columns a 10-pixel border, they'll be wider than the parent element because 50% + 50% + 20px + 20px equals 100% + 40px.*

Finishing This Round

At this point, we can take the visualization backgrounds out. (Just delete them from the style sheet altogether.) It also seems like the sidebar title and borders should be a variant of the page's background color instead of just plain gray.

```
h4 {font-size: 100%; margin: 0; padding: 0.33em 0 0;
   border-bottom: 1px solid rgb(50%,50%,33%);
   color: rgb(50%,50%,35%);}
p {line-height: 1.66; margin: 0.5em 0 1em 3em;}
div#entry {margin: 0 33% 1em 7%; padding: 0;}
div#sidebar {margin: 0; padding: 0; float: right; width: 25%;}
div#sidebar a {display: block; padding: 8px 0 2px 10px; margin: 0;
   border-left: 1px solid rgb(50%,50%,35%);}
```

With these changes, we've hit our design target! The result is visible in Figure 9.7, and the complete style sheet is provided in Listing 9.2.

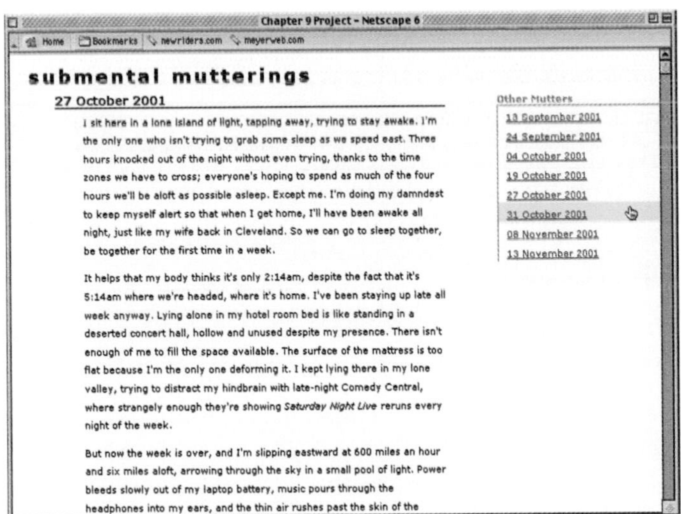

FIGURE 9.7
Our little diary, all dressed up.

Listing 9.2 The Full Style Sheet

```
<style type="text/css">
html {margin: 0; padding: 0;}
body {font: 11px Verdana, Arial, Helvetica, sans-serif;
   margin: 0; padding: 0;
   background: rgb(95%,95%,80%); color: black;}
h1 {font-size: 200%; text-transform: lowercase; letter-spacing: 3px;
   margin: 0.66em 0 0.33em 3%; padding: 0;}
h3 {font-size: 133%; margin: 0; padding: 0;
   border-bottom: 1px solid black;}
h4 {font-size: 100%; margin: 0; padding: 0.33em 0 0;
   border-bottom: 1px solid rgb(50%,50%,35%);
   color: rgb(50%,50%,35%);}
p {line-height: 1.66; margin: 0.5em 0 1em 3em;}
div#entry {margin: 0 33% 1em 7%; padding: 0;}
div#sidebar {margin: 0; padding: 0; float: right; width: 25%;}
div#sidebar a {display: block; padding: 8px 0 2px 10px; margin: 0;
   border-left: 1px solid rgb(50%,50%,35%);}
div#sidebar a:hover {background: rgb(85%,85%,70%);}
</style>
```

Styling the Document with Positioning

Floating the sidebar to the right was pretty easy, and for this kind of layout it's often the best choice. It should be noted, however, that it also depends on the order of the content. If the links had been placed at the bottom of the page after the entry, we couldn't have floated them as we did in the previous section.

In such circumstances, positioning is a better option than floating, so let's remove the `div#sidebar` rule from the style sheet and use positioning to reproduce the look we had in the previous section.

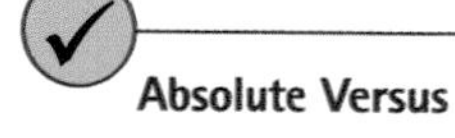

Absolute Versus Fixed

There is a tendency to think that `position: absolute` means an element will stay in place while the document scrolls. Not so! That would be `position: fixed`. `absolute` causes the element to be placed at an "absolute" position within its containing block. If that containing block is part of the document and scrolls with it, then the absolutely-positioned element will scroll with it.

From Floating to Positioning

Having taken out the rule that floats the sidebar, we end up with the sidebar wedged between the `h1` and the entry, as shown in Figure 9.8.

The best type of positioning for this situation is absolute positioning. That means the element will be positioned with respect to the top-left corner of its containing block. In this case, because the sidebar doesn't have any positioned parents, its containing block is the root element, which some browsers take to be `html` and others take to be `body`. That's why we set both elements to have no margin and no padding—that way, they're effectively the same shape. This removes any possible confusion about the edges of the containing block.

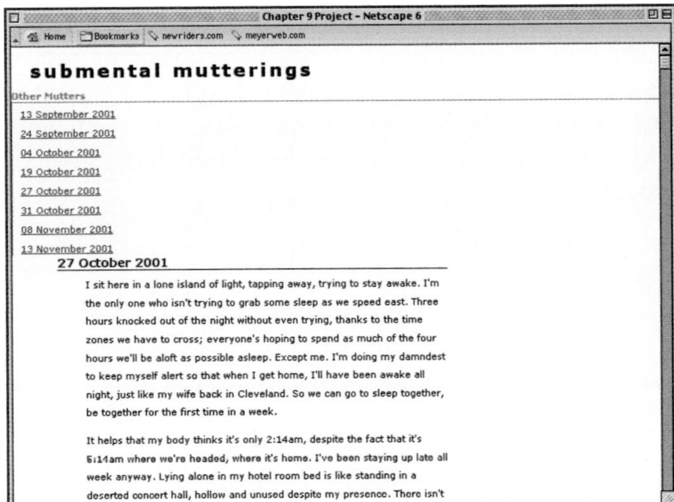

Figure 9.8 *The unfloated sidebar in an otherwise styled document.*

Because we actually want the sidebar to be on the right, we should use the `right` and `top` to place it. Let's give it a pale blue background so we can see its extent a little better, as illustrated in Figure 9.9.

```
div#entry {margin: 0 33% 1em 7%; padding: 0;}
div#sidebar {position: absolute; top: 0; right: 0; width: 20%;}
div#sidebar {background-color: rgb(85%,85%,95%);}
div#sidebar a {display: block; padding: 8px 0 2px 10px; margin: 0;
   border-left: 1px solid rgb(50%,50%,35%);}
```

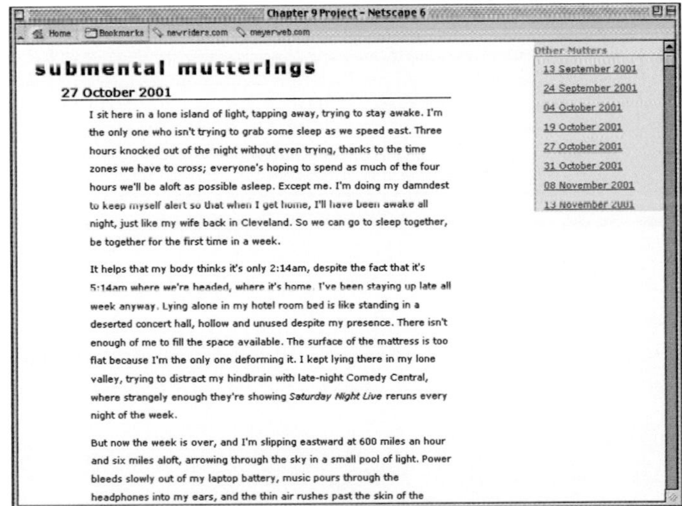

Figure 9.9 *The sidebar's been positioned but needs to be moved.*

Now it's in the top-right corner of the document. We need to move it down, but by how much?

Well, we know that the `h1` element is 200% normal size and has top and bottom margins of `0.66em` and `0.33em`, respectively, which adds up to `0.99em`. For simplicity's sake, let's call it `1em`. Because the definition of the `em` unit for margins depends on the `font-size` of the element, we realize that the height of the `h1` element (including margins) is `2em` in relation to itself. That's twice 200%, or 400% normal size, which is equivalent to `4em`.

```
div#sidebar {position: absolute; top: 4em; right: 0; width: 20%;
   font-size: 11px;}
```

Why did we declare the `font-size` again? To make sure browsers know what an `em` means for this element. This ensures that they'll calculate the value `4em` using the same yardstick by which our other distances were measured. (Some browsers are a little buggy about this.)

Now we can remove the temporary visualization backgrounds and get back our basic design, as seen in Figure 9.10.

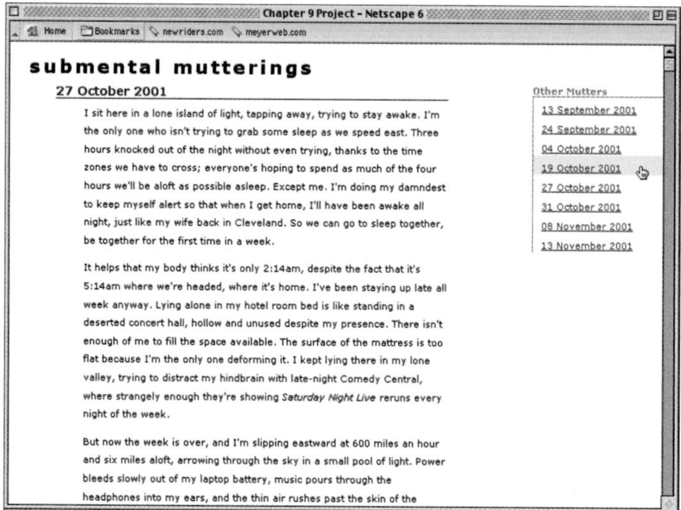

FIGURE 9.10

It looks so familiar and yet...

Notice that the sidebar and the entry aren't quite lined up like they were before. This is because we haven't accounted for the effects of the `line-height` for the heading elements. Because every browser will have a different default that can vary from `1.0` to `1.2` or even higher, we need to neutralize the variable effects it can cause.

```
h4 {font-size: 100%; margin: 0; padding: 0.33em 0 0;
   border-bottom: 1px solid rgb(50%,50%,35%);
   color: rgb(50%,50%,35%);}
h1, h3, h4 {line-height: 1em;}
p {line-height: 1.66; margin: 0.5em 0 1em 3em;}
```

We could have set the `line-height` of all elements to be `1em`, but that would be overkill in this case. All we really need to worry about here is the headings. By setting all headings to have a `line-height` of `1em`, we've made sure that their content is exactly as tall as their `font-size` and no taller.

A desire to avoid the kind of slipperiness that `line-height` and other properties can cause is what drives many authors to position with pixels instead of ems. This involves sacrificing layout flexibility for a certain degree of consistency. But imagine what would happen if we positioned with pixels and then decided to change the `font-size` for the `body`: We'd have to recalculate and rewrite all of our positioning statements.

Why the Change?

This variability wasn't an issue with the floated sidebar because it didn't have to worry about the height of the `h1` element. Because it was floating from a spot below the `h1`, it got shifted up or down as the `h1` got bigger or smaller. When positioning, the element is removed from the document's flow altogether, so placement doesn't depend on the size of other elements.

Advantage: Positioning

So why did we go to all that effort to use positioning when we'd already used `float` to achieve the same effect and didn't have nearly as much to worry about? Because now we have much more flexibility in terms of where the sidebar markup can appear. With `float`, the sidebar had to come before the entry. Now its markup can be anywhere from before the `h1` to after the entry.

Even with the sidebar markup placed at the very end of the document, our positioning rules will still place the sidebar precisely as shown in Figure 9.10. Whereas `float` effects are highly dependent on source order, positioning is fairly insensitive to source order. That's a huge advantage and is not one to be tossed aside lightly.

Other Ways to the Same Position

We do have some alternatives in terms of how we define the width of the sidebar. One such possibility is as follows:

```
div#sidebar {position: absolute; top: 4em; right: 0; left: 80%;
   font-size: 11px;}
```

Alternatively, we could drop the property `right` and add `width` with an appropriate value:

```
div#sidebar {position: absolute; top: 4em; left: 80%; width: 20%;
   font-size: 11px;}
```

Either one of these would have the same effect as the rule we actually used. That's because although each rule leaves different things implicit, they all imply the same thing. If we were to write out the rule with nothing left implicit, we would have the following:

```
div#sidebar {position: absolute; top: 4em; right: 0; left: 80%;
   width: 20%; padding: 0; margin: 0; font-size: 11px;}
```

Regardless of which path we choose, the end result is the same. In this case, we've put enough margin on the entry to leave room for the positioned element as opposed to leaving enough room for the float. Either way, we get the layout we want.

Styling Three Columns

Four and More

Although it's certainly possible to have any number of columns, physical constraints will eventually come into play: There are only so many pixels available on a monitor, let alone in a browser window. In the majority of cases, any more than three columns will be too many.

Now that we've successfully created a two-column layout in two different ways, let's add another column to the mix and see what happens. We'll add in a set of links that refer to the site as a whole and place them on the left side of the page. This left-side sidebar should be styled in a way that makes it obviously different from the rest of the page.

Adding the Markup

The first thing we need to do is get the actual HTML added to our document. Despite our desire for a different look, we're going to use essentially the same markup as was used for the "Other Mutters" sidebar, just to increase the challenge. And just for an extra bit of fun, we're going to put the site navigation links at the very beginning of the document *before* the `h1` element. This will give us Figure 9.11.

```
<body>
<div id="sitenav">
<h4>our web site</h4>
<a href="home.html">site home</a>
<a href="eric.html">eric</a>
<a href="kat.html">kat</a>
<a href="gallery.html">photos</a>
<a href="humor.html">humor</a>
<a href="links.html">favorites</a>
</div>
<h1>Submental Mutterings</h1>
```

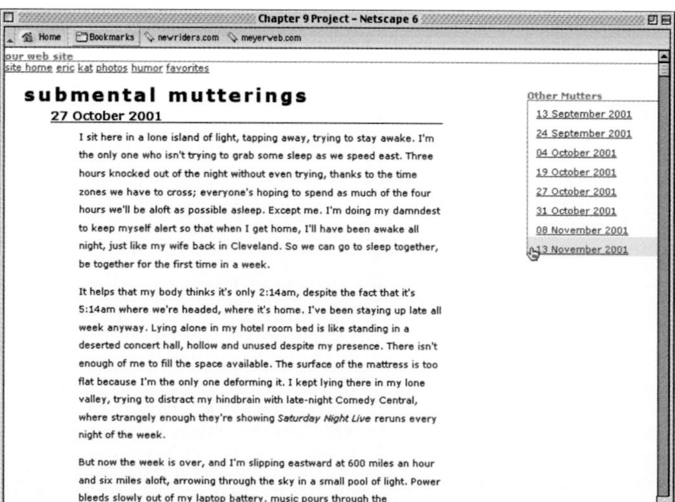

FIGURE 9.11

Another "column" enters the fray.

It's pretty obvious that we can recycle some of the same ideas that were used in the right sidebar: block-level links, for example. We can't just blindly reuse all of the "Other Mutters" styles for two reasons:

- If we want the look to be distinctive, we'll have to use new styling ideas.
- Because this sidebar will be on the left, we probably want to right-justify or center the links and title text.

So we'll have to write new styles to make this sidebar stand on its own.

Placing the Elements

First things first, though. Let's position this sidebar and move the entry text over a bit to give it room. To keep everything clear, we're going to assign temporary backgrounds to the entry and both sidebars.

```
div#sidebar a:hover {background: rgb(85%,85%,70%);}
div#entry {background-color: rgb(95%,85%,85%);}
div#sidebar, div#sitenav {background-color: rgb(85%,85%,95%);}
</style>
```

Now we'll position the sidebar and alter the left margin of the entry `div` to provide room. This sidebar's links are short words, so we'll keep the overall sidebar narrow.

```
h1, h3, h4 {line-height: 1em;}
div#sitenav {position: absolute; top: 1em; left: 0; width: 12.5%;
   font-size: 11px;}
div#entry {margin: 0 33% 1em 20%; padding: 0;}
div#sidebar {position: absolute; top: 4em; right: 0; width: 20%;
   font-size: 11px;}
```

Note that we've placed the `sitenav` sidebar so that its top is only `1em` below the top of the containing block, which is the root element. This means we'll have to shove the `h1` element over so that there isn't any overlap. While we're at it, let's redistribute our spacing between padding and margins. This will let us create a vaguely interesting effect before we're done.

```
h1 {font-size: 200%; text-transform: lowercase; letter-spacing: 3px;
   margin: 0 33% 0 16%; padding: 0.66em 0 0.33em 0;}
```

Add it all up and you get Figure 9.12.

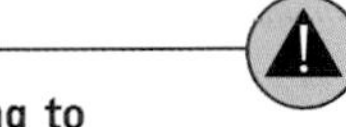

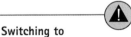

Switching to Padding

There's another reason to use padding on the `h1` here: The top margin would be incorrectly ignored in Netscape 6.x. The bug's profile is that if you absolutely position the first element in the document, as we did, the top margin of the next element is ignored. But we really are going to use the padding to our advantage later on!

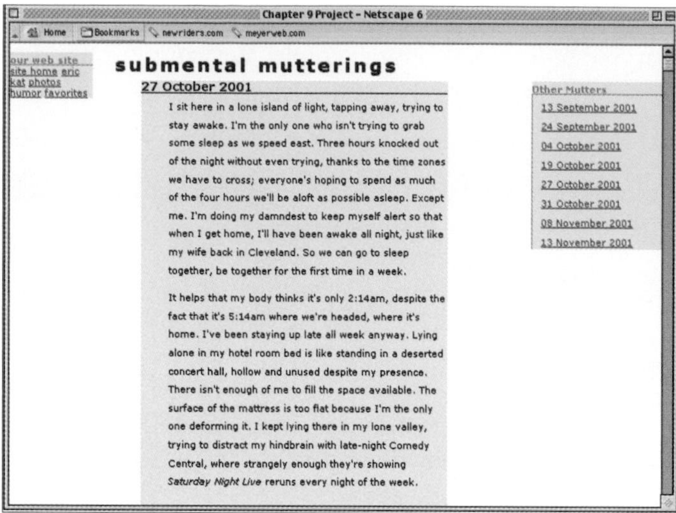

FIGURE 9.12

Three columns in a transitional state.

It's fairly obvious that we still need to do something about those links. We also need to make the sidebar a little less like everything else on the page.

A Distinctive Look

Because the `sitenav` sidebar is supposed to be distinct from the rest of the page, let's really set it apart. We'll give it a border and a visible background, turn the `h4` into a "cap" element, and maybe one or two other things. First let's make those links blocky! We'll also right-align and pad them as well as remove the underlines.

```
div#sitenav {position: absolute; top: 2em; left: 0; width: 12.5%;
   font-size: 11px;}
div#sitenav a {display: block; padding: 4px 8px; margin: 0;
   text-decoration: none; text-align: right;}
div#entry {margin: 0 33% 1em 20%; padding: 0;}
```

Taking Out the Underlines

We've explicitly removed the underlines from these links because that will make them look more like buttons and also because the underlining would look strange so close to the borders between the links.

All right. Now we need to put a border on the sidebar itself and add borders to the top of each link. We'll also add a white background to the sidebar, which means removing the blue visualization background. That's all right. We don't need it any more anyway, as we can see in Figure 9.13.

```
div#sitenav {position: absolute; top: 2em; left: 0; width: 12.5%;
   font-size: 11px; background-color: white;
   border: 1px solid black;}
div#sitenav a {display: block; padding: 4px 8px; margin: 0;
   text-decoration: none; text-align: right;
   border-top: 1px solid gray;}
```

FIGURE 9.13

Making the site navigation stand out.

With a couple of extra touches, we'll be there. First, of course, we want to give the links a highlight color (we'll use a light orange-red this time around). Let's also style the `h4` element in this sidebar to be white text on a dark background, and let's center the text.

```
div#sitenav a {display: block; padding: 4px 8px; margin: 0;
   text-decoration: none; text-align: right;
   border-top: 1px solid gray;}
div#sitenav a:hover {background: #FB9;}
div#sitenav h4 {background: rgb(33%,33%,33%); color: white;
   text-align: center; margin: 0; padding: 0.25em 0 0.125em 0;}
div#entry {margin: 0 33% 1em 20%; padding: 0;}
```

Note that we had to redefine the margin and padding of the `h4` so that it would look better with its light-on-dark style.

Tweaking the New Layout

With this new configuration for the page, it would be visually more appealing to make the entry `div` a little wider. This will bring its right edge closer to the "Other Mutters" sidebar, but with the introduction of the `sitenav` sidebar, we need to redistribute things a little anyway.

```
div#entry {margin: 0 25% 1em 20%; padding: 0;}
```

Before we're done, we obviously want to get rid of the red and blue visualization backgrounds, so let's go ahead and delete those now. With these changes, we have the design shown in Figure 9.14.

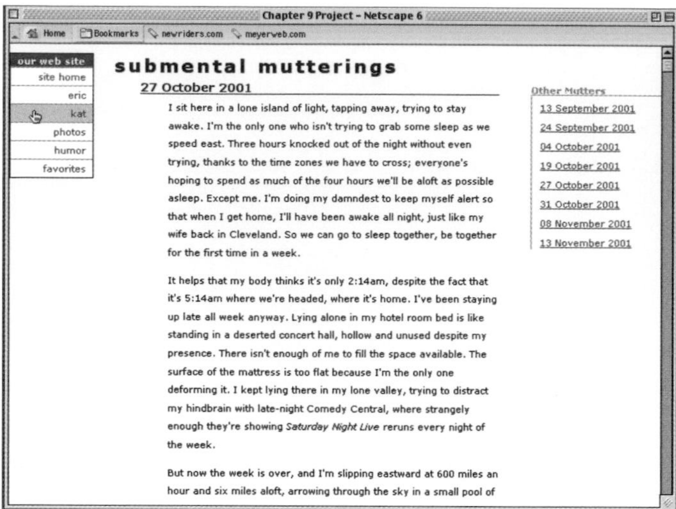

FIGURE 9.14

The adjusted layout with the entry column better balanced than before.

Taking Advantage of Our Positioning

Remember when we changed the `h1` so that it used padding instead of margins? Although it was done in part to avoid a bug in NS6.x, the other (and more interesting) reason was so we could jazz up the top of the page. We start by changing the margins of the `h1` even more and giving it a visible background. This also requires us to change the padding; otherwise, the `h1` text will overlap with the `sitenav` sidebar.

```
h1 {font-size: 200%; text-transform: lowercase; letter-spacing: 3px;
   margin: 0; padding: 0.66em 0 0.33em 16%;
   background: rgb(85%,85%,70%);}
```

To go with that background, we're also going to set a background on the date entry. Because the `h1` has no margins, the `h3` and the `h1` will touch, and their backgrounds will appear to be a single irregularly shaped area, as we can see in Figure 9.15.

```
h3 {font-size: 133%; margin: 0; padding: 0;
   border-bottom: 1px solid black;
   background: rgb(85%,85%,70%);}
```

The bottom border on the date looks kind of goofy now, so let's delete it. (Go ahead and remove it from your project file. I'll wait.) We should also give it some padding on the left side so that the text isn't hard up against the edge of the background color.

```
h3 {font-size: 133%; margin: 0; padding: 0 0 0 0.5em;
background: rgb(85%,85%,70%);}
```

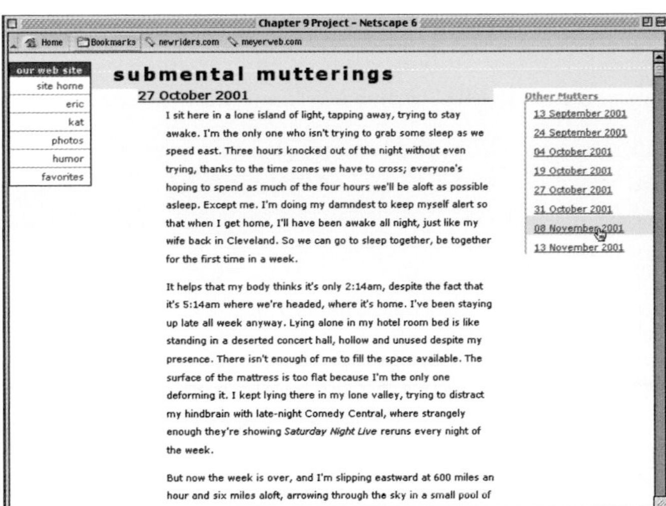

FIGURE 9.15

Shading in the backgrounds at the top.

Take another look at Figure 9.15. The way the date and the "Other Mutters" sidebar line up is kind of interesting and almost begs to be exploited. Let's connect the two! We can do this by making the entry `div` so wide that its right edge abuts the left edge of the sidebar.

```
div#entry {margin: 0 20% 1em 20%; padding: 0;}
div#sidebar {position: absolute; top: 4em; right: 0; width: 20%;
   font-size: 11px;}
```

What Slides Beneath

Note that the background of the `h1` element slides under the `sitenav` sidebar. This is to be expected when one element is positioned over another, and it can be used to accomplish a variety of design tricks.

Having done this, we need to give the paragraphs inside the entry enough of a right margin that they don't get too close to the sidebar. We could do some percentage math to figure out a good percentage value to assign, but let's just go with ems instead.

```
p {line-height: 1.66; margin: 0.5em 3em 1em 3em;}
```

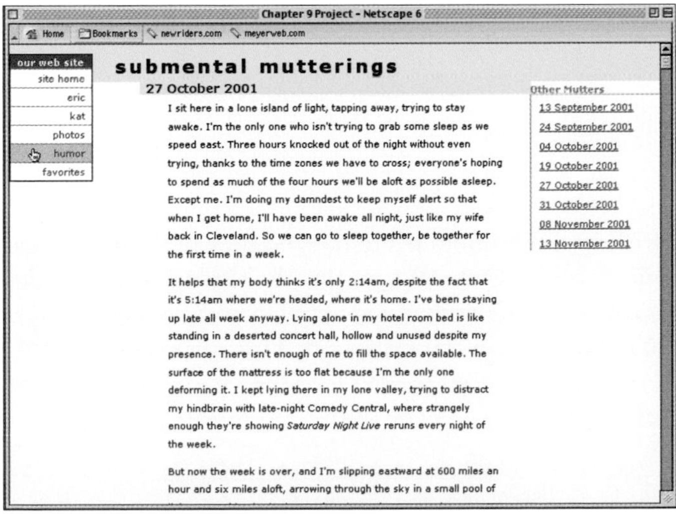

FIGURE 9.16

Bringing two columns very close together to make the top of the page seem more integrated.

Small Gaps and Overlaps

If you look very closely at the top of the "Other Mutters" title, you might see a slight gap between the bottom of the `h1` element and the top of the Mutters `h4`. This can happen when using ems to specify positioning and element sizes because fractional ems might be rounded in unexpected ways. This is why most positioning is done with pixels despite the loss of layout fluidity that pixels enforce.

Although our "punch-out" effect is somewhat interesting, it looks a little odd with the inverted-L border just beneath it. Rather than abandon those borders, let's adapt them and restyle the "Other Mutters" title to fit in.

It would be interesting to fill in the background of the `h4` with a darker variant of the background we set on the `h1` and `h3` elements. We'll want to remove the bottom border from the `h4` and also make sure its margin and padding are explicitly defined.

```
div#sidebar {position: absolute; top: 4em; right: 0; width: 20%;
   font-size: 11px;}
div#sidebar h4 {background: rgb(70%,70%,55%); color: black;
   margin: 0; padding: 0.25em 0 0 0.5em; border-width: 0;}
div#sidebar a {display: block; padding: 8px 0 2px 10px; margin: 0;
   border-left: 1px solid rgb(50%,50%,35%);}
```

Now that we've done that, the color of the hyperlinks' left border doesn't match the background of the `h4`. That's a quick fix, and it leads us to the result in Figure 9.17.

```
div#sidebar a {display: block; padding: 8px 0 2px 10px; margin: 0;
   border-left: 1px solid rgb(70%,70%,55%);}
```

FIGURE 9.17

Getting the right sidebar to mesh with the overall effect.

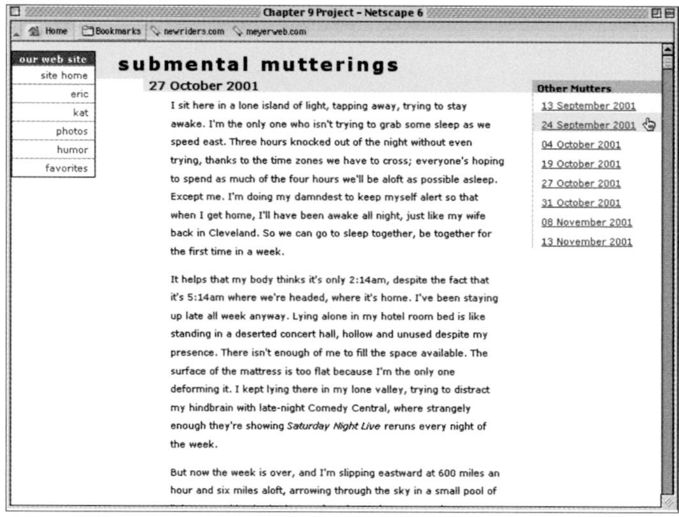

Doing the Math

Obviously, the "wild guess" is based on more than luck. We know the `h1` is `4em` tall, and the "our web site" `h4` is `1em` tall. It has `0.375em` of vertical padding, and there are the borders on the `h4` and the `div` itself to consider. That brings the bottom of the `h4` roughly `1.555em` below the top of the `div` that contains it. This would seem to imply `top: 2.455em`, but to pull the sidebar up just a little more, we rounded the value down to `2.33em`.

Cleaning Up

There are only a few minor things left to do, and they're almost unnecessary. You might have noticed from previous figures that the `sitenav` sidebar is positioned so that the border between "site home" and "eric" comes close to lining up with the bottom edge of the `h1` element's background. That suggests an idea: We could try aligning the border at the bottom of "our web site" with the bottom of the `h1`. Let's take a wild guess and change the value of `top` by a little bit.

```
div#sitenav {position: absolute; top: 2.33em; left: 0; width: 12.5%;
   font-size: 11px; background-color: white;
   border: 1px solid black;}
```

Finally, just to make sure we've left nothing to chance, let's give the sidebars values for `z-index`. By giving them these values, we make it much less likely that they'll be overlapped by other elements. This really is playing it safe because browsers typically won't let nonpositioned elements overlap positioned elements. But you never know what a future browser might do, and besides, we might add more positioned elements to the design in the future. Let's give the left sidebar a `z-index` of `10` and the right one a `z-index` of `11`. Because the sidebars don't overlap, we could have given the same value, but that could lead to trouble if a future design change brought them close enough to overlap. In such a case, the right sidebar would overlap the left one, because its `z-index` is higher and they share the same parent element.

These last few changes give us the style sheet provided in Listing 9.3 and the layout shown in Figure 9.18.

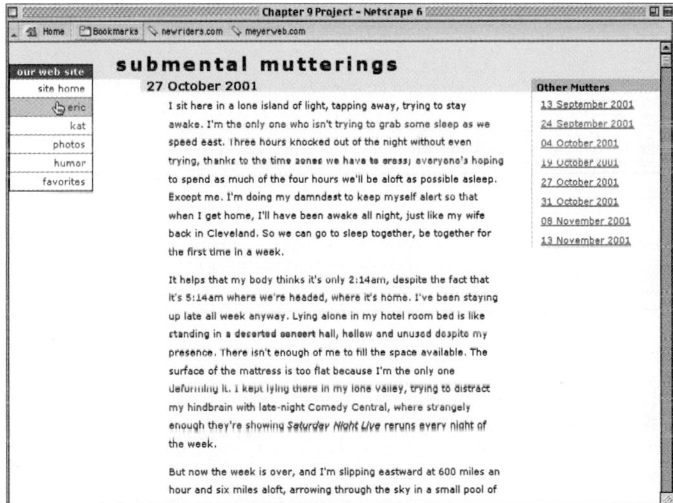

FIGURE 9.18

The positioned design as it finally stands.

Listing 9.3 The Fully Positioned Style Sheet

```
<style type="text/css">
html {margin: 0; padding: 0;}
body {font: 11px Verdana, Arial, Helvetica, sans-serif;
   margin: 0; padding: 0;
   background: rgb(95%,95%,80%); color: black;}
h1 {font-size: 200%; text-transform: lowercase; letter-spacing: 3px;
   margin: 0; padding: 0.66em 0 0.33em 16%;
   background: rgb(85%,85%,70%);}
h3 {font-size: 133%; margin: 0; padding: 0 0 0 0.5em;
   background: rgb(85%,85%,70%);}
h4 {font-size: 100%; margin: 0; padding: 0.33em 0 0;
   border-bottom: 1px solid rgb(50%,50%,35%);
   color: rgb(50%,50%,35%);}
h1, h3, h4 {line-height: 1em;}
p {line-height: 1.66; margin: 0.5em 3em 1em 3em;}
```

continues

Listing 9.3 Continued

```
div#sitenav {position: absolute; top: 3em; left: 0; width: 12.5%;
   font-size: 11px; background-color: white;
   border: 1px solid black; z-index: 10;}
div#sitenav a {display: block; padding: 4px 8px; margin: 0;
   text-decoration: none; text-align: right;
   border-top: 1px solid gray;}
div#sitenav a:hover {background: #FB9;}
div#sitenav h4 {background: rgb(33%,33%,33%); color: white;
   text-align: center; margin: 0; padding: 0.25em 0 0.125em 0;}
div#entry {margin: 0 20% 1em 20%; padding: 0;}
div#sidebar {position: absolute; top: 4em; right: 0; width: 20%;
   font-size: 11px; z-index: 11;}
div#sidebar h4 {background: rgb(70%,70%,55%); color: black;
   margin: 0; padding: 0.25em 0 0 0.5em; border-width: 0;}
div#sidebar a {display: block; padding: 8px 0 2px 10px; margin: 0;
   border-left: 1px solid rgb(70%,70%,55%);}
div#sidebar a:hover {background: rgb(85%,85%,70%);}
</style>
```

Refloating the Design

Positioning is certainly interesting, and in some cases, it's the only option available. With the particular design we've created, however, floating is still an option even with three columns. So let's convert the positioned sidebars back to floated sidebars partly for the heck of it but also to spend a little more time exploring the differences between positioning and floating elements.

Bringing Back the Float

The first step is probably the most obvious. We can take the rule for `div#sidebar` found in Listing 9.2 and use it to replace the positioning rule in Listing 9.3.

```
div#entry {margin: 0 20% 1em 20%; padding: 0;}
div#sidebar {margin: 0; padding: 0; float: right; width: 25%;}
div#sidebar h4 {background: rgb(70%,70%,55%); color: black;
   margin: 0; padding: 0.25em 0 0 0.5em; border-width: 0;}
```

Because of all the effort we undertook to position the sidebar in the same place it would have floated, there should be no visible change due to this code alteration.

When it comes to the `sitenav` sidebar, however, we have a bit more work to do. Here's our new rule, which is interesting as much for what got dropped as for what's been changed. Note that we got rid of the properties `top`, `left`, and `z-index`, all of which only apply to positioned elements, not floated elements. We can see the result in Figure 9.19.

```
div#sitenav {float: left; width: 12.5%;
   font-size: 11px; background-color: white;
   border: 1px solid black;}
```

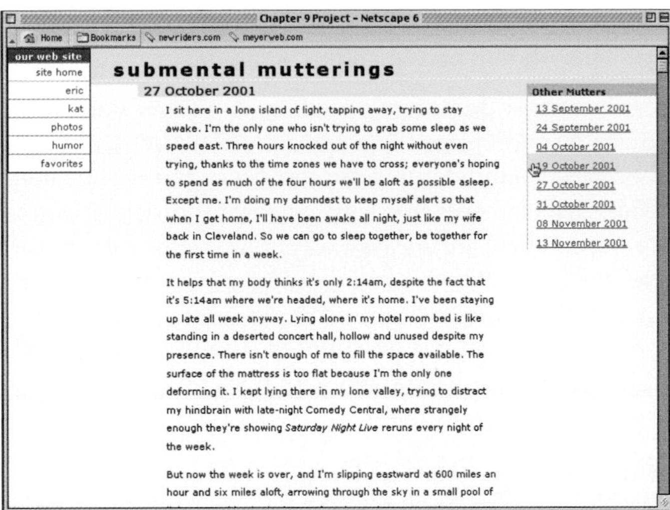

FIGURE 9.19

Floating instead of positioning.

The fix is simple enough: We look up the value we had for `top` when the element was positioned, and we make its top margin that very same value.

```
div#sitenav {float: left; width: 12.5%; margin-top: 2.33em;
   font-size: 11px; background-color: white;
   border: 1px solid black;}
```

With that, we're back to the same look we had when the sidebars were positioned.

What Slides Beneath: The Sequel

As before, the background of the `h1` is sliding under the sidebar. That's because floated elements are considered to be "above" the normal flow of the document, even though they affect text layout. Thus, the backgrounds and borders of elements in the normal flow will slide under floated elements just as they will with positioned elements.

Differences and Similarities

The change from floating to positioning and back isn't as remarkable for what's different as for what stays the same. Before we finish this project, it's worth taking a look back to compare the two approaches:

- Either way, the margins on the entry column—the main text, if you prefer—were crucial to staying out of the way of the side columns. After we'd determined how we wanted the page laid out, the entry margins only changed once, and that was when we added the third column.
- The big advantage to positioning is that it isn't nearly as dependent on the placement of an element in the document. With floating, you can only float to the left or right, and the placement of the float might depend on what elements come before it. Positioned elements can be put anywhere in relation to their containing block.
- Floated elements permit the backgrounds and borders of other elements to slide beneath them but not the text content. Positioned elements let anything slide under them. This makes it much easier for positioned elements to obscure text.

- Some properties (such as `top` and `z-index`) only apply to positioned elements. They should have no effect at all on floated elements.
- Whether floating or positioning a column, browser bugs make it almost a requirement that you place the column's `div` without any border, padding, margin, or background. Simply use the `div` as an invisible construct inside which you place elements that have whatever borders, margins, and so on that they need. There are always exceptions to this rule, but it's the best way to start.

Also remember that although our design used columns to create sidebars, these columns could as easily have been filled with text, images, funny quotes, or anything else you care to put in them.

Despite the differences between the two approaches, we can still get good designs either way. Consider Figure 9.20: Does it use floats or positioning to achieve the layout effects we see? Only its hairdresser knows for sure!

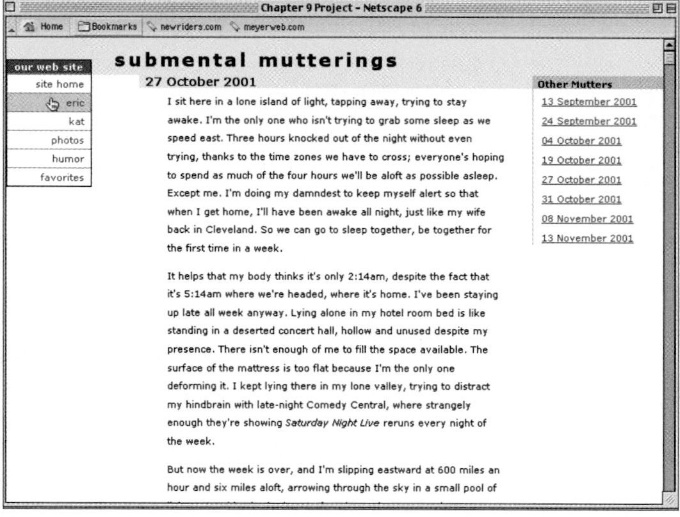

FIGURE 9.20

Floated or positioned, the design still looks good!

Branching Out

When it comes to floats and positioning, there are almost too many choices to make, since you can do almost anything. Here are but a few ideas to get you thinking.

1. Return to the style sheet shown in Listing 9.2 and alter it to link up the borders beneath the entry date and the "Other Mutters" sidebar. (Also try the same for the styles that produced Figure 9.14.) If the borders don't quite line up, remember that you might have to nail down the height of one or more headings with `line-height`. Then try moving the border from the links to the `div` itself and try playing with the widths and margins of the entry and sidebar `div`s.

2. Using the style sheet in Listing 9.2, change the font and font size defined for the `body` element and make the `h1` element larger (such as `250%` instead of `200%`). Note what has to be changed—and what doesn't—before making any necessary adjustments to the styles. Now make the same changes to the style sheet in Listing 9.3. Remember that the sidebars had their font sizes declared independently and again note what changes need to be made before making any. Do your best to work out why you have to change what you do and (just as importantly) why you don't have to make other changes.

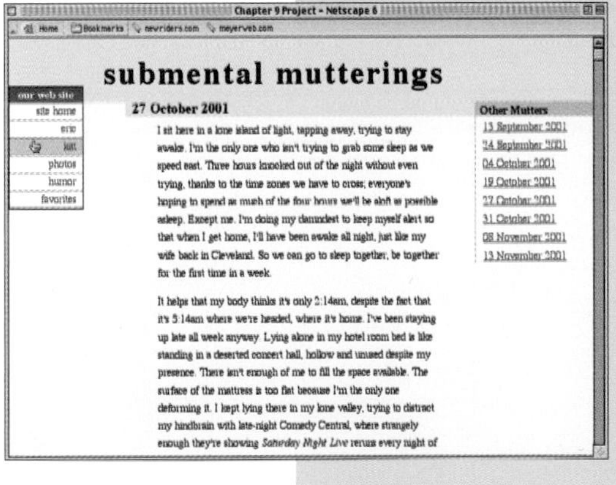

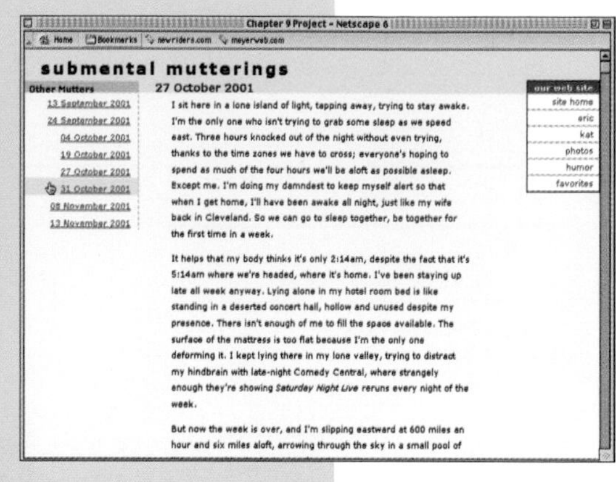

3. Try flipping the left and right columns of the three-column layout. This involves switching not only text alignment and border placement but also the width of the entry column, the placement of the background on the entry date, the padding on the `h1` element, the margins of the entry paragraphs, and potentially more. Try it with both positioning and floating styles and observe the different factors that have to be tracked in each case. Remember to prevent overlap of the column contents.

10

Sneaking Out of the Box

I'll turn him into a flea. A small, harmless little flea. Then I'll put that flea into a box and put that box inside another box, and then I'll mail that box to myself, and when it arrives I'll SMASH IT WITH A HAMMER! It's brilliant brilliant brilliant, I tell you! Genius, I say!

—*The Emperor's New Groove* (2000)

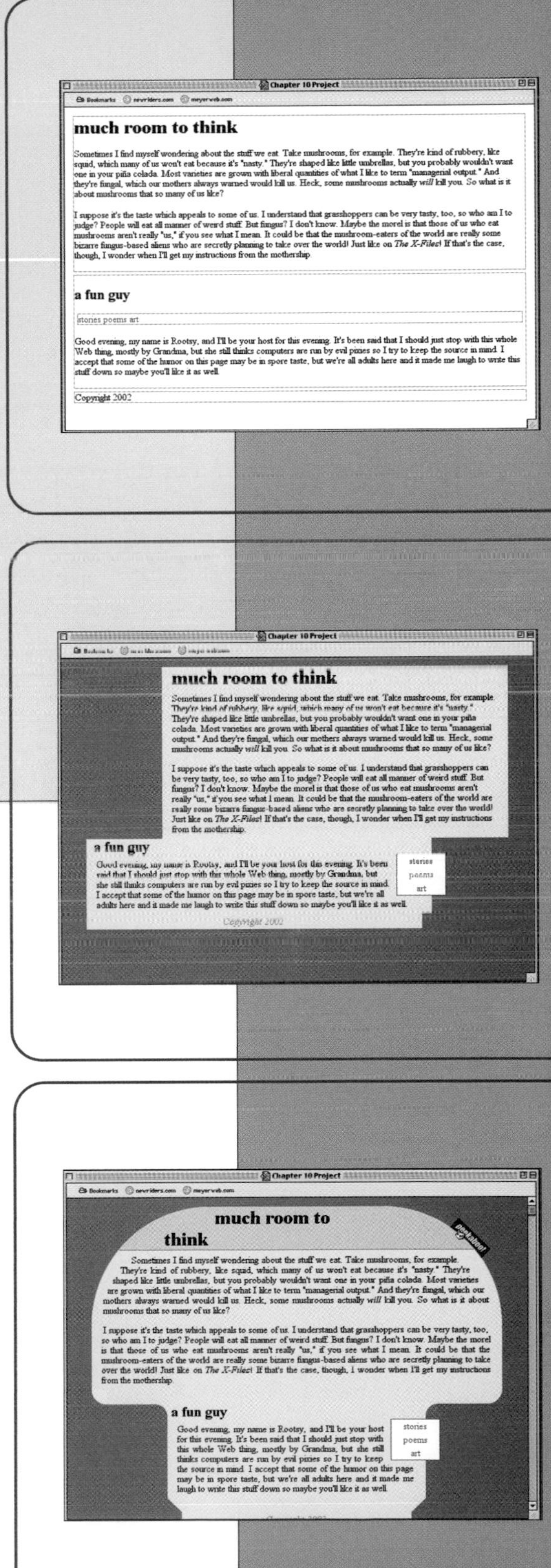

The history of Web design to date has been one of overcoming confinement. When you get right down to it, the tools we've been given to accomplish compelling design are woefully limited because HTML elements generate nothing but rectangular boxes. Headings, paragraphs, and even lists are all a series of boxes at their core.

The granddaddy of all boxiness is the table, of course. We've spent years taking an inherently gridlike structure and doing our utmost to bend it into something less rigid. How many designers have taken an image and split it up into two, three, or more pieces just so that it can straddle some cell divisions and provide the illusion that the page isn't composed of a series of boxes? How many of us have wished that, just once, we could have a table cell with a rounded corner?

It's also true that CSS does not fundamentally change things. In fact, Chapter 8 of the Cascading Style Sheets, Level 2 Specification (`www.w3.org/TR/REC-CSS2/`), devoted to describing how elements are laid out, is titled "Box

Model." As of yet, CSS is still an inheritor of HTML's rectangular legacy, but that doesn't mean it doesn't offer some relief. Thanks to some almost completely unknown subtleties of CSS, it's possible to create diagonal lines without graphics and have text flow along a curve. This project will explore some ways to do both.

Project Goals

A friend who maintains a site of humorous little observations has asked for an example of an eye-catching, unusual layout that he could use on his Web site. After making sure his visitors are all using post-version 4 browsers, we ask for and receive a sample document.

For this project, we have only the vaguest of instructions from our client. He's a big fan of the color purple, and most of his current site is designed around different shades of purple, so we need to carry that through into our design. (Because he doesn't have a consistent set of shades, we get to pick our own in this project.) Our friend has also asked that the layout be, "You know, cool and organic without being too out there. Unusual. Something nobody's ever seen before. That should be easy for you, right?"

Preparation

See the Introduction for instructions on how to download files from the Web site.

Download the files for Project 10 from this book's Web site. If you're planning to play along at home, load the file `ch10proj.html` into the editing program of your choice. This is the file you'll be editing, saving, and reloading as the project progresses.

Laying the Groundwork

The project is, as usual, fairly short, but this time it has a somewhat unusual structure. There are two main sections to the text—each wrapped in a `div` element—and a final `div` for the footer. In addition, the menu comes partway through the page. Listing 10.1 shows the basic page skeleton, and Figure 10.1 shows the page with temporary borders set for all the `div` elements.

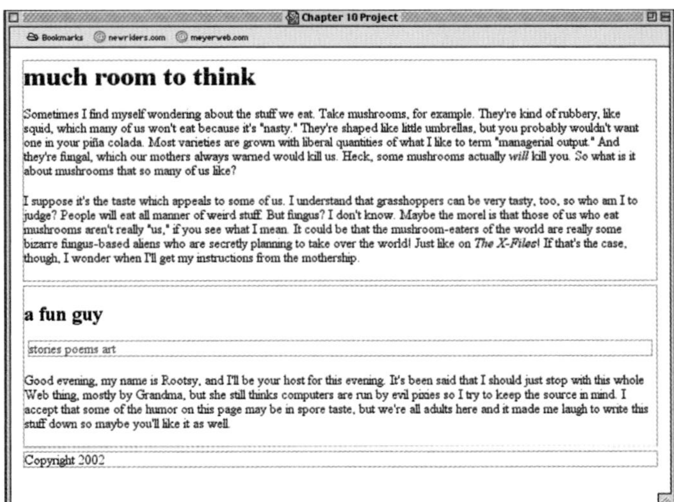

FIGURE 10.1

The project file in its raw, barely styled state.

Class Plus ID

Although uncommon, it's perfectly legal to give an element both a `class` and an `id`. As we'll see in this project, this can be incredibly useful in certain circumstances.

Listing 10.1 The Page's Basic Structure

```
<body>
<div class="wrap" id="p1">
</div>
<div class="wrap" id="p2">
  <div id="menu">
  </div>
</div>
<div class-"wrap" id-"footer">
</div>
</body>
```

There are a few things of interest to note about this particular markup structure:

- The three main sections of the page all share the class `wrap`. This will be highly useful for giving them all a common set of styles.
- The menu `div` is a descendant of the second of the three top-level `div` elements. At this point in the project, only the menu `div` does not have this class or indeed any class at all.
- Every `div` has an `id` value. This makes it simple to apply any styles meant specifically for a given `div` without interfering with the others.

With this in mind, we can proceed to setting up the page's styles.

Styling the Document

Because we don't have a lot in the way of specific guidance, we're mostly going to have to make things up as we go. It's a good thing we have a lot of practice in that arena. We'll start out by setting some basic background and color styles, fiddling with the margins on the various sections of the document, and seeing where the results lead us.

Separation Anxiety

We're going for a purple-colored page as decided earlier, but it would be good to keep black text on a light background. That calls for giving the "wrappers" a lighter variant of the document's background color.

First we need to remove the medium-gray borders that were used in Figure 10.1 to help us understand the page's structure. To get a wine-colored background, we'll go with a `body` background color of `#969`, which is a decently dusky purple. For the actual content, we'll give the `div`s a background of `#FDF`. For both, we'll make the text color black. All of this has the result seen in Figure 10.2.

```
<title>Chapter 10 Project</title>
<style type="text/css">
body {background: #969; color: black;}
div.wrap {background: #FDF; color: black;}
</style>
</head>
```

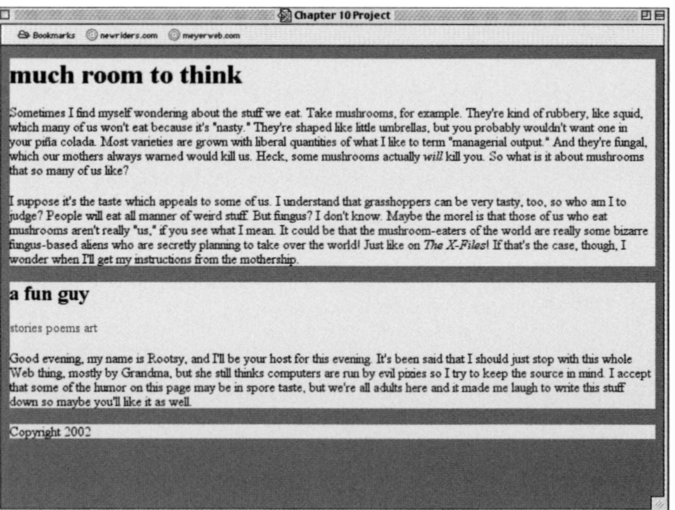

Chapter 10 Project

Bookmarks newriders.com meyerweb.com

much room to think

Sometimes I find myself wondering about the stuff we eat. Take mushrooms, for example. They're kind of rubbery, like squid, which many of us won't eat because it's "nasty." They're shaped like little umbrellas, but you probably wouldn't want one in your piña colada. Most varieties are grown with liberal quantities of what I like to term "managerial output." And they're fungal, which our mothers always warned would kill us. Heck, some mushrooms actually *will* kill you. So what is it about mushrooms that so many of us like?

I suppose it's the taste which appeals to some of us. I understand that grasshoppers can be very tasty, too, so who am I to judge? People will eat all manner of weird stuff. But fungus? I don't know. Maybe the morel is that those of us who eat mushrooms aren't really "us," if you see what I mean. It could be that the mushroom-eaters of the world are really some bizarre fungus-based aliens who are secretly planning to take over the world! Just like on *The X-Files*! If that's the case, though, I wonder when I'll get my instructions from the mothership.

a fun guy

stories poems art

Good evening, my name is Rootsy, and I'll be your host for this evening. It's been said that I should just stop with this whole Web thing, mostly by Grandma, but she still thinks computers are run by evil pixies so I try to keep the source in mind. I accept that some of the humor on this page may be in spore taste, but we're all adults here and it made me laugh to write this stuff down so maybe you'll like it as well.

Copyright 2002

Figure 10.2

Making the page wine a bit.

Color Safe?

Although the page's background color is Web safe, the `div` backgrounds are not. The closest safe color would be `#FCF`. In this particular project this will not be a problem, but it could be in any project that seeks to mix a lot of graphics and CSS-based colors.

We can immediately see a problem: the gaps between the `div`s. This is happening because of the margins of the paragraphs, which are used to determine separation between elements. This doesn't happen in every browser, but it happens in enough of them that it's a concern for us. The fix is easy: Set paragraph margins to zero and enforce the separation using padding instead.

```
div.wrap {background: #FDF; color: black;}
p {margin: 0; padding: 0.5em 1em;}
</style>
```

This new rule not only helps fix our gap problem, it also pushes the paragraph content inward from the edges of the divs, which looks better anyway. We'd better get rid of the heading element's top margins, which could give us more separation problems.

```
p {margin: 0; padding: 0.5em 1em;}
h1, h2 {margin: 0; padding: 0 0.5em;}
</style>
```

With these changes in place, the divs effectively run together, creating the illusion of a single block of content instead of three distinct sections. We can see this in Figure 10.3.

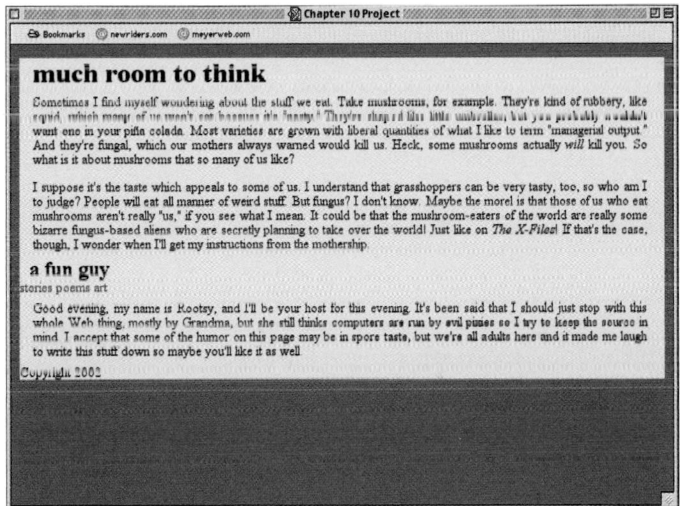

FIGURE 10.3

Bringing the pieces of the page together makes them seem to be one big element.

Now that we've achieved this wonderful visual unity, it's time to start breaking it up (but in a good way!).

►► MARGINS, PADDING, AND SEPARATION

To keep the usual one em separation between paragraph text, we've had to give each one a top and bottom padding of `0.5em`*. This is because padding does not overlap but vertically adjacent margins do. Most authors don't think about this aspect of layout, but it's an important point.*

For example, consider the case of one `div` *that follows another, with both* `div`*s having a margin set.*

continues

continued

```
<div style="margin: 1em;">div one</div>
<div style="margin: 1em;">div one</div>
```

How much space would you expect to appear between the text of the two `divs`*? Most people would say one em, and that's what CSS says, too. But if the first* `div` *has a bottom margin of* `1em` *and the second a top margin of* `1em`*, why aren't there two ems of space between the* `div` *text?*

This happens because when margins are vertically adjacent, as they are in the preceding sample code, the margins effectively overlap. The distance between the borders of two elements will be equal to the larger of the adjacent margins. Thus, if the first `div` *had a bottom margin of* `1px` *and the second a top margin of* `15px`*, the distance between the two would be* `15px`*.*

This is all fairly obvious once you stop to think about it. However, padding does not behave in this way. Suppose we change our example from margins to padding.

```
<div style="padding: 1em;">div one</div>
<div style="padding: 1em;">div one</div>
```

Now there really will be two ems of space between the two. Therefore, to keep the layout consistent, we would have to cut the amount of top and bottom padding in half—and that's just what we did in our project.

Moving the Edges

It's time to take our big box of a page and make it a little less boxy. The first step is simply to push the edges of the content away from the edges of the browser window.

```
div.wrap {background: #FDF; color: black; margin: 0 2em;}
```

That's all it takes to make the content a bit narrower. That leads to the next step: Why give all of the `divs` the same margins? If we vary them from section to section, the box won't be quite so boxy anymore, as shown in Figure 10.4.

```
h1, h2 {margin: 0; padding: 0 0.5em;}
div#p1 {margin: 0 2em 0 10em;}
div#p2 {margin: 0 10em 0 2em;}
div#footer {margin: 0 11em 0 2em;}
</style>
```

In a sense, we've made the two main sections of the page into mirrors of each other. The first part has a `2em` right margin and a `10em` left margin; with the second part, the values are reversed. Then, just to keep the footer a little different, we made its left side match up with the `div` right above it but pushed its right side in a little further (with `11em`).

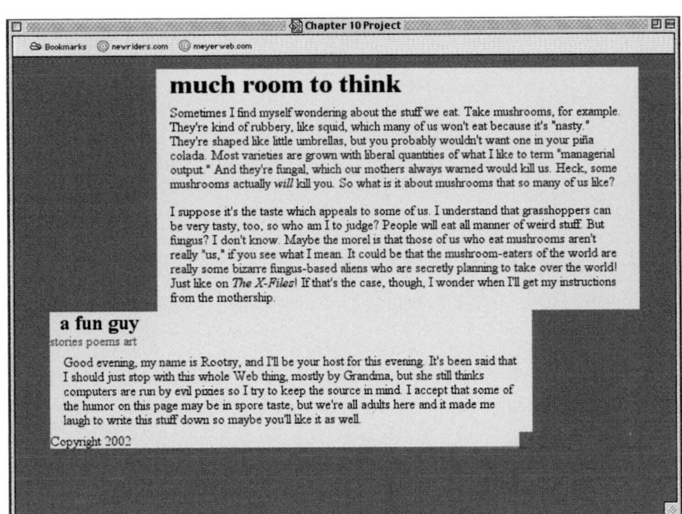

FIGURE 10.4

Breaking up the box.

There are two things in Figure 10.4 that stand out as needing some help: the menu and the footer. Let's quickly style the footer because all we really need is to give it some padding and maybe center the text. Well, okay, let's also italicize it and make its color match the body's background.

```
div#footer {margin: 0 11em 0 2em; padding: 0.25em;
   text-align: center; font-style: italic; color: #969;}
```

With that done, let's give the menu a workover.

Menu Magic

With three links in a `div`, the menu is actually pretty simple. Let's try floating the `div` itself to the right and seeing how that turns out (see Figure 10.5). Remember that when you float a text element, you need to give it a `width`. Because the links are fairly short, let's make the menu fairly narrow. We'll also give it a black border and a white background so that we can visualize its position on the page a little better.

```
div#p2 {margin: 0 10em 0 2em;}
div#menu {float: right; width: 5em;
   border: 1px solid black; background: white;}
div#footer {margin: 0 11em 0 2em; padding: 0.25em;
   text-align: center; font-style: italic; color: #969;}
```

Well, it's a start. Let's make sure the text doesn't get too close to the menu itself by giving it some margins. Let's also pull the menu to the right with a negative margin. This will cause it to stick out into the dark purple background. We'll also set the padding to zero just to be certain.

```
div#menu {float: right; width: 5em;
   padding: 0; margin: 0 -1.5em 0.25em 0.5em;
   border: 1px solid black; background: white;}
```

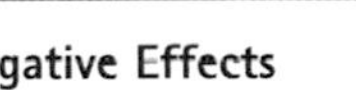

Negative Effects

For some reason, IE5.x/Win treats negative right and left margins as if they were larger than they really are. In some cases, it practically doubles the distance specified. This makes negative margins on floats of limited value, although it's still possible in some designs (like this one) to use them without major problems. Any design that requires the precise placement of an element shouldn't use floats with negative side margins.

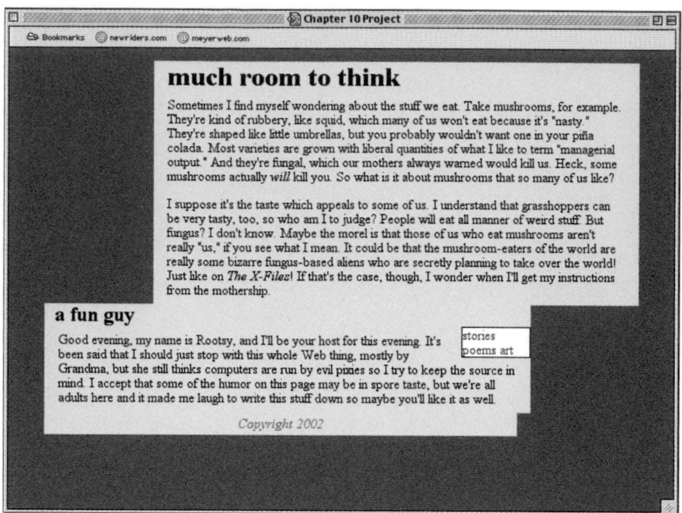

FIGURE 10.5

Floating the menu to the right.

The black border on the menu is a little harsh, especially when it's surrounded by all that purple. Let's soften it up bit by changing the border's color to something a little darker than the page background. We'll just take the body's background color of `#969` and drop the digits two each.

```
div#menu {float: right; width: 5em;
   padding: 0; margin: 0 -1.5em 0.25em 0.5em;
   border: 1px solid #747; background: white;}
```

Of course, the links are all running together like regular text because they're inline elements. If we want each one on its own line, we're going to have to do something about it ourselves. Rather than inserting `<br>` elements, we'll just turn them into block-level elements (see Project 5, "How to Skin a Menu," for more information). Let's add in some padding and center the link text while we're at it; the result is shown in Figure 10.6.

```
div#menu {float: right; width: 5em;
   padding: 0; margin: 0 -1.5em 0.25em 0.5em;
   border: 1px solid #747; background: white;}
div#menu a {display: block; text-align: center;
   padding: 0.2em 0.5em;}
div#footer {margin: 0 11em 0 2em; padding: 0.25em;
   text-align: center; font-style: italic; color: #969;}
```

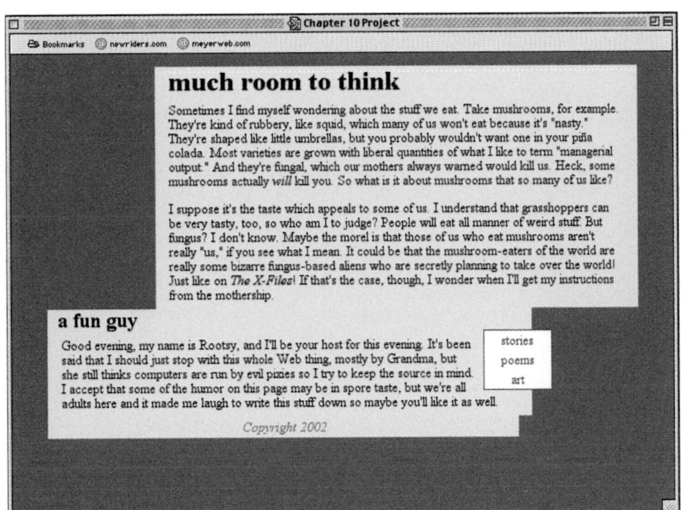

FIGURE 10.6

Moving the menu out of its parent and blocking out the links.

Thinking at an Angle

Our design isn't too bad, all things considered. Granted, we're still seeing a lot of straight lines and sharp corners, but the effect is of having an irregular polygon instead of the usual rectangles. Still, it would be pretty nifty if we could put in some diagonal lines. That would break up the straight lines of the layout we have so far. It would be even cooler to not use images to create these diagonals but instead coax them out of the combination of regular HTML elements and some minimal styling.

Impossible, you say? In fact, it's quite possible using nothing more than what's found in CSS1. For the current project, let's alter the end of the page a bit. We'll make the footer narrower than the `div` before it, and we'll tie the two together with diagonal lines. The best part is that we can do this simply by styling the footer `div` itself.

First we'll alter the footer's margins so that they match the margins of the `div#p2`, and then we'll give the footer a really thick border with amazingly loud colors, as shown in Figure 10.7.

```
div#footer {margin: 0 10em 0 2em; padding: 0.25em;
   text-align: center; font-style: italic; color: #969;
   border: 1.5em solid; border-color: red lime blue cyan;}
```

FIGURE 10.7

The footer gets some very loud borders.

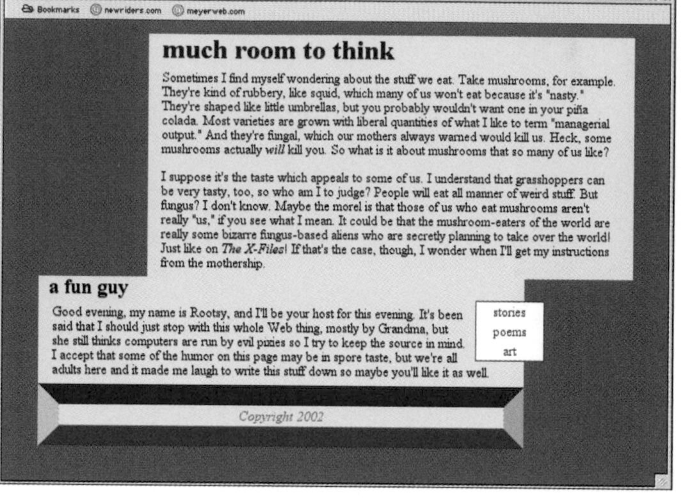

How Did He Think of That?

The inspiration for this effect came from the demonstration titled "An Exercise in Regular Polygons," which can be found at `www.tantek.com/CSS/Examples/`. Tantek Çelik's brilliant insight in demonstrating that CSS-based diagonals are possible set the stage for effects such as the one we're using in this project.

Wow, that's ugly. It's also temporary and is intended solely to help show how we're going to get to our goal. Take a close look at the corners of the footer. See the diagonal boundaries that are created where the colors meet? They've always been there, existing at the corners of every element's border. Because so few of us ever make our borders more than a pixel or two wide or set different colors for each border side, these diagonals have gone largely unnoticed. Now that we've found them, we can put them to use.

The key lies in manipulating the colors and widths of the individual borders so that we get the effect we desire. Rather than red/lime/blue/cyan, we need to use the two colors that are adjacent to this `div`. Therefore, we need to set the side borders to match the `body` background and the top border to match the `div` background above it.

```
div#footer {margin: 0 10em 0 2em; padding: 0.25em;
   text-align: center; font-style: italic; color: #969;
   border: 1.5em solid; border-color: #FDF #969;}
```

More Separation

Notice that this has created extra space between the text and the footer. The top border creates this space (a fact easily verified by setting the footer's top border color to some obvious color like `yellow`), so it can't be eliminated. We could reduce it by making the border narrower, but that would reduce the width of the side borders as well as the top border.

With the colors set, there is only one more thing to take care of. Right now, the bottom border of the footer widens the light purple area back out, which isn't quite the effect we're after.

We have two choices. One is to make the bottom border's width `0`. This would cause it to effectively cease to exist and would get rid of the extra light purple that we don't want. The other choice is to set the bottom border's color to match the `body`'s background, which causes it to disappear visually. It doesn't really matter which option we choose, but changing the color involves less typing, so we'll go with that solution. The result can be seen in Figure 10.8.

```
div#footer {margin: 0 10em 0 2em; padding: 0.25em;
   text-align: center; font-style: italic; color: #969;
   border: 1.5em solid; border-color: #FDF #969 #969;}
```

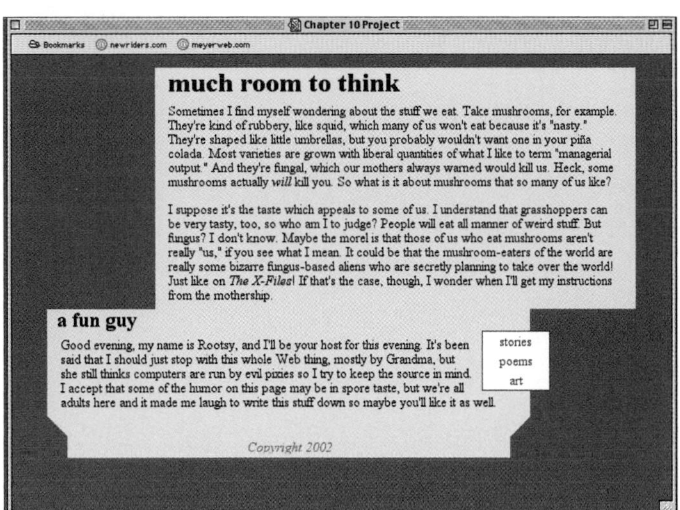

FIGURE 10.8

Diagonal lines for your viewing pleasure.

As cool as this trick is, it really only works in situations like this one in which you want to bridge the gap between two elements by widening or narrowing the background color they share. If they have different colors or there are already borders, the effect doesn't work as well. It also breaks down in most situations where a background image is being used.

The result of our labor thus far can be seen in Listing 10.2. We're about to move on to the next step: curves.

Listing 10.2 The Style Sheet So Far

```
<style type="text/css">
body {background: #969; color: black;}
div.wrap {background: #FDF; color: black; margin: 0 2em;}
p {margin: 0; padding: 0.5em 1em;}
h1, h2 {margin: 0; padding: 0 0.5em;}
div#p1 {margin: 0 2em 0 10em;}
div#p2 {margin: 0 10em 0 2em;}
div#menu {float: right; width: 5em;
   padding: 0; margin: 0 -1.5em 0.25em 0.5em;
   border: 1px solid #747; background: white;}
div#menu a {display: block; text-align: center;
   padding: 0.2em 0.5em;}
div#footer {margin: 0 10em 0 2em; padding: 0.25em;
   text-align: center; font-style: italic; color: #969;
   border: 1.5em solid; border-color: #FDF #969 #969;}
</style>
```

Curves Ahead

So far, we've seen how to put boxes together to create irregular shapes and how to use borders to create diagonal lines. What about curves, though? Is it possible to coax HTML elements into showing curves?

The basic answer is "no." But with simple images and some creative styling, we can set up curved corners and even have text flow along a curve instead of inside boxes.

Pulling Up a Toadstool

Given the topic being discussed on the page, it would be kind of nifty to create a mushroom-shaped layout, wouldn't it? Of course it would. So let's fiddle with a few margins to get the basic toadstool shape out of our layout (see Figure 10.9).

```
div#p1 {margin: 0 2em;}
div#p2 {margin: 0 10em;}
div#menu {float: right; width: 5em;
   padding: 0; margin: 0 -1.5em 0.25em 0.5em;
   border: 1px solid #747; background: white;}
div#menu a {display: block; text-align: center;
   padding: 0.2em 0.5em;}
div#footer {margin: 0 10em; padding: 0.25em;
   text-align: center; font-style: italic; color: #969;
   border: 1.5em solid; border-color: #FDF #969 #969;}
```

Figure 10.9

A few simple edits lead to major layout changes.

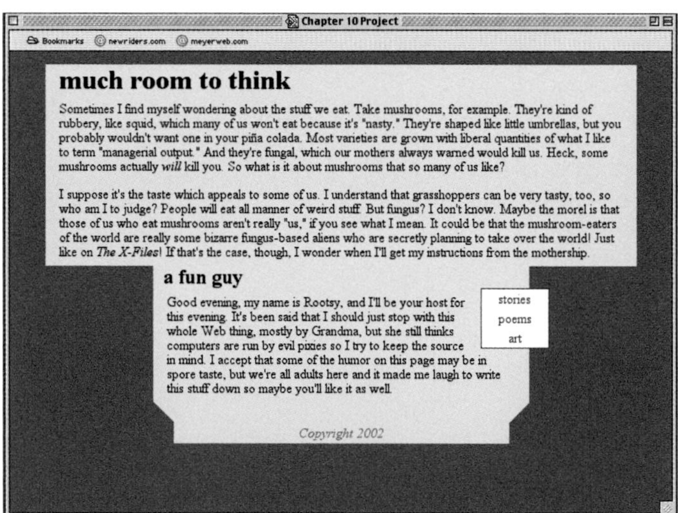

All right, so it's really more of a "T" shape than a toadstool shape. To get a nice morel layout, we need to round off the various sharp corners, mostly in the "cap" part of the layout (`div#p1`). That won't necessarily be simple, but it will definitely be interesting.

The Bottom of the Cap

Let's start out by rounding off the bottom corners of the mushroom's cap. We'll need two separate images to pull this effect off, with both of them being placed in a single div. The images are shown in Figure 10.10 at four times their normal size.

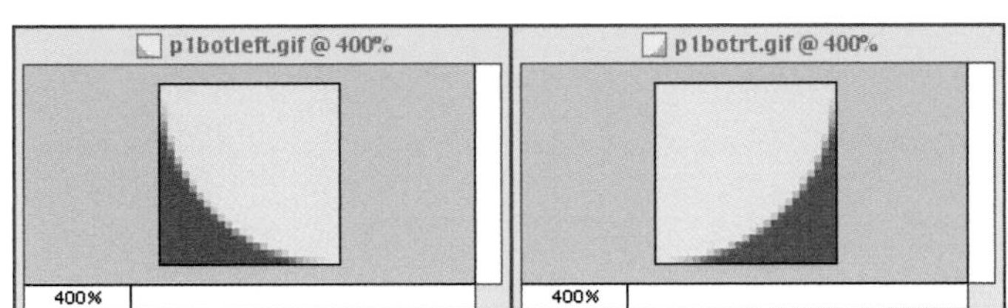

FIGURE 10.10

The two GIF files we'll use to round off the cap.

Our first step will be to add a bit of markup to the document itself. What we want is a div that contains the bottom-right corner image, not the bottom left.

```
<p>
I suppose it's the taste which appeals to some of us.  I understand that
grasshoppers can be very tasty, too, so who am I to judge?  People will eat all
manner of weird stuff.  But fungus?  I don't know.  Maybe the morel is that
those of us who eat mushrooms aren't really "us," if you see what I mean.  It
could be that the mushroom-eaters of the world are really some bizarre fungus-
based aliens who are secretly planning to take over the world!  Just like on
<cite>The X-Files</cite>!  If that's the case, though, I wonder when I'll get
my instructions from the mothership.
</p>
<div id="p1end"><img src="p1botrt.gif" alt=" "></div>
</div>
```

Removing Whitespace

We've eliminated any spaces between the img and the div tags to make sure no extra space opens up in the div. Some browsers, most notably IE5.x/Win, will interpret even carriage returns as a space that needs to be placed on the page. This may or may not be correct, but we can sidestep the potential problem by eliminating unneeded spaces.

Now we have an appropriately identified div containing an image. Of course, the image will be left-aligned unless we do something to change that. We can put it in the right corner with a simple text-align style, but while we're at it, let's put the other corner in place.

```
div#p1 {margin: 0 2em;}
div#p1end {text-align: right; margin: 0; padding: 0;
  background: #FDF url(p1botleft.gif) bottom left no-repeat;}
div#p2 {margin: 0 10em;}
```

The important part here is that we've moved the p1botrt.gif image to the right side of the div and put the p1botleft.gif image in bottom-left corner of the div. Because the div is the last thing in the cap, both images will end up in the corners, as you can see in Figure 10.11.

Just like that, we've managed to give our design some curvy corners. Let's continue with the idea by rounding off the corners where the cap meets the stem.

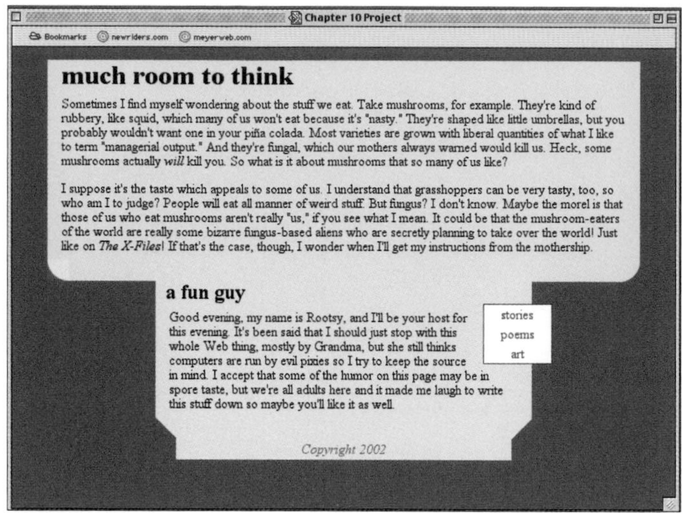

FIGURE 10.11

A rounded cap bottom softens the design.

A Rounded Heading

We could insert another `div` at the top of the `div#p2` to put in our curves, but there's no need: We already have an element right there that will do the job. The `h2` element simply needs an image and a little style.

Actually, it needs two new images because the ones we used in the mushroom's cap won't do here. The images we'll be working into the `h2` are shown in Figure 10.12.

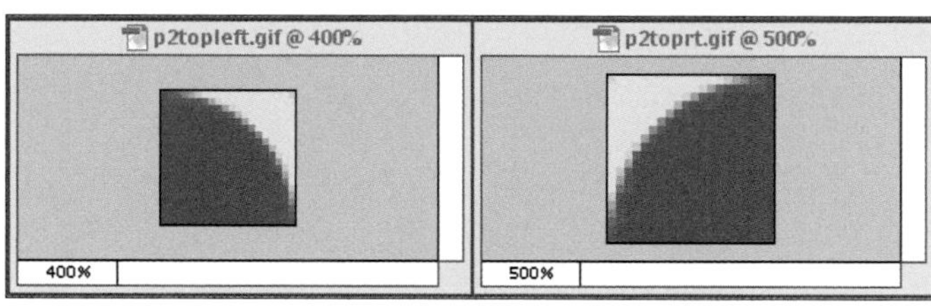

FIGURE 10.12

The two GIF files we'll use to blend cap with stem.

Blank `alt`

We're giving these images a blank `alt` value because they don't contribute anything to the content of the page and don't need to be described in any way by screen readers for the blind. This might be different if we were placing logos or buttons, but we aren't.

However, we can't do this the same way as the `div#p1end` worked. If we try to right-align the `h2` to put the right-side curve in, the text in the `h2` will right-align as well, and we don't want that. Therefore, the top-left corner for the stem will go into the beginning of the `h2` element.

```
<h2><img src="p2topleft.gif" alt=" "> a fun guy</h2>
```

Note that we put a space between the image and the text. That's to keep the text from bumping up next to the image.

Now we need to drop the top-right corner curve into the top-right corner of the h2's background. While we're at it, we need to make sure the top-left curve will be aligned with the top of the h2 element.

```
h1, h2 {margin: 0; padding: 0 0.5em;}
h2 {background: transparent url(p2toprt.gif) right top no-repeat;}
h2 img {vertical-align: top;}
div#p1 {margin: 0 2em;}
```

Being Transparent

We've deliberately set the background color to be transparent so that any background colors can show through the h2. This will become crucial before we're done.

So now we have one curve in the top-left corner of the h2's content and another in the top-right corner of the background. There's only one problem: This places the curves inside the stem. They need to be outside it for the illusion to work.

We know that the curve images are 20 pixels on a side and that we can't let the h2 have any padding. Padding will push the top-left corner away from the place it needs to be. Therefore, we need to set the padding to zero and the right and left margins of the h2 to be -20px. This will pull the left and right edges of the h2 out of the stem, taking the corner images right along with them. We can see this effect in Figure 10.13.

```
h2 {margin: 0 -20px; padding: 0;
   background: transparent url(p2toprt.gif) right top no-repeat;}
```

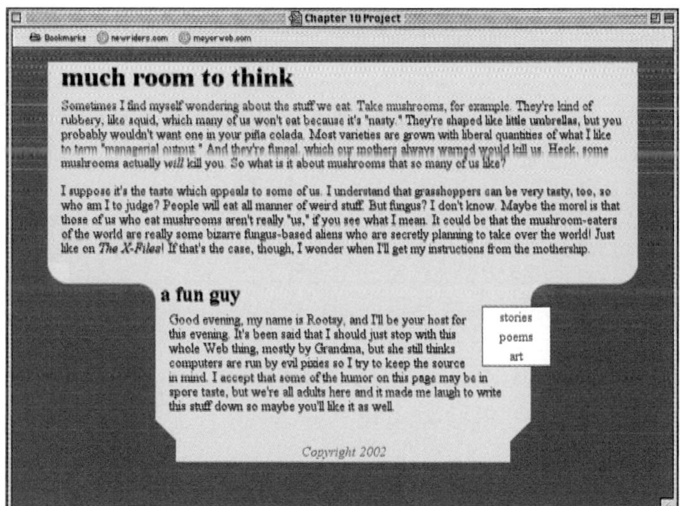

FIGURE 10.13

Negative margins and no padding put the curves right where they need to be.

The cap and stem have some nice curves to them, but we aren't done yet. The bottom of the cap is done, but what about the top? It's still awfully blocky.

Capping the Cap

Looking at the top of the cap, it seems fairly obvious that we could just stick rounded corners into the `h1` and call it done. So, of course, that's not what we're going to do. Instead, we're going to take the idea of curves in Web design to a whole new level. We're not only going to put large curves into the top corners of this design, we're going to get the text to flow along with those curves. Really.

First we need a curve graphic big enough for our purposes. A 200×200 graphic would be just about the right size. Then we need to divide it into a number of layers. For our purposes, we've going to divide it into eight sections, as illustrated in Figure 10.14.

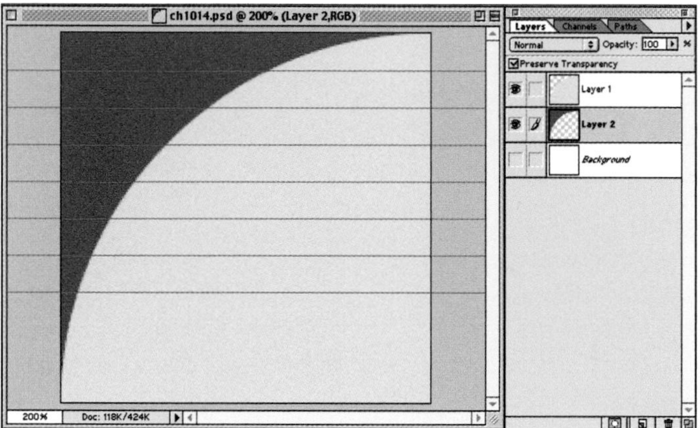

FIGURE 10.14

The top-left curve (as seen in Adobe Photoshop).

We could have gone to 10 sections, each one 20 pixels tall, but the bottom of the curve can be just as easily captured in the 60-pixel-tall section shown.

Now here's the tedious part. For each curve section, select an area just big enough to encompass the dark purple area. (You'll understand why in a moment.) Save that selected area as a GIF file and make the light purple color in each graphic transparent. An example of the results can be seen in Figure 10.15, which shows two of the curve graphics.

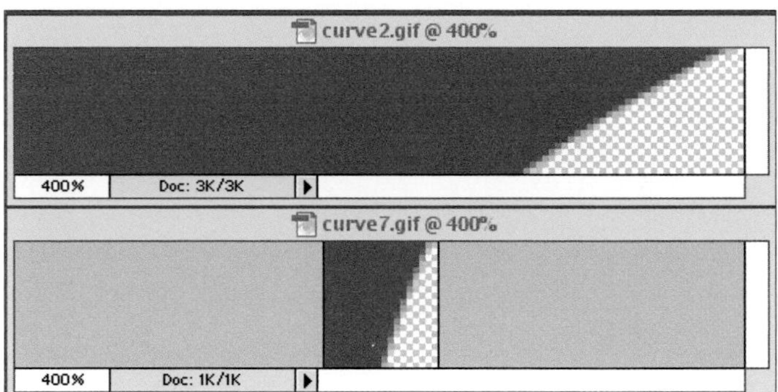

FIGURE 10.15

Two sections of the curve; the checkerboard pattern indicates transparency.

When we have all eight graphics (call them `curve1.gif` through `curve8.gif`), we put them in a folder called `curve-l`. To get them into the document, we'll need to add some markup.

```
<body>
<div class="wrap" id="p1">
<img src="curve-l/curve1.gif" alt=" " class="curve-l">
<img src="curve-l/curve2.gif" alt=" " class="curve-l">
<img src="curve-l/curve3.gif" alt=" " class="curve-l">
<img src="curve-l/curve4.gif" alt=" " class="curve-l">
<img src="curve-l/curve5.gif" alt=" " class="curve-l">
<img src="curve-l/curve6.gif" alt=" " class="curve-l">
<img src="curve-l/curve7.gif" alt=" " class="curve-l">
<img src="curve-l/curve8.gif" alt=" " class="curve-l">
<h1>much room to think</h1>
```

Now that we have them in the document, we need to assemble them into a curve. As they are now, the pieces will just be shown one after another in a line or two because they're inline elements. We need to fix that, but we need to be clever about it. Rather than making them block-level elements, we can float them all to the left.

```
div#footer {margin: 0 10em; padding: 0.25em;
   text-align: center; font-style: italic; color: #969;
   border: 1.5em solid; border-color: #FDF #969 #969;}
img.curve-l {float: left;}
</style>
```

That isn't enough, though. If we want the pieces of the curve to stack up, we have to make sure each one floats to the left and below the image that came before it. That will require nothing more complicated than `clear`. To be able to see what's going on, we'll set a temporary border on these images (see Figure 10.16).

```
img.curve-l {float: left; clear: left;
   border: 1px solid gray;}
```

FIGURE 10.16

The pieces assemble themselves into a curve.

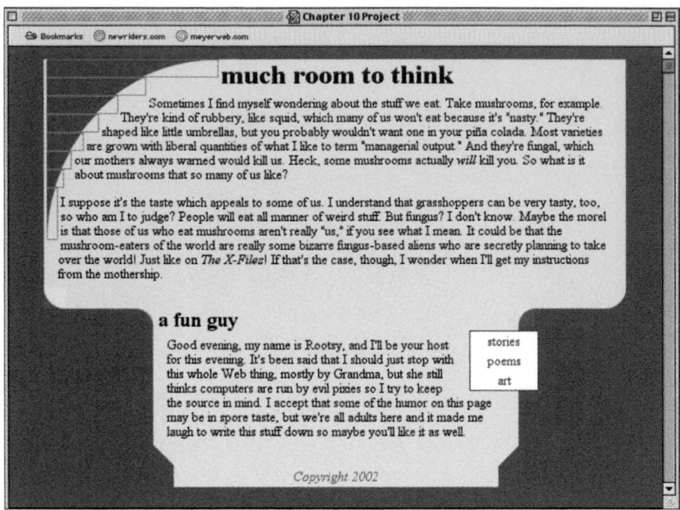

Notice the text filling in the space next to the images. The effect is that it flows along with the curve. Pretty cool, no?

Of course, there are a few things to take care of. The images need to be all the way to the left side of the `div#p1`; otherwise, the illusion is ruined. We should also give them a small right margin to make sure no text gets too close to the curve. And those icky gray borders have to go.

```
img.curve-l {float: left; clear: left; margin: 0 0.5em 0 0;}
```

Let's also give the page's title a bit of extra style. A slightly darker background and a bottom border would be a decent effect and would also illustrate something fascinating about the curve we've created.

```
h1, h2 {margin: 0; padding: 0 0.5em;}
h1 {background-color: #EBE; border-bottom: 1px solid #969;}
h2 {margin: 0 -20px; padding: 0;
   background: transparent url(p2toprt.gif) right top no-repeat;}
```

Remember that the `h1` is flowing past the floated curve. If you've already gone through Project 9, "Multicolumn Layout," you probably know what will happen here. Check Figure 10.17 to see if you're right.

Now we see why we went to the effort of making the light purple areas of the curve graphics transparent. If we hadn't, there would be big blocks of light purple overwriting the background of the `h1` element. Instead, it "slides under" the floated elements. The big advantage is that no matter how big or small we make the text—and thus no matter how tall or short the `h1` element becomes—this effect will still hold true.

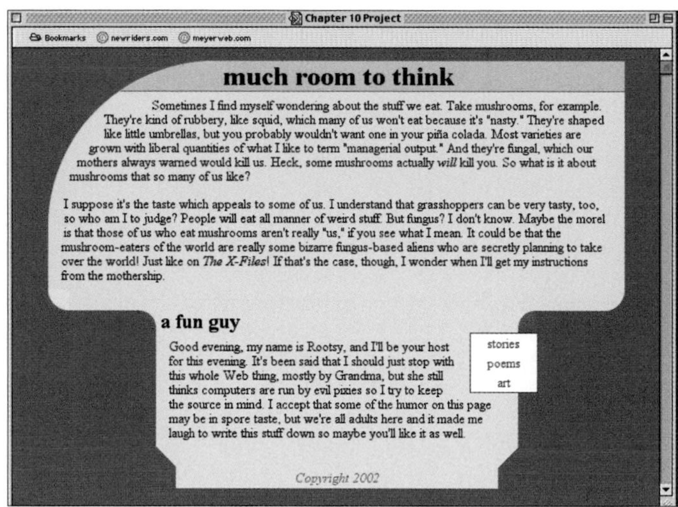

FIGURE 10.17

A seamless curve and a titular cap.

The Other Cap Curve

As cool as this is, our work is only half done: The top-right corner of the cap is still sharp and boxy. We need to give it a mirror curve. The approach is fairly obvious, but we need to go about it the right way.

Obviously, we're going to need another large curve graphic to slice up. We could just reuse the left curve and horizontally flip each graphic, but we're going to be a little more difficult about it and use the graphic shown in Figure 10.18.

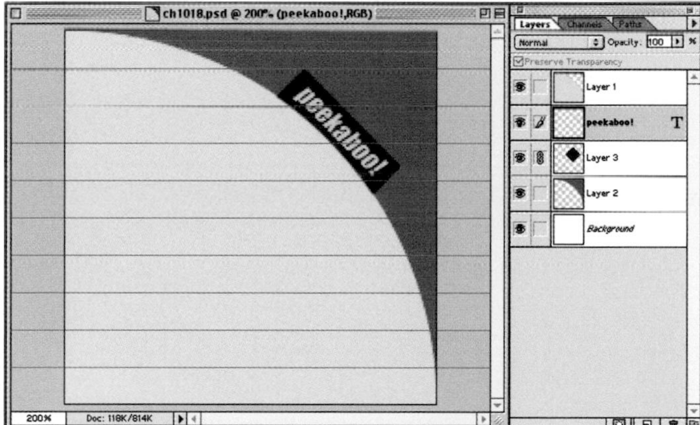

FIGURE 10.18

The other cap curve (as seen in Adobe Photoshop).

See that little "peekaboo!" box sticking out beyond the curve? It's part of the graphic, of course. We'll make use of it in a bit. First, go through the same procedure as with the first curve: Select just enough of each section to encompass the dark purple curve, save it as a GIF with the light purple made transparent, and dump the files into a folder named `curve-r`.

Now we add the markup. Note that it must be added exactly as shown here:

```
<img src="curve-l/curve1.gif" alt=" " class="curve-l">
<img src="curve-r/curve1.gif" alt=" " class="curve-r">
<img src="curve-l/curve2.gif" alt=" " class="curve-l">
<img src="curve-r/curve2.gif" alt=" " class="curve-r">
<img src="curve-l/curve3.gif" alt=" " class="curve-l">
<img src="curve-r/curve3.gif" alt=" " class="curve-r">
<img src="curve-l/curve4.gif" alt=" " class="curve-l">
<img src="curve-r/curve4.gif" alt=" " class="curve-r">
<img src="curve-l/curve5.gif" alt=" " class="curve-l">
<img src="curve-r/curve5.gif" alt=" " class="curve-r">
<img src="curve-l/curve6.gif" alt=" " class="curve-l">
<img src="curve-r/curve6.gif" alt=" " class="curve-r">
<img src="curve-l/curve7.gif" alt=" " class="curve-l">
<img src="curve-r/curve7.gif" alt=" " class="curve-r">
<img src="curve-l/curve8.gif" alt=" " class="curve-l">
<img src="curve-r/curve8.gif" alt=" " class="curve-r">
<h1>much room to think</h1>
```

Why are they interleaved? Because, according to CSS, no floated element can be higher than the top of any previously floated element. Thus, if we put all of the right-curve images after the left-curve images, the top of the right curve would be even with the top of the last image in the left curve. Not really the effect we want.

Then again, without the correct styles, we won't get the effect we want anyway. All we need is a mirror of the left-curve styles: floating and clearing to the right instead of the left and with the margins rearranged so that there's no right margin and a 0.5em left margin. The result is shown in Figure 10.19.

```
img.curve-l {float: left; clear: left; margin: 0 0.5em 0 0;}
img.curve-r {float: right; clear: right; margin: 0 0 0 0.5em;}
</style>
```

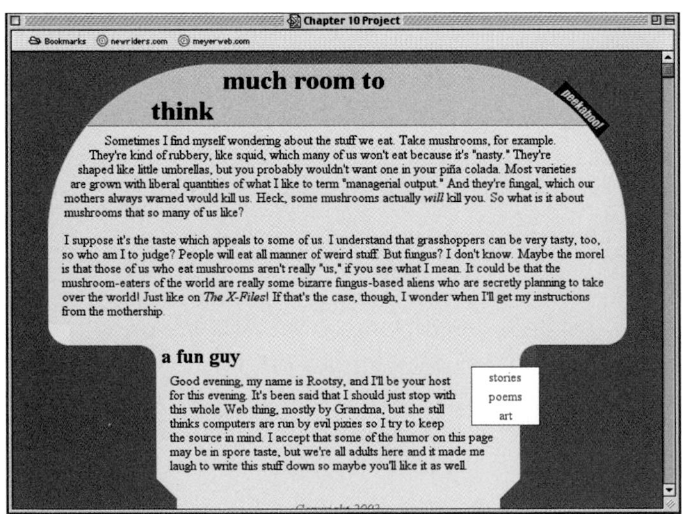

FIGURE 10.19

Our mushroom has been very nicely capped.

Keeping the Cap Whole

There is one potential danger with our design as it stands. If the text were ever to become small enough, the cap could become shorter than the two large curves that dominate it. In such a case, the curves would stay intact but would protrude out of the bottom of the cap.

Thanks to an earlier design effect, we can easily prevent this. The end of the cap, the `div` with an `id` of `p1end`, can be styled so that no floated elements can appear on either side of it.

```
div#p1end {text-align: right; margin: 0; padding: 0; clear: both;
  background: #FDF url(p1botleft.gif) bottom left no-repeat;}
```

This will always keep the cap whole, even if it means a large amount of blank space between the end of its text and the beginning of the stem.

Linkaboo

It isn't enough to add a "peekaboo!" to the curve graphic and just leave it there, static and boring. After all, it does look like a tab that one should be able to use, doesn't it? We'll turn it into a link in a jiffy.

The trick is in figuring out which graphics in the right curve need to be linked. Examining the graphics shows that pieces of the "peekaboo!" appear in `curve2.gif` through `curve5.gif`. Thus, we need to wrap those images in hyperlink elements.

```
<img src="curve-l/curve2.gif" alt=" " class="curve-l">
<a href="peekaboo.html"><img src="curve-r/curve2.gif"
   alt="peekaboo!" class="curve-r"></a>
<img src="curve-l/curve3.gif" alt=" " class="curve-l">
<a href="peekaboo.html"><img src="curve-r/curve3.gif"
   alt=" " class="curve-r"></a>
<img src="curve-l/curve4.gif" alt=" " class="curve-l">
<a href="peekaboo.html"><img src="curve-r/curve4.gif"
   alt=" " class="curve-r"></a>
<img src="curve-l/curve5.gif" alt=" " class="curve-l">
<a href="peekaboo.html"><img src="curve-r/curve5.gif"
   alt=" " class="curve-r"></a>
<img src="curve-l/curve6.gif" alt=" " class="curve-l">
```

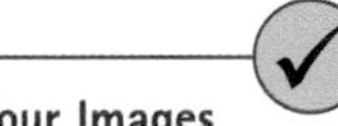

Sizing Your Images

Once you've finished a design like this, it's a good idea to add in the HTML attributes `height` and `width` for each image. You could try to set the image sizes with CSS, but it would be a lot more effort than it's worth because you'd have to give each image its own `id` and then write a rule for each image. Using the HTML attributes is a more direct method.

This will make the "peekaboo!" (and the portions of the purple curve to its right) into a usable link. There is the danger, though, that a browser could decide to draw borders around these links. That would mess up our nice curve, so we'll add a style to prevent that from happening.

```
img.curve-r {float: right; clear: right; margin: 0 0 0 0.5em;}
img {border-width: 0;}
</style>
```

Actually, this will prevent borders from appearing on all of the images in the page, including the smaller curves at the bottom of the cap and the top of the stem. That's fine, of course. We wouldn't want borders appearing on those graphics anyway.

A Little Justification

As one last touch, let's give the paragraph text full justification. This will cause the text in each line to stretch out as wide as it possibly can. The final effect is that the right and left edges of each line of text line up with each other—or they would if the curves didn't interfere. Then again, this makes the text more obviously flow along the top-right curve in the page, as we can see in Figure 10.20.

```
p {margin: 0; padding: 0.5em 1em; text-align: justify;}
```

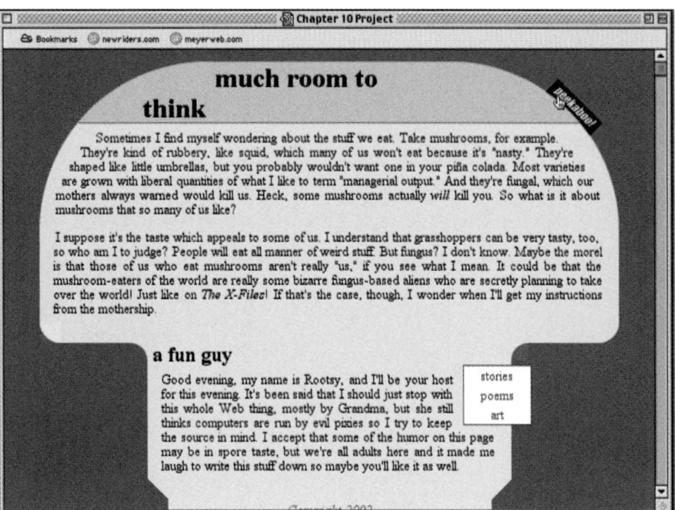

FIGURE 10.20

Fully justifying the text in our layout.

With this last little tweak, we're left with the styles shown in Listing 10.3.

Listing 10.3 The Final Style Sheet

```
<style type="text/css">
body {background: #969; color: black;}
div.wrap {background: #FDF; color: black; margin: 0 2em;}
p {margin: 0; padding: 0.5em 1em; text-align: justify;}
h1, h2 {margin: 0; padding: 0 0.5em;}
h1 {background-color: #EBE; border-bottom: 1px solid #969;}
h2 {margin: 0 -20px; padding: 0;
   background: transparent url(p2toprt.gif) right top no-repeat;}
h2 img {vertical-align: top;}
div#p1 {margin: 0 2em;}
div#p1end {text-align: right; margin: 0;
  background: #FDF url(p1botleft.gif) bottom left no-repeat;
```

```
  clear: both;}
div#p2 {margin: 0 10em;}
div#menu {float: right; width: 5em;
   padding: 0; margin: 0 -1.5em 0.25em 0.5em;
   border: 1px solid #747; background: white;}
div#menu a {display: block; text-align: center;
   padding: 0.2em 0.5em;}
div#footer {margin: 0 10em; padding: 0.25em;
   text-align: center; font-style: italic; color: #969;
   border: 1.5em solid; border-color: #FDF #969 #969;}
img.curve-l {float: left; clear: left; margin: 0 0.5em 0 0;}
img.curve-r {float: right; clear: right; margin: 0 0 0 0.5em;}
img {border-width: 0;}
</style>
```

Branching Out

There are many other ways to utilize the principles explored in this project. Here are a few suggestions:

1. Go back to the layout from Figure 10.8 (before we started on the mushroom idea) and rework it so that each section links to the other with a set of diagonals like the one already there. This will mean changing the margins of every top-level `div` and giving borders to the second part. As for the bottom of the `div#p2`, remember the other way to make bottom borders disappear.

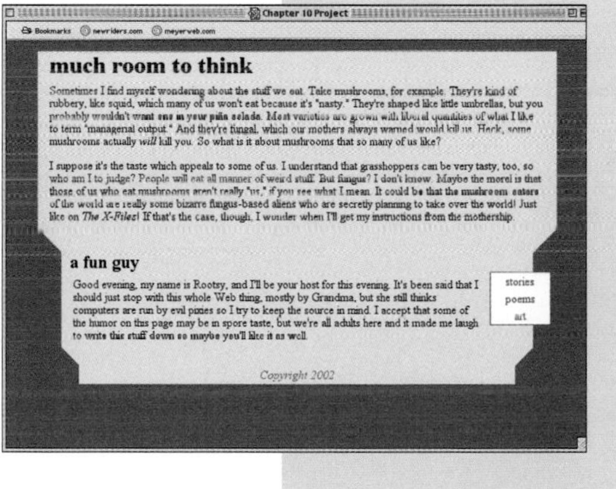

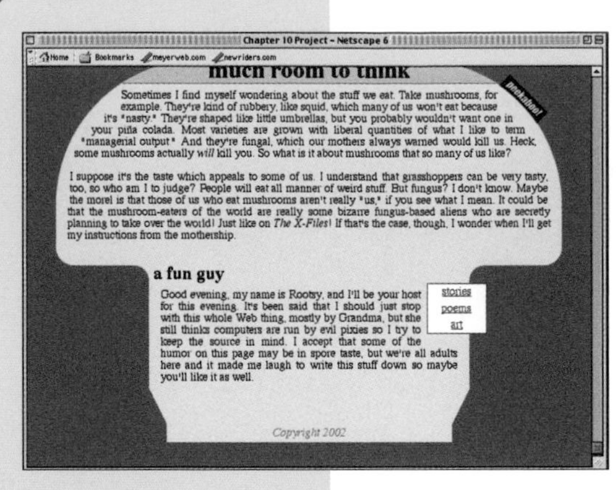

2. Try varying the width of the footer's top border and see how it affects the way the diagonal lines are drawn. For example, make the top border `3em` wide and then `0.75em` wide. Consider what the ratios between the side- and top-border widths will mean in terms of the angles that result.

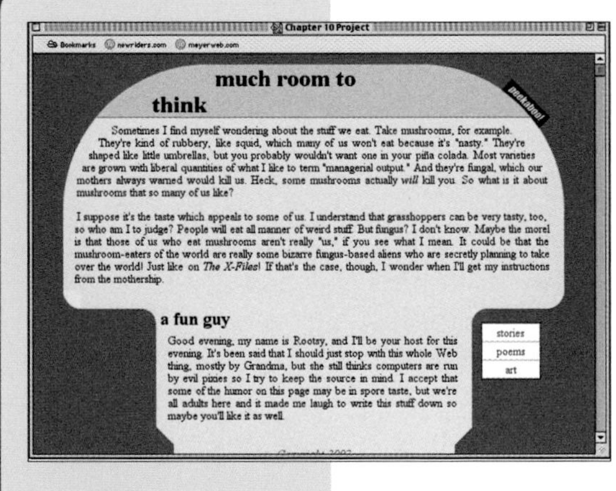

3. Try putting the menu someplace other than where it is now, such as completely inside the stem and shifted upward. You could also move it completely outside the stem if that seems more interesting. Also consider extra styling for the links within the menu so that they stand out slightly better.

11

POSITIONING A BETTER DESIGN

Like tables, there is another highly limiting structure that's composed of rows and cells: a prison. It's time for designers to break out.

ERIC A. MEYER

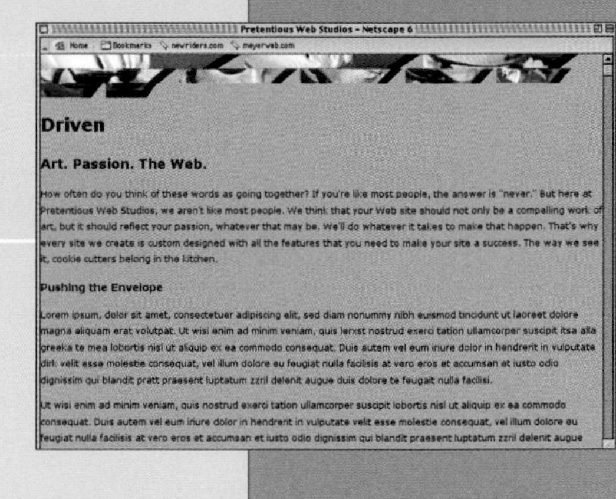

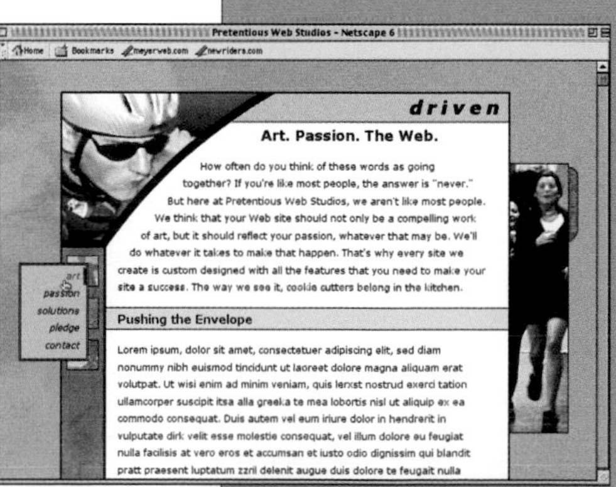

WE'VE BEEN USING TABLES for years now, warping them into ever more complicated arrangements just to get interesting visual effects. The classic approach of nesting tables within tables and slicing up images to be slotted into various cells of a complex table was all we had. The thought might occur from time to time that this was no way to run a railroad, but since there were no other tracks, we followed them—more or less blindly.

Happily, this is no longer true. CSS positioning offers a much more sane alternative to table-based layouts—or it would if browsers acted in a consistent fashion. Despite these hurdles, there is still plenty we can do that doesn't trip across browser bugs. The result is a much cleaner way to design and a lot less image slicing.

Project Goals

We've been hired on a temporary basis to help create a new look for our latest client, Pretentious Web Studios. (There's nothing like truth in advertising.) Their client base is typically companies who want cutting-edge Web sites that use the latest technology.

The entire point of this project is to take a raw HTML document that contains everything we need to create a great design and simply rearrange the pieces until we have one. We will skip the usual steps of analyzing the structure and looking for places to put `class`es and `id`s—that's already been done for us—and will instead dive straight into the styling.

Along the way, we'll use the following new techniques to get our layout:

- Placing elements so that they overlap one another and determining which one goes "on top"
- Accomplishing on-the-fly adjustment of layout with nothing more than a few edits of our styles
- Working around browser bugs both subtle and gross

The real point, though, is to demonstrate just how flexible positioning can be. Although browser limitations prevent us from doing the really fancy stuff, there's still more than enough room for design possibilities that leave tables in the dust.

Preparation

See the Introduction for instructions on how to download files from the Web site.

Download the files for Project 11 from this book's Web site. If you're planning to play along at home, load the file `ch11proj.html` into the editing program of your choice. This is the file you'll be editing, saving, and reloading as the project progresses.

Laying the Groundwork

First let's get a look at our unstyled document (see Figure 11.1). Remember that we already have all the pieces in place to create the entire document, so it's going to look pretty crazy right now.

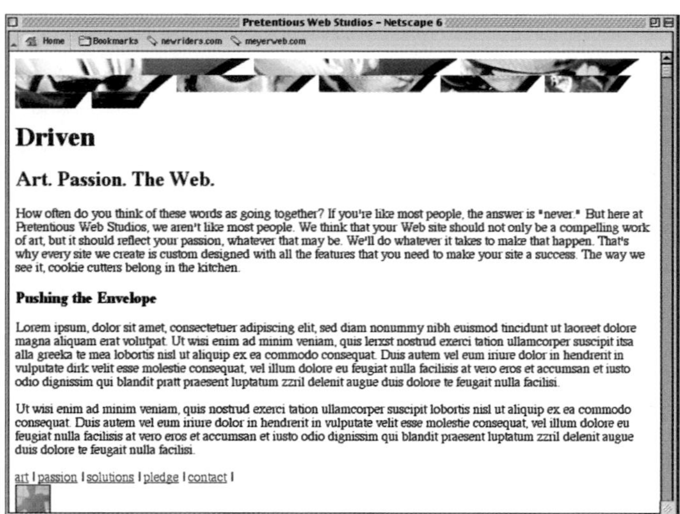

FIGURE 11.1

The project in its rawest form.

Up at the top, we can see the shattered pieces of a curve that we'll be assembling. If you scroll down past the text to the part that doesn't appear in Figure 11.1, you'll find three images. First there's a single image containing three boxes, then there's a tall picture of some running women, and finally there's a sort of paddle-shaped image with rounded corners and some text along its edges. These three images, plus two more background images, are all we'll need. (Not counting the 10 images in the curve, that is.)

Floating Curves

For details on how to create a curve in a Web document, see Project 10, "Sneaking Out of the Box."

Listing 11.1 shows us the document structure; the paragraph text has been replaced with temporary placeholders for clarity's sake.

Listing 11.1 The Document's Basic Structure

```
<!DOCTYPE HTML PUBLIC "-//W3C//DTD HTML 4.0 Transitional//EN"
                  "http://www.w3.org/TR/REC-html40/loose.dtd">
<html>
<head>
<title>Project 11</title>
</head>
<body>
<div id="wrap">
  <img src="curve/slice1.gif" class="curve" alt="">
  <img src="curve/slice2.gif" class="curve" alt="">
  <img src="curve/slice3.gif" class="curve" alt="">
  <img src="curve/slice4.gif" class="curve" alt="">
  <img src="curve/slice5.gif" class="curve" alt="">
  <img src="curve/slice6.gif" class="curve" alt="">
  <img src="curve/slice7.gif" class="curve" alt="">
  <img src="curve/slice8.gif" class="curve" alt="">
  <img src="curve/slice9.gif" class="curve" alt="">
  <img src="curve/slice10.gif" class="curve" alt="">
  <h1>Driven</h1>
  <h2>Art.  Passion.  The Web.</h2>
  <p>(text)</p>
```

continues

Listing 11.1 Continued

```
    <h3>Pushing the Envelope</h3>
    <p>(text)</p>
    <p>(text)</p>
    <div id="menu">
      <a href="link1.html">art</a><b> | </b>
      <a href="link2.html">passion</a><b> | </b>
      <a href="link3.html">solutions</a><b> | </b>
      <a href="link4.html">pledge</a><b> | </b>
      <a href="link5.html">contact</a><b> | </b>
    </div>
    <img src="left-side.gif" id="ls" alt="">
  </div>
  <img src="right-side.gif" id="rs" alt="">
  <a href="run.html" id="rp" title="run, don't walk"><img src="rightpanel.gif"
  alt=""></a>
  </body>
  </html>
```

You might wonder what those <b> elements are doing here because CSS is supposed to make things like boldface tags obsolete. They aren't meant for display in modern browsers, if that's any consolation. We'll get to all that later in this project in the section titled "Degrading Gracefully."

alt and Accessibility

For more information on accessibility, including advice on alt values, see http://www.w3.org/TR/WCAG10/, particularly Guideline 1.

Also, you might notice that all of the images have blank alt values. That's because none of the images really has anything to do with the content of the page and because it makes the structure a little simpler to read. You might want to consider adding in some sort of alt text to the mandatory alt attributes in your own designs, but let your better judgement be your guide.

A key feature of this structure is the way that most, but not all, of the content is enclosed by the div with an id of wrap. The last two images are not, however. There's a good reason for this, and we'll find out all about it when we start placing elements so that they overlap each other.

Identifying the div

Admittedly, wrap is not the most descriptive id we could have chosen. Other possibilities include main-text, content, or layout-frame.

Finally, take note of the various id values throughout the document. They'll get a lot of use in this project.

Styling the Document

Because we don't have to mess around with the markup, we'll get right to laying out the document itself. As is typical for our projects, we'll work our way down through the document, establishing the overarching styles first and then drilling down to the details. Where better to start than with the document's body?

Styling the Body

The text of the document indicates a very dynamic image, so we'll use reddish tones to reinforce that idea. We don't want to go into bright reds, though, because those can be very hard on the eyes when displayed on a computer monitor. We'll settle on deep, rich reds and reddish tans for the design.

```
<head>
<title>Pretentious Web Studios</title>
<style type="text/css" media="all">
body {background: rgb(75%,66%,66%);}
</style>
</head>
```

We also want to minimize the effect that browser styles can have on our later positioning, so we need to eliminate the margins and padding on the `body` element. We'll also go ahead and lay down some `font` styles.

```
body {background: rgb(75%,66%,66%);
  margin: 0; padding: 0;
  font: 12px/1.5 Verdana, Arial, sans-serif;}
```

In addition to the font family, we've declared a basic `font` size for the `body` element and supplied a value of `1.5` for the `line-height` property, which will push the lines of text a little further apart than usual (see Figure 11.2).

Applying to All Media

You might notice that we've included a `media="all"` attribute on our `style` element. This will enable it to be seen in all media but not in all browsers. This is a relatively common way of hiding advanced styles from Navigator 4.x.

See "Tricking Browsers and Hiding Styles" on the Web site for more information.

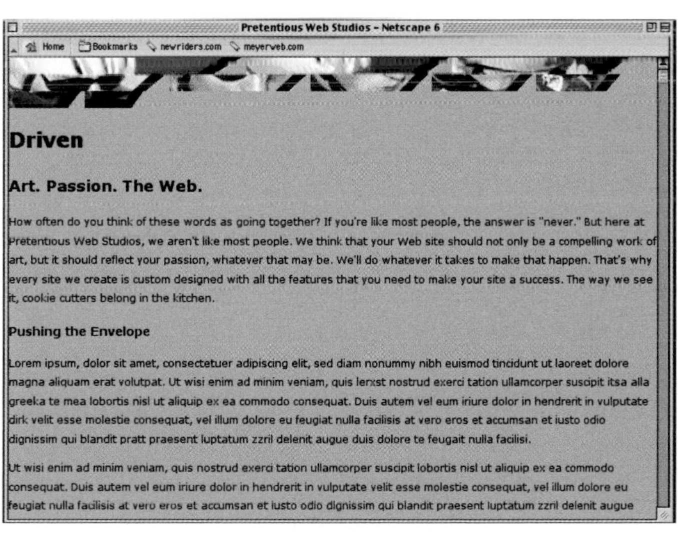

FIGURE 11.2

The background and font begin the styling process.

Framing Our Content

The “framing” in this section doesn’t mean using the `<frame>` tag, but instead it refers to making the wrapper `div` stand out and provide a framework inside which the content can be styled. A white background with a strong black border would be a great start.

```
<style type="text/css" media="all">
body {background: rgb(75%,66%,66%);
  margin: 0; padding: 0;
  font: 12px/1.5 Verdana, Arial, sans-serif;}
div#wrap {border: 2px solid black;
  background: white;}
</style>
```

This is nice, but it also will have the `div` filling out the entire browser window. We could simply give it margins to push it away from the browser window’s edges, but that limits our options. If we position the `div`, later on we can put other elements in front of or behind it; this will prove important as we move forward. So let’s position the wrapper `div`. This will prove to be a little trickier than you might first think, although the process starts easily enough.

```
div#wrap {border: 2px solid black;
  background: white;
  position: absolute;
  margin: 0; padding: 0 0 2em 0;}
```

No Padding Required

The wrapper `div` will never receive top, bottom, or left padding. Instead, the text elements within will be pushed inward with margins.

At this point, the only real change in layout is the bottom padding on the `div`. As before, it has no padding on its top, right, and left sides, and it still hasn’t moved away from the edges of the browser window. A few offset properties should take care of that, as illustrated in Figure 11.3.

```
div#wrap {border: 2px solid black;
  background: white;
  position: absolute;
  margin: 0; padding: 0 0 2em 0;
  left: 80px; right: 80px; top: 40px;}
```

We haven’t defined `bottom` for a reason: By leaving it and `height` at their default values, the positioned element is able to expand around its own content. If we explicitly set either or both values, the `div`’s height would be a certain fixed amount, no matter how tall or short the content might be.

So, at this point, the side of the `div` should be `80px` away from the edges of the browser window, and the top should be `40px` down from the window’s top. Unfortunately, that won’t be the case in Internet Explorer for Macintosh, where the right edge of the `div` is for some reason up against the right edge of the browser window.

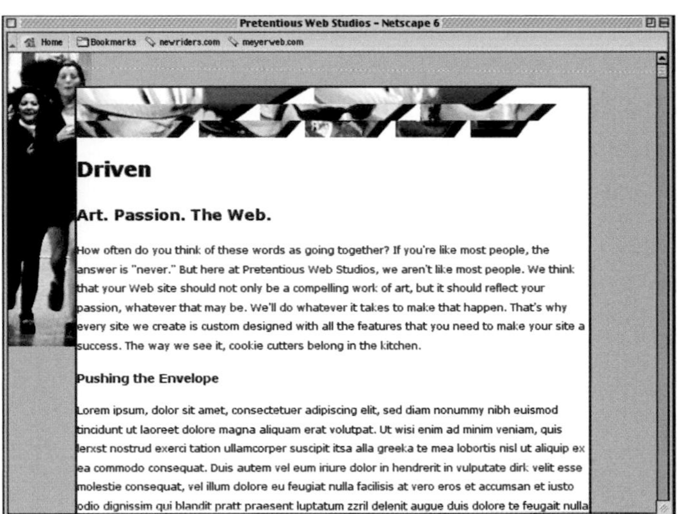

FIGURE 11.3

A positioned `div` with offset properties and no margins.

Hey, Ladies!

The picture of the running women that just appeared in the upper-left corner of the screen used to be below the wrapper `div`. Why did it suddenly jump up there? Because we took the entire content `div` out of the document's flow. We'll talk about this in detail later in the project.

This is where the workarounds get a little thick. The first step is to supply a value that IE5/Mac likes. Changing `right` won't really help, but changing the right margin of the `div` will.

```
div#wrap {border: 2px solid black;
  background: white;
  position: absolute;
  margin: 0 80px 0 0; padding: 0 0 2em 0;
  left: 80px; right: 80px; top: 40px;}
```

The Containing Block

As discussed in Project 8, "Creating an Online Greeting Card," any positioned element is positioned with respect to its containing block. Because the wrapper `div` doesn't have an ancestor element that's been positioned, its containing block is the root element. That's either the `body` or `html` element, depending on the browser.

This change "fixes" the display in IE5/Mac, and it remains unchanged in IE for Windows, but in Mozilla-based browsers (such as Netscape 6), there are now 160 pixels of space between the right edge of the `div` and the right edge of the browser window. That's because the value of `right` is supposed to define the offset between the edge of the containing block and the outer edge of the element's margins. (The same is true for `top`, `left`, and `bottom` with regard to their respective sides.) Thus, the two `80px` values get added together.

As it turns out, the two versions of Explorer are ignoring different things. The Windows edition ignores the value set for the right margin, and the Macintosh edition ignores the value of `right` itself. And so we come to the final step in our little dance: using the `voice-family` hack.

```
div#wrap {border: 2px solid black;
  background: white;
  position: absolute;
  margin: 0 80px 0 0; padding: 0 0 2em 0;
  left: 80px; right: 80px; top: 40px;
  voice-family: "\"}\"";
  voice-family:inherit;
  right: 0;}
```

For a discussion of the `voice-family` hack and other ways to use browser bugs to your advantage, see "Tricking Browsers and Hiding Styles" on the Web site.

With this last addition, we get consistent display in the various mainstream browsers. It works because…

- IE5/Win uses the first value for `right` but not the second and ignores the right margin.
- IE5/Mac uses the value set for the right margin and ignores both values of `right`.
- Mozilla sees all the values for `right` and the right margin, but they string together just so and get us the desired result.

It's a heck of a way to run a railroad, no doubt about it, but at least we got to the final destination with a minimum of scarring.

Assembling the Curve

Now that we (finally!) have the main `div` laid out as we'd like, it's time to take that shattered curve at the top of the content and turn it into something useful. We'll just reuse the techniques learned in Project 10, with the result shown in Figure 11.4.

```
div#wrap {border: 2px solid black;
  background: white;
  position: absolute;
  margin: 0 80px 0 0; padding: 0 0 2em 0;
  left: 80px; right: 80px; top: 40px;
  voice-family: "\"}\"";
  voice-family:inherit;
  right: 0;}
div#wrap img.curve {float: left; clear: left;
  margin: 0 15px 0 0; padding: 0;
  height: 20px;}
</style>
```

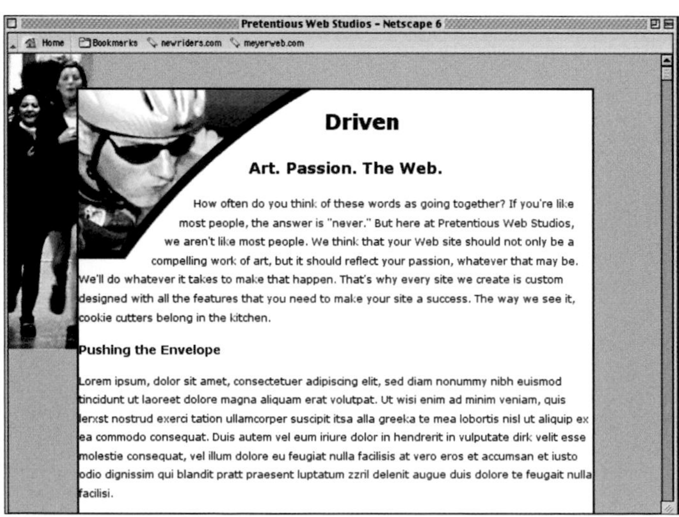

FIGURE 11.4

The curved image assembled with text already flowing along it.

With the 15-pixel right border on each piece of the curve, the text flowing past is kept an aesthetically pleasing distance from the visible pieces of the images.

The text flowing beneath the bottom of the curve is an expected effect because text will always flow as close to the sides of its parent element as possible. We could set padding on the wrapper `div` to push the text inward, but that would also push the curve inward, and we definitely don't want that (at least, not in this design). The only other option is to set margins on the paragraphs themselves, as we'll see after the next section.

Trimming the Top

With our curve in place, let's take care of those headlines at the top of the content. For the word "Driven," enclosed in an `h1` element, we'll set it apart with a background color and a dark gray-red bottom border. We should also remove its margin so that it snuggles right up to the top of the wrapper `div`, and a little padding wouldn't be amiss.

```
div#wrap img.curve {float: left; clear: left;
  margin: 0 15px 0 0; padding: 0;
  height: 20px;}
h1 {border-bottom: 2px solid rgb(45%,35%,35%);
  background: rgb(90%,75%,75%);
  margin: 0; padding: 0.125em 0.25em;}
</style>
```

Just to give it more pep, let's right-align and italicize the text. We'll also demonstrate the near-total hipness of our client by lowercasing the text in the element and spreading the letters apart a little bit, as shown in Figure 11.5.

```
h1 {border-bottom: 2px solid rgb(45%,35%,35%);
  background: rgb(90%,75%,75%);
  margin: 0; padding: 0.125em 0.25em;}
  text-align: right; text-transform: lowercase;
  font-style: italic; letter-spacing: 0.25em;}
```

In examining Figure 11.5, it would seem that the height of the `h1` is larger than we might have expected. This is because the element is inheriting a `line-height` value of `1.5` from the `body` styles. (Remember that?) If we want to bring that back under control, we'll need to explicitly assign a value. While we're at it, let's give the `h1` a specific `font-size` to make it a little more consistent between browsers.

```
h1 {border-bottom: 2px solid rgb(45%,35%,35%);
  background: rgb(90%,75%,75%);
  margin: 0; padding: 0.125em 0.25em;
  text-align: right; text-transform: lowercase;
  font-style: italic; letter-spacing: 0.25em;
  font-size: 200%; line-height: 1.25em;}
```

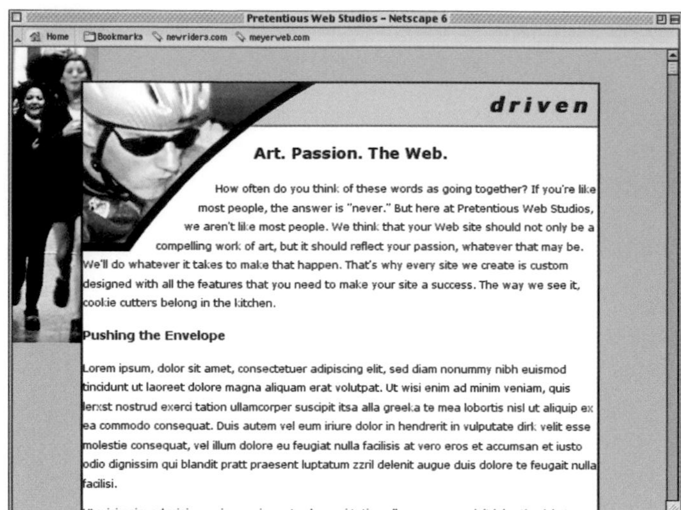

FIGURE 11.5

Making the top headline look hip with some text styles.

Now we need to work on the `h2` that immediately follows the "driven" headline. Its placement really isn't too bad, but it could stand to get a little closer to the border just above it. We should also give it a specific `font-size` value as was done with the `h1`. In this case, we'll put it halfway between the size of the `h1` and the size of the paragraphs. We really don't need much else, as illustrated by Figure 11.6.

```
h1 {border-bottom: 2px solid rgb(45%,35%,35%);
  background: rgb(90%,75%,75%);
  margin: 0; padding: 0.125em 0.25em;
  text-align: right; text-transform: lowercase;
  font-style: italic; letter-spacing: 0.25em;
  font-size: 200%; line-height: 1.25em;}
h2 {font-size: 150%; margin: 0;}
</style>
```

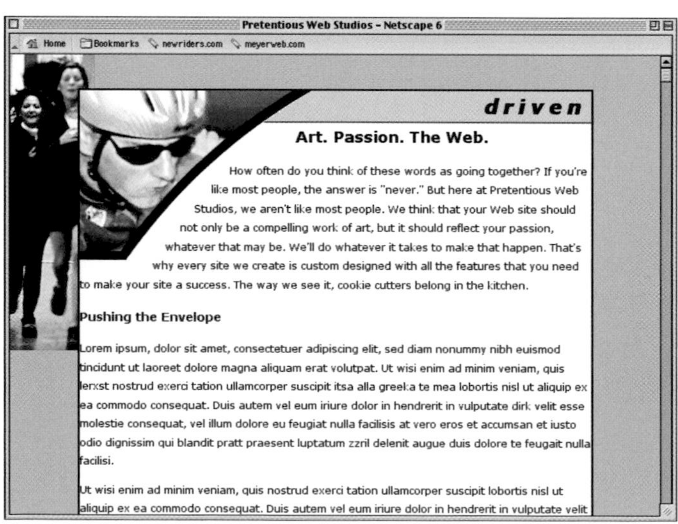

FIGURE 11.6

Now both headlines are nicely placed without crowding each other.

Content Margins

It's about time to get the text pushed away from the edges of the wrapped `div`, so that's what we'll do. After we get past the top two headlines (the ones we just finished styling), the rest of the text content proves to be found in either `p` or `h3` elements. We'll give them consistent side margins using a pixel value, but what value should we use?

If we measure the flat bottom edge of the curve image, we find that it's 56 pixels across. Let's set the side margins on the content elements to be just over half that distance.

```
h2 {font-size: 150%; margin: 0;}
h3, p {margin: 1em 30px;}
</style>
```

That's not a bad effect, but having the text wrap halfway under the bottom edge of the curve turns out to be not quite as nice as we might have hoped. Let's increase the left margin of these elements so that it exactly matches that 56-pixel distance, as shown in Figure 11.7.

```
h3, p {margin: 1em 30px 1em 56px;}
```

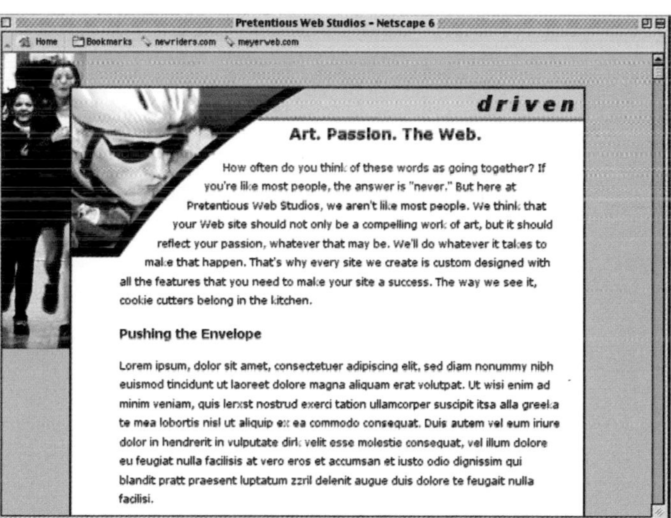

FIGURE 11.7 *Pushing the text content away from the edges of the wrapper* `div`.

That's better, but it's still not great because there's too much of a jump from the second-to-last line of the first paragraph to the last line. What we need to account for is the 15-pixel margin on the curve images themselves. Instead of increasing the margin further, we'll add 15 pixels of left padding instead.

```
h3, p {margin: 1em 30px 1em 56px; padding-left: 15px;}
```

Why add padding instead of margins? Patience, grasshopper. All will be revealed in the fullness of time.

Decorating the Wrapper

Now that we've pushed the paragraph and h3 text over from the left edge of the wrapper div, there's this empty column of whitespace that looks a little odd. If only we had a suitable background image, we could lay it down in a vertical stripe and increase the visual appeal of the page while also filling in that blank space. If only we had such an image… Oh, wait, we do! It's shown in Figure 11.8.

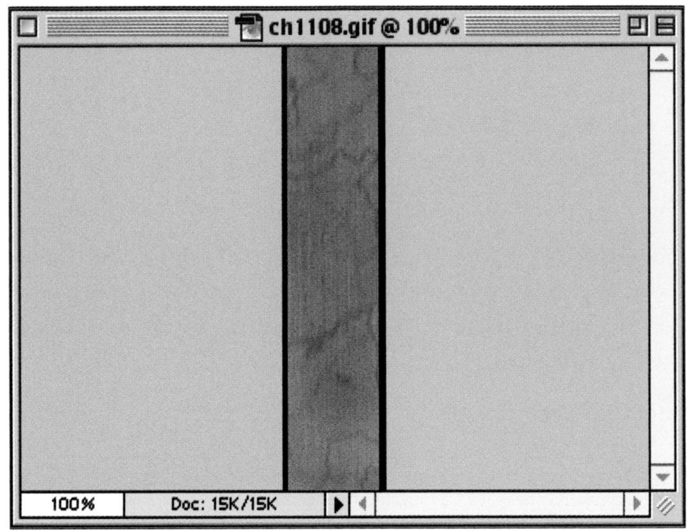

FIGURE 11.8

The background image for the wrapper div.

```
div#wrap {border: 2px solid black;
  background: white url(wrap-bg.gif) top left repeat-y;
  position: absolute;
  margin: 0 80px 0 0; padding: 0 0 2em 0;
  left: 80px; right: 80px; top: 40px;
  voice-family: "\"}\"";
  voice-family:inherit;
  right: 0;}
```

There's only one problem with the preceding styles and this particular image—the image doesn't quite line up with the bottom of the curve image in every browser. It turns out that some browsers think a background image should start in the top-left outer corner of the border, whereas others believe it should start at the top-left corner of the padding, just inside the border.

Placing the Background Image

So which is it, the padding or the border? According to section 14.2.1 of CSS2, background images should be placed in relation to the padding corner, not the border corner.

It doesn't actually matter who's right or wrong because we have to deal with the situation either way. However, a close examination of the image wrap-bg.gif will reveal that it's actually 58 pixels wide and has a 2-pixel black strip along its left side. This is because we're going to sneak around browser disagreements by getting rid of the left border on the wrapper div and using the background image to supply it for us. If we drop the left border's width to zero and increase the left padding to 2px, the leftmost 2 pixels of the background image will stick out past the curve images. Because those 2 pixels are all black, we get the border back through a little sleight of hand, as illustrated in Figure 11.9.

```
div#wrap {border: 2px solid black; border-left-width: 0;
  background: white url(wrap-bg.gif) top left repeat-y;
  position: absolute;
  margin: 0 80px 0 0; padding: 0 0 2em 2px;
  left: 80px; right: 80px; top: 40px; z-index: 100;
  voice-family: "\"}\"";
  voice-family:inherit;
  right: 0;}
```

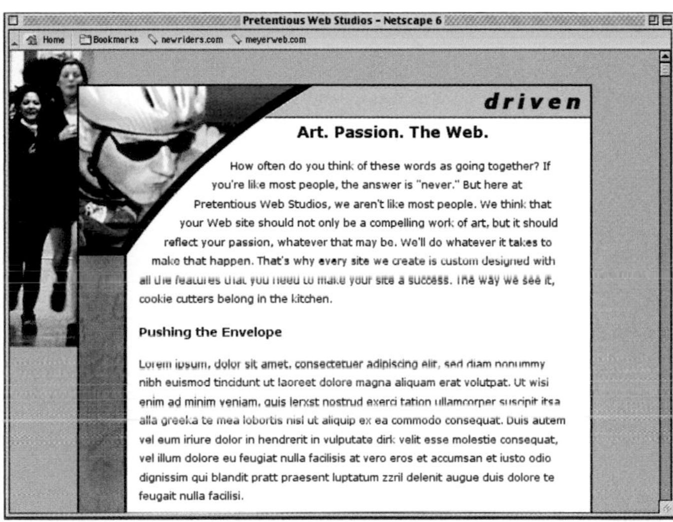

FIGURE 11.9

Using a background image to simulate the left border of the wrapper and avoid browser inconsistencies.

Sprucing Up the Section Head

That `h3` element ("Pushing the Envelope") looks sort of dull just sitting there, so let's give it some extra style. Because it functions as a section heading, we'll use it to separate parts of the page. Again, we'll apply a background and borders to the element and set an explicit `font-size` value.

```
h3, p {margin: 1em 30px 1em 56px; padding-left: 15px;}
h3 {border: 1px solid black; border-width: 1px 0;
  background: rgb(93%,85%,85%); font-size: 125%;}
</style>
```

Now we see why we added those extra 15 pixels on the left side as padding instead of margin: The border and background just touch the right edge of the background image. Unfortunately, the right side of the `h3` doesn't come anywhere close to the right edge of the wrapper `div`, thanks to the `30px` right margin set by the `h3, p` rule. We'll have to override it.

```
h3 {border: 1px solid black; border-width: 1px 0;
  background: rgb(93%,85%,85%); font-size: 125%;
  margin-right: 0;}
```

These changes, taken together, give us the effect shown in Figure 11.10.

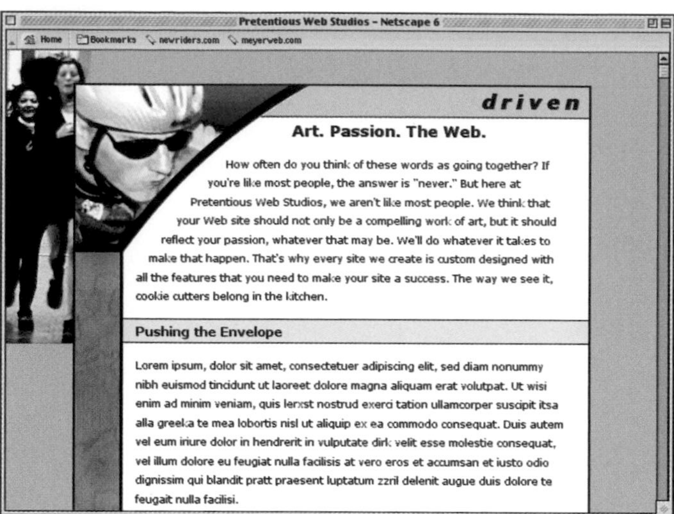

FIGURE 11.10

Bringing the section head into contact with the borders to its sides.

Relocating the Ladies

Although the ladies look just fine where they are, we actually need to clear out the upper-left corner of the document for a later effect, so we'll need to move our fair image to some other location.

The question some of you might be asking is how they got there in the first place. Remember that this image follows the wrapper `div` in the document, which means the women are not actually a part of that `div`. When the wrapper was absolutely positioned, it was completely removed from the normal flow of the document. This meant that the first element in the normal flow was the ladies' picture, which moved to the top left of the `body` element's content-area. This would have happened no matter what element followed the `div`.

Because this image is not part of the wrapper `div`, it will (like the `div`) be positioned with respect to the root element. In other words, the image and the `div` share the same positioning context. If we want to move the ladies over to the top-right corner, it's a simple matter.

```
h3 {border: 1px solid black; border-width: 1px 0;
  background: rgb(93%,85%,85%); font-size: 125%;
  margin-right: 0;}
img#rs {position: absolute;
   top: 0; right: 0;}
</style>
```

That's not really where we want them, however. Let's shift them downward and over to the left a bit by defining offsets from the top and right (as shown in Figure 11.11).

```
img#rs {position: absolute;
   top: 11em; right: 33px;}
```

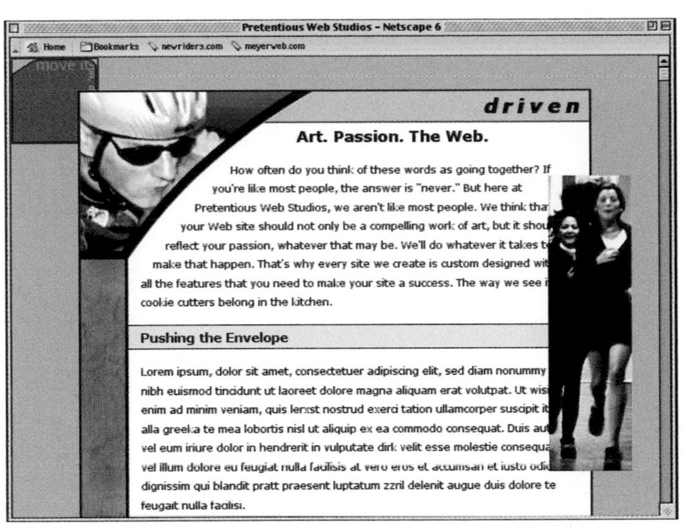

Figure 11.11

The ladies have shifted to the right, but they're overlapping our content, and another image has taken their place!

Suddenly we have even more problems than before. In the first place, moving the women's image out of the top-left corner has allowed another image to appear there. How did that happen? That's the second image that follows the wrapper `div`. It's been hidden underneath the `div` all this time, sitting just to the right of the women. After they were positioned and thus taken out of the document flow, the "move it" image became the last element actually in the normal flow. That's why it landed in the top-left corner. We'll deal with it in just a moment.

Our second problem is that the women are now overlapping the wrapper `div` and its contents. Unlike floated elements, positioned elements do not cause text to flow around them. We'll have to do something to fix this, and the most obvious solution is to drop the women behind the `div`.

To do this, we actually have to add styles to both the wrapper `div` and the women's picture. Both of these images need to be given values for `z-index` so that we're sure the wrapper will be in front of the image. First the wrapper:

```
div#wrap {border: 2px solid black; border-left-width: 0;
  background: white url(wrap-bg.gif) top left repeat-y;
  position: absolute; z-index: 100;
  margin: 0 80px 0 0; padding: 0 0 2em 2px;
  left: 80px; right: 80px; top: 40px;
  voice-family: "\"}\"";
  voice-family:inherit;
  right: 0;}
```

And now for the ladies:

```
img#rs {position: absolute; z-index: 10;
   top: 11em; right: 33px;}
```

The Z-Axis

The value of `z-index` places a positioned element along the *z-axis*, an imaginary line running from the back of your monitor straight out of its face and through you. It's analogous to the x (horizontal) and y (vertical) axes, but the z-axis effectively measures depth. More mathematically, it's a line drawn perpendicular to the plane of the monitor's display.

It actually doesn't matter what `z-index` numbers we give these two elements, as long as both numbers are above zero and the wrapper's value is higher than the ladies'. That will place the `div` in front of (or on top of) the image. Let's also add a black border to the image, as shown in Figure 11.12.

```
img#rs {position: absolute; z-index: 10;
   top: 11em; right: 33px;
   border: 1px solid black;}
```

FIGURE 11.12

Placing elements along the `z-index` *can cause some to overlap others.*

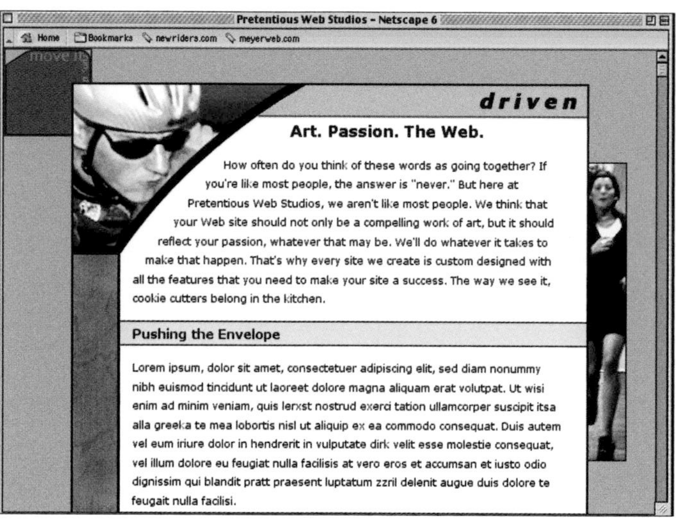

Negative `z-index` Problems

If you give an element a negative value for `z-index` and its containing block is the root element, there is a high probability that it will disappear altogether. That happens because you've placed the element behind the `body` itself!

Now we need to get that "move it" image out of the top-left corner and get rid of its blue border while we're at it. By now, positioning the element is easy work:

```
img#rs {position: absolute; z-index: 10;
  top: 11em; right: 33px;
  border: 1px solid black;}
a#rp {position: absolute; z-index: 5;
  top: 10em; right: 10px;}
</style>
```

Note that we've moved it close to the same location as the ladies. Its offsets are a little smaller, however, so its top-right corner will be placed 1em above and 23 pixels to the right of the women's top-right corner. Because the "move it" has a `z-index` value of `5`, though, that will put it behind the women, who have a `z-index` of `10`.

To get rid of the border, we'll augment our previous rule and write a new one, just to cover all our bases.

```
a#rp {position: absolute; z-index: 5;
  top: 10em; right: 10px;
  border-width: 0;}
a#rp img {border-width: 0;}
</style>
```

By reducing the `border-width` values for both the link and the image within it to `0`, we avoid any potential problems with unusual browser configurations. For most browsers, eliminating the border on the image itself would be sufficient, but one can never be too careful.

Despite being positioned and placed behind another element, the "move it" graphic is still a link and can be used as such. If you look closely, this can be seen in Figure 11.13.

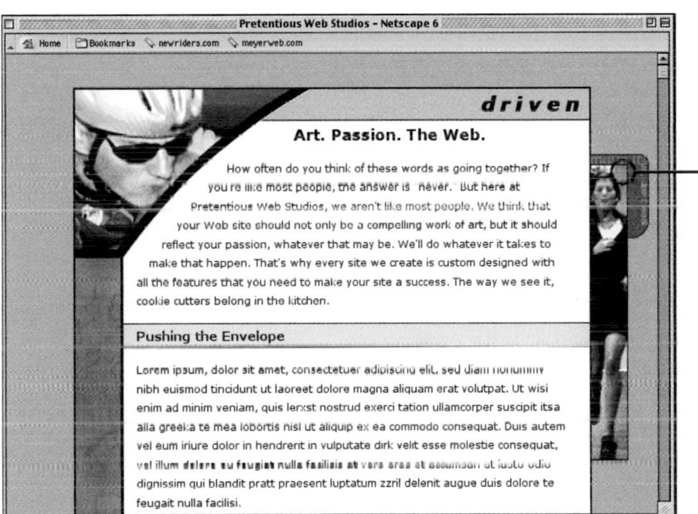

FIGURE 11.13

The tab is moved behind the ladies, and its border is removed.

▸▸ Positioning, Flow, and Element Heights

With this latest change, there are now no elements whatsoever in the normal flow of the document. The `body` *element had only three children: the wrapper* `div`*, the women's picture, and the linked image we just positioned. By taking all of the content out of the normal flow, the* `body` *now has an effective height of zero because there is no content to make it grow.*

It's important to keep this in mind when you're absolutely positioning elements. Many an author has been working happily along and then suddenly discovered that an enclosing `div`*, having had all its children absolutely positioned, is suddenly zero pixels tall. This can be circumvented by assigning the element in question a length value for* `height` *(such as* `div#main {height: 250px;}`*) or by not absolutely positioning all of its children. The latter approach is the basis of Project 9, "Multicolumn Layout," in which one of the columns was not floated or positioned but instead left in the document's flow.*

continues

> *continued*
>
> *So if the* `body` *has no height, how is it that the background is still a dull red? This occurs because browsers are permitted to carry background styles set on the* `body` *throughout the browser window, regardless of the actual size of the* `body` *element itself. Effectively, the* `body` *styles are inherited* upward *in the document structure to the* `html` *element, and yes, it's possible in some browsers to style* `html` *separately from* `body`*. This is the only occurrence in CSS of styles inheriting to an ancestor instead of a child, and it only happens because of specific wording to that effect in CSS2.*

Placing the Menu and Other Images

Almost forgotten in all of our work have been the menu and the triple-stack image down at the bottom of the wrapper `div`. They're shown in Figure 11.14, patiently waiting their turn.

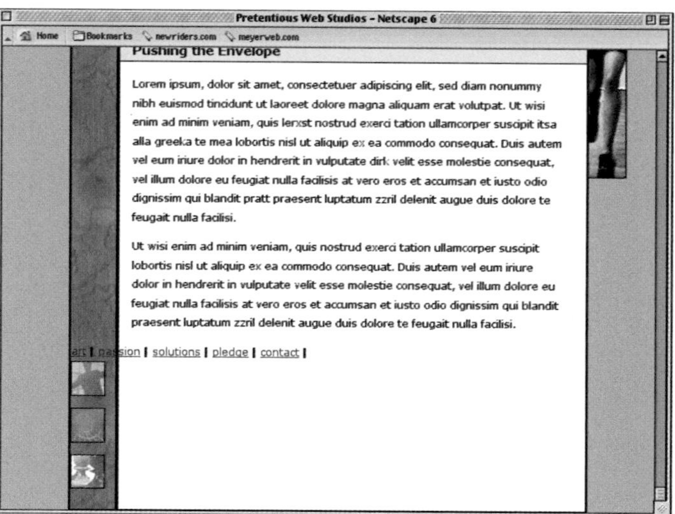

FIGURE 11.14

The menu and miscellaneous images are still loitering at the bottom of the document, waiting to get some style.

We'll take care of the menu first. Let's move it over by the women so that we can illustrate a few concepts. We start out with the following:

```
a#rp img {border-width: 0;}
div#menu {position: absolute; z-index: 7;
  width: 7em; top: 200px; right: 0;}
</style>
```

We've given it a semirandom value for `z-index` because we can. The values for `top` and `right` should put the menu right up against the right side of its containing block and `200px` down from the top.

The catch here is that the menu's containing block is the wrapper `div`, not the browser window. That happened because the wrapper `div` is itself a positioned element, and thus it establishes a containing block for its descendant elements. The menu, being one such descendant, is therefore positioned with respect to the `div` itself.

We can get the menu to stick out of the containing block, of course, either with a negative value of `right` or a negative right margin. Let's try the latter and give the menu a background and border, too. The result is shown in Figure 11.15.

```
div#menu {position: absolute; z-index: 7;
  width: 7em; top: 220px; right: 0;
  margin-right: -4.5em; padding: 0.25em 0 0.5em;
  border: 3px double black; background: rgb(80%,77%,66%);}
```

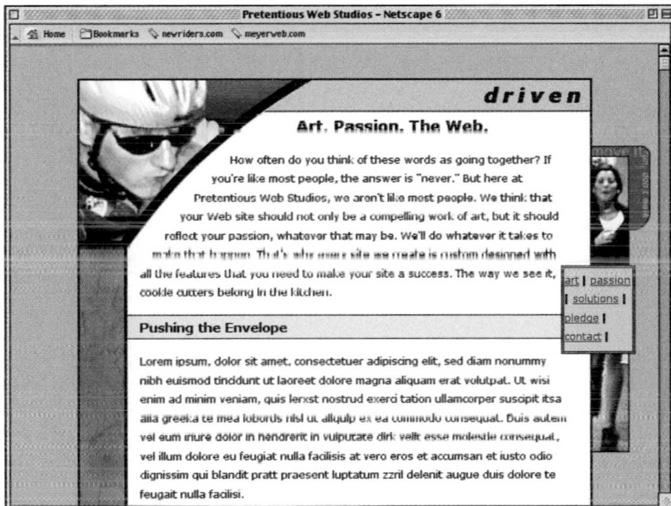

FIGURE 11.15

The menu is hanging out of its containing block, overlapping the women in the process.

So how does the menu, with a `z-index` value of `7`, get to be on top of the image with a `z-index` of `10`? Because the containing block of the menu has a `z-index` value of `100`.

Think of it this way: Every containing block is like a layer in a program such as Canvas, Freehand, or Illustrator. There can be multiple shapes in such layers, and they have their own stacking order, but every shape in a layer is stacked on top of all the shapes in a lower layer. In the same way, a positioned element keeps all of its descendants grouped with it. In this case, if we were to give the menu a negative value for `z-index`, it would be placed behind the wrapper `div`, but it would still be on top of the women's picture.

Things are getting a little too crowded on the right side, so let's shift the menu over to the left. All it takes is a couple of edits to property names.

```
div#menu {position: absolute; z-index: 7;
  width: 7em; top: 220px; left: 0;
  margin-left: -4.5em; padding: 0.25em 0 0.5em;
  border: 3px double black; background: rgb(80%,77%,66%);}
```

We certainly ought to clean up the way the links look and do something about those black vertical bars. The easiest thing to do is jettison the bars altogether and make the links block level.

```
div#menu {position: absolute; z-index: 7;
  width: 7em; top: 220px; left: 0;
  margin-left: -4.5em; padding: 0.25em 0 0.5em;
  border: 3px double black; background: rgb(80%,77%,66%);}
div#menu b {display: none;}
div#menu a {display: block;}
</style>
```

We'll see at the end of the project why we bothered to have these bars in the markup, only to turn off their display. In the meantime, the links need some help, so let's give them a good working over (see Figure 11.16).

```
div#menu a {display: block;
  color: black; background: transparent;
  margin: 0; padding: 0 8px;
  text-align: right; font-style: italic;
  text-decoration: none;}
```

FIGURE 11.16

Repositioning and cleaning up the menu.

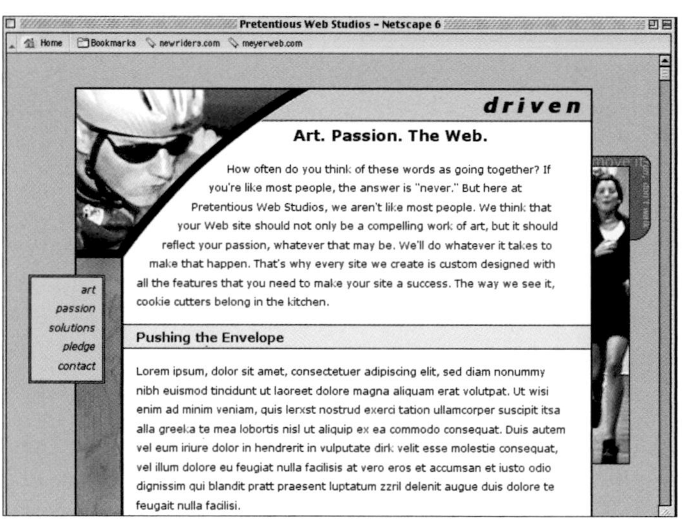

Hovering and Borders

To learn more about creating layout effects by manipulating borders and padding when a link is hovered, see Project 5, "How to Skin a Menu."

To make the menu a little more interactive, let's define a hover style that not only changes the color of the link but also adds a little red bar at the right edge of the menu.

```
div#menu a {display: block;
  color: black; background: transparent;
  margin: 0; padding: 0 8px;
  text-align: right; font-style: italic;
  text-decoration: none;}
div#menu a:hover {color: #943;
  padding-right: 4px; border-right: 4px solid #732;}
</style>
```

With the menu now complete, let's turn to the triple-stack image still waiting for us to pay it some attention. If you remember from Figure 11.14, it had been placed at the left edge of the `div` and thus was drawn inside the column defined by the `div`'s background image. Let's keep that idea going but move the image up so that it slides partway under the menu.

```
div#menu a:hover {color: #943;
  padding-right: 4px; border-right: 4px solid #732;}
img#ls {position: absolute; z-index: 1;
   top: 210px; left: 8px;}
</style>
```

Because both the menu and this image are children of the wrapper `div`, they are stacked in relation to each other (and the `div`), and their `z-index` values will determine which one goes in front. Because the menu's `z-index` is higher, it wins out, as we can see in Figure 11.17.

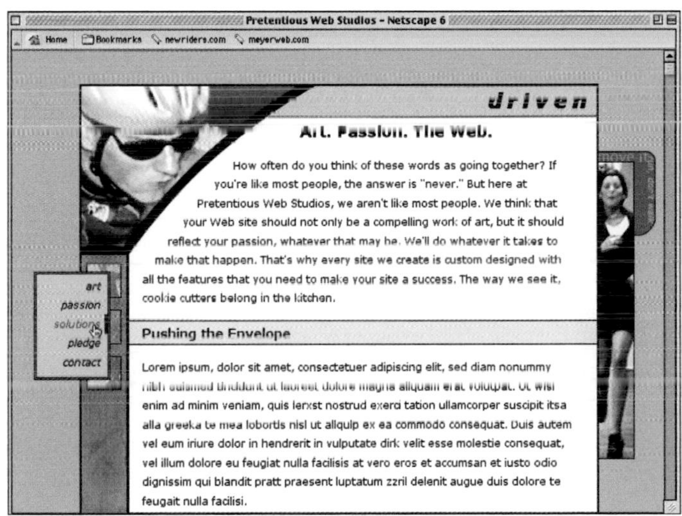

Figure 11.17

The three-box image is placed beneath the menu; note also the hover effect in the menu.

Again, it's fairly easy to decide where to place the image in relation to the other elements on the screen. In this case, we needed to measure the height of the curve image (200 pixels) and add some sort of offset, which here was 10 pixels. Then we had to decide how far in we wanted to offset the image (in this case, `8px`). With those distances known, the rule became a snap to write.

> **What if the One Had Been Three?**
>
> If the triple-stack image had instead been three separate images, it would have been easy to get the same effect as in Figure 11.17. It just would have required us to position each image individually.

Tweaking the Layout

Let's carry out a couple of tweaks just to illustrate how easy it is to alter the layout of a positioned page. Rather than have just the one woman running, let's reveal at least some of the second woman (remember her?) by increasing the right offset on the wrapper `div`.

```
div#wrap {border: 2px solid black; border-left-width: 0;
  background: white url(wrap-bg.gif) top left repeat-y;
  position: absolute; z-index: 100;
  margin: 0 110px 0 0; padding: 0 0 2em 2px;
  left: 80px; right: 110px; top: 40px;
  voice-family: "\"}\"";
  voice-family:inherit;
  right: 0;}
```

That's all it takes; the wrapper `div` gets a little narrower, and the ladies stay right where they were. It's just that now we can see more of them. Of course, we could have picked any value we wanted up to the point of revealing the entire picture. This is pretty good as it is, so we'll leave it.

The "move it" image, however, looks a little odd now. Actually, it looks more odd than it already did. Let's turn it into a tab by sliding more of it underneath the women's picture. In this case, we'll line up the top offsets of the two images and then add a little top margin to push the image down even further, as shown in Figure 11.18.

```
a#rp {position: absolute; z-index: 5;
  top: 11em; right: 23px;
  border-width: 0; margin-top: 5px;}
```

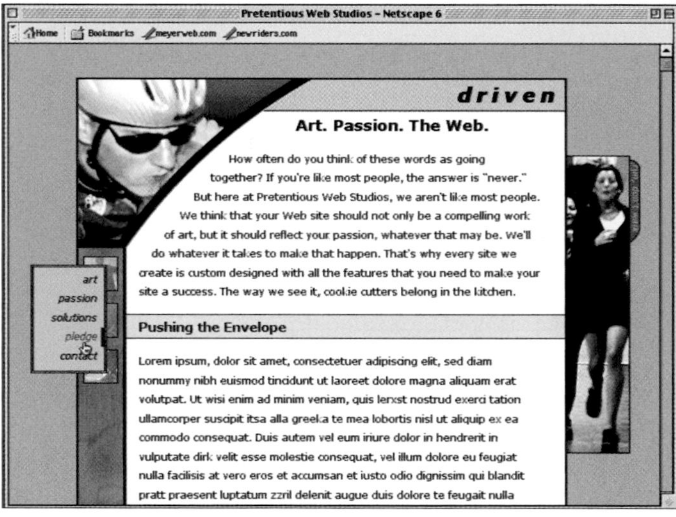

FIGURE 11.18

More of the women's picture is revealed, and the "move it" image becomes a linked tab.

Dynamic Effects

With a little bit of JavaScript (which is beyond the scope of this book), it would be fairly simple to dynamically change positioning values to let elements slide smoothly out from under other elements and then slide away when they aren't needed.

For more information about JavaScript, see *JavaScript Design* by William B. Sanders (New Riders, 2001).

The portion of the image still sticking out ("run, don't walk") can still be used as a link. We could continue to play with these values for quite a while, experimenting with different layout effects—that's part of what makes positioning so appealing. Its very flexibility makes it a powerful design tool as well as a fascinating way to lay out Web pages.

To cap off the experience, let's give the `body` a background image to go with its color. It just so happens that we have an image handy that will visually extend the curve image in the top-left corner of the content `div`, so let's add it in and see the results in Figure 11.19.

```
body {background: rgb(75%,66%,66%) url(page-bg.jpg) top left no-repeat;
  margin: 0; padding: 0;
  font: 12px/1.5 Verdana, Arial, sans-serif;}
```

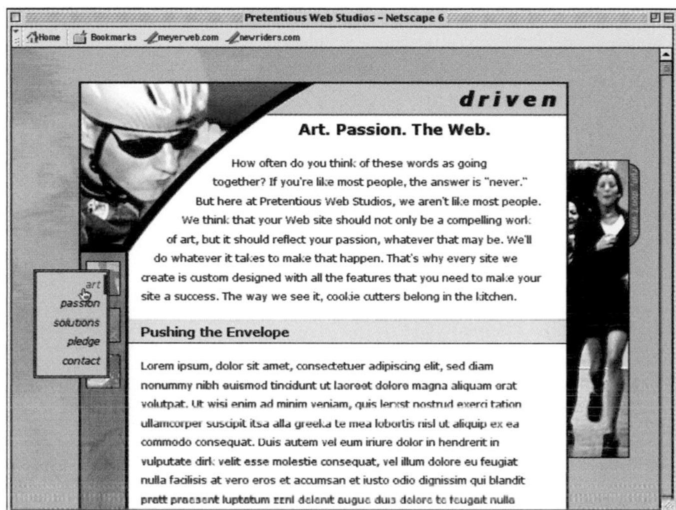

FIGURE 11.19 *Adding a background image that ties into the foreground content.*

Of course, it wasn't just random chance that the background lined up with the foreground, but this illustrates another of the advantages of positioning: the capability to place an element at a precise coordinate and thus line it up with another image. Once you do that, it becomes harder to move things around for fear of having images not line up, but this is usually the last step in the design process anyway. If you aren't sure about your design placement, it's probably a bad time to be tweaking elements to line up with backgrounds.

With that, we've completed our work on this design. You can see the end result of all our work in Listing 11.2.

Listing 11.2 The Complete Style Sheet

```
<style type="text/css" media="all">
body img {display: block;}
body {background: rgb(75%,66%,66%) url(page-bg.jpg) top left no-repeat;
  margin: 0; padding: 0;
  font: 12px/1.5 Verdana, Arial, sans-serif;}
div#wrap {border: 2px solid black; border-left-width: 0;
  background: white url(wrap-bg.gif) top left repeat-y;
  position: absolute; z-index: 100;
  margin: 0 110px 0 0; padding: 0 0 2em 2px;
  left: 80px; right: 110px; top: 40px;
  voice-family: "\"}\"";
  voice-family:inherit;
  right: 0;}
div#wrap img.curve {float: left; clear: left;
  margin: 0 15px 0 0; padding: 0;
  height: 20px;}
```

continues

Listing 11.2 Continued

```
h1 {border-bottom: 2px solid rgb(45%,35%,35%);
  background: rgb(90%,75%,75%);
  margin: 0; padding: 0.125em 0.25em;
  text-align: right; text-transform: lowercase;
  font-style: italic; letter-spacing: 0.25em;
  font-size: 200%; line-height: 1.25em;}
h2 {font-size: 150%; margin: 0;}
h3, p {margin: 1em 30px 1em 56px; padding-left: 15px;}
h3 {border: 1px solid black; border-width: 1px 0;
  background: rgb(93%,85%,85%); font-size: 125%;
  margin-right: 0;}
img#rs {position: absolute; z-index: 10;
  top: 11em; right: 33px;
  border: 1px solid black;}
a#rp {position: absolute; z-index: 5;
  top: 11em; right: 23px;
  border-width: 0; margin-top: 5px;}
a#rp img {border-width: 0;}
div#menu {position: absolute; z-index: 7;
  width: 7em; top: 220px; left: 0;
  margin-left: -4.5em; padding: 0.25em 0 0.5em;
  border: 3px double black; background: rgb(80%,77%,66%);}
div#menu b {display: none;}
div#menu a {display: block;
  color: black; background: transparent;
  margin: 0; padding: 0 8px;
  text-align: right; font-style: italic;
  text-decoration: none;}
div#menu a:hover {color: #943;
  padding-right: 4px; border-right: 4px solid #732;}
img#ls {position: absolute; z-index: 1;
   top: 210px; left: 8px;}
</style>
```

Degrading Gracefully

A few last words about the vertical bars—and switching off their display—are in order. The whole point of these bars is to provide some separation of the links in Netscape Navigator 4.x, which will see none of the styles we wrote (thanks to `media="all"` in the `style` element).

However, it will still load the images, which would lead to a right mess. So to make the degradation of the page a little more graceful, we're going to add a style sheet that NN4.x can read and that turns off the images.

```
<head>
<title>Project 11</title>
<style type="text/css">
img {display: none;}
</style>
<style type="text/css" media="all">
```

If we do this, the images will disappear in newer browsers unless we take steps to counter it. Thus, we add the following to the top of our main style sheet:

```
<style type="text/css" media="all">
body img {display: block;}
body {background: rgb(75%,66%,66%);
  margin: 0; padding: 0;
  font: 12px/1.5 Verdana, Arial, sans-serif;}
```

This will make the images visible in modern browsers that can read the main style sheet.

This is a step that you don't necessarily have to take, depending on the type of audience your site draws. If you get a comparatively large number of Navigator 4.x users, you'll probably want to consider taking this step. The result is shown in Figure 11.20.

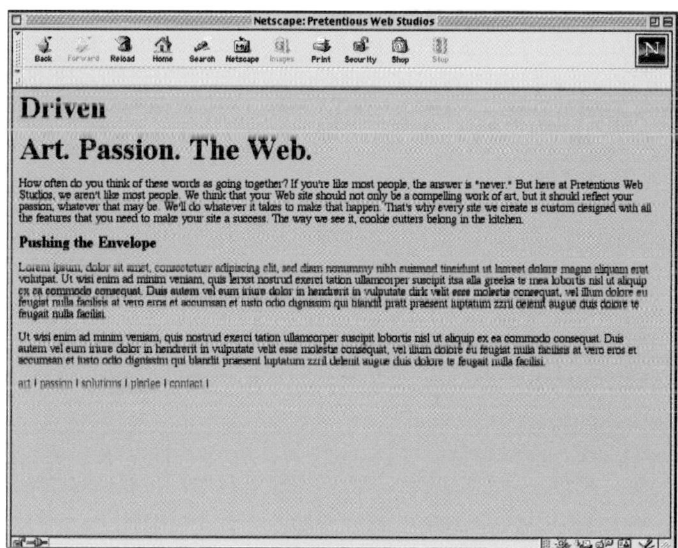

FIGURE 11.20

The "degraded" page layout.

It might not be pretty, but it is totally legible and accessible. It's also a great place to start work on a print style sheet! You can try adding a few styles that NN4.x will use, if you're so inclined. The layout in Figure 11.20 isn't an end; it's a possible beginning. How far you take it is up to you.

Print Styles

For more information on creating print-media stylesheets, see Project 6, "Styling for Print."

Branching Out

The move to positioning opens up a vast new realm of possible layout effects. Here are a few starting points to explore:

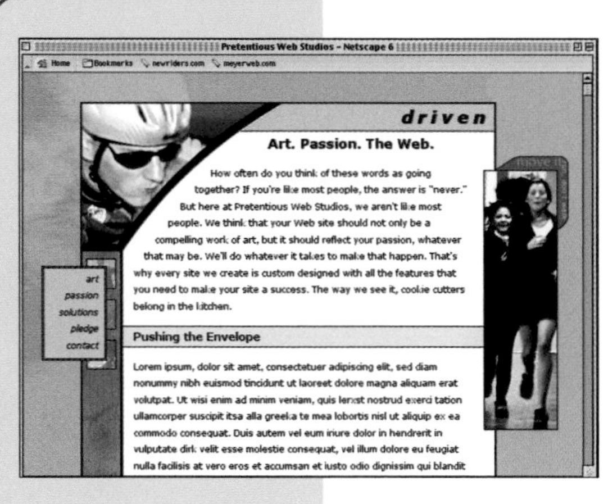

1. Reposition the "move it" tab back out so that more of it is visible around the top corner and then change the `z-index` values of the women's picture and the "move it" image so that they're above the wrapper `div`. Make sure to narrow the `div` so that no text is obscured. Then move the women and the tab so that the top of the tab is lined up with the top of the wrapper `div`.

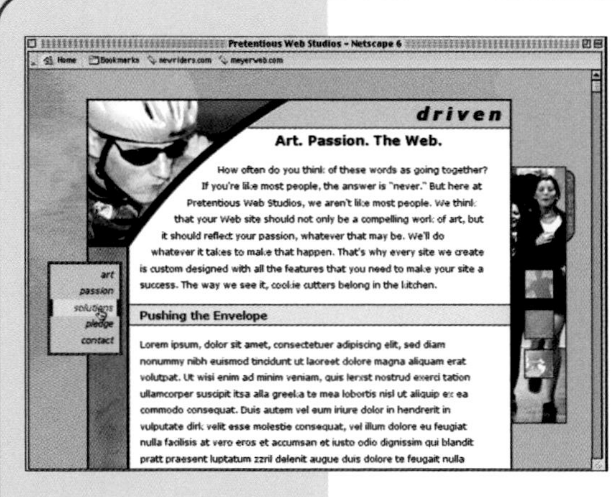

2. Move the triple-stack image so that it's centered in the visible portion of the women's picture (wherever it might be located) and expand the menu a bit to fill in the space it leaves behind. Try adding a few more hover effects to the menu links while you're at it.

3. Try flipping the menu to the right and the women to the left. Because the "run, don't walk" tab won't work with the women's picture now that it's been moved to the left, either place it somewhere else in the design or hide it where the user won't be able to see it.

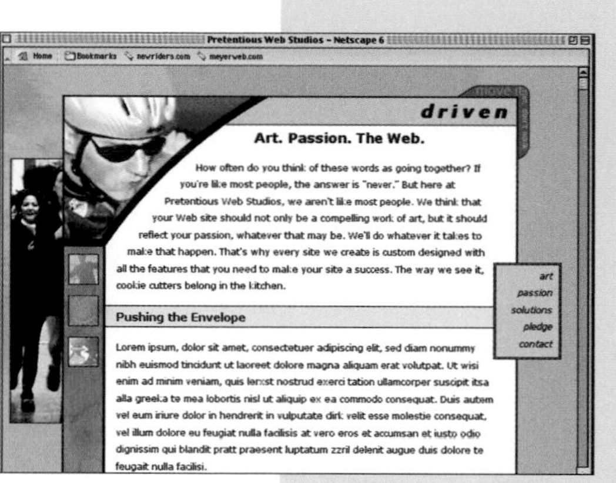

12

Fixing Your Backgrounds

I have the world's largest collection of seashells. I keep it scattered on beaches all over the world. Maybe you've seen some of it.
—*Steven Wright*

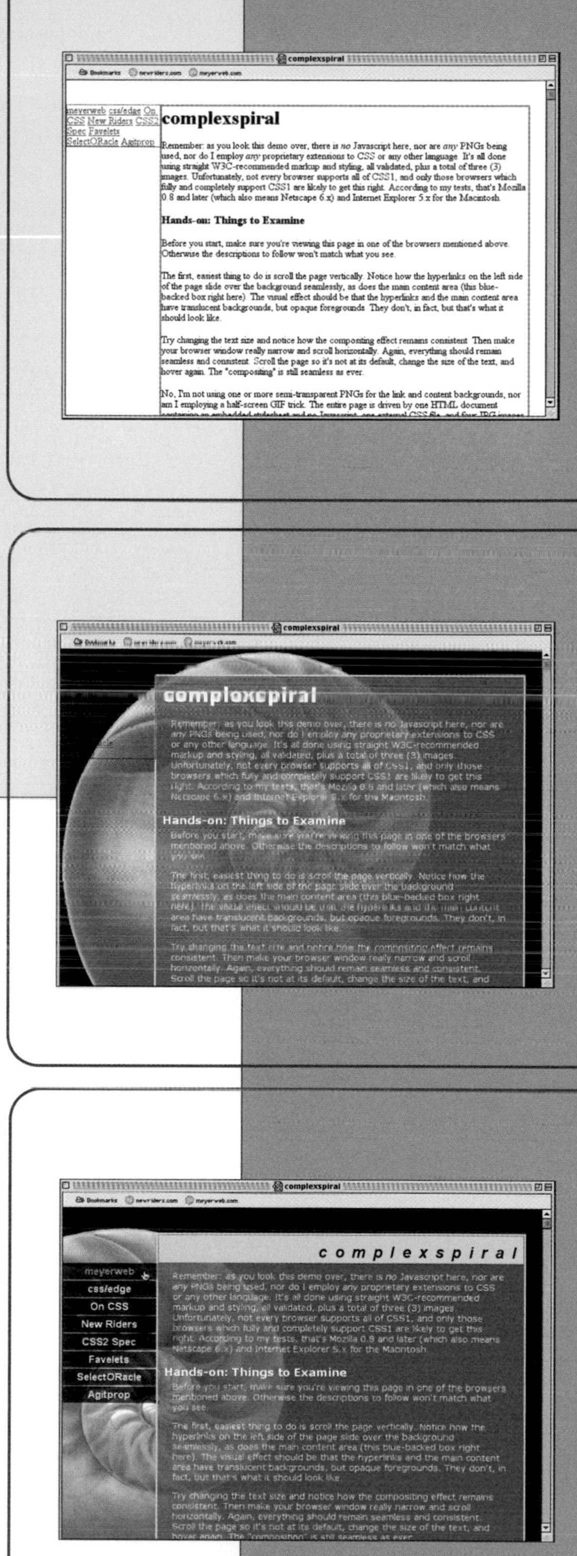

For all its power, HTML-based design has some severe limitations. A sufficiently clever (or desperate) designer can work around these limitations but generally at the expense of hideously complicated tables and a lot of sliced-up images. This has been the norm for years; indeed, best-selling design tools have been built around this need to easily slice up a single large image into many small pieces, all for the purpose of having a Web browser reassemble the slices into an apparent whole.

As we've seen in other projects, CSS can free us from the need for complex table structures and convoluted markup. So far, however, we've looked at ways to replace HTML-based tricks with much less complicated CSS-based effects. Although these are certainly useful and can make the designer's life a lot simpler, it might occur to ask: Doesn't CSS offer anything new? Can it enable us to do anything that was truly impossible to achieve with HTML alone?

The answer to these questions is simple: Yes. Certainly, CSS does this in a myriad of small ways, like its capability to alter the spacing between letters or to change the style of a link that has a mouse pointer over it, but CSS also has some really spectacular tricks up its sleeve. Let's explore just one of them.

Project Goals

This project will be a little different than the others in this book. Instead of creating a cross-browser design, we'll be pushing hard at one of the capabilities that CSS has to offer—even though the majority of browsers available (as of this writing) will fail to display the design correctly. In a sense, this is a look forward to what should be possible when browsers finally implement all of CSS1.

This is not to say that the techniques explored in this project are useless. It might be necessary to work around the limitations of some browsers, but a clever designer can do this without seriously upsetting the page's appearance. To search for these clever design tricks, it's necessary to understand how things are supposed to work, so that's what we're going to do in this project.

Our goals this time around are simple: to stretch our wings a little bit, to play on the edge of what's possible, and to find out just what CSS can do if it's given the chance.

Preparation

See the Introduction for instructions on how to download files from the Web site.

Download the files for Project 12 from this book's Web site. If you're planning to play along at home, load the file `ch12proj.html` into the editing program of your choice. This is the file you'll be editing, saving, and reloading as the project progresses.

Laying the Groundwork

Breaking News!

Although the text is correct in stating that Internet Explorer for Windows does not support the techniques demonstrated in this project, it has become possible to add such support—thus allowing IE/Win to re-create this project's figures! See the aside at the end of the project for details.

There isn't much to do in terms of changing the document this time, but this is a good point at which to pause and talk about the aforementioned browser limitations. If you're using Internet Explorer for Windows up through IE6 or Opera up through version 6.01, the figures in this project won't match what you see onscreen. That's because the techniques we'll be exploring aren't supported by these browsers. Before the project is done, though, we'll have figured out ways to work around these limitations.

The following browsers are known to support the techniques explored in this project:

- Mozilla 0.8 or later and any browser based on it
- Netscape 6.x
- Internet Explorer 5.x for Macintosh

If you're planning to try the examples yourself while reading, you'll need to use one of these browsers.

The document in its unstyled state is pretty ordinary. Note that there are some hyperlinks at the end of the file. These are not visible in Figure 12.1, but they will be very shortly.

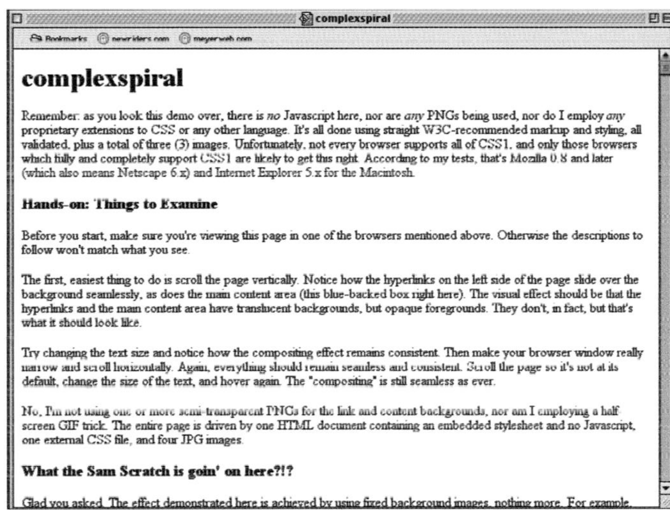

FIGURE 12.1

The unstyled document.

Styling the Document

As has been the case for many of our projects, we'll start by placing elements where we want them and then style them a step at a time. By the time we're done, we should have an artistic design that offers effects that have been heretofore impossible in HTML-based Web design.

Blocking Out the Design

The first step is to get the two main pieces of the page where we want them. The document we have to work with is split into two `div` elements: one with an `id` of `content` and a second with an `id` of `links` that follows the content `div`. Let's position the links on the left side of the page and move the content `div` out of its way.

```
<head>
<title>complexspiral</title>
<style type="text/css">
div#content {margin: 40px 25px 25px 150px;}
div#links {position: absolute; top: 40px; left: 0; width: 150px;}
</style>
</head>
```

The margins on the content `div` will keep it from getting too close to the edges of the browser window, with the large left margin preventing overlap between content and links.

More on Positioning

See Project 8, "Creating an Online Greeting Card," and Project 11, "Positioning a Better Design," for more information about positioning and containing blocks.

Remember that the containing block of any positioned element is either the nearest ancestor element that's been positioned or the root element if there are no positioned ancestors. In this case, the only positioned element is the one with the links, which means we're positioning our links relative to the root element.

We want to make sure the `body`'s styles don't mess up our design in various browsers, so we'll eliminate both margins and padding from the `body` element.

```
<style type="text/css">
body {margin: 0; padding: 0;}
div#content {margin: 40px 25px 25px 150px;}
```

At this point, we could use some help with visualizing the layout, so let's give our two `div` elements some borders so that we can see where they've been placed in the browser (see Figure 12.2).

```
div#content {margin: 40px 25px 25px 150px;
   border: 3px solid gray;}
div#links {position: absolute; top: 40px; left: 0; width: 150px;
   border: 1px dotted black;}
```

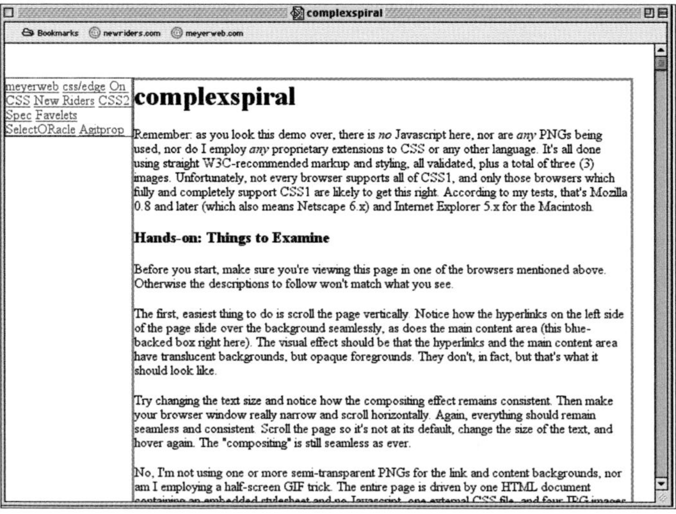

FIGURE 12.2

A touch of positioning creates the design's skeleton.

Instead of letting the links run together, let's make them block-level elements so that they'll "stack up."

```
div#links {position: absolute; top: 40px; left: 0; width: 150px;
   border: 1px dotted black;}
div#links a {display: block;}
</style>
```

Block-Level Links

See Project 5, "How to Skin a Menu," for a detailed exploration of making links into block-level elements and the design advantages that can provide.

Fixing Backgrounds

Now it's time to add a background image to the `body` element itself. For this purpose, we already have an image ready to go (called `shell-bg.jpg`) and have only to write the styles to put it in place. This time, we're going to do something just a little different and write a new `body` rule that is concerned solely with the background. We'll put this rule at the end of the style sheet.

The background images are all derived from a single Photoshop file called `cspiral.psd`. This file, along with the HTML files and JPG background images used to generate the figures in this project, can be downloaded from this book's Web site.

```
div#links a {display: block;}
body {background: black url(shell-bg.jpg) 0 0 no-repeat fixed;}
</style>
```

Much of this might be familiar: the keyword `no-repeat` to keep the image from repeating (or tiling), and the position keywords `0 0` to place the image in the top-left corner. The question is, the top left corner of what?

Background images usually are placed relative to the top-left corner of the element to which they've been applied. This isn't the case with our new rule. The keyword `fixed` is the difference. If you make a background image `fixed` (one of the values of the property `background-attachment`), then it's actually placed in relation to the browser window itself, not the element. This has a number of surprising consequences, all of which we'll explore as we continue on.

For now, let's check Figure 12.3 to see the results of our new rule.

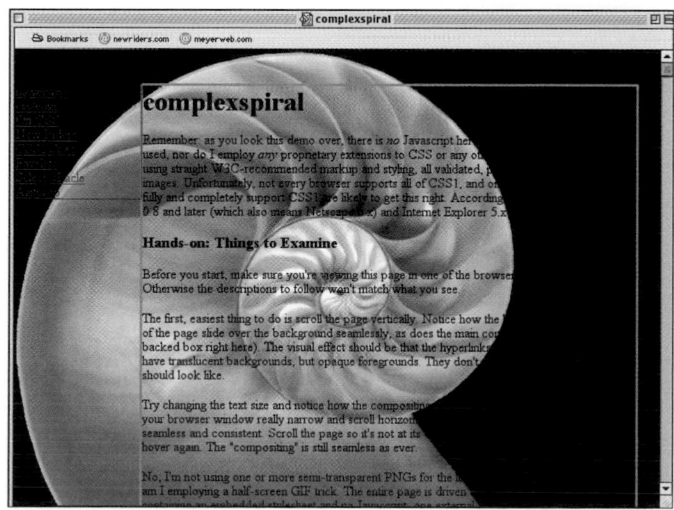

FIGURE 12.3

Giving the body a background leads to some legibility problems.

Okay, so setting a black background for a document with black text might not have been the best idea. We'll fix that in moment. For now, try scrolling the document up and down in your browser. The background image should stay firmly in place, not moving so much as a pixel, as you move through the document.

Fixed Like Fixed

The fact that the keyword `fixed` is used to place background images relative to the browser window parallels the use of `position: fixed` to position elements relative to the browser window.

The unmoving nature of this background image is a result of the keyword `fixed`. As previously mentioned, the image has been positioned in the top-left corner of the browser window, not the `body` element. This is why it doesn't move when the document is scrolled. Among other things, this demonstrates that the browser window is not the same thing as the `body` element and vice versa.

This is a tricky point, and it's easier to explain it using other elements as examples. To that end, let's give the content `div` its own fixed background image, this one called `shell-blue.jpg`. The possibly surprising result is shown in Figure 12.4.

```
body {background: black url(shell-bg.jpg) 0 0 no-repeat fixed;}
div#content {background: #468 url(shell-blue.jpg) 0 0
   no-repeat fixed;}
</style>
```

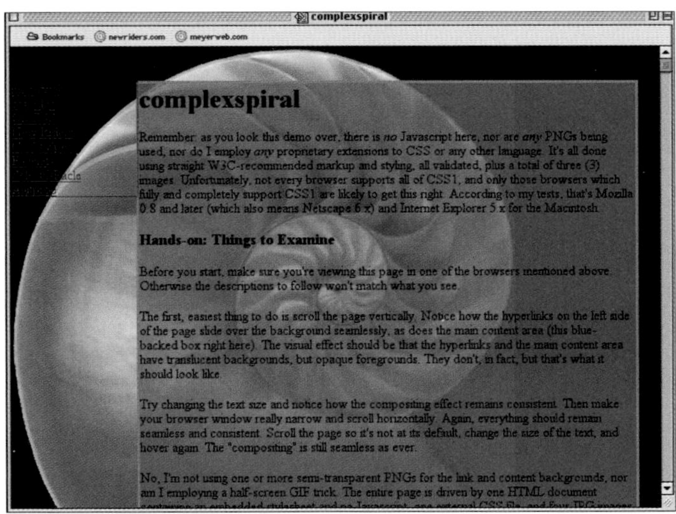

complexspiral
Bookmarks
newriders.com
meyerweb.com
complexspiral
Remember: as you look this demo over, there is *no* Javascript here, nor are *any* PNGs being used, nor do I employ *any* proprietary extensions to CSS or any other language. It's all done using straight W3C-recommended markup and styling, all validated, plus a total of three (3) images. Unfortunately, not every browser supports all of CSS1, and only those browsers which fully and completely support CSS1 are likely to get this right. According to my tests, that's Mozilla 0.8 and later (which also means Netscape 6.x) and Internet Explorer 5.x for the Macintosh.
Hands-on: Things to Examine
Before you start, make sure you're viewing this page in one of the browsers mentioned above. Otherwise the descriptions to follow won't match what you see.
The first, easiest thing to do is scroll the page vertically. Notice how the hyperlinks on the left side of the page slide over the background seamlessly, as does the main content area (this blue-backed box right here). The visual effect should be that the hyperlinks and the main content area have translucent backgrounds, but opaque foregrounds. They don't, in fact, but that's what it should look like.
Try changing the text size and notice how the compositing effect remains consistent. Then make your browser window really narrow and scroll horizontally. Again, everything should remain seamless and consistent. Scroll the page so it's not at its default, change the size of the text, and hover again. The "compositing" is still seamless as ever.
No, I'm not using one or more semi-transparent PNGs for the link and content backgrounds, nor am I employing a half-screen GIF trick. The entire page is driven by one HTML document

FIGURE 12.4

Adding a fixed background image to the content creates the illusion of a translucent background.

Browser Limitations

This is the part where IE/Win and Opera stumble because their support for fixed background images is limited to the `body` element only. When you try to apply fixed backgrounds to other elements, things quickly go haywire. (This problem can be avoided in IE/Win; see the "Fixing Backgrounds in Explorer" aside at the end of the chapter for details.)

Just glancing at Figure 12.4, you might think at first that the content has simply been given a translucent (partly transparent) background color, but CSS doesn't permit translucency in any form. There are proprietary ways to make entire elements translucent, but we aren't using those here.

So what's happening? The keyword `fixed` is the key to all this. Remember that fixed-attachment background images are placed in relation to the browser window. That's true no matter where the element is actually drawn. However, the image is still only visible in the actual background of the `div`. In other words, although the `div`'s background image is placed in the top-left corner of the browser window, we can see only that part of the background image that intersects with the background area of the `div`.

Because we're using variants of the same basic image and are placing them in the top-left corner of the browser window, they line up and create the illusion of translucency. We can scroll the document, as shown in Figure 12.5, and the illusion will hold.

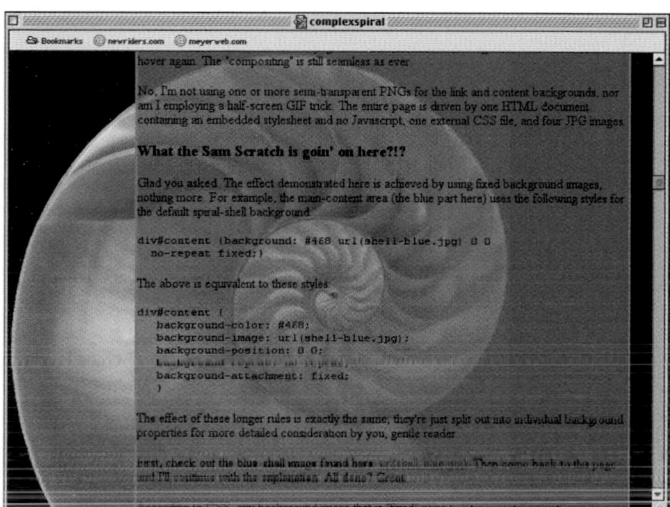

FIGURE 12.5

Scroll the document as far as you'd like, but the background images won't move.

One way to check this for yourself is to change the left margin on the content `div` and reload the page. No matter how big or small you make the value for the `div`'s left margin, the illusion will be maintained. This is because changing the margin values changes the shape of the `div` and thus the area its background covers, but the image itself never moves from the top-left corner of the browser window.

Polishing the Content

Before we start improving the appearance of the links, let's touch up the content. We can color the text in a very light yellow, picking up on the colors in the shell, and we can also change the border's color to match the shell a bit more nicely. In addition, a little padding on the `div` will keep the text from crowding the border too closely.

```
div#content {margin: 40px 25px 25px 150px;
   color: #FFE; font: 14px Verdana, sans-serif; padding: 10px;
   border: 3px solid #FFCC99;}
```

In addition, some margins for the `h3` and `p` elements would be nice. If we give the paragraphs left and right margins, they'll effectively indent themselves and leave the `h3` elements hanging out a bit. In addition, if we set the paragraphs to have no top margin and a `1em` bottom margin and set a reduced bottom margin for the `h3` elements, the paragraphs and headings will be able to move closer together (see Figure 12.6).

```
div#content {margin: 40px 25px 25px 150px;
   color: #FFE; font: 14px Verdana, sans-serif; padding: 10px;
   border: 3px solid #FFCC99;}
h3 {margin-bottom: 0.25em;}
p {margin: 0 1em 1em;}
div#links {position: absolute; top: 40px; left: 0; width: 150px;
   border: 1px dotted black;}
```

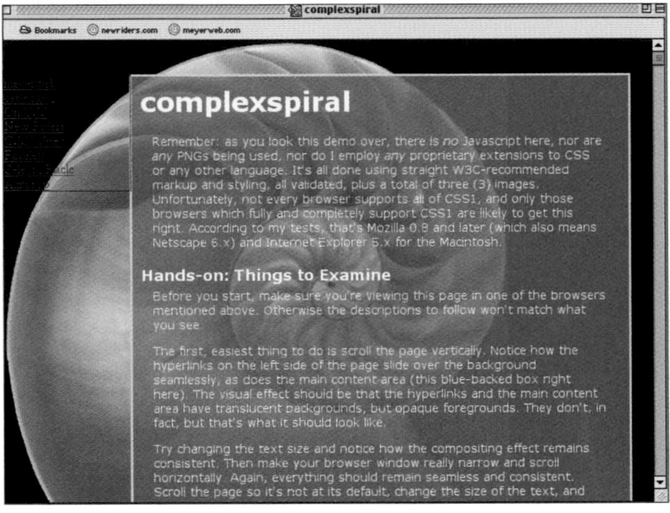

FIGURE 12.6

Making the content a bit more readable.

Combining States

The combination of link states (for example, `a:visited:hover`) was introduced in CSS2 and can be very handy. Unfortunately, very few browsers support this feature of CSS2. As it happens, two browsers that do are Mozilla/Netscape 6.x (and their cousins) and IE5/Mac, which are the browsers that natively support fixed-attachment backgrounds. Therefore, although we're combining link states in this project, they are better avoided in most public designs.

We should also style the links within the content `div` because the default blue and purple colors will be very hard to read against the current background. While we're at it, we'll make them two different shades of yellow and assign a different hover style for the unvisited and visited states.

```
p {margin: 0 1em 1em;}
div#content a:link {color: #FF9;}
div#content a:visited {color: #CC9;}
div#content a:link:hover {color: #FF0;}
div#content a:visited:hover {color: #CC0;}
div#links {position: absolute; top: 40px; left: 0; width: 150px;
   border: 1px dotted black;}
```

There's one more thing to do with the content `div` and that's make the title look a little nicer.

Setting the Title Apart

Although the title "complexspiral" certainly doesn't look awful, it would probably look better with some styles to set it apart. Let's give it a light background based on the color of the content `div` and give it dark blue text to match. We'll also set values for the margin and padding. Let's zero out the top and side margins of the title in an attempt to get its background up against the edges of the `div`.

```
div#content {margin: 40px 25px 25px 150px;
   color: #FFE; font: 14px Verdana, sans-serif; padding: 10px;
   border: 3px solid #FFCC99;}
h1 {background: #ACE; color: #024;
   margin: 0 0 0.5em; padding: 15px 0 5px;}
h3 {margin-bottom: 0.25em;}
```

It would also be a good idea to explicitly set the size and styling of the text within the `h1`. Let's change its default font to Arial, which looks better at larger sizes, and give the text an exact size of `25px`. We'll also set the value of `line-height` to be equal to the `font-size` and make the text both bold and italic (see Figure 12.7).

```
h1 {background: #ACE; color: #024;
   margin: 0 0 0.5em; padding: 15px 0 5px;
   font: italic bold 25px/25px Arial, sans-serif;}
```

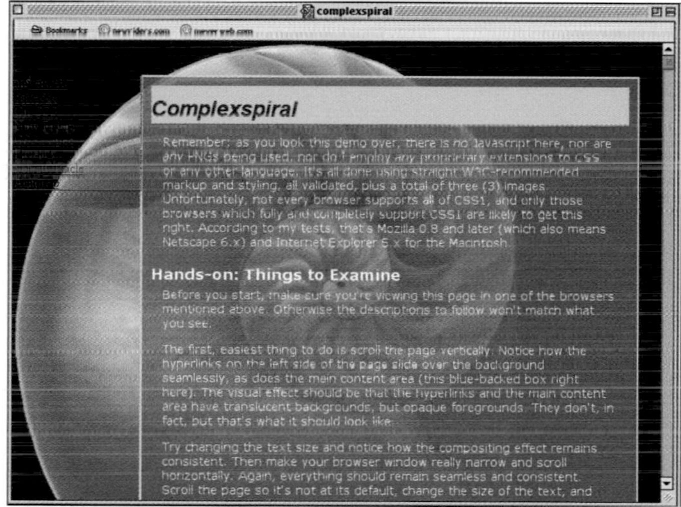

FIGURE 12.7

The title's background and foreground colors definitely set it apart.

It turns out that setting the top and side margins to zero wasn't enough to make the `h1` cozy up to the edges of the `div`. That's because of the `10px` padding we gave the `div` earlier in the project. Rather than remove that padding, which would force us to adjust the margins of the `h3` and `p` elements, let's just use negative margins on the `h1` to pull it up and out. We'll actually give it margins `-9px` wide so that it doesn't quite touch the borders of the `div`.

```
h1 {background: #ACE; color: #024;
   margin: -9px -9px 0.5em; padding: 15px 0 5px;
   font: italic bold 25px/25px Arial, sans-serif;}
```

Actually, the title's text could use a little more work. It might look more hip if we right-aligned it, spread the letters out a bit, and made the whole thing lowercase, as shown in Figure 12.8.

```
h1 {background: #ACE; color: #024;
   margin: -9px -9px 0.5em; padding: 15px 0 5px;
   font: italic bold 25px/25px sans-serif;
   letter-spacing: 0.5em; text-align: right;
   text-transform: lowercase;}
```

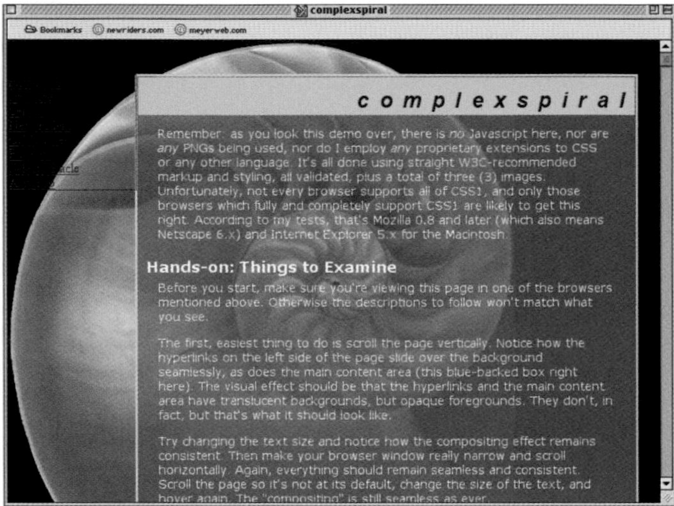

FIGURE 12.8

Bringing the content to its full potential.

With our content in hand, let's turn to styling the links on the left side of the page and give them a fixed background while we're at it.

Styling the Links

Before we even touch the links, let's get rid of the border around the `div` that contains them. We don't need it anymore, and it will just get in the way if we let it hang around, so let's rewrite the `div#links` rule to eliminate the `border` declaration.

```
div#content a:visited:hover {color: #CC0;}
div#links {position: absolute; top: 40px; left: 0; width: 150px;}
div#links a {display: block;}
```

Now it's time to take on the links. Back at the beginning of the project, we made the links on the left side of the page into block-level elements, and now we're going to take advantage of that. Because they're elements like paragraphs or `div`s, we can do nifty things like center the link text and apply margins and padding (see Figure 12.9).

```
div#links a {display: block;
   padding: 5px 10px; margin: 0 0 2px; border-width: 0;
   text-align: center; font: bold 17px/17px sans-serif;
   text-decoration: none; color: #FFC;}
```

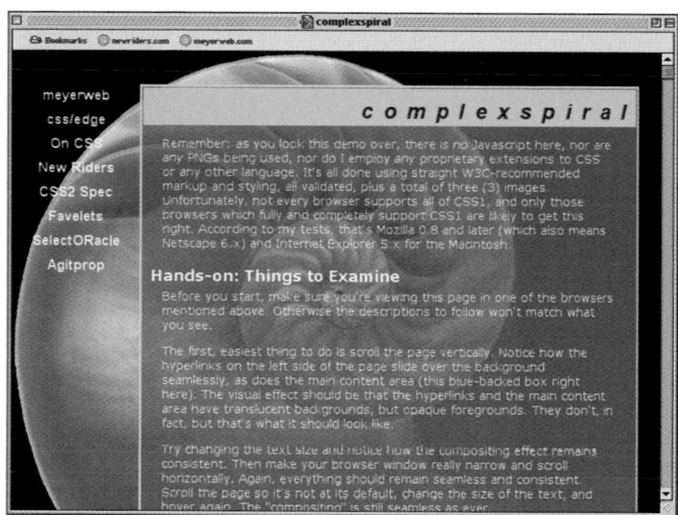

FIGURE 12.9

The links start to show some real style.

A little interactivity would be nice, so let's give these links a hover style. It won't be anything fancy, just a simple change of color to a nice golden tone.

```
div#links a {display: block;
   padding: 5px 10px; margin: 0 0 2px; border-width: 0;
   text-align: center; font: bold 17px/17px sans-serif;
   text-decoration: none; color: #FFC;}
div#links a:hover {color: #F93;}
body {background: black url(shell-bg.jpg) 0 0 no-repeat fixed;}
```

Now it's time to bring in another fixed background. This calls for a third variant of our basic shell image, this time one that's been faded. (Thus, we call it `shell-fade.jpg`.) The trick here is that we'll apply this background to the links themselves, not to the `div` holding them.

```
div#content {background: #468 url(shell-blue.jpg) 0 0
   no-repeat fixed;}
div#links a {background: black url(shell-fade.jpg) 0 0
   no-repeat fixed;}
</style>
```

Now we have a situation in which a single image, `shell-fade.jpg`, has been placed in the top-left corner of the browser window and will only be visible in the background of any `a` element contained within the `div` with an `id` of `links`. This is illustrated in Figure 12.10.

As before, we can scroll the document up and down, but the fixed background images won't move. The elements themselves move and thus reveal different parts of the background images associated with the various elements.

FIGURE 12.10

Fixing a background image for the links makes them look translucent as well.

Simple Markup for Complex Designs

Remember that the effect we've achieved here has been accomplished with exactly three JPG images and some CSS. That's all!

Let's take advantage of our positioned link `div` and add borders to the links. If we do this right, it will look as if pieces of the content `div`'s border light up when we mouse over the links on the left.

To make this happen, first we have to give our links right-side borders and make the style exactly match the appearance of the border on the content `div`. Then we can give the border a highlight color when the links are hovered.

```
div#links a {display: block;
   padding: 5px 10px; margin: 0 0 2px; border-width: 0;
   border-right: 3px solid #FC9;
   text-align: center; font: bold 17px/17px sans-serif;
   text-decoration: none; color: #FFC;}
div#links a:hover {color: #F93; border-color: #F93;}
```

This isn't quite enough, however. Remember that the `div` containing the links is `150px` wide, the same as the left margin of the content `div`. This means the link borders will actually be drawn just to the left of the content's border because the link border will appear inside the `div` that contains the links. The easiest fix here is to simply increase the width of the link `div`, causing the borders to overlap.

```
div#links {position: absolute; top: 40px; left: 0; width: 153px;}
```

Stacking Order

If the content `div` had also been positioned, we would have had to give the link `div` a `z-index` value to make sure it ended up "on top." See Project 11 for more information.

Because the link `div` has been positioned, it will appear "on top" of the content `div`, so the link borders will be drawn over the content's border. Normally this can't be seen visually, but if we hover one of the links, its border changes color, as shown in Figure 12.11.

FIGURE 12.11

Precisely placing borders on the links allows for interesting effects.

Moving Fixed Backgrounds

Although a fixed background image won't move when the document scrolls, it is possible to move it by changing its position. After all, not every design will benefit from images in the top-left corner of the browser window.

It seems a little distracting to have the center of the nautilus shell's spiral near the middle of the content, so let's move it over so that the spiral's center is right underneath the left border of the content `div`. A quick check in a graphics editor tells us that the distance between the two is 237 pixels, so we need to move the content's background image 237 pixels to the left (see Figure 12.12).

```
div#content {background: #468 url(shell-blue.jpg) -237px 0
   no-repeat fixed;}
```

Horizontal and Then Vertical

When using length (or percentage) values for `background-position`, the horizontal value always comes first and is followed by the vertical value. Thus, to move an image over 50 pixels and down 100, you must write the values as `50px 100px`.

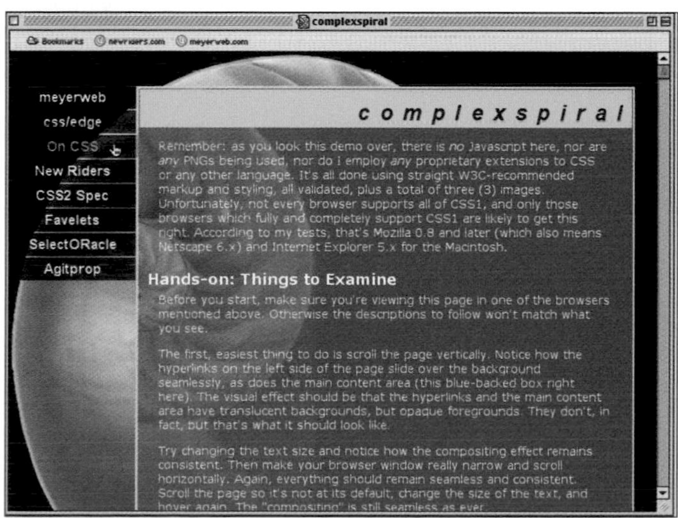

FIGURE 12.12

Moving the content's background image is fine, but we seem to have forgotten the other images.

Whoops! We did indeed move over the content's background, but we didn't do anything to move the other two background images. Thus, they stayed in place, and now the overall effect isn't nearly so pretty.

The fix is simple enough: Just make sure the `background-position` keywords match for the three fixed background images.

```
body {background: black url(shell-bg.jpg) -237px 0 no-repeat fixed;}
div#content {background: #468 url(shell-blue.jpg) -237px 0
   no-repeat fixed;}
div#links a {background: black url(shell-fade.jpg) -237px 0
   no-repeat fixed;}
```

With all three images, we've placed the background image so that its left edge is `237px` to the left of the left edge of the browser window. This has much the same effect as setting a negative margin on an element, although background images do not have margins. As we can see in Figure 12.13, setting the images to have the same `background-position` values has brought them back into alignment.

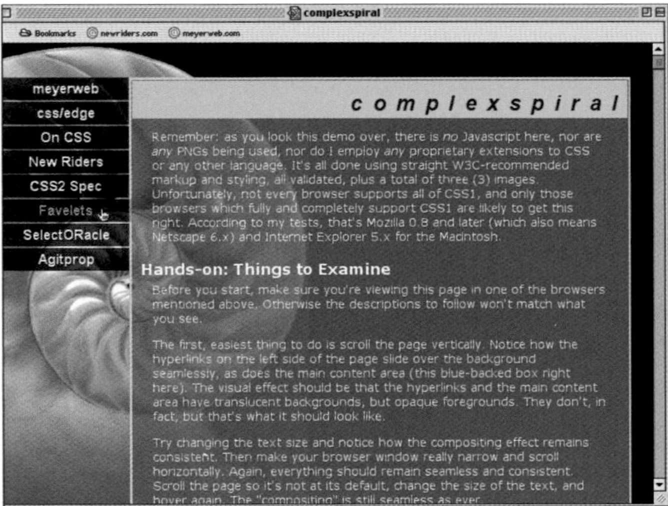

FIGURE 12.13

With the position values all the same, the background images l ine up again and our illusion is restored.

With this change, it's now a lot easier to see the smoked-glass effect caused by the links' background image because more of the shell is now visible in their backgrounds.

Adjusting the Layout

Now that we've proven we can move background images around, let's shift them downward so that the edge of the spiral intersects with the corner of the content `div`. This requires that the images move `30px` downward (see Figure 12.14).

```
body {background: black url(shell-bg.jpg) -237px 30px no-repeat fixed;}
div#content {background: #468 url(shell-blue.jpg) -237px 30px

   no-repeat fixed;}
div#links a {background: black url(shell-fade.jpg) -237px 30px
   no-repeat fixed;}
```

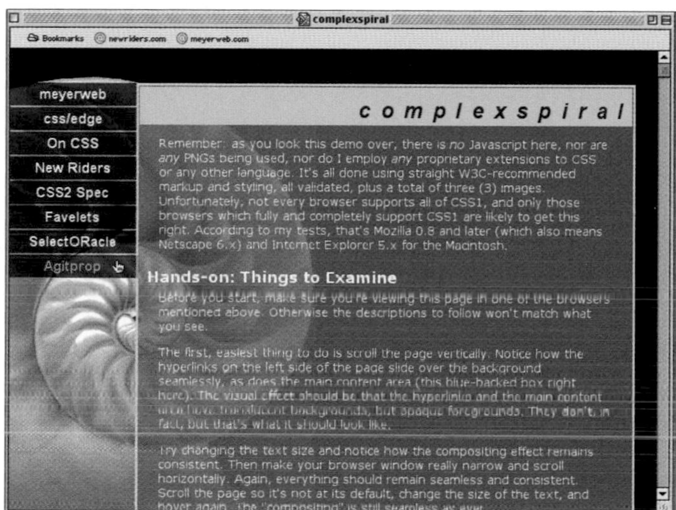

FIGURE 12.14

The background images are all moved downward the same distance.

Right away, we can see that even though we moved the background images without moving the pieces of the design, they still line up and maintain the illusion of translucency.

This would hold true if we did the reverse: left the images in place and moved one or more pieces of the design. Because we have moved the background images downward, it might be a good idea to move the links downward as well. As it is, you can't really appreciate the effect of the content's border growing out of the edge of the spiral because the topmost link's background clutters up the area. Let's move the links downward to make the top of the first link line up with the bottom of the "complexspiral" `h1`.

We know that the content `div` has a `40px` top margin and a `3px` top border. The `h1` itself is `25px` tall (that's the value of its `line-height`) and has `20px` of padding on its top and bottom, making its overall height `45px`. If we add all that together we get `89px`, but we'll round that up by one just for the heck of it. Now all we have to do is change the value of `top` for the link `div`, and it will be shifted downward.

```
div#links {position: absolute; top: 90px; left: 0; width: 153px;}
```

Even though we've moved the entire element, we don't have to do anything to adjust the position of the background images. Thanks to the way fixed-attachment backgrounds work, moving the links just means they reveal different parts of the background image that the links all share, as we can see in Figure 12.15.

Dancing Around Browser Limits

Another good reason to shift the background images downward is to avoid the limitations of older browsers, like Navigator 4.x. Because these browsers place all background images in relation to the top-left corner of the elements, they create a nasty repetition effect in the links. If the images are pushed downward so that they're past the bottom of the links, the links will just show pure black backgrounds—not ideal but better than the alternative.

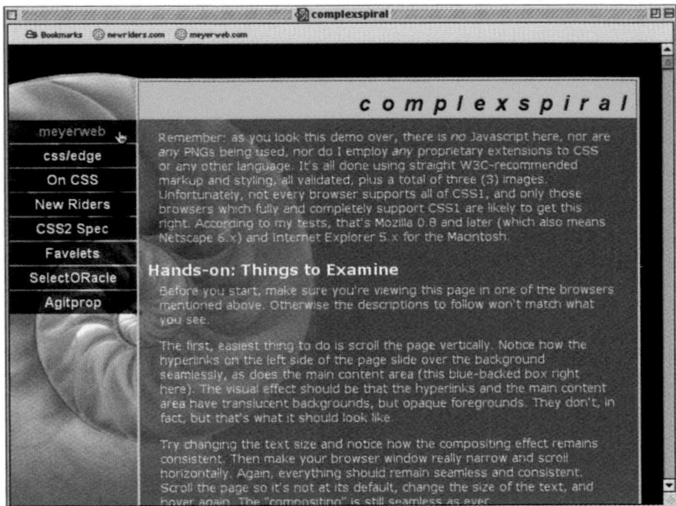

FIGURE 12.15

The links have been moved, but the translucent illusion still remains.

As it happens, the bottom of the last link does intersect the center of the spiral, but for once, that's purely a coincidence. Of course, if the size of the links changed, the margins were adjusted, or a link ran to two lines, this particular alignment would be thrown off, but the translucent-background effect would be preserved.

The result of all our hard work is given in Listing 12.1. Note that most of the styles are concerned with element placement and other text effects. The real meat of the style sheet, the fixed backgrounds, is found in the humble last three lines.

Listing 12.1 The Complete Style Sheet

```
<style type="text/css">
body {margin: 0; padding: 0;}
div#content {margin: 40px 25px 25px 150px;
   color: #FFE; font: 14px Verdana, sans-serif; padding: 10px;
   border: 3px solid #FFCC99;}
h1 {background: #ACE; color: #024;
   margin: -9px -9px 0.5em; padding: 15px 0 5px;
   font: italic bold 25px/25px Arial, sans-serif;
   letter-spacing: 0.5em; text-align: right;
   text-transform: lowercase;}
h3 {margin-bottom: 0.25em;}
p {margin: 0 1em 1em;}
div#content a:link {color: #FF9;}
div#content a:visited {color: #CC9;}
div#content a:link:hover {color: #FF0;}
div#content a:visited:hover {color: #CC0;}
div#links {position: absolute; top: 90px; left: 0; width: 153px;}
div#links a {display: block;
```

```
    padding: 5px 10px; margin: 0 0 2px; border-width: 0;
    border-right: 3px solid #FC9;
    text-align: center; font: bold 17px/17px sans-serif;
    text-decoration: none; color: #FFC;}
div#links a:hover {color: #F93; border-color: #F93;}
body {background: black url(shell-bg.jpg) -237px 30px no-repeat fixed;}
div#content {background: #468 url(shell-blue.jpg) -237px 30px
    no-repeat fixed;}
div#links a {background: black url(shell-fade.jpg) -237px 30px
    no-repeat fixed;}
</style>
```

The Power of Fixed Backgrounds

The advantages of fixed-background designs like this one are hard to overstate. With just a few simple rules, it's possible to produce composite effects that rival the most sophisticated visual design tools available. Here are just a few of the advantages:

- The link text can be changed or the links reordered, and the illusion will still work without any extra effort.
- No matter how tall, short, skinny, or wide an element might become, it will always reveal just the parts of its background image that intersect with its background area.
- Similar effects using sliced-up images are possible, but in those designs the background images scroll with the elements. Furthermore, they require a large number of small image files, which increase server load. With fixed-attachment backgrounds, complex effects can be achieved with a very small number of moderately sized images.

The only real drawback to this sort of design is that if you change the background colors, you have to re-create the background images. Of course, this is true of just about any design that uses background images. In fact, this points out another advantage: Rather than having to re-create dozens of background images, you only have to produce a small handful.

Fixing Backgrounds in Explorer

As this book went through its final edits, Andrew Clover published a JavaScript fix for IE/Win's lack of support for fixed-attachment backgrounds (and fixed-position elements). You can find the script at `http://doxdesk.com/software/js/fixed.html`. *By linking Andrew's incredible script into the project file(s), you can get IE/Win to correctly display the figures in this project, and use this technique in your own designs!*

Branching Out

A great many possibilities are available to authors who use this technique. Here are some examples of things to try:

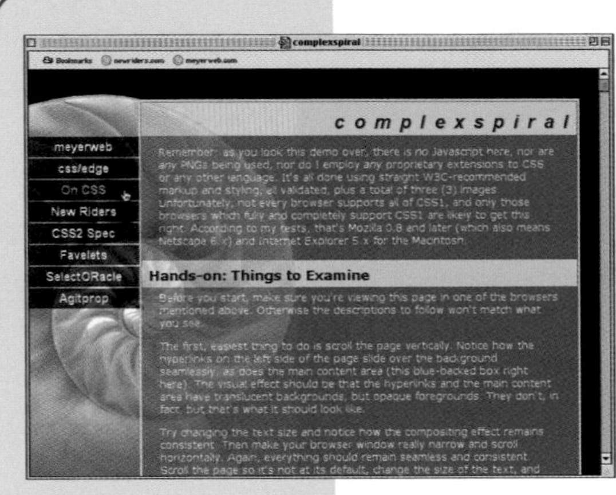

1. Add variant background images for the `h1` and `h3` elements within the content. This will help them stand apart and will increase the illusion of a set of translucent elements placed over a single image. You could reuse the faded background from the links or come up with a new background image to use.

2. Flip the design around so that the links are on the right and the shell is still in their background. This will require you to reposition not only the content and link `div`s but the background images as well.

3. Distort one or more of the images used in the design. For example, a ripple effect in the content area could make it appear as though the content's background is filled with a sheet of glass. This effect could be particularly striking if combined with a color inversion, for example.

13

Eric Meyer on CSS in CSS

Self-plagiarism is style.

—Alfred Hitchcock

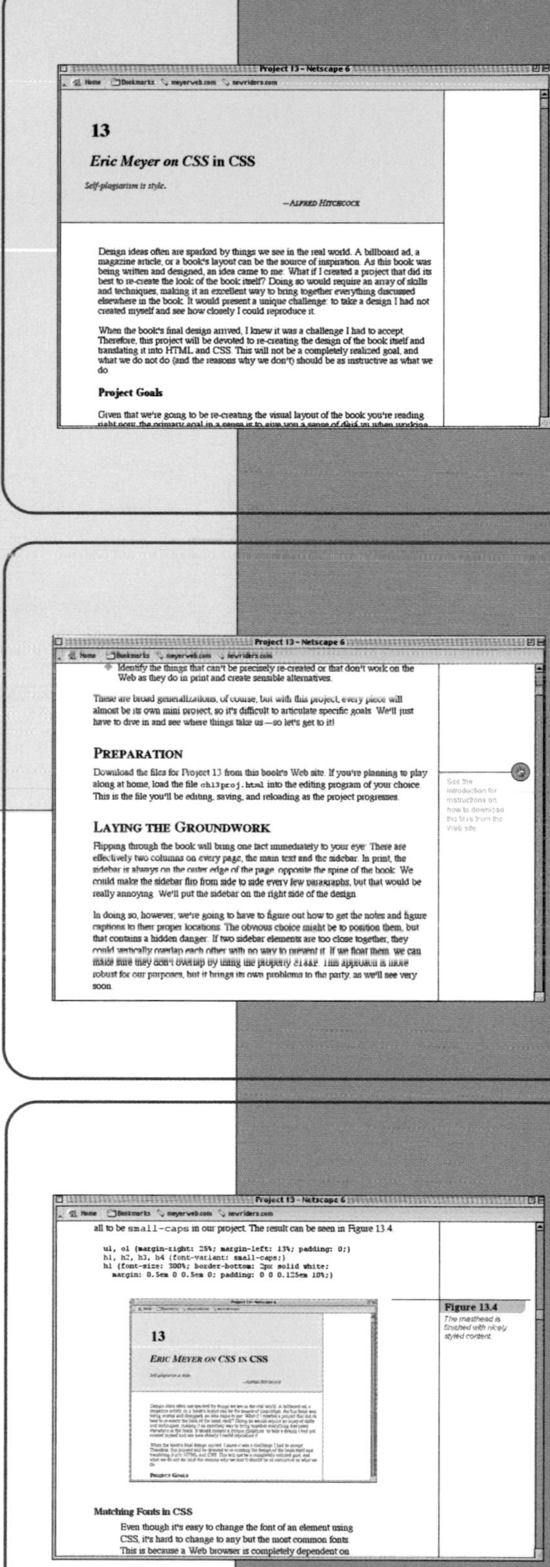

Design ideas often are sparked by things we see in the real world. A billboard ad, a magazine article, or a book's layout can be the source of inspiration. As this book was being written and designed, an idea came to me: What if I created a project that did its best to re-create the look of the book itself? Doing so would require an array of skills and techniques, making it an excellent way to bring together everything discussed elsewhere in the book. It would present a unique challenge: to take a design I had not created myself and see how closely I could reproduce it.

When the book's final design arrived, I knew it was a challenge I had to accept. Therefore, this project will be devoted to re-creating the design of the book itself and translating it into HTML and CSS. This will not be a completely realized goal, and what we do not do (and the reasons why we don't) should be as instructive as what we do.

Project Goals

Given that we're going to be re-creating the visual layout of the book you're reading right now, the primary goal in a sense is to give you a sense of déjà vu when working through the project. On a more practical level, the goals are twofold:

- Use CSS and HTML to simulate the book's layout as closely as possible.
- Identify the things that can't be precisely re-created or that don't work on the Web as they do in print and create sensible alternatives.

These are broad generalizations, of course, but with this project, every piece will almost be its own mini project, so it's difficult to articulate specific goals. We'll just have to dive in and see where things take us—so let's get to it!

Preparation

See the Introduction for instructions on how to download files from the Web site.

Download the files for Project 13 from this book's Web site. If you're planning to play along at home, load the file `ch13proj.html` into the editing program of your choice. This is the file you'll be editing, saving, and reloading as the project progresses.

Laying the Groundwork

Flipping through the book will bring one fact immediately to your eye: There are effectively two columns on every page, the main text and the sidebar. In print, the sidebar is always on the outer edge of the page, opposite the spine of the book. We could make the sidebar flip from side to side every few paragraphs, but that would be really annoying. We'll put the sidebar on the right side of the design.

In doing so, however, we're going to have to figure out how to get the notes and figure captions to their proper locations. The obvious choice might be to position them, but that contains a hidden danger: If two sidebar elements are too close together, they could vertically overlap each other with no way to prevent it. If we float them, we can make sure they don't overlap by using the property `clear`. This approach is more robust for our purposes, but it brings its own problems to the party, as we'll see very soon.

Beyond that, it's a matter of making sure the content itself is properly structured so that it can be styled. Paragraphs should be contained in the `p` element, section headings in `h3` and `h4` elements, sidebar notes in appropriately `classed` `divs`, and so on. Instead of trying to figure all that out ahead of time, we'll just look at each piece and then style it.

Styling the Document

Because our goal is to reproduce the book's layout, we can use it as a point of comparison as we work through the project. There are many ways to attack this problem, but we'll start by addressing the fundamental basis of the book's design: the two-column layout it uses to put notes and captions into a sidebar.

The Sidebar

In setting up the sidebar, we really only need to ensure that there's a border separating it from the main content and that the notes and captions actually make it into the sidebar. This turns out to be a lot trickier than one might have hoped.

We could wrap all of the content in a `div` and then give the sidebar elements a negative right margin to pull the floats into the sidebar. That would let us set a right border on the content `div`, thus ensuring that the border would be as tall as the main content itself. The floats, with their negative margin, would be placed just outside the border. Unfortunately, taking that approach trips across a number of bugs in Internet Explorer for Windows that exist through IE6. These bugs are bad enough that they lead to a near-complete breakdown of the layout in IE/Win, and working around the bugs causes a similar breakdown in almost any other browser.

We could break the content up into multiple `div`s with `class` values like `main` and `sidebar`. This would avoid most of IE/Win's bugs and would make it a lot easier to work around the rest. That's an awful lot of structural hacking, though, so let's not do that either.

Here's a thought: How about giving the various "top-level" elements in the document a wide right margin to open up the space? That way, we can avoid adding a `div` for the sole purpose of creating the columns and can also avoid IE/Win's flaws. It's important to make sure we get all of the elements that are children of the `body` element, but fortunately, the content lends itself fairly well to such an effort. Creating the first rules in our style sheet has the result shown in Figure 13.1.

```
<head>
<title>Project 13</title>
<style type="text/css">
body {margin: 0; padding: 0; color: black;
  background: white;}
h1, h2, h3, h4, h5, p, pre, table, div {margin-right: 22%;
  margin-left: 8%; padding: 0;}
ul, ol {margin-right: 25%; margin-left: 13%; padding: 0;}
div.listing pre {margin: 0;}
</style>
</head>
```

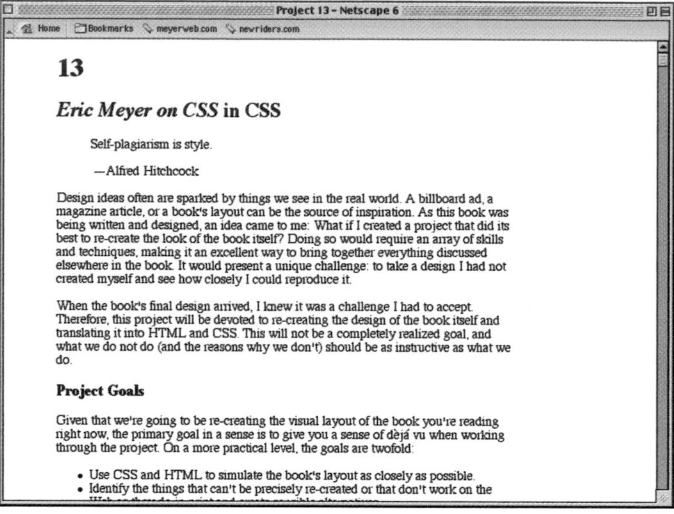

FIGURE 13.1

Applying margins to elements within the `body` *to create a column effect.*

Extra Indentation

The masthead is indented further than the rest of the text because it's all enclosed in a `div`. Thus the elements inside the masthead `div` get offset by both the left margin on the `div` and their own left margins. We'll fix that in the next section.

This results in a content column that's 70% of the width of the `body` element. It's not really a column, of course, but it creates the illusion of one. The reason for using the value `22%` for the right margin will become clear in just a bit. The list margins are made a little bit wider than other elements because we want them to be indented a bit as compared to the normal text flow. The rule for `div.listing pre` has been inserted to avoid problems in IE/Win as we move forward. (It's a rule we would have written anyway, but including it now will prevent confusion as we work on the project.)

Now all we need to do is figure out how to draw a line between the main column and the sidebar. We could try to draw a right border on every element to which we just gave a `22%` right margin, but then we'd have to enforce vertical separation with padding, and it would start to get messy. Furthermore, not all elements touch the separator line. If the line were created from the borders of content elements, they would all be touching it.

Instead, let's borrow a trick from the old days of Web design and rework it a bit. Remember single-pixel GIF tricks? We're going to use one here by taking a 1-pixel GIF that's the appropriate shade of blue and applying it to the background of the `body` element. If we position it correctly and then only tile it vertically, we'll get a separator line, as shown in Figure 13.2.

```
<style type="text/css">
body {margin: 0; padding: 0; color: black;
  background: white url(blue.gif) 80% 0 repeat-y;}
h1, h2, h3, h4, h5, p, pre, table, div {margin-right: 22%;
  margin-left: 8%; padding: 0;}
```

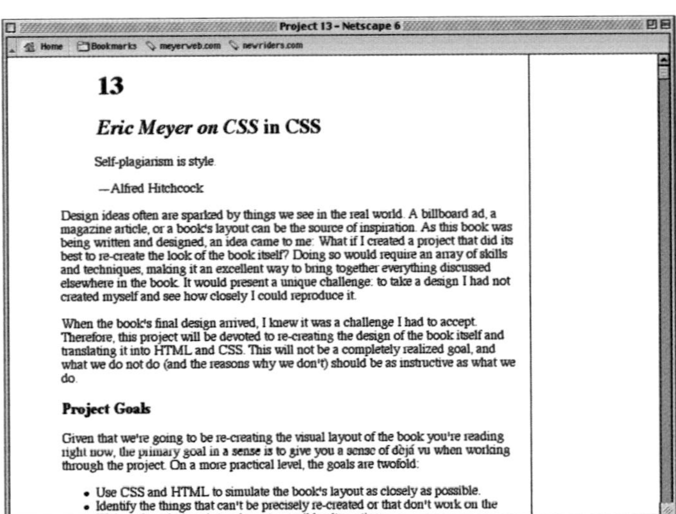

FIGURE 13.2

A simple background image on the `body` *creates the separation between "columns."*

Remember setting all those right margins to be `22%`? Because the right margins are all `22%` and the line has been placed at 20% of the distance from the right edge of the `body` element, there's a `2%` space between the element edges and the line. Thus, we've created the slight distance between the content and the separator line.

The Masthead

With the content column set up, let's turn to the masthead: the light blue box that leads off every project with the number, title, and epigram for that project. If we look at the markup for the masthead, we find this:

```
<div id="masthead">
<h1>13</h1>
<h2><cite>Eric Meyer on CSS</cite> in CSS</h2>
<blockquote>Self-plagiarism is style.</blockquote>
<div id="attrib">&mdash;Alfred Hitchcock</div>
</div>
```

Delayed Images

The three preview images that also appear on the project's first page are not part of the masthead, nor are they even present in the current project file. We'll get to them in the next section.

Thanks to the `div` that encloses the masthead's content, creating the blue box is fairly simple. We want the masthead to fill the entire space between the left edge of the `body` and the separator line, and we can do this with margins. The border is simple as well: Set up a 1-pixel border on the right and bottom edges of the masthead. Finally, to keep the content from getting too close to the top or bottom of the masthead, we'll give the `div` some padding.

```
ul, ol {margin-right: 25%; margin-left: 13%; padding: 0;}
div#masthead {margin: 0 20% 2.5em 0; padding: 2em 0 1.5em 0;
  border: 1px solid #006; border-width: 0 1px 1px 0;
  background: #BDF;}
</style>
```

To style the epigram, all we need is a few styles. The quotation, enclosed in a `blockquote`, should be slightly smaller than normal and italicized. The attribution should be the same, plus it needs to be over to the right and set in a small-caps font, as illustrated in Figure 13.3.

```
div#masthead {margin: 0 20% 2.5em 0; padding: 2em 0 1.5em 0;
  border: 1px solid #006; border-width: 0 1px 1px 0;
  background: #BDF;}
div#masthead blockquote {font-size: 90%; font-style: italic;}
div#attrib {font-size: 90%; font-style: italic;
  text-align: right; font-variant: small-caps;}
</style>
```

FIGURE 13.3

Laying down the basics of the masthead with some borders and a background.

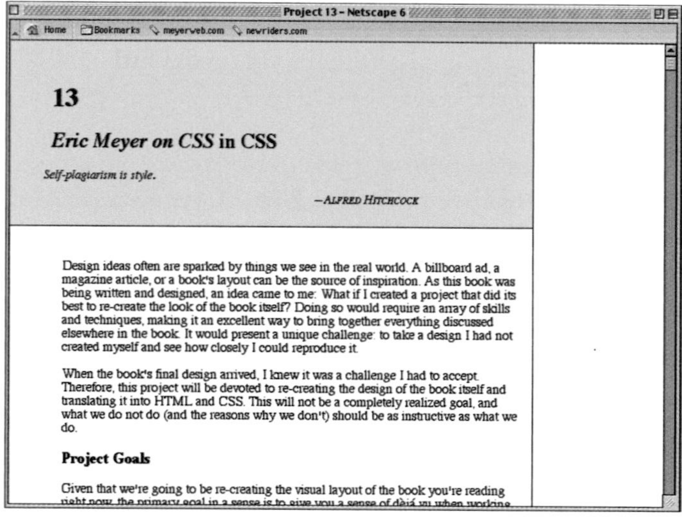

Different-Size Caps

IE5 for Windows will render `small-caps` text in all uppercase letters. This is technically permitted in CSS1, but it might not be a desirable effect. We'll keep using `small-caps` text in this project, but exercise caution in your own projects.

Things are shaping up pretty well except for the left edge of the content, where things are a bit ragged. It would be nice to have everything line up, but this would require giving them all the same left margin. Let's start out with the `blockquote` and its left margin along with the rest of its sides.

```
div#masthead blockquote {font-size: 90%; font-style: italic;
  margin: 2em 22% 0.5em 10%;}
```

The top and bottom margins just help keep it separate from the other masthead content, of course. The right margin is large enough to make sure a long quotation doesn't get too close to the separator line, and the left margin will line up the quotation with the main content. Let's make similar changes to the `h1` and `h2` elements and set their font sizes.

```
ul, ol {margin-right: 25%; margin-left: 13%; padding: 0;}
h1 {font-size: 300%; margin: 0.5em 0 0.5em 10%;}
h2 {font-size: 200%; margin: 0 0 0.66em 10%;}
div#masthead {margin: 0 20% 2.5em 0; padding: 2em 0 1.5em 0;
  border: 1px solid #006; border-width: 0 1px 1px 0;
  background: #BDF;}
```

At first glance this seems fine, but there's a small mistake lurking in our styles. To reveal it, we need only give the `h1` a bottom border:

```
h1 {font-size: 300%; border-bottom: 2px solid white;
  margin: 0.5em 0 0.5em 10%;}
```

The problem is that the border stretches from the separator line to just to the left of the number 13—instead of continuing on to the left edge of the browser window. To fix this, we'll need to eliminate the `h1`'s left margin and compensate with left padding.

```
h1 {font-size: 300%; border-bottom: 2px solid white;
  margin: 0.5em 0 0.5em 0; padding: 0 0 0.125em 10%;}
```

Finally, we should change the font of the title to look a little more like what we have in print. Using the exact same font isn't really a possibility, but we could roughly approximate the feel of the print version by using `small-caps`. Because all of the titles and headings (except for `h5` elements) in the book look the same, we'll set them all to be `small-caps` in our project. The result can be seen in Figure 13.4.

```
ul, ol {margin-right: 25%; margin-left: 13%; padding: 0;}
h1, h2, h3, h4 {font-variant: small-caps;}
h1 {font-size: 300%; border-bottom: 2px solid white;
  margin: 0.5em 0 0.5em 0; padding: 0 0 0.125em 10%;}
```

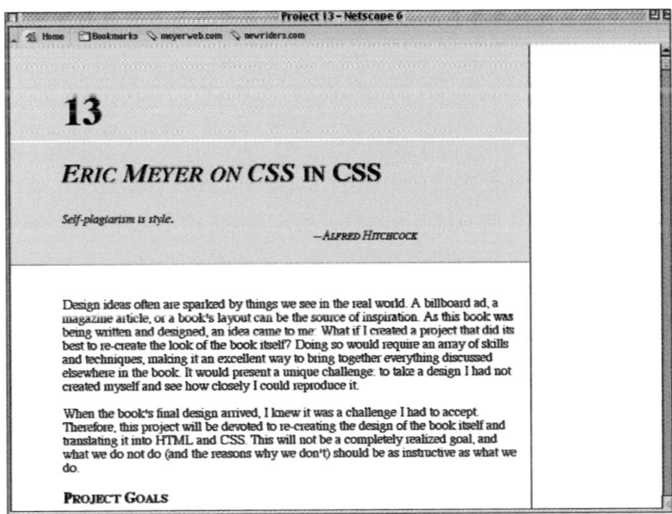

FIGURE 13.4

The masthead is finished with nicely styled content.

▸▸ Matching Fonts in CSS

Even though it's easy to change the font of an element using CSS, it's hard to change to any but the most common fonts. This is because a Web browser is completely dependent on the fonts installed on the user's machine. You can specify that an element should be displayed using the font New Century Schoolbook, as follows:

```
p {font-family: "New Century Schoolbook", serif;}
```

This will work fine on any computer that has the font installed. If the font isn't available, however, the user's default font will be used instead. This is why we aren't trying to precisely reproduce the title font used in the book.

Obviously, this dilemma could be solved if the author could specify a font to be downloaded and used in a Web page. At the height of the browser wars, Netscape and Microsoft each invented its own method for font downloading, and neither one supported the other. When CSS2 was released, it provided font description and downloading features that matched neither Microsoft nor Netscape's mechanisms. For the time being, cross-browser downloadable fonts remain solidly in the realm of wishful thinking.

Placing the Previews

There's one last thing to do here at the top of the document and that's drop in the three preview images that appear on the first page of each project. These previews are reproductions of figures that appear elsewhere in the project. Here, we'll just point to the images we want and place them appropriately.

It's important to put the images at the correct spot in the markup, however. Because we want them to start out next to the masthead and we need to float them over to the side, we need to insert the images before the masthead itself.

```
<body>
<div id="previews">
<img src="13CSS03.jpg" alt="preview 1">
<img src="13CSS10.jpg" alt="preview 2">
<img src="13CSS15.jpg" alt="preview 3">
</div>
<div id="masthead">
<h1>13</h1>
```

Now all we have to do is float the `div` and size the images.

```
div#attrib {font-size: 90%; font-style: italic;
  text-align: right; font-variant: small-caps;}
div#previews {float: right; width: 33%; margin: 0; text-align: center;}
div#previews img {width: 80%; margin-top: 1em;}
</style>
```

You might note that the `div` is wider than the `20%` margins set for the main content. That's because, as in the print version, we want the preview images to stick out of the sidebar. We've made the images `80%` of the width of their containing `div`, and the `text-align` value will center them in the `div`. This will push them away from the edge of the `body` (see Figure 13.5).

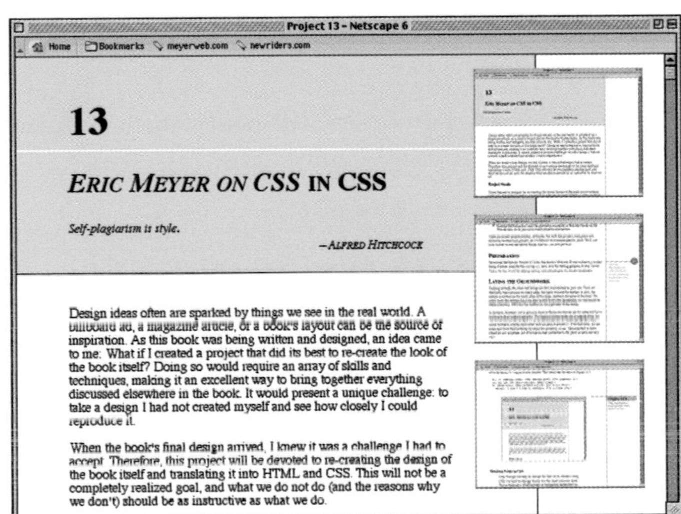

FIGURE 13.5

Re-creating the preview images with a few changes that make life easier.

This isn't exactly the same as the print version, of course. We're still missing the rounded-corner boxes that surround the images and the dark blue background for the sidebar. We could attempt to re-create these effects, but we won't. Why not? For the boxes, it would take a great deal of effort and structural hacking to make them look right, and it just isn't worth the effort for so small a part of the design. The dark blue background, on the other hand, is being omitted because it would look fairly strange to have the dark blue suddenly stop just below the images and leave an empty sidebar below it. So we're going to skip re-creating those effects and move on to the main content.

Title Spacing

As soon as we hit the first heading, "Project Goals," we can see that the spacing is off as compared to the print version. It needs to be moved down closer to the text following and further away from the paragraph before it. The same is true of all `h3`, `h4`, and `h5` elements, so we'll style them all together.

```
h1, h2, h3, h4 {font-variant: small-caps;}
h3, h4, h5 {margin-top: 1.25em; margin-bottom: 0;}
h1 {font-size: 300%; border-bottom: 2px solid white;
  margin: 0.5em 0 0.5em 0; padding: 0 0 0.125em 10%;}
```

Interparagraph Spacing

Although we've reduced the top margin on paragraphs, two paragraphs in a row will still be about `1em` apart because the default bottom margin for paragraphs is still in effect. Because vertically adjacent margins collapse and the distance between element borders is always the greater of the two margins, the `1em` bottom margin will preserve traditional interparagraph spacing.

That in itself isn't enough, though. If we want the titles to get close to the following text, we also need to reduce the top margin on paragraphs. While we're at it, we'll also set a slightly larger `line-height`.

```
h2 {font-size: 200%; margin: 0 0 0.66em 10%;}
p {margin-top: 0.5em; margin-bottom: 1em; line-height: 1.2em;}
div#masthead {margin: 0 20% 2.5em 0; padding: 2em 0 1.5em 0;
  border: 1px solid #006; border-width: 0 1px 1px 0;
  background: #BDF;}
```

We also ought to increase the size of the `h3` element, which is bigger in print as compared to the normal text size (see Figure 13.6).

```
h2 {font-size: 200%; margin: 0 0 0.66em 10%;}
h3 {font-size: 150%;}
p {margin-top: 0.5em; margin-bottom: 1em; line-height: 1.2em;}
```

FIGURE 13.6

Touching up the paragraphs and setting the title spacing to match the book.

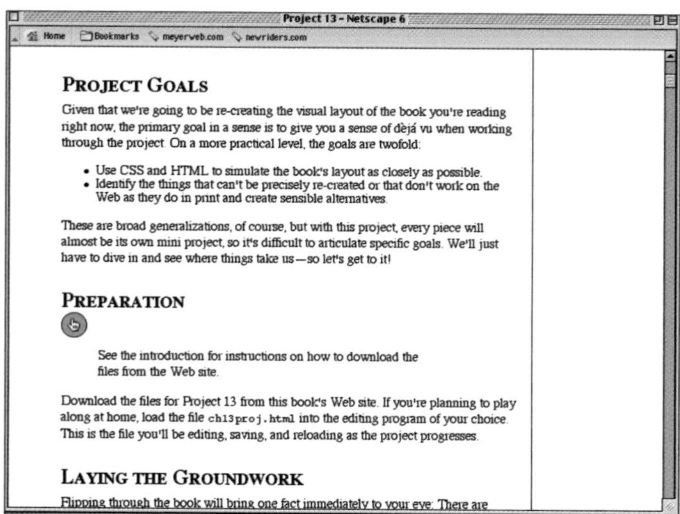

Since we've started sizing heading elements, let's fill in sizes for the rest of them. That way, we won't have to worry about it later on.

```
h3 {font-size: 150%;}
h4 {font-size: 110%;}
h5 {font-size: 100%;}
p {margin-top: 0.5em; margin-bottom: 1em; line-height: 1.2em;}
```

With that accomplished, let's figure out how to liven up our lists.

Lists

Just a little bit into the "Project Goals" section, we find an unordered list. In this book, such lists have small blue diamonds for bullets instead of the usual block dot. So long as we have an appropriately sized graphic file that shows a blue diamond on a white background, we can make use of it.

```
div#previews img {width: 80%; margin-top: 1em;}
ul li {list-style: outside square url(diamond.gif);}
</style>
```

It's also the case that such lists are separated a little bit from each other. We could fiddle around with the `line-height` of the list items, but there is a better way: increasing either the margin or the padding of the list items. The only real difference between the two is that if we ever wanted to set background colors on the lists, with an increased margin, the backgrounds would touch and create one big block of color. We won't be doing that, however, because it's not how lists look in this book, so we'll increase the bottom margin of the `li` elements. This has the result shown in Figure 13.7.

```
ul li {list-style: outside square url(diamond.gif);
  margin-bottom: 0.5em;}
```

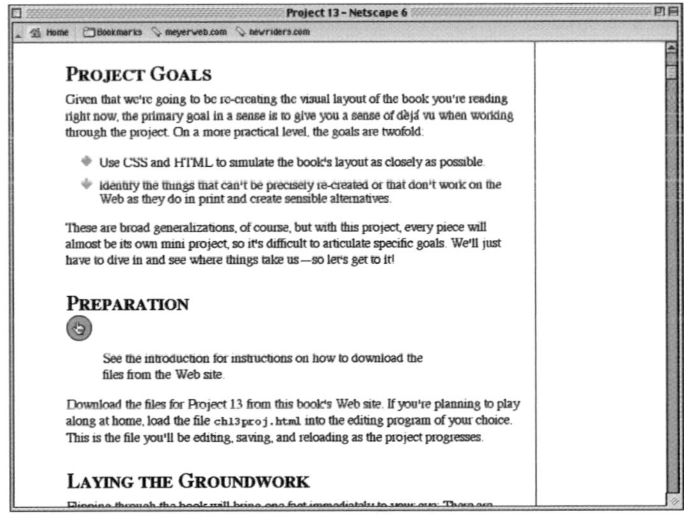

FIGURE 13.7

Using images to replace boring bullets with dazzling diamonds.

Sidebar Notes

Moving into the "Preparation" section, we find our first sidebar note. This is one of the green Web site notes, and it is unusual compared to the blue notes and red warnings for one reason: Web notes don't have titles. Here's the markup for the Web note:

```
<div class="note web">
<img src="web-icon.gif" alt="Web">
<p>
See the introduction for instructions on how to download the files
from the Web site.
</p>
</div>
```

Here's the markup for one of the blue notes:

```
<div class="note tip">
<img src="tip-icon.gif" alt="Tip">
<h5>Delayed Images</h5>
<p>
The three "preview" images that also appear on the project's first page
are not a part of the masthead, nor are they even present in the current
project file.  We'll get to them in the next section.
</p>
</div>
```

Structurally speaking, the only difference between the two is the `h5` element. Of much greater importance are the `class` values for these two notes. We can see that both have the word `note`, and a quick search through the HTML shows that all sidebar notes share this value. Then comes another word that describes the kind of note (the possibilities being `web`, `tip`, and `warn`).

Thus, any styles that are common to all notes can be written into one rule, and the styles specific to each type will go into its own rules. We want to float the notes into the sidebar, but we also want to make sure that any note will appear below another note and not to its left. If we throw in a `width` and some margins, we have the start depicted in Figure 13.8.

```
ul li {list-style: outside square url(diamond.gif);
  margin-bottom: 0.5em;}
div.note {float: right; clear: right; border-width: 0;
  width: 19%; margin: 0 1% 0 0; padding: 0;}
</style>
```

It turns out that Explorer for Windows has a bit of trouble with the styles we've just added; it thinks for some reason that `19%` plus `1%` equals more than `20%`. So we'll use the `voice-family` trick to give IE/Win the value it needs while still delivering the correct number to other, more robust browsers.

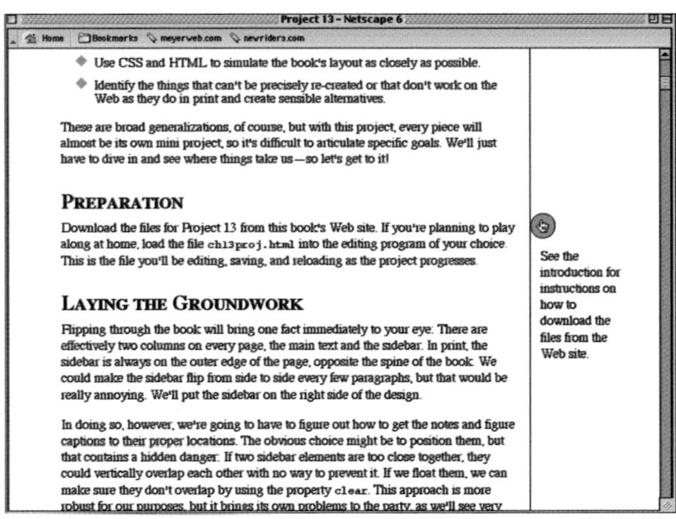

FIGURE 13.8

The first steps toward styling sidebar notes to match the print version.

```
div.note {float: right; clear: right; border-width: 0;
  width: 18%; margin: 0 1% 0 0; padding: 0;
  voice-family: "\"}\""; voice-family:inherit;
  width: 19%;}
```

Obviously, we're going to want to move the icon over to the right. Because images are inline content just like text, we could right-align it using `text-align`. However, we want the title and paragraph text to be left-justified.

```
div.note {float: right; clear: right; border-width: 0;
  width: 18%; margin: 0 1% 0 0; padding: 0;
  text-align: right;
  voice-family: "\"}\""; voice-family:inherit;
  width: 19%;}
div.note h5, div.note p {text-align: left;}
</style>
```

We still need to make the text smaller than normal and set it in a sans-serif font like the one used in the book. It's easiest to do this on the `div` itself.

```
div.note {float: right; clear: right; border-width: 0;
  width: 18%; margin: 0 1% 0 0; padding: 0;
  text-align: right; font: 80% Arial, Verdana, Helvetica, sans-serif;
  voice-family: "\"}\""; voice-family:inherit;
  width: 19%;}
```

Now let's turn our attention back to the actual contents of the notes. The image element lacks the attributes `height` and `width`, so we need to supply those values through CSS. Also, we want to make sure the text in the notes stands a little bit away from the sidebar's border and runs over to the right edge of the note's `div`. This yields the following:

```
div.note h5, div.note p {text-align: left; margin-left: 1em; margin-right: 0;}
div.note img {height: 30px; width: 30px; margin: 0;}
</style>
```

For a discussion of the `voice-family` trick and other ways to use browser bugs to your advantage, see "Tricking Browsers and Hiding Styles" on the Web site.

Finally, we need to connect the icon to the separator line with a dark blue horizontal line. Why not reuse the trick employed to create the separator line itself? We know the icon is `30px` tall and is in the top-right corner of the note. Therefore, we can draw a line in the background of the `div` that's `15px` from the top of the `div` by repeating the single-pixel file in the horizontal direction, as shown in Figure 13.9.

```
div.note {float: right; clear: right; border-width: 0;
  width: 18%; margin: 0 1% 0 0; padding: 0;
  text-align: right; font: 80% Arial, Verdana, Helvetica, sans-serif;
  background: transparent url(blue.gif) 50% 15px repeat-x;
  voice-family: "\"}\""; voice-family:inherit;
  width: 19%;}
```

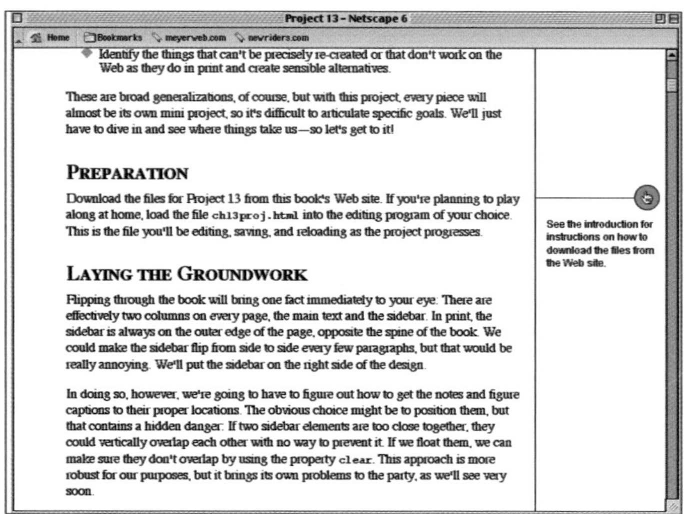
Project 13 - Netscape 6

Home | Bookmarks | meyerweb.com | newriders.com

- Identify the things that can't be precisely re-created or that don't work on the Web as they do in print and create sensible alternatives.

These are broad generalizations, of course, but with this project, every piece will almost be its own mini project, so it's difficult to articulate specific goals. We'll just have to dive in and see where things take us—so let's get to it!

PREPARATION

Download the files for Project 13 from this book's Web site. If you're planning to play along at home, load the file `ch13proj.html` into the editing program of your choice. This is the file you'll be editing, saving, and reloading as the project progresses.

See the introduction for instructions on how to download the files from the Web site.

LAYING THE GROUNDWORK

Flipping through the book will bring one fact immediately to your eye: There are effectively two columns on every page, the main text and the sidebar. In print, the sidebar is always on the outer edge of the page, opposite the spine of the book. We could make the sidebar flip from side to side every few paragraphs, but that would be really annoying. We'll put the sidebar on the right side of the design.

In doing so, however, we're going to have to figure out how to get the notes and figure captions to their proper locations. The obvious choice might be to position them, but that contains a hidden danger: If two sidebar elements are too close together, they could vertically overlap each other with no way to prevent it. If we float them, we can make sure they don't overlap by using the property `clear`. This approach is more robust for our purposes, but it brings its own problems to the party, as we'll see very soon.

FIGURE 13.9

With only a very few styles, we've gotten close to reproducing the note's original look.

Now all we need to do is set the color for the text and pull the text upward so that it's closer to the line we just drew. We shouldn't assign the same `color` value to all notes, though; remember that each type of note has different-colored text. This is where the second word in each note's `class` comes in handy.

```
div.note img {height: 30px; width: 30px; margin: 0;}
div.web {color: #399;}
div.tip {color: #006;}
div.warn, div.warn code {color: maroon;}
</style>
```

Inheriting Styles

Another way to get warning `code` text to match its parent would be to use the value `inherit` in a new rule: `div.warn code {color: inherit;}`. This value is fairly well supported by browsers, and we didn't use it solely because it wasn't any more efficient than the method we chose.

We've added in a selector to color any `code` text in a warning the same as the text that surrounds it. This overrides an earlier rule that made all `code` elements dark blue.

As for moving the text upward a bit, that calls for some caution. We can just set a negative top margin to accomplish this, but we don't want text to overlap the icons. Therefore, we need to make sure that whatever element comes first in the various types of notes has a right margin that leaves space for the icon. In Web notes, the first element is always a paragraph.

```
div.note img {height: 30px; width: 30px; margin: 0;}
div.web p {margin: -10px 30px 0 1em;}
div.web {color: #399;}
```

The right margin of `30px`, being the exact width of the icon, should prevent any overlap between text and image. We need to apply similar styles to the first element of blue notes and red warnings, always an `h5`. These note titles are not in small-caps text, so let's get rid of that styling and make them normal again.

```
div.note img {height: 30px; width: 30px; margin: 0;}
div.note h5 {margin: -5px 30px 0 1em; padding: 0;
  font-variant: normal;}
div.web p {margin: -10px 30px 0 1em;}
```

The `padding: 0;` set for the note titles is mostly for insurance because one never knows when a browser might decide to use padding instead of margins to open up space around heading elements.

We also need to make sure any `code` text within the notes is legible. In many browsers, `code` text is smaller than normal text. In the context of the notes, we want it to be about the same size as the paragraph text, as illustrated in Figure 13.10.

```
div.web p {margin: -10px 30px 0 1em;}
div.note code {font-size: 100%;}
div.web {color: #399;}
```

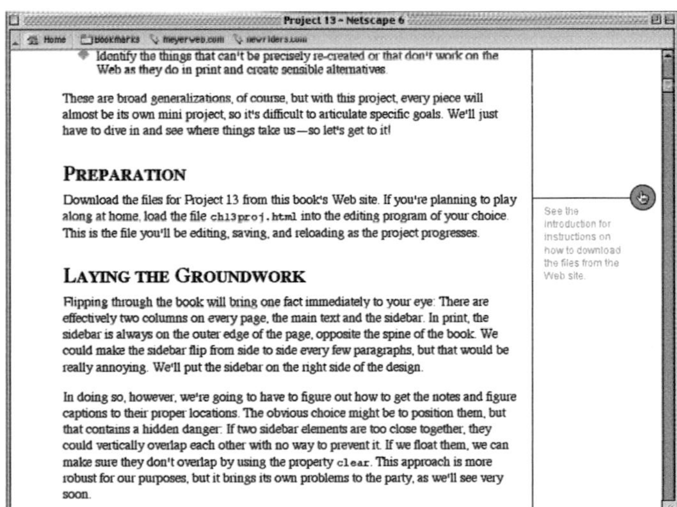

FIGURE 13.10

A blue note that mirrors the printed version closely.

Of course, the lines won't break in exactly the same places in the Web version as they do in print, and this can make notes taller or shorter than they are on the page. Even so, the resemblance is close enough to move on to making code, changed or otherwise, stand out.

Code Blocks and Fragments

In the section titled "Laying the Groundwork," we find that some text has been enclosed in `code` elements. Consider, for example, the third paragraph:

```
<p>
Beyond that, it's a matter of making sure the content itself is properly
structured so that it can be styled.  Paragraphs should be contained in
the <code>p</code> element, titles in <code>h3</code> and
<code>h4</code> elements, sidebar notes in appropriately
<code>class</code>ed <code>div</code>s, and so on.  Instead of trying to
figure all that out ahead of time, we'll just look at each piece, figure
out how it should be structured, and then style it.
</p>
```

In the book, such pieces of code are set in a monospace font and are colored dark blue. That's incredibly simple to reproduce, of course, but let's wait a moment. Blocks of code are set in the same monospace font as the `code` elements, but they aren't blue. Looking at the source, we find that these blocks are `pre` elements. So we'll write the following:

Fighting Code Spread

Depending on the monospace font that gets used by the browser, the `code` elements might look a bit spread out. One way to fix this would be with a negative value for `letter-spacing`.

```
p {margin-top: 0.5em; margin-bottom: 1em; line-height: 1.2em;}
code, pre {font-family: "Courier New", Courier, monospace;}
code {color: #006;}
div#masthead {margin: 0 20% 2.5em 0; padding: 2em 0 1.5em 0;
  border: 1px solid #006; border-width: 0 1px 1px 0;
  background: #BDF;}
```

In the book, code blocks often have portions that are dark red, indicating changes that are being made to the project. Let's take a closer look at one of the code blocks from the HTML document.

```
<pre>
ul li {list-style: outside square url(diamond.gif);
  <b>margin-bottom: 0.5em;</b>}
</pre>
```

It's interesting that changes are marked using a `b` element, which is the deprecated boldface element. In the book, the changes are dark red and not boldfaced. Rather than try something complicated like replacing the `b` elements with `span`s, let's just work with what we have. In addition, let's make sure the code block text is indented a bit as compared to normal text and is smaller as well (see Figure 13.11).

```
code {color: #006;}
pre {margin-left: 10%; font-size: 80%;}
pre b {color: maroon; font-weight: normal;}
div#masthead {margin: 0 20% 2.5em 0; padding: 2em 0 1.5em 0;
  border: 1px solid #006; border-width: 0 1px 1px 0;
  background: #BDF;}
```

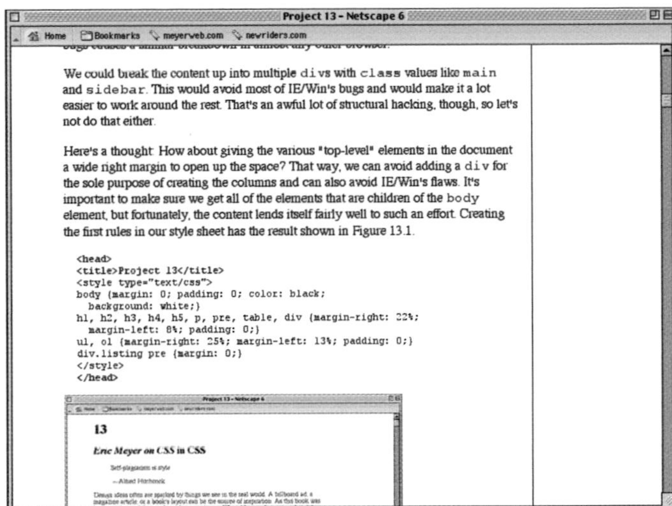

FIGURE 13.11

Code fragments and code blocks stand out better thanks to their new styles.

Figures

Now, at long last, we come to one of the most challenging parts of this project: figures and their captions. Handling the layout of these structures will require not only CSS but a little bit of added HTML as well.

First let's examine the markup we already have for figures, using the figure from earlier in the project.

```
<div class="figure">
<img src="13CSS04.jpg" height="300" width="400" alt="figure">
</div>
<div class="caption">
<h5>Figure 13.4</h5>
<p>
The masthead is finished with nicely styled content.
</p>
</div>
```

Although there are many ways in which a figure and its caption could be structured, this one is actually very useful. Because the figure is in one div and the caption is in another, we can easily float them next to each other, sending the picture to the left and the caption to the right. Let's do the figure first.

```
div.warn {color: maroon;}
div.figure {float: left; width: 75%; margin: 0; padding: 0;}
</style>
```

In doing this, we leave enough room for the caption to go into the sidebar plus 5% more. (This avoids some problems in IE/Win.) Let's now float the caption to the right, using the same basic declarations as we did with the notes. Our progress to date is shown in Figure 13.12.

Why We Float

Although it might seem like we can just let the caption flow into the space to the right of the figure itself, doing so would have severe drawbacks in this situation, as we'll see shortly.

```
div.figure {float: left; width: 75%; margin: 0; padding: 0;}
div.caption {float: right; width: 18%; padding: 0 1% 0 0; margin: 0;
voice-family: "\"}\""; voice-family:inherit;
  width: 19%;}
</style>
```

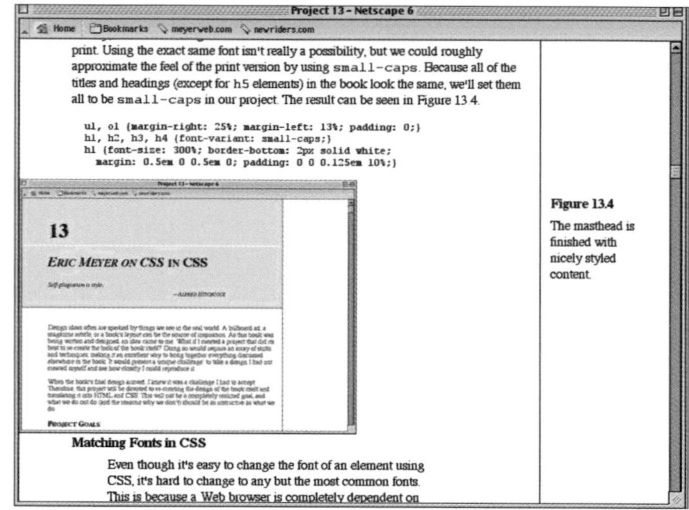

FIGURE 13.12

The figure and its caption have been floated, but there's still much work to be done.

The figure is out of alignment, but let's worry about that after the caption is styled. The simplest part is the actual caption text, which is contained in a `p` element. Re-creating its appearance is a snap.

```
div.caption {float: right; width: 18%; padding: 0 1% 0 0; margin: 0;
  voice-family: "\"}\""; voice-family:inherit;
  width: 19%;}
div.caption p {font: italic 80% Arial, Verdana, Helvetica, sans-serif;
  color: #555;}
</style>
```

Re-creating the top border of the caption might seem simple because we have to set a top border on the `div` itself. What makes it a little bit trickier is the way in which the line sticks into the main column. We'll set the border and see how close we get to the look we want.

```
div.caption {float: right; width: 18%; margin: 0 1% 0 0; padding: 0;
  border-top: 1px solid #006;
  voice-family: "\"}\""; voice-family:inherit;
  width: 19%;}
```

That gets us a top border that stops at the separator line. If we hadn't floated the caption, the line would have gone all the way across the page to the left side of the screen, thanks to the way floats affect backgrounds and borders. By floating the caption, we avoided that problem.

To extend the line to the left, we'll have to add some left-side padding. In the course of doing so, we need to adjust the first `width` value so that IE/Win doesn't mess things up too much. Unfortunately, it thinks that any padding on a floated element is calculated with respect to the size of the float, so if we said `25%` left padding, it would make the content very skinny. It would also be far too much padding for browsers that calculate padding correctly. A great deal of trial and error leads us to the following combination of values (illustrated in Figure 13.13).

```
div.caption {float: right; width: 30%; margin: 0 1% 0 0;
  padding: 0 0 0 40%;
  border-top: 1px solid #006;
  voice-family: "\"}\""; voice-family:inherit;
  width: 19%; padding-left: 10%;}
```

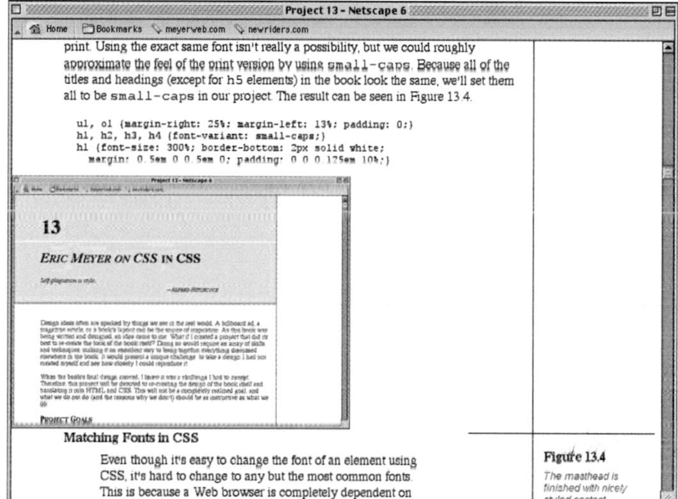

FIGURE 13.13

Extending the caption's top border into the main column with some padding.

Whoops! The caption has suddenly dropped below the figure. This is because the padding has made the caption wide enough that its element box overlaps the box created by the floated figure's `div`. Floats are not allowed to overlap, so the second one (the caption) is placed below the first. We can avoid this simply by reducing the `width` of the figure's `div`. Technically, we could use `70%` because the caption totals a width of `30%`, but let's make sure they don't overlap by dropping the value lower.

```
div.figure {float: left; width: 67%; margin: 0; padding: 0;}
```

This brings the caption back up where it's supposed to be, but some of the following paragraph comes up along with it! That's because before our most recent changes, the figure `div` was wide enough that there was no room for following content to flow next to it. Thanks to the demands of our caption styles, that's no longer true.

This development points out a related problem. Suppose a note comes just before a figure, and the bottom of the note is lower than the top of the figure. The figure's caption would float down below the end of the note, which would look a little odd. There isn't any way to say in CSS that two floated elements have to line up with each other, but we can add a little bit of HTML that will serve the same purpose.

```
<hr>
<div class="figure">
<img src="13CSS04.jpg" height="300" width="400">
</div>
<div class="caption">
<h5>Figure 13.4</h5>
<p>
The masthead is finished with nicely styled content.
</p>
</div>
<hr>
```

Just adding an `hr` element before every figure and after every caption is enough for our needs. We'll just set such elements to `clear: both` and prevent them from appearing (see Figure 13.14).

```
div.warn {color: maroon;}
hr {clear: both; visibility: hidden;}
div.figure {float: left; width: 67%; margin: 0; padding: 0;}
```

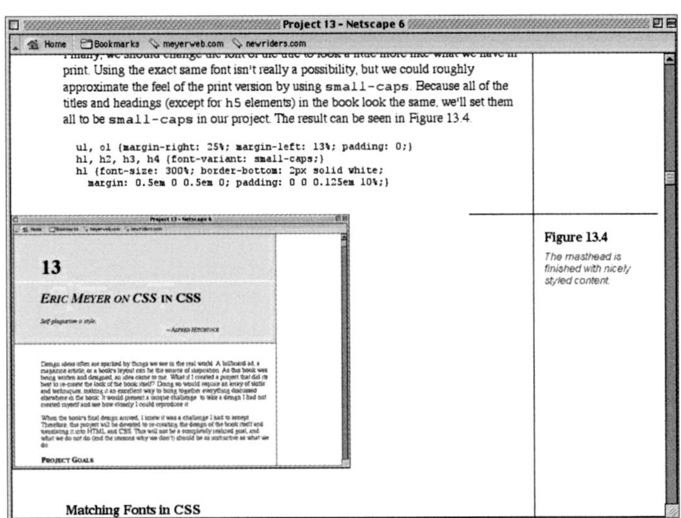

Figure 13.14

Invisible `hr` elements keep the figures and captions lined up and standing alone.

Hidden Elements

The difference between `visibility: hidden` and `display: none` is that the former simply makes elements invisible while allowing them to affect the layout of the document. The latter completely removes an element from the layout, preventing it from having any layout effects.

Now all we need to do is style the caption's label (for example, "Figure 13.4"). A quick glance at the book tells us that the label needs to line up with the sidebar's separator line, look like a blue tab, and not stretch all the way to the end of the caption's top border. Creating the tab look requires inserting a small background graphic into the bottom-right corner of the `h5` element and setting a background color. Let's also spread out the letters just a touch.

```
div.caption {float: right; width: 30%; margin: 0 1% 0 0;
  padding: 0 0 0 40%;
  border-top: 1px solid #006;
  voice-family: "\"}\""; voice-family:inherit;
  width: 19%; padding-left: 10%;}
div.caption h5 {letter-spacing: 1px; color: black;
  background: #9BD url(captioncurve.gif) bottom right no-repeat;}
div.caption p {font: italic 80% Arial, Verdana, Helvetica, sans-serif;
  color: #555;}
```

Rounding Off Corners

For a detailed exploration of using background images to round off corners, see Project 10, "Sneaking Out of The Box."

With a little padding and margins, we'll be there. To make the label text line up with the paragraph, we need to figure out the paragraph's margins. The rule that sets the margins for the caption's paragraph is as follows:

```
h1, h2, h3, h4, h5, p, pre, table, div {margin-right: 22%;
  margin-left: 8%;}
```

Although these work okay for the paragraphs, they won't do for the caption label. We need to set new margins for the `h5` element, and to keep things consistent, we'll apply similar margins to the paragraphs. At the same time, we'll make the label into small-caps text, because that's what appears in the book's design.

```
div.caption h5 {margin: 0 1em 0 0; padding: 0.33em 10px 0 1em;
  color: black; letter-spacing: 1px; font-variant: small-caps;
  background: #9BD url(captioncurve.gif) bottom right no-repeat;}
div.caption p {font: italic 80% Arial, Verdana, Helvetica, sans-serif;
  color: #555; margin: 0; padding: 0.25em 1em;}
```

Circle Gets the Boot

As for the small circle placed on every caption label, we aren't going to reproduce that effect in this project. It would certainly be possible to do so, but as with the boxes around the preview images, the effort would be too great for so small an aspect of the design.

As with the sidebar notes, we need to make sure that any `code` text within our captions is the same size as its surrounding text. We'll do this by adding a selector to the rule that already exists for the note text.

```
div.note code, div.caption code {font-size: 100%;}
```

The last thing we need to do is get the figure over toward the center of the text. Unfortunately, due to all the workarounds we had to use, it isn't possible to just center the image and have that work. Recall that the `div` enclosing the figure is now only `67%` of the width of the `body` element. Instead, we'll right-align the figure, putting its right edge against the right edge of the `div` (see Figure 13.15).

```
div.figure {float: left; width: 67%; margin: 0; padding: 0;
  text-align: right;}
```

It isn't perfect, but it will work fairly well in most browsers, and it ensures a small but noticeable separation between the figure and the caption's top border, just like in the book.

FIGURE 13.15

The finishing touches for styling figures and captions.

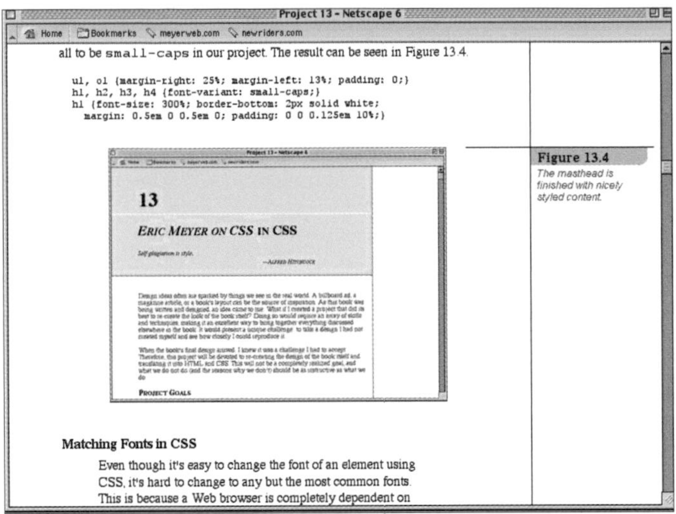

Code Listings and Tables

To wrap up our project, we'll look at two very different structures that end up having very similar styles: code listings and tables. Listing 13.1 provides an example of what we need to re-create.

Listing 13.1 A Sample Listing

```
div.web {color: #399;}
div.tip {color: #006;}
div.warn {color: maroon;}
```

Just in glancing at the printed version of the listing, the markup necessary to re-create it is almost obvious, except perhaps for the heading. Let's put it into an `h5` element and wrap a `span` around the listing number itself. This leads to:

```
<h5><span>Listing 13.1</span> An example listing</h5>
```

Now we can color the listing numbers and give the `span` a right margin to push the listing title away from the number.

```
h5 {font-size: 100%;}
h5 span {color: #006; margin-right: 0.5em;}
p {margin-top: 0.5em; margin-bottom: 1em; line-height: 1.2em;}
```

There is one fly in our ointment: The `h5` element has a left margin of `22%`, and it's contained inside a `div` that also has a `22%` left margin. We need to change that to prevent the `h5` from being massively indented, so we'll replace the left margin of the `h5`.

```
div.listing pre {border: 1px solid #006; border-width: 1px 0;
  padding: 0.5em 1em; margin: 0.125em 0 1.5em;}
div.listing h5 {margin-left: 0.5em;}
ul, ol {margin-right: 25%; margin-left: 13%; padding: 0;}
```

As for the listed code, having it in a `pre` element makes the most sense. In fact, we already have a `div.listing pre` rule that had to be added at the beginning of the project to avoid problems in IE5/Windows. We'll just rewrite it to add the top and bottom borders and to massage the margins and padding a bit (see Figure 13.16).

```
div.listing pre {border: 1px solid #006; border-width: 1px 0;
  padding: 0.5em 1em; margin: 0.125em 0 1.5em;}
```

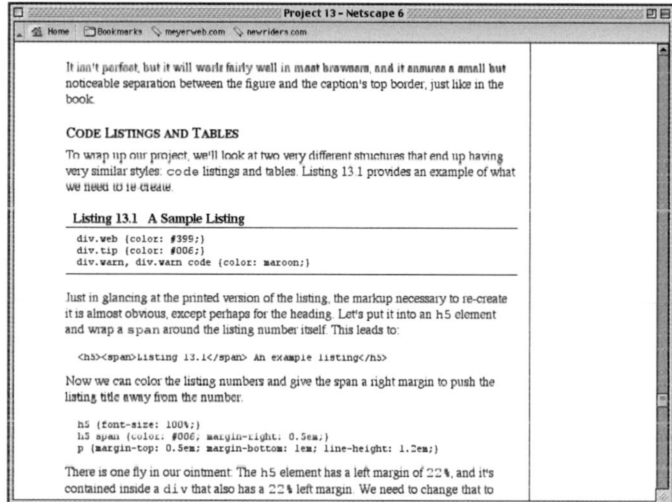

FIGURE 13.16

Styling the listings is a matter of a just a few simple rules.

Tables are very similar to listings in that they have top and bottom borders and a title just above the top border. There are a few differences, though, as Table 13.1 illustrates.

Table 13.1 A Sample Table

Column 1	Column 2	Column 3
This	is	an
example	table	K?

The title is the same as with a listing, and because we're dealing with a table, the markup will involve a `table`.

```
<h5><span>Table 13.1</span> An example table</h5>
<table cellspacing="0">
<tr>
<th>Column 1</th><th>Column 2</th><th>Column 3</th>
</tr>
<tr>
<td>This</td><td>is</td><td>an</td>
</tr>
<tr>
<td>example-</td><td>table</td><td>K?</td>
</tr>
</table>
```

You might be tempted to add a `class` to the `table`, but there's no reason to do so. The only `table` elements in our design will be the ones that enclose tables like Table 13.1. So we'll give them top and bottom borders, reduce the font size slightly, tack on a bottom margin to keep other text away, and declare a `width`.

Giving Width to Tables

In many browsers, tables by default are made only as wide as they need to be to display their contents. That's why we've explicitly given our `table`s a `width`: to override default browser behavior.

```
div.listing h5 {margin-left: 0.5em;}
table {border: 1px solid #006; border-width: 2px 0;
  font-size: 90%; margin-bottom: 1.5em; width: 70%;}
ul, ol {margin-right: 25%; margin-left: 13%; padding: 0;}
```

The column headings are all that remain to be styled. The rule we add will have to set the color and left alignment of the text as well as draw a border underneath it.

```
table {border: 1px solid #006; border-width: 2px 0;
  font-size: 90%; margin-bottom: 1.5em; width: 70%;}
th {color: #006; border-bottom: 1px solid #006; text-align: left;}
ul, ol {margin-right: 25%; margin-left: 13%; padding: 0;}
```

As a last touch, we'll give our table cells a little bit of padding so that their contents will be less likely to jam up next to each other. The results are shown in Figure 13.17.

```
th {color: #006; border-bottom: 1px solid #006; text-align: left;}
th, td {padding: 0.125em 0.66em;}
ul, ol {margin-right: 25%; margin-left: 13%; padding: 0;}
```

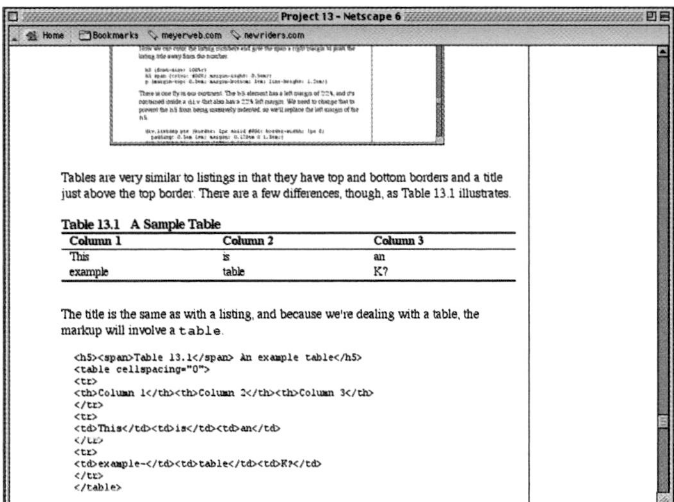

FIGURE 13.17

Re-creating table layout is as simple as writing three new rules.

Postproject Analysis

Although we've gotten close to reproducing the look of the book with CSS, a few things were left out. The inability to download fonts is one of the basic design limitations of the Web, although in a way it's a blessing in disguise. Because designers can't count on a certain font being used, they're encouraged to think in terms of more flexible design principles.

The other big stumbling block in doing such a design is, as always, browser limitations. In this particular project, Internet Explorer for Windows was the big problem, but depending on the project you're attempting, any browser could end up playing that role. Fortunately, browsers are advanced enough that it's usually possible to create a minimal workaround that doesn't mess up other browsers.

We also left out five different design aspects:

- The running head at the top of each project wasn't even attempted. Page numbers are irrelevant on the Web, and it was not necessary to include the project number beyond that found in the masthead and the `title` element.
- The boxes and dark background behind the preview images were omitted due to the difficulty in re-creating them and because they don't work as well in a Web browser.
- The omission of the small circles on each caption label was due almost entirely to the amount of effort that re-creating them would have required.
- The "Branching Out" section and the blue aside boxes (for example, "Matching Fonts in CSS" in this project) were cut from the project chiefly for length.

All told, however, there was very little we had to leave out and a great deal we were able to re-create. The final style sheet we've created is provided in Listing 13.2.

Listing 13.2 The Complete Style Sheet

```
<style type="text/css">
body {margin: 0; padding: 0; color: black;
  background: white url(blue.gif) 80% 0 repeat-y;}
h1, h2, h3, h4, h5, p, pre, table, div {margin-right: 22%;
  margin-left: 8%;}
div.listing pre {border: 1px solid #006; border-width: 1px 0;
  padding: 0.5em 1em; margin: 0.125em 0 1.5em;}
div.listing h5 {margin-left: 0.5em;}
table {border: 1px solid #006; border-width: 2px 0;
  font-size: 90%; margin-bottom: 1.5em; width: 70%;}
th {color: #006; border-bottom: 1px solid #006; text-align: left;}
th, td {padding: 0.125em 0.66em;}
ul, ol {margin-right: 25%; margin-left: 13%; padding: 0;}
h1, h2, h3, h4 {font-variant: small-caps;}
h3, h4, h5 {margin-top: 1.25em; margin-bottom: 0;}
h1 {font-size: 300%; border-bottom: 2px solid white;
  margin: 0.5em 0 0.5em 0; padding: 0 0 0.125em 10%;}
h2 {font-size: 200%; margin: 0 0 0.66em 10%;}
h3 {font-size: 150%;}
h4 {font-size: 110%;}
h5 {font-size: 100%;}
h5 span {color: #006; margin-right: 0.5em;}
p {margin-top: 0.5em; margin-bottom: 1em; line-height: 1.2em;}
code, pre {font-family: "Courier New", Courier, monospace;}
code {color: #006;}
pre {margin-left: 10%; font-size: 80%;}
pre b {color: maroon; font-weight: normal;}
div#masthead {margin: 0 20% 2.5em 0; padding: 2em 0 1.5em 0;
  border: 1px solid #006; border-width: 0 1px 1px 0;
  background: #BDF;}
div#masthead blockquote {font-size: 90%; font-style: italic;
  margin: 2em 22% 0.5em 10%;}
div#attrib {font-size: 90%; font-style: italic;
  text-align: right; font-variant: small-caps;}
div#previews {float: right; width: 33%; margin: 0; text-align: center;}
div#previews img {width: 80%; margin-top: 1em;}
ul li {list-style: outside square url(diamond.gif);
  margin-bottom: 0.5em;}
div.note {float: right; clear: right; border-width: 0;
  width: 18%; margin: 0 1% 0 0; padding: 0;
  text-align: right; font: 80% Arial, Verdana, Helvetica, sans-serif;
  background: transparent url(blue.gif) 50% 15px repeat-x;
  voice-family: "\"}\""; voice-family:inherit;
  width: 19%;}
div.note h5, div.note p {text-align: left;
  margin-left: 1em; margin-right: 0;}
div.note img {height: 30px; width: 30px; margin: 0;}
div.note h5 {margin: -5px 30px 0 1em; padding: 0;
  font-variant: normal;}
div.web p {margin: -10px 30px 0 1em;}
```

```
div.note code, div.caption code {font-size: 100%;}
div.web {color: #399;}
div.tip {color: #006;}
div.warn, div.warn code {color: maroon;}
hr {clear: both; visibility: hidden;}
div.figure {float: left; width: 67%; margin: 0; padding: 0;
  text-align: right;}
div.caption {float: right; width: 30%; margin: 0 1% 0 0;
  padding: 0 0 0 40%;
  border-top: 1px solid #006;
  voice-family: "\"}\""; voice-family:inherit;
  width: 19%; padding-left: 10%;}
div.caption h5 {margin: 0 0.5em 0 0; padding: 0.33em 7px 0 0.5em;
  color: black; letter-spacing: 1px;
  background: #9BD url(captioncurve.gif) bottom right no-repeat;}
div.caption p {font: italic 80% Arial, Verdana, Helvetica, sans-serif;
  color: #555; margin: 0; padding: 0.25em 0.5em;}
</style>
```

Branching Out

There isn't as much room for change when you're trying to re-create a book's design, but here are a few suggestions for things to try anyway.

1. Reduce the amount of vertical space the masthead consumes without making it look significantly different than in the printed version. Don't worry about making the borders line up with the preview images since they won't line up in most cases anyway.

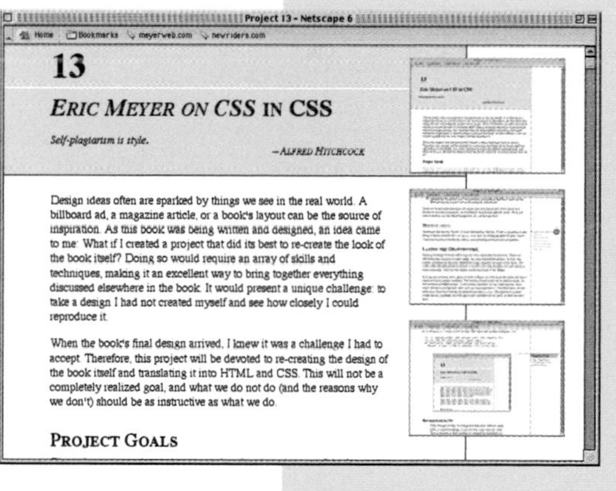

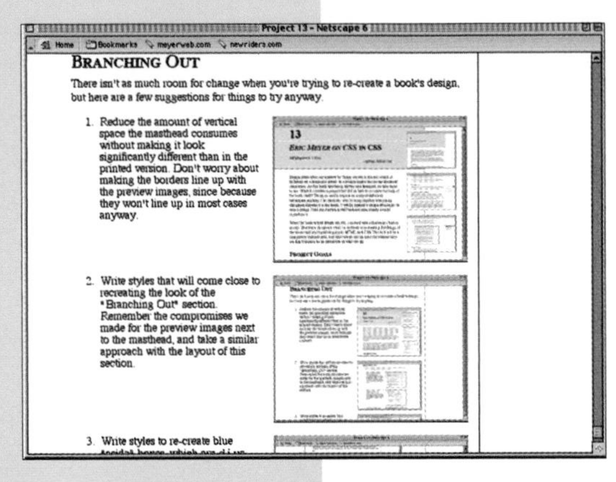

2. Write styles that will come close to recreating the look of the "Branching Out" section. Remember the compromises we made for the preview images next to the masthead, and take a similar approach with the layout of this section.

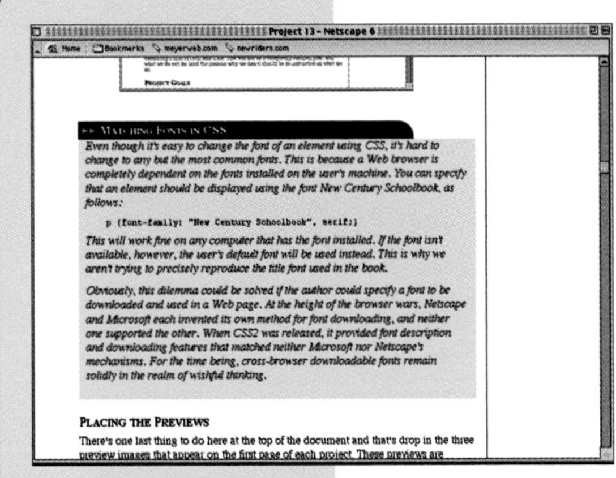

3. Write styles to re-create blue aside boxes, which are `div`s with a `class` of `aside`. It will require two images to carry off the full effect—with both of them used in the heading of the aside. Although you won't be able to put both in the background of the heading, try to find creative ways to manipulate the HTML so that both images can be placed using CSS and not involving an `img` element in the HTML.

INDEX

C

D

E

F

G

H

I

J-L

M

N-O

P-Q

R

S

T

U-V-W

X-Z

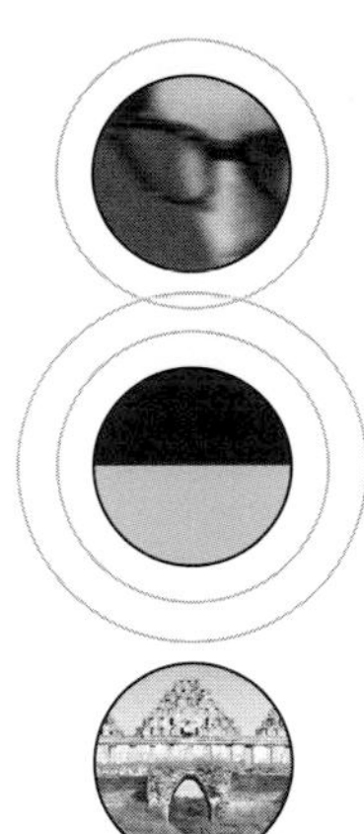

VOICES THAT MATTER

HOW TO CONTACT US

VISIT OUR WEB SITE

WWW.NEWRIDERS.COM

On our Web site you'll find information about our other books, authors, tables of contents, indexes, and book errata. You will also find information about book registration and how to purchase our books.

EMAIL US

Contact us at this address: **nrfeedback@newriders.com**

- If you have comments or questions about this book
- To report errors that you have found in this book
- If you have a book proposal to submit or are interested in writing for New Riders
- If you would like to have an author kit sent to you
- If you are an expert in a computer topic or technology and are interested in being a technical editor who reviews manuscripts for technical accuracy
- To find a distributor in your area, please contact our international department at this address. **nrmedia@newriders.com**
- For instructors from educational institutions who want to preview New Riders books for classroom use. Email should include your name, title, school, department, address, phone number, office days/hours, text in use, and enrollment, along with your request for desk/examination copies and/or additional information.
- For members of the media who are interested in reviewing copies of New Riders books. Send your name, mailing address, and email address, along with the name of the publication or Web site you work for.

BULK PURCHASES/CORPORATE SALES

The publisher offers discounts on this book when ordered in quantity for bulk purchases and special sales. For sales within the U.S., please contact: Corporate and Government Sales (800) 382-3419 or **corpsales@pearsontechgroup.com**. Outside of the U.S., please contact: International Sales (317) 428-3341 or **international@pearsontechgroup.com**.

WRITE TO US

New Riders Publishing
1249 Eighth Street
Berkeley, CA 94710

CALL US

Toll-free (800) 571-5840. Ask for New Riders.
If outside U.S. (317) 428-3000. Ask for New Riders.

WWW.NEWRIDERS.COM

companion web site at www.ericmeyeroncss.com

Visit the Web Site for:

Eric Meyer on CSS

This book is meant to be worked with, not just read (although you can certainly do that as well). If you're ready for the hands-on learning experience this book is meant to deliver, visit the companion Web site at `http://www.ericmeyeroncss.com/` to download project files for each one of the 13 projects in the book.

These project files include all the graphics needed to re-create the design in each project. The files also include an unstyled version of the markup so that you can follow along with the text and make the same changes to the project files that I did in writing the projects. In the process, you can keep hitting "Reload" in a Web browser to see the effects of each change, which is like having hundreds of figures for a project instead of just 15 or 20. You can also download the files that were used to generate the actual figures in the book!

You will also find "Picking a Rendering Mode" and "Tricking Browsers and Hiding Styles," which are of a more practical and theoretical nature than the projects themselves. Plus, you will find a short Glossary of terms.

Beyond the projects, the Web site is a great place to:

- Get links to CSS tools and resources
- Find forums for discussing CSS and its use in the real world
- Check for any errata or updates to the book
- And more

You can also find a link to this companion Web site at `http://www.newriders.com`.

Here are a few basic CSS links:

- CSS2 Specification—`http://www.w3.org/TR/REC-CSS2`
- CSS2 Validator—`http://jigsaw.w3.org/css-validator/`
- W3C "Core" Style Sheets—`http://www.w3.org/StyleSheets/Core/`
- CSS1 Support Charts—`http://www.webreview.com/style/`
- css/edge—`http://www.meyerweb.com/eric/css/edge/`

www.newriders.com

www.ericmeyeroncss.com